مقرنس MUQARNAS

مقرنس

Muqarnas

An Annual on Islamic Art and Architecture

EDITED BY OLEG GRABAR

VOLUME 2

Sponsored by The Aga Khan Program
for Islamic Architecture at
Harvard University and the
Massachusetts Institute of Technology
Cambridge, Massachusetts

Yale University Press
NEW HAVEN AND LONDON
1984

The Renaissance of Islam
The Art of the Mamluks

Selected papers from a symposium sponsored by the Center for Advanced Study in the Visual Arts, National Gallery of Art; Freer Gallery of Art; Smithsonian Institution; and held at the National Gallery of Art, Washington, D.C., May 13–16, 1981.

Designed by James J. Johnson
and set in Times Roman type by
Santype International Ltd., Salisbury, Wiltshire,
Great Britain.
Printed in the United States of America by Halliday Lithograph, West Hanover, Massachusetts.

LC 83–643765
ISSN 0732–2992
ISBN 0–300–03137–8

The paper in this book meets the guidelines for permanence and durability of the Committee on Production Guidelines for Book Longevity of the Council on Library Resources.

10 9 8 7 6 5 4 3 2 1

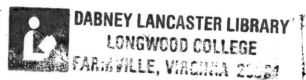

NOTE TO CONTRIBUTORS:

Muqarnas will consider articles on all aspects of Islamic art and architecture, historical and contemporary. Certain issues will be devoted to specific themes, but nonthematic issues can include articles on any topic concerning the arts of the Muslim world.

Articles should be no more than 50 double-spaced, typed pages (including footnotes) and should have no more than 20 black-and-white illustrations. All articles are subject to review by an editorial board and by the Yale University Press. For further information, write to the publications office of the Aga Khan Program, Room 10–390, M.I.T., Cambridge, Mass. 02139.

Contents

THE ART OF THE MAMLUKS

OLEG GRABAR

Reflections on Mamluk Art

The exhibition of Mamluk art organized by Esin Atıl and the symposium held in Washington, D.C., at its opening were both memorable occasions. Jointly they provided one of the very few opportunities in the slowly growing field of Islamic art for the collective attention of a large number of art historians and a smaller number of historians to focus on a single period. This volume of *Muqarnas* records much of the material that was presented there at the symposium.

As is both common and appropriate in a new field, the overwhelming majority of the papers are taxonomic; they seek to organize a quantity of objects or monuments of architecture into formal, technical, or other categories, to provide accurate definitions of those categories, to propose and justify dates, and to suggest an evolution of style and function. One cannot quarrel with those objectives, but at the same time Mamluk objects, whether or not they were in the exhibition, and the great masterpieces of Mamluk architecture raise more complex questions of meaning and perhaps require more speculative treatment. In answering those questions and in suggesting different interpretations we can perhaps add to our understanding both of the nature of Islamic art and of the methods of the history of art in general.

A priori, few periods of Islamic history lend themselves as well to a thorough and detailed analysis as does the Mamluk period in Egypt and the Levant.[1] Its chronological framework is clearly defined by major political events: although one can quibble over whether 1250 or 1260 signaled its beginning, there is general agreement that 1517 marks its end. Its geographical spread is equally clearly defined. Egypt was its center; Syria, Palestine, and most of the Arabian peninsula were its provinces. Compared with the territorial uncertainties of the beyliks of Anatolia or of the contemporary Turkic and Mongol dynasties of Iran, the Mamluks were tied to a reasonably well-demarcated area, to which they introduced a reasonably well-oiled administrative structure. Although subject to numerous changes and at times to devastating crises, the economic foundations of Mamluk wealth—primarily as middlemen in the transit trade from the East to the West—remained fairly secure. Cairo was the largest metropolitan center in the world throughout these two-and-a-half centuries. It was also a haven for refugees from the whole of Muslim western Asia, especially during the first half-century of Mamluk rule, and its stature as a major intellectual center was maintained throughout the Mamluk period as Muslims from independent North Africa and Spain came there to learn and to work. Many of the intellectual, religious, and legal leaders of the budding Ottoman world were trained there.

The Mamluk period is superbly documented. Chronicles abound in great variety, permitting a reconstruction of events that is more balanced than is possible for earlier centuries, for which so often a single source predominates. Although less accessible, legal and archival documents are also numerous,[2] and there are masses of literary, pietistic, scientific, philosophical, and even popular compendia, studies, and texts of all kinds. Mamluk coins and inscriptions have by and large been published. Mamluk history, society, trade, and institutions have been the subjects of numerous studies and—a rare phenomenon in Islamic historiography—of actual scholarly debate. Most important for our purposes, the monuments of Mamluk times are visible. Cairo, Tripoli, and Jerusalem are very much Mamluk cities, and Damascus, Aleppo, and the holy cities of Mecca and

Medina were enormously modified during Mamluk times. According to the estimate of Michael Meinecke, nearly a third of some 3,300 identifiable Mamluk construction projects (new buildings and restorations) have been, at least in part, preserved.[3] Thousands of Mamluk objects fill the galleries and reserves of museums all over the world. In contrast to the situation for Iran, India, or the Muslim West, studies of the architectural monuments and, to a lesser degree, of smaller objects are available in books or articles. From the grand volumes of Napoleon's *Expédition de l'Egypte* to recent monographs on individual buildings or objects, the bibliography on Mamluk art is extensive and, however critical one may be of its intellectual shortcomings, for the most part reasonably accurate.[4]

The Mamluk period coincides with the most extraordinary changes in the arts and culture of Eurasia, which begin as the Pisani cautiously discover antique sculpture, as Gothic cathedrals cover northern Europe, as Anatolian architecture hones its Seljuq models, and as literate and sophisticated Sung painting still rules in China. It ends in the time of Raphael and Leonardo, when northern Europe and Spain discover Italy, when the Ottoman dome is ready for Sinan's perfection, and after two brilliant centuries of Persian painting. In the thirteenth century the Crusaders were finally and definitively defeated, and Western awareness of Asia depended on Marco Polo and some lonely Dominican friars; by the beginning of the sixteenth, Portuguese and Spanish vessels sailed the entire Indian Ocean, and the Ottoman fleet was barely able to stand up to Italian and Spanish navies in the Mediterranean Sea.

Thus, for three different reasons—internal cohesion and continuity; quantity, variety, and availability of information; and concomitant historical and cultural changes elsewhere—the Mamluk period offers opportunities for research that are rare in other areas or for other times.

Methodologically, problems of this period are simple enough and, on the whole, hardly unusual. Some result from the sheer quantity of documents: determining the qualitative range of Mamluk art, for surely with so many examples it is unlikely that the same quality was maintained throughout; identifying paradigmatic works through which other works can be evaluated; and establishing the social range of Mamluk art, as it is highly improbable that different kinds of patrons sponsored or acquired the same kinds of objects.

Other problems are essentially historical: the sources of Mamluk art, its stylistic evolution, the relationship between the Cairene center and the provinces or among the provinces themselves. A more specific subject arises from contrasting the two-and-a-half centuries of Mamluk art with the changes wrought in Anatolia, Iran, and Italy over the same period. Both Anatolian-Ottoman and Iranian art are characterized by clear-cut and at times irreversible changes, while Mamluk art impresses one by its secure conservatism, by its numerous variations on the same themes. How valid is that impression? If it is valid, should it be explained in social terms, as the visual and functional contract accepted by a stable society for an unusually long period of time, or in cultural terms, as evidence that inventions and new searches elsewhere simply did not reach the Mamluk world? Why did the Mamluk world appear so static and so stable in a Mediterranean world, both Christian and Muslim, in cultural ferment? The comparison with the Ottomans is particularly striking, as both cultures shared similar Sunni religious directions tinged with newly (at least in the Levant) fashionable Sufism, drew their elites from a comparable ethnic stock, and were in continuous, if not always friendly, contact with each other.

What posing these questions tells us, it seems to me, is that, however useful and indeed essential it may be to fulfill the taxonomic requirements of scholarship, these endeavors lose something of their import if they are bereft of their social, ideological, or aesthetic contexts and divorced from their methodological implications. The variety of Mamluk forms that greets anyone visiting Cairo or Jerusalem, looking at the exhibition of Mamluk art in its many different locations, or perusing its catalog provides a sumptuous feast to the eyes, but how does one recognize in these forms the will or the taste of the Mamluk world? I shall start with a number of almost random observations on some of the objects in the exhibition, then make a few remarks on Mamluk architecture, and finally sketch out a possible approach to Mamluk art as a whole.

Let me begin by comparing two objects in brass, a basin (plate 1; c. 1330) from the time of Nāṣir al-Dīn Muḥammad in the British Museum and a candlestick (plate 2; dated 1482–83) in Cairo's Museum of Islamic Art donated by Qāytbāy to the mosque of Medina.[5] Both are decorated with a single band broken up by several strongly accentuated medallions and framed by narrow bands above and below. The primary decorative motif consists in writing set over or contrast-

PLATE 1. Basin, c. 1330. British Museum, London, no. 51, 1–41.

ing with vegetal ornament. The visual coherence of the decorative schemes, the powerful stress on movement within circular objects seen respectively as a ring and a cylinder, the contrast between the forcefully proclaimed identification of a prince in the inscriptions and the more complex but also more static and repetitive elaboration of ornamental details are all features of a Mamluk style. They are also found in Koranic pages, glass lamps, textiles, and architectural ensembles of the Mamluk period,[6] and they are different from the stylistic

PLATE 2. Candlestick, 1482–83. Museum of Islamic Art, Cairo, no. 4297.

characteristics of similar objects in the twelfth and thirteenth centuries from Egypt, Syria, or Iran.[7]

The differences between the objects, such as the more elaborate and mannered style of writing on Qāytbāy's candlestick, the technique of engraving in the later object versus that of inlaying in the earlier one, and the simplified ornamental motifs, represent differences of subperiods within a single style. There is no difficulty in establishing some of the same stylistic distinctions by comparing al-Nāṣir's architecture to Qāytbāy's or by surveying sequences of Mamluk domes.[8] Objects such as the Baptistère de St. Louis (no. 21),[9] the candlestick in the Walters Art Gallery (no. 16),[10] the Rasulid basin (no. 22), the great basins, bowls, and candlesticks from Çairo (nos. 27, 28, 29, 30, 31) can all be identified and interpreted as personal, qualitative, or social variants of a single formal matrix. The penbox in the British Museum made by Muḥammad ibn Sunqūr in 1281 (no. 13) would be a transitional piece, and the one by Muḥammad ibn Ḥasan al-Mawṣūlī made in 1269 (no. 10) a fascinating attempt to meet an emerging new taste with the fussy details of another style. The establishment of a set of formal characteristics for Mamluk metalwork (or, for that matter, any other technique), however broad, allows the traditional techniques of connoisseurship to operate, so that dating and evaluation of objects can result. For instance the basin in the Victoria and Albert Museum (no. 18) has an interior decoration which appears to be a pastiche of all the motifs of classical Islamic metalwork, and one ewer in the Museum of Islamic Art (no. 19; plate 3) exhibits a striking and atypical contrast between the upper and lower parts of the body's decoration. In both instances the question is raised of the genuineness of the whole object or of parts of it.

PLATE 3. Ewer, c. 1300. Museum of Islamic Art, Cairo, no. 15089.

Three brasses, however, complicate matters somewhat. Two are penboxes, one in the Louvre (no. 23; plate 4), the other in the Museum of Islamic Art in Cairo made for Abū'l-Fida (no. 24); the third is a Koran box also in Cairo (no. 25; plate 5). All three are dated or datable to the first third of the fourteenth century, and all three bear some relationship to our hypothetical type, especially through the presence of large and powerful inscriptions. But all three also have areas of intricate and sophisticated designs whose effect is not immediately striking from a distance, as it is in the vessels from the times of al-Nāṣir and Qāytbāy; rather, they require close scrutiny and a personal, almost solitary, attention to the object. The inscriptions on two of these objects clearly indicate that they were meant for private use. Even if the name of the owner of the Louvre penbox can no longer be read, its long statement about the glories of penmanship suggests a testimonial in honor of years or decades of writing services. The Koran box is covered with carefully chosen Koranic inscriptions; the commonly known Throne Verse is in bold letters, but less frequently quoted passages are visible only at close quarters.

From these random observations on a few brass objects, the working hypothesis can be proposed that several modes coexisted in Mamluk times using a vocabulary of forms from different sources. Some were earlier than the Mamluks; others were new inventions. One mode was strong, outer-directed, impersonal; the other was intimate, inner-directed, personal. At times, as on a late Mamluk lamp from Cairo (no. 32; plate 6) the two modes can be found on the same object. It is perhaps too risky to suggest that one mode was official, the other private, but the possibility is not excluded. They may also reflect two levels of piety, one official and proclamatory, the other individual and perhaps mystical, in their use respectively of well-worn and uncommon Koranic quotations.

I began talking about the style of two types of objects and then went on to identify them, as well as others, through modes. Without wishing to fall into the difficulties encountered by so many art historians in recent years in trying to define style, I wonder whether the identification of modes—that is, of combinations of subjects and forms adapted to a particular function—does not better suit the historian's need to understand objects as active

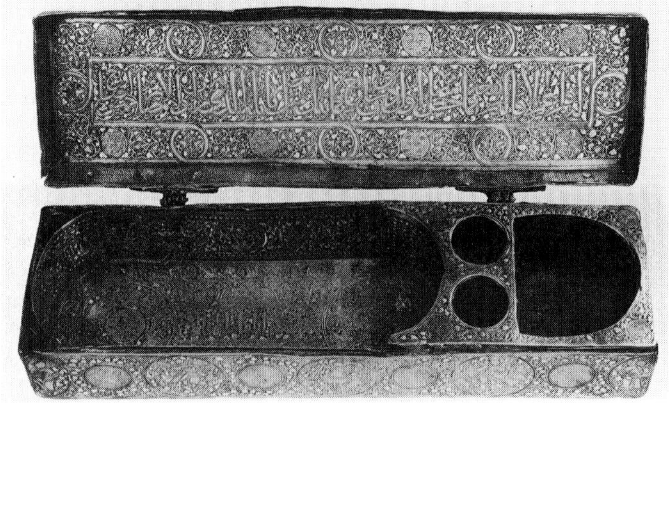

PLATE 4. Penbox, 1304–05. Louvre, Paris, no. 3621.

PLATE 5. Koran box, c. 1330. Museum of Islamic Art, Cairo, no. 183.

components of their contemporary life, especially when most of Mamluk art falls into the category of objects or buildings with primarily practical functions.

PLATE 6. Lamp, second half of the 14th century. Museum of Islamic Art, Cairo, no. 15123.

The problem of stylistic or modal definition is far more complex when one turns to the illumination and especially the frontis- and finispieces of spectacular Mamluk Korans,[11] such as the magnificent ones of 1370 and 1334 (nos. 4 and 5; plates 7 and 8). Here the primary task, it seems to me, is not to describe them, nor to proclaim that they beautify the holy book, nor even to identify the sources or evolution of this or that motif in their decoration. The problem is first of all one of formal definition: what type or types of design are found in these manuscripts? Book pages are two-dimensional, finite surfaces, and these examples illustrate two characteristic ways of covering those surfaces: in the 1370 Koran a single motif growing from a center, and in the 1334 Koran an all-over repeat pattern of medallions. Both types of design occur on other flat surfaces, in ceramics (nos. 69 and 72) or textiles (nos. 116, 121, 125, 127), in Mamluk art and at other times or places as well. Once this level of formal generality is established, then detailed analyses of individual motifs and their origins serve to identify the historical and possibly cultural or social dimensions of a given page.

But neither formal typology nor historical morphology manages to answer a much more fundamental question: what led patrons of the same social and intellectual level (ruling princes), at roughly the same time (c. 1370) and for the same text (the Koran), to require or appreciate different kinds of illuminations? To postulate different religious meanings for these forms—for instance, esoteric and Sufi or establishment and Sunni—makes

PLATE 7. Frontispiece, Koran, c. 1370. Egyptian National Library, Cairo, MS 54, fol. 2a.

sense because such meanings would reflect different interpretations of the holiness of the Koran, but no investigation, as far as I know, has identified the processes by which these or any other visual forms relate to piety. The argument that these fancy frontispieces indicate royal patronage is weakened by the frontispiece of al-Busiri's *Kawākib* in the Chester Beatty Library (no. 9), where Qāytbāy makes it perfectly clear that he is the patron of the manuscript by highlighting inscriptions proclaiming his titles and his sponsorship. Perhaps we have no choice but to see these designs simply as means of sensuous attraction or as homage to the holy text through rich and intricate designs. Illumination is in this case an attribute given to a book and not, like an illustration, issuing from it.

One last observation on Mamluk objects concerns their inscriptions. Metalwork in particular displays not merely a large number of inscriptions but an unusual variety of inscription types, ranging from straightforward statements of rank to personal statements or signatures. In the other media, only glass objects occasionally give a written indication of function, patronage, or location. Why is this so? With some hesitation, one might suggest that something about a hierarchy of media can be inferred from the presence or absence of inscriptions: not necessarily or simply a hierarchy of quality—that brass or glass were "higher" techniques than ceramics or textiles or ivory—but one reflecting the relative ability to display individuality and peculiarities of taste. Metalwork demonstrated that quality as early as the middle of the twelfth century.[12]

Why these two media? Perhaps because, in contrast with ceramics, textiles, and even architecture, the last stages of their ornamentation were artisanal and not industrial: the finishing touches, enameling or chasing, on glass or metal could be used to apply decoration at the whim of a single patron when the object was almost finished. This may explain, for instance, why the Baptistère de St. Louis, the most elaborate work of early Mamluk *Prachtkunst*, depicting (or so it seems) the whole Mamluk court, has no royal inscription.[13] It did not need one, because it was made for an immediate and specific purpose, self-evident to those who used it.[14] The basin's maker, on the other hand, wanted to ensure that he was remembered so that he could receive new commissions: his signature can be found on the basin six times. As to the two other inscriptions on the Baptistère—the identification of a penbox as a penbox and of another vessel as one to carry food—they probably commemorate some concrete event that escapes us.

One conclusion we might draw from these remarks is that inscriptions serve to determine the

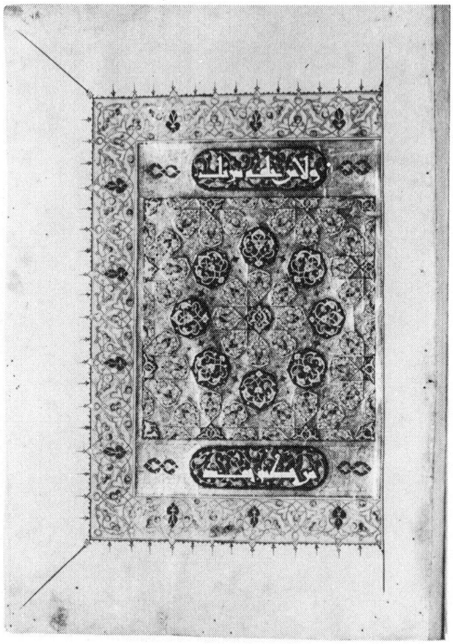

PLATE 8. Finispiece, Koran, 1334. Egyptian National Library, Cairo, MS 81, fol. 378a.

rarity or uniqueness of an object. Thus it is likely that the tray in the Metropolitan Museum made for al-Mu'ayyad (no. 22) was one of many similar objects, but unlikely that Abū'l-Fida's fancy pencase (no. 24) had any mates. A second conclusion is that inscriptions and other types of motifs were chosen to complement each other: with the exceptions of a problematic candlestick in the Walters Art Gallery (no. 16) and the basin in the Victoria and Albert Museum (nos. 16 and 18), the fewer figures depicted, the more elaborate the inscriptions. Furthermore, the later the object, the less likely it is to have representations. Does this mean that the Mamluk period witnessed the replacement of one kind of visual vocabulary (representations) by another (writing) without necessarily implying changes in content? Or did the need for a different content for decoration lead to changes in vocabulary? The answer lies either in specific cultural and historical circumstances or in the mutually exclusive properties of certain visual terms.

Hypotheses such as those based on or derived from observations of individual objects can easily be multiplied to form a variety of combinations, which can then comprise what may be called the connoisseurship of Mamluk art. Connoisseurship is here defined as the web of impressions and associations triggered by a single object, which then, after appropriate comparisons with other objects, return to it as an attribution that is an explanation of place, function, patron, and artist. Until now, however, our discussions of objects have not really elucidated any one individual object so much as they have identified themes, motifs, and questions addressed either to a class of objects or to elements of design and decoration seen independently of an object.

Another possible approach both to objects and to monuments of architecture is to group them by period and then to identify discrete Mamluk substyles. An opportunity to do just that arose when the Mamluk exhibition was shown at the Metropolitan Museum in New York, where the objects were arranged in roughly chronological order.[15] One rapid exercise using this approach will suffice. The reign of Qāytbāy (1468–96) was the last fairly prosperous and relatively quiet period of Mamluk history, and it is notable for a large number of surviving monuments and objects. The monuments are fairly accessible, and some preliminary studies have been devoted to them.[16] They include some thirty buildings in Cairo alone, numerous constructions in Jerusalem, and the rebuilding of the holy places in Arabia.[17] About two dozen bronzes are attributed directly to Qāytbāy's patronage or to his time,[18] as are many objects in glass and ivory, many manuscripts, and a quantity of textiles.

All these works display a number of common and consistent features. One is a sophisticated arabesque design that uses various motifs but always manages to transform surfaces in a way that makes the material of manufacture—whether stone, metal, paper, or fabric—lose its material quality and become a luxurious pattern, brilliantly reacting to the movement of sources of light, as Christel Kessler has so well shown for architecture.[19] Another is the predominance of certain vegetal designs, such as the three-petaled leaf, and of compositions based on coordinated medallions at different angles. Typical also are thick letters with playful finials, especially on the hastae, and an extremely complex geometry. Yet it is still very difficult to combine these details into a definition of style, mainly because not one of these features seems sufficiently anchored in Qāytbāy's reign to justify identifying it exclusively with that time.

In short, the strategies of traditional connoisseurship or of characterizing period styles do not seem appropriate to the study of Mamluk objects. Except in the case of the Baptistère, the analysis of a Mamluk object leads, not to a better understanding of any individual object, but to hypotheses, ideas, and concepts valid for classes of objects (lamps, basins, pencases) or for classes of specific decorative motifs (calligraphic bands, cartouches, peonies, geometric order), or, more rarely, to the identity of an owner or an artisan.[20] Nearly the same conclusion can be reached about Mamluk architecture. Such otherwise dissimilar scholars as Alexander Papadopoulo and the late K. A. C. Creswell seem to have been almost instinctively drawn to compiling sequences of domes and minarets (they could have used gates just as well), as though those elements could be studied apart from the buildings to which they belonged.[21] The reason for this attitude is not difficult to find. Aside from some of the early monuments of Mamluk architecture (the mosque of Baybars, for example, or some of Qalā'ūn's or al-Nāṣir's buildings) whose forms have deliberately archaizing features,[22] the hundreds of Mamluk monuments of Cairo, Jerusalem, Aleppo, Damascus, and Tripoli have a sameness of purpose, of form, of ornament, and of effectiveness—or, in Humphreys's words, "expressive intent"[23]—that is striking.

PLATE 9. Shari' Bayn al-Qaṣrayn, Cairo.

So far as function is concerned, they are mosques, madrasas, khanqahs, or more rarely hospitals or ribats, and nearly always associated with the mausoleums of founders. They illustrate the high Muslim ideal of an architecture of social service, supported by charity in the form of the economic and legal conditions of the waqf system and inspired by the ideological and religious reform of the Muslim system that began in the eleventh century and assumed many regional variants.[24] The problem with all these Mamluk foundations is that there are so many of them, located so close to each other—as in the Shari' Bayn al-Qaṣrayn in Cairo (plate 9), on the western and northern sides of the Ḥaram al-Sharīf in Jerusalem (fig. 1), and in Cairo's eastern cemeteries—that one begins to doubt their actual social, religious, or intellectual uses and usefulness. At best, there is an apparent contradiction between the cost and quality of these buildings and their likely value to the surrounding population.

In form as well, the sequence of a large gate with a flanking minaret, a dark passageway, a court, a variety of public, covered areas (hypostyles or iwans), a smaller number of more restricted living or functional spaces (cells, libraries, lavatories, and the like), and an exteriorized mausoleum dome repeats itself hundreds of times. Changes in, for example, the construction of domes or the ornamentation of minarets do occur, and even sudden innovations, such as the appearance of loggias in the fifteenth century, are apparent, as are occasional returns to older models. On the whole, however, we are dealing with a circumscribed number of set pieces organized according to a very limited number of formulas. The existence of one or more types with variations is, of course, true of any "classical" period. It is as true of Ottoman architecture in the sixteenth and seventeenth centuries as it is of Gothic architecture in the thirteenth. But if it is correct to conclude that Mamluk architecture is also such a classical moment of formal poise and equilibrium, then the question must be asked why this stage was reached in Mamluk Islam, but not in contemporary Turkish or Iranian Islam.

Mamluk ornament is not a subject I have studied in detail, but I suspect that, just as with three-dimensional forms, ornamental motifs can fairly easily be broken down into a relatively small

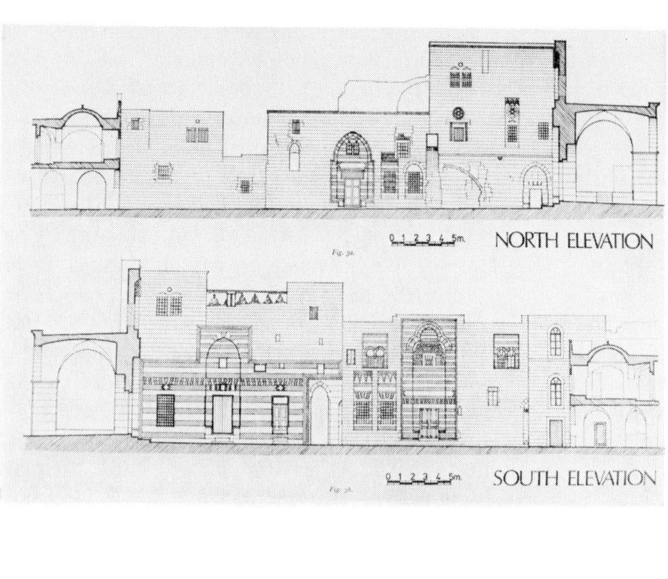

FIGURE 1. Ḥaram al-Sharīf, Jerusalem; elevations. (Drawing by Michael Burgoyne.)

PLATE 10. Madrasa of Faraj ibn Barqūq, Cairo; airview.

number of elements and treated in a relatively limited number of ways, and that, with occasional variations, exceptions, innovations, and returns to older models, nearly the same motifs and visual interpretations of motifs prevailed for over two centuries.

Effectiveness or expressive intent is a combination of three separate things: the message conveyed by the monuments, the means used to convey that message, and the quality of those means. To identify the message itself, the only hypothesis we so far have for the Mamluks is the one developed by Humphreys: theirs is an architecture that embodies tension between religious function and secular form because it is there to communicate to the population that the military aristocracy of the Mamluks, by accepting Islam and glorifying its precepts through buildings, asserts its political and economic domination of the local population. Aside perhaps for a few early buildings, this interpretation still seems entirely applicable and has been confirmed by subsequent investigations.[25]

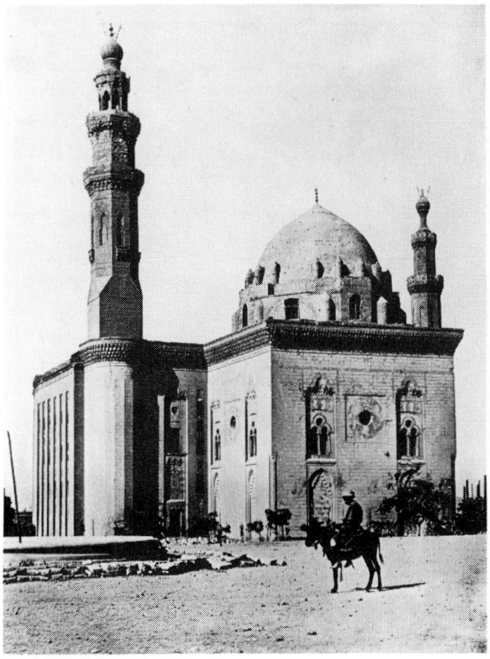

PLATE 11. Madrasa of Sultan Ḥasan, Cairo.

The means used to convey that message are more difficult to identify, but one possibly relevant observation is that, with the partial exception of the Sultan Ḥasan madrasa, which is anomalous in so many ways, a Mamluk building is very rarely perceived as a whole building, as almost any Ottoman mosque is, but rather as a small number of repetitive parts (dome, gate, minaret) which presuppose a building but are not necessarily visually integrated into it. Even an isolated building like the mausoleum and khanqah of Faraj ibn Barqūq (plate 10) can be grasped as an architectonic entity only if it is seen from the air; on the ground, its separate sides have a fascinating asymmetry in the arrangement of the entrance, the minarets, and the domes.[26] The powerful use of a continuous muqarnas molding around the whole building and perhaps a more spectacular siting in the city, which, among other things, makes it visually accessible from the height of the Citadel, differentiate the madrasa of Sultan Ḥasan (plate 11) from that norm, but even there the eccentricities of the plan (fig. 2)—the location of the gate complex, for example—are fully in accord with it. This Mamluk

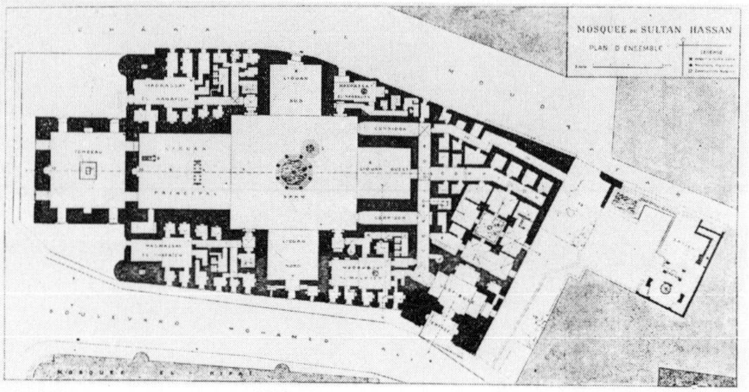

FIGURE 2. Madrasa of Sultan Ḥasan, Cairo; plan.

architectural norm consisted of a small number of signs (gates projecting into the street, minarets leading from one monument to the next, domes focusing on the presence of a benefactor or a holy man, muqarnas establishing some sort of qualitative hierarchy, long bands of Koranic or royal proclamations) that are all essentially the same. At best, like faces in a crowd, they are recognizable and identifiable only after a social or affective relationship has been established.

For all these reasons a qualitative evaluation of Mamluk architecture is not, I think, an appropriate exercise, in spite of the large number of monuments. Aside from the Sultan Ḥasan madrasa and possibly a few others, it is not appropriate because the synchronic intent of the monuments was social and ideological and not aesthetic. Perhaps this is why nineteenth-century descriptions of Cairo, whether that of Prisse d'Avennes, of Roberts, or of one of the many other observers, almost always deal with streets or other urban settings that include monuments (plate 12),[27] but not with a monument alone. Perhaps that is why, also, when the great world expositions of the second half of the nineteenth century wanted to reproduce the Muslim world in Philadelphia, Chicago, or Paris, they picked the monumental streets of Cairo rather than the imperial monuments of Istanbul.[28]

Always granting such exceptions as Sultan Ḥasan's madrasa and the Baptistère de St. Louis, the artistic creativity of the Mamluk world did not express itself in individual monuments or objects made or built to glorify a specific individual or occasion. Its aim was to fulfill a range of functions, from financial investment and piety to such mundane occupations as heating and lighting a room or a mosque or writing a book. In this sense the best works of Mamluk art—its architecture, its bronzes, its illuminated books—were often technically brilliant continuations, maybe even culminations, of medieval Islamic (and in many ways also Western Christian) art, but they hardly paved the way for the kind of development that just a few decades after the end of the Mamluk regime made an ensemble like the Süleymaniye in Istanbul possible. Except in a minor way for rugs, Mamluk objects had nothing to do with the explosion of *Prachtkunst* found in the new imperial worlds of Islam. However interesting they may be archaeologically, the illustrated manuscripts of the Mamluk period show neither the vivacity of thirteenth-century Arab paintings nor the sophisticated brilliance of Iranian ones.

Why is this so? Only prolonged scholarly debate will provide the answer, but I can at least

PLATE 12. Nineteenth-century drawing of a street in Cairo. (Drawing after Prisse d'Avennes.)

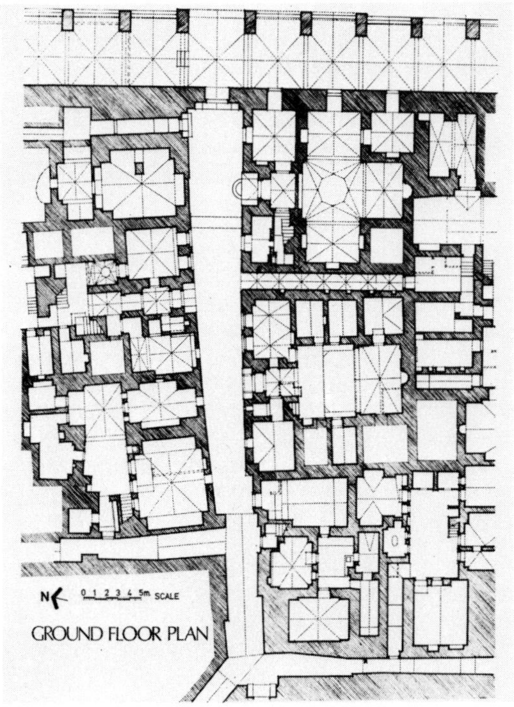

FIGURE 3. Reconstruction of a street in Jerusalem; plan. (Drawing by Michael Burgoyne.)

contribute two tentative hypotheses to that discussion.

The first is that, whether or not meaning can be given to any particular object or monument, the real concern of Mamluk patrons, artisans, and users lay not in the buildings built or the objects made, but in the cities ruled by the sultans and amirs and the lives of the several social classes who inhabited them. In Jerusalem, the whole Ḥaram al-Sharīf with its attendant street was the object of Mamluk attention and care.[29] As any drawing shows (fig. 3), the several buildings are blurred into a single street façade to form a mass, rather than a group of individual monuments. In Cairo, Mamluk minarets and gates guide and accompany one from the Ḥākim mosque to the Citadel.[30] Rather than ends in themselves (as they have become in museums), the objects should be seen as intermediaries between people and activities, as expressions of an attitude toward artistic creativity much more characteristic of bourgeois than of princely art. Perhaps one of the paradoxes of Mamluk art is that it was a princely art that maintained and developed the visual forms not of princely or imperial ideas but of an urban elite.

A second hypothesis is that the disappearance of alien threat that followed the final defeat of the Crusaders and the Mongols allowed the city dwellers of Egypt and the Levant to establish an equilibrium among social, intellectual, religious, and economic structures that could remain unchallenged from both inside and outside. That equilibrium leaves the historian who looks only for changes and evolutions without a task, because all one can do is penetrate Mamluk life and not seek in it some element of vitality that was never there. The implication of this conclusion extends beyond Mamluk art, for it raises the fundamental question whether the methods or strategies to be used in studying any one period should be determined by universal principles or by the cultural idiosyncrasies of a particular moment of history.

HARVARD UNIVERSITY
CAMBRIDGE, MASSACHUSETTS

NOTES

1. Esin Atıl's catalog, *Renaissance of Islam: Art of the Mamluks* (Washington, D.C., 1981), contains an extensive bibliography of secondary works that can easily serve as an introduction to Mamluk studies in general (pp. 266–82). For primary sources only piecemeal introductions are available, such as Donald P. Little's *An Introduction to Mamluk Historiography for the Reign of al-Nāṣir* (Wiesbaden, 1970), and Barbara Schäfer, *Beiträge zur mamlukischen Historiographie* (Freiburg, 1971).

2. See Muḥammad M. Amīn, *Catalogue des documents d'archives du Caire* (Cairo, 1981), and Donald P. Little, "The Significance of the Ḥaram Documents," *Der Islam* 57 (1980).

3. "Regional Architectural Traditions," paper presented at The Renaissance of Islam: The Art of the Mamluks, National Gallery of Art, Washington, D.C., May 13–16, 1981.

4. What constitutes acceptable accuracy in publication is a complicated question. New surveying methods and the development of new technical knowledge about painting and the decorative arts have introduced into art-historical research an expectation of precision that seems to require that nearly everything be restudied. While I am hardly willing to argue in favor of insufficient or incomplete information, I question whether a historian who studies taste and culture (as distinct from a historian who studies technology) necessarily profits from a surfeit of detailed information about some point that had no importance in its own time. For instance, to know where and even when certain ceramics were made is only pertinent to the historian of a culture if evidence exists to show that the time and place of manufacture were important within the culture itself. The same point could be made for masonry techniques and a number of other features. On the other hand, technical precision is essential if the objective of the investigation is to understand and explain modes of production, sources of materials, division of labor, technological know-how, and other similar issues.

5. Atıl, *Renaissance*, nos. 26, 34; it is with purpose, if slightly perversely, that I write, "from the time of" the sultan. Since we have at least one formula, *mimmā ʿumila* (as on no. 28), that identifies an object as being by or for a specific individual, should not objects like these with a simple royal identification be put in a somewhat different category, at least when determining patronage?

6. Ibid., nos. 1, 53, 122. In architecture the same kind of equilibrium between writing and other types of decoration occurs in most examples, such as the Barqūq and Shaykhū ensembles; Louis Hautecoeur and Gaston Wiet, *Les Mosquées du Caire* (Paris, 1932), pls. 147, 166ff.

7. Arthur U. Pope and Phyllis Ackerman, *A Survey of Persian Art* (London, 1939), vol. 6, pls. 1321, 1324, 1332, for Iranian examples; Hayward Gallery, *The Arts of Islam* (London, 1976), nos. 146, 198, 200, for Ayyubid examples.

8. For instance, the structure of the dome of Nāṣir's mosque, Hautecoeur and Wiet, *Mosquées* (pl. 86), is different from Qāytbāy's, though a beautiful late fifteenth-century rug in the Metropolitan Museum (1970.105) contains a design strikingly similar to that of the wooden ceiling in Qāytbāy's funerary complex. For the whole series of domes, see Christel Kessler, *The Carved Masonry Domes of Medieval Cairo* (London, 1976).

9. This number and similar ones in the text refer to Esin Atıl, *Renaissance*.

10. Several problems surround the identification of this object, including that posed by the socket and neck from Cairo which are supposed to belong to it (no. 15): the neck of the Cairo piece has a pseudowriting which is more Ayyubid than Mamluk, as are the medallions with astral symbols on the base of the candlestick. The possibility that both these objects were made by sticking fragments of different origins together cannot be excluded.

11. I am purposely avoiding dealing with calligraphy, as the techniques for appropriate judgment of this prototypical form of expression in the Muslim world have not been worked out. This is not meant as a criticism of the various publications of recent years that deal with calligraphy, such as Martin Lings and Y. H. Safadi, *The Qur'ān*, British Library Exhibition (London, 1976), or Hassan Massoudy, *Calligraphie arabe vivante* (Paris, 1981). All of them make useful and sometimes very important contributions to the history and techniques of scripts, but they do not provide all we need for developing critical terms to understand such texts as the one found in Qadi Ahmad, *Calligraphers and Painters*, trans. Vladimir Minorsky (Washington, D.C., 1959), pp. 57–59.

12. L. T. Giuzalian, "The Bronze Qalamdan of 542/1148 from the Hermitage Collection," *Ars Orientalis* 7 (1968).

13. Atıl, *Renaissance*, no. 21.

14. In spite of its masterful publication by D. S. Rice (*The Baptistère de St. Louis* [Paris, 1953]), the Baptistère is far from having been explained.

15. The exhibition was arranged by Marilyn Jenkins and contained additional examples from the Metropolitan Museum, the Madina Collection, and private and public collections from Kuwait.

16. See Atıl, *Renaissance*, passim.

17. Hautecoeur and Wiet, *Mosquées*, pp. 307ff; Michael M. Burgoyne, *The Architecture of Islamic Jerusalem* (Jerusalem, 1976), for a list.

18. A. Souren Melikian-Chirvani, "Cuivres inédits de l'époque de Qā'itbāy," *Kunst des Orients* 6 (1969).

19. Especially for bronzes and domes (Kessler, *Carved Masonry Domes*).

20. This conclusion is not an original one for Islamic art, but one may wonder whether it is not so because much of the perception of Islamic art developed from Western knowledge of Egypt, which was familiar to us earlier than any other part of the Muslim world.

21. Alexander Papadopoulo, *L'Islam et l'art musulman* (Paris, 1976), figs. 243–49, 267–70; K. A. C. Creswell, *The Muslim Architecture of Egypt*, vol. 2 (Oxford, 1959), pls. 121ff.

22. The mosque of Baybars is the subject of a forthcoming reevaluation by Jonathan Bloom; in the meantime, see Creswell, *Muslim Architecture of Egypt*, pp. 155ff.

23. R. S. Humphreys, "The Expressive Intent of the Mamluk Architecture of Cairo," *Studia Islamica* 35 (1972).

24. There is as yet no easily accessible study of the changes that began in the eleventh century. The best, but very difficult and often controversial, book on those times is Marshall G. S. Hodgson, *The Venture of Islam* (Chicago, 1974). Some important studies have been done on building functions, such as Jacqueline Chabbi on the ribat, "La fonction du ribat à Bagdad du Ve siècle au début du VIIIe siècle," *Revue des Études Islamiques* 42 (1974).

25. Oleg Grabar, "The Inscriptions of the Madrasah-Mausoleum of Qāytbāy," *Near Eastern Numismatics, Iconography, Epigraphy, and History*, ed. D. K. Kouymjian (Beirut, 1974).

26. The works of Faraj ibn Barqūq have been admirably published by S. Lamei Mostafa, in *Kloster und Mausoleum des Farağ ibn Barqūq in Cairo* (Glückstadt, 1968), and in *Moschee des Farağ ibn Barqūq* (Glückstadt, 1972).

27. The general public visiting the exhibition appeared to look almost as much at the large reproductions of Cairo from nineteenth-century drawings as at the Mamluk objects.

28. For instance, the Chicago exhibition, as in Halsey C. Ives, *The Dream City: A Portfolio of Photographic Views* (St. Louis, 1894), unpaginated.

29. For the monuments of Mamluk Jerusalem, consult the articles of Archibald Walls, Amal Abu'l Hajj, and especially Michael Burgoyne in *Levant* 2–12 (1968–80).

30. The visual structure of Cairo is only now beginning to be investigated. I owe my conclusions to papers presented in a seminar at Harvard University in 1980 by Katherine Fischer and Hazem Sayyed and to a visual study by Nezar al-Sayyad, *The Streets of Islamic Cairo*, Aga Khan Program for Islamic Architecture Studies in Islamic Architecture 2 (Cambridge, Mass., 1981).

KARL STOWASSER

Manners and Customs at the Mamluk Court

Egypt had just thwarted another invasion of a Crusader army, the second within thirty years, when, on 2 May 1250, Mamluk troops staged their coup d'état in Cairo. It was a time of grave peril for Islam. Emboldened by the obvious success of the *reconquista* in the west, Christendom had for some time entertained a most audacious plan. Relying more on rumor and wishful thinking than on knowledge of the geopolitical and geographic realities, they hoped for the conquest and occupation of Egypt and a link, at Aswan, with the Christian powers of Nubia and Ethiopia, in alliance, perhaps, with the Mongol heathens. The terrifying Mongol armies had already brought ruin and destruction to vast portions of the Eastern Caliphate and reduced the most powerful Muslim state of the day, the empire of the Anatolian Seljuqs, to the status of a protectorate. The Christians hoped for no less, in short, than the elimination, once and for all, of Islam.

None of this came about, of course. A mere decade later, Mamluk troops had brought the tide of the seemingly invincible Mongol hordes to a halt in Galilee, and before the century was over they had driven the last remnants of the Crusader army from Muslim soil. The Mamluk slave warriors, with an empire extending from Libya to the Euphrates, from Cilicia to the Arabian Sea and the Sudan, remained for the next two hundred years the most formidable power of the eastern Mediterranean and the Indian Ocean—champions of Sunni orthodoxy, guardians of Islam's holy places, their capital, Cairo, the seat of the Sunni caliph and a magnet for scholars, artists, and craftsmen uprooted by the Mongol upheaval in the east or drawn to it from all parts of the Muslim world by its wealth and prestige. Under their rule, Egypt passed through a period of prosperity and brilliance unparalleled since the days of the Ptolemies. The titles and honorifics of their sultans reflected pride in their achievements: "pillar of the world and of the faith, sultan of Islam and of the Muslims, lord of kings and sultans, slayer of infidels and polytheists, supporter of the truth, helper of mankind, ruler of the two seas, lord of the qibla and servant of the Holy Places, reviver of the illustrious caliphate, the shadow of God on earth, partner of the Commander of the Faithful, Baybars, son of ʿAbd-Allah, the former slave of al-Ṣāliḥ, may God strengthen his authority."

They ruled as a military aristocracy, aloof and almost totally isolated from the native population, Muslim and non-Muslim alike, and their ranks had to be replenished in each generation through fresh imports of slaves from abroad. Only those who had grown up outside Muslim territory and who entered as slaves in the service either of the sultan himself or of one of the Mamluk amirs were eligible for membership and careers within their closed military caste. The offspring of mamluks were freeborn Muslims and hence excluded from the system; they became the *awlād al-nās*, the "sons of respectable people," who either fulfilled scribal and administrative functions or served as commanders of the non-Mamluk *ḥalqa* troops. The exceptions were the sultans' sons, who for the sake of stability were allowed to succeed their fathers in the post of chief mamluk; beginning with Sultan Qalā'ūn al-Alfī (1279–90), and until the end of the "Turkish period" in 1382, the empire was ruled by a Mamluk royal dynasty.

Some two thousand slaves were imported annually: Qipchaq, Azeri, and Uzbek Turks, Mongols, Avars, Circassians, Georgians, Armenians, Greeks, Bulgars, Albanians, Serbs, Hungarians. Sultan Lājīn (1297–99) apparently came from the Baltic area; the father of Sultan Barqūq (1382–89, 1390–99) was a peasant in the Danube region. Khān Masrūr was the slave market in Cairo, and a year-round market solely for Mongol slaves was maintained in Alexandria. Genoese and Venetian traders vied with each other as chief suppliers. Up to 100,000 dirhams, we are told, were paid toward the purchase of a single slave; the maintenance costs for the slaves amounted to 70,000 dirhams per month during al-Nāṣir Muḥammad's second reign (1299–1309) and had more than tripled by the time his son al-Ḥasan ascended the throne in 1347. Exaggerated as these figures may seem, there can be no doubt that the number of slave warriors owned by an amir—his *ṭulb*—meant not only strength and prestige, but often survival in the almost continual power struggle within the Mamluk system. In Qalā'ūn's words, "All kings have done something for which they are remembered. Some amassed treasures, others erected edifices. I have built 'walls' and 'strongholds' for myself and my descendants—the Mamluks."

Most of the slaves, especially the Qipchaq Turks, were brought in while still at a young and malleable age. After assignment to barracks—there were twelve of these *ṭibāq* in the Citadel alone, each comprising several buildings and accommodating about a thousand mamluks—they received instruction in Muslim faith and practice, including some rudiments of Islamic jurisprudence, by selected members of the indigenous clergy. Their commandant was the *muqaddam al-mamālīk*; their supervisors were palace eunuchs. During their training period, they received monthly stipends ranging from three to ten dinars, in addition to food rations and clothing allowances. Discipline was strict; all contact with the local population was prohibited. Qalā'ūn's mamluks were not allowed to leave the Citadel at any time. The rules were somewhat relaxed under al-Ashraf Khalīl (1290–94), who granted occasional daytime leaves, only to be tightened again by al-Nāṣir Muḥammad, whose mamluks, by rotation, were marched under the close supervision of their eunuchs to a weekly bath in town. Such iron discipline carried over into palace service later on: amirs and mamluks in attendance on the sultan were not permitted to speak to each other, nor as much as exchange a glance. Joint excursions by two or more royal mamluks, on a hunting trip, for instance, were not only discouraged, but could mean banishment from court and even more drastic punishment for those involved, had they failed to obtain the sultan's prior permission. On the other hand, the sultans as a rule lavished every attention on the well-being of their mamluk trainees. Qalā'ūn even went to the length of periodically inspecting and tasting their food in person.

Toward the end of the fourteenth century, the steady supply of young slaves began to dry up, owing to the upheavals caused by Tamerlane's invasions in the east and demographic changes in the Qipchaq steppe, and the system found itself compelled to fill the ranks with mostly adult mamluks from other parts—"ex-sailors, bakery helpers, water carriers, and their ilk," in the words of the contemporary historian Maqrīzī—who were neither capable nor willing to fit into this strict regimen. Rules had to be relaxed, the standards of training lowered, and, by the time of the second reign of Sultan al-Nāṣir Faraj (1405–12), the royal mamluks, once the elite, had become an impoverished, despicable, ignorant rabble, "more promiscuous than monkeys," laments Maqrīzī, "more larcenous than mice, more destructive than wolves."

In the earlier system, once the young trainees had reached a certain age, instruction in the martial arts was added to their curriculum: fighting with lance and spear, sword and dagger; archery; and, above all, horsemanship. These skills were then constantly honed, not only in routine practice on their barracks grounds, but in frequent contests under the eyes of the sultan on specially designated and prepared fields (*mayādīn*), such as the Mīdān al-Kabīr below the Citadel, the Mīdān al-Qabaq east of Cairo, the Mīdān al-Nāṣirī in the area now occupied by Garden City and Taḥrīr Square, and the Mīdān Siryāqūs north of Cairo. There the mamluks and their amirs would demonstrate their military prowess and daredevil horsemanship. Sultan Baybars al-Bunduqdārī (1260–77), a first-rate archer himself, made *qabaq* contests—*qabaq* (from Turkish *qabāq*, "pumpkin") designated a wooden, disk-shaped target mounted on top of a very tall pole at which the contestants, each lying supine on the back of a galloping horse, fired their arrows—a daily afternoon event, and later sultans, Qalā'ūn, Khalīl, and al-Nāṣir Muḥammad, continued the practice. The winners were rewarded with robes of honor or fully bridled and caparisoned horses. Slaves were sometimes given their freedom on such occasions.

Manumission by the sultan meant integration into the mamluk command structure and the beginning of a career in court and palace service, in the military, or as an administrator in the provinces. Advancement and promotion depended almost entirely on the sultan's favor, and often his whim, as did demotion and disgrace. There was little room for friendship in such a system. Even the camaraderie of the *khushdāshiyya*, that is, slaves who had served under the same master, seems to have remained binding only as long as the stakes in advancement were not too high. At the same time, the system excluded nepotism and favoritism: each on his own must claw and intrigue his way up the career ladder. Yet in spite of all this competing for position, the constant realignment of rival factions, and the brutal power struggle that could spill over into pitched battles in the streets of Cairo, toward the outside world the mamluks never failed to display a remarkable esprit de corps, combined with an aristocratic aloofness. No mamluk would deign to eat at the same table with "natives," no matter what their rank and station.

Whether in military, administrative, or court service, the ranks were the same: amir of five, of ten, of forty, of a hundred. The actual number of mamluks under the command of an amir fluctuated. An amir of a hundred, for instance, could be in charge of as many as five hundred mamluks and traditionally had the additional title of "commander of a thousand," which designated his function in times of war. Fiefs, with an annual tax yield of between more than 200,000 dinars in the case of senior amirs of a hundred and 9,000 dinars or less for amirs of ten, furnished their material support: one-third belonged to the fief-holder, two-thirds was to be set aside for the upkeep and equipment of the mamluks in his charge. Those in court service were entitled to regular allocations in cash and kind commensurate with their rank, the nature of their assignment, and their degree of closeness to the sultan. A court assignment could be quite lucrative, if one played one's cards right. A certain ʿAlī ibn al-Ṭabbākh, who for thirty-seven years had faithfully served al-Nāṣir Muḥammad as master of the table (*khwān-salār*), left at his death, in addition to a sizable fortune (the man had drawn five hundred silver dirhams per day), twenty-five pieces of real estate in choice locations.

A strictly hierarchical system and meticulous attention to rank and status, dress and appearance, protocol and ceremonial, characterized the Mamluk regime. This is hardly surprising, given their diverse ethnic backgrounds and their lack of shared traditions. Some of their offices and functions, their customs and manners, were obviously carried over from earlier Islamic practices either in Egypt or in the Eastern Caliphate; others had distinctly Asiatic—Turkish, Mongol, Caucasian—origins. Especially striking is the similarity with Fatimid institutions. Unlike their former Ayyubid masters, who, as restorers of orthodox Sunnism, went out of their way to eradicate the memory of two hundred years of Shiite rule, the Mamluks felt free to reach back to the older institutions and adapt and expand them to suit both their own needs and their role as rulers of Sunni Islam's supreme power. A minutely organized court ensured discipline and enhanced royal dignity; pomp and ostentation on public occasions were designed to impress their own subjects as much as visitors from abroad with the spectacle of regal splendor and military might.

An elaborate, almost modern, protocol governed the visit of a foreign dignitary or emissary from the moment he was admitted on Egyptian soil. In the case of a visiting monarch, the sultan might himself ride out to meet his guest on his arrival in Cairo or might delegate a high-ranking amir, such as the viceroy (*nā'ib al-salṭana*) or the chief chamberlain (*ḥājib al-ḥujjāb*), for that purpose. The sultan would dismount and, after an exchange of greetings, drape his royal visitor in a robe of silk brocade; this ceremony was customarily followed by a large banquet. Lesser dignitaries and diplomatic emissaries were received by the *mihmandār*, the "meeter and greeter" of the royal court. Ranking visitors were accommodated in one of the royal palaces overlooking the polo field below the Citadel, envoys and lesser dignitaries in the royal mansion (*al-dār al-ṣulṭāniyya*), a carry-over from the vizier's residence (*dār al-wizāra*) of Fatimid and Ayyubid days. In charge of these guesthouses was the superintendent of hospitality (*nāẓir al-ḍiyāfa*), who provided the visitors with horses and fodder, rations and money allowances, even female companionship on occasion. He was likewise responsible for making out a report on the guests, for recording the gifts they had brought, and, if they were non-Muslims or came from an enemy country, for tightening security.

On the day set for the royal audience, the visitor, previously instructed in the proper etiquette, was stripped of his arms and ushered by chamberlains through several anterooms lined with soldiers to the great portico (*īwān*) of the Citadel. On such occasions, the sultan was seated on the most awesome throne, the *takht al-mulk*, an elevated structure similar to the pulpit of a mosque, flanked on either side by the amirs—resplendent in their finery and carefully arranged according to rank—and guarded by the captains of the guard (*ru'ūs al-nawb*). As he approached the sultan, the visitor, unless he was a king, was expected to kiss the ground three times, beginning at his end of the carpet that led to the throne. The *kātim al-sirr*, or head of the chancery, who had issued the invitation to the audience, would then formally present him to the sultan. Only in rare instances was a visitor allowed to sit in the royal presence. Interpreters and translators would stand by to translate documents and act as linguistic intermediaries, although the sultan rarely addressed a visitor directly. Rather, he spoke through the *mushīr*, or counselor, who otherwise acted as the sultan's mouthpiece during sessions of the royal council (*majlis al-salṭana, al-mashwara*), a body composed of the commander-in-chief of the armed forces (*atābeg al-ʿasākir*) as chairman, the caliph, the vizier in his capacity as head of the bureaucracy, the justices of the four orthodox rites, and the amirs of a hundred, which would convene by royal summons to deliberate on vital matters of state, such as war and peace. The reason, we are told, was to safeguard royal dignity, since the sultan might be overruled by the council. On the other hand, since quite a number of sultans had only a somewhat shaky command of Arabic and some of the later ones spoke no Arabic at all, it may have been deemed wiser that they open their mouths as little as possible.

The relationship between the sultan and the Abbasid caliph as "partners" remained ambivalent. While the spiritual weight of the caliph's office was needed to lend the regime an aura of respectability and legitimacy, its holder could obviously not be tolerated as co-ruler and had to be relegated to a purely ceremonial function without power. Sultan Baybars, who in 1261 installed a descendant of the house of Abbas in Cairo, was the man who established the tradition of the monthly audience: on the first day of every month, the caliph, at the head of religious dignitaries and representatives of the Sufi orders, would betake himself to the Citadel to felicitate the sultan on the completion of the month just past and to extend his blessing for the month to come. When the caliph attended the Friday prayer, the sultan would assign amirs to escort him as, riding on a mule, he approached the Great Mosque of the Citadel. There the sultan would go forth and meet him with every sign of respect and honor, even kissing his hand at times, and invite him to join him in the royal enclosure. On such occasions, the caliph would deliver the sermon, perhaps exhorting the worshipers, at least in the early years, to join in holy war against the infidel Mongols and Crusaders and the heretic Ismaʿilis.

Equally fraught with intended symbolism was the ceremony attending the accession of a new sultan. Black—signifying the Abbasid caliphate—was the dominant color as the ruler-to-be, escorted by the amirs of his retinue on foot, made his way on horseback from his residence to the great portico of the Citadel: he wore the *takhfīfa*, a small, round, black turban, its two ends dangling between his shoulders (as distinguished from the *nāʿūra*, an oversized turban worn, as the equivalent of a crown, on special ceremonial occasions only), rode a horse with a black neck caparison and saddle blanket, and was flanked by two standard-bearers carrying black banners. Heralds (*jāwīshiyya*) cleared the way for the sultan-to-be, who was surrounded by halberdiers (*ṭabardāriyya*); the *shabbāba*, a small silver trumpet, was sounded to announce his coming, and the *ghāshiya*, a highly ornamented cushionlike saddle cloth of cotton and quilted leather, was carried before him as an emblem of royalty.

Inside, he would take his seat on the imperial throne, the *takht al-mulk*, and the amirs, in succession of rank and followed by the commanders of the *ḥalqa*, or corps of non-Mamluk professional soldiers, would approach him, first kissing the ground and then his hand. (This form of obeisance, which was to be observed by all except kings who approached the sultan, survived until the time of Sultan Barsbāy [1422–37], who changed it to a simple hand kiss preceded by a genuflection and the placing of a finger on the ground as a symbolic gesture of ground-kissing.) Next, the caliph made his appearance and joined the sultan on the throne in order to place the black caliphal robe of honor (*al-khilʿa al-khalīfiyya, al-sawād al-khalīfatī*) over the sultan's green *farajiyya*, a flowing, long-sleeved atlas robe. The head of the chancery then read the caliph's investiture of the sultan as ruler of the Muslim territories under Mamluk sway and of lands yet to be conquered from the infidels.

After the formal witnessing of the document by the four justices and an exhortatory speech by the caliph, the assembled amirs would again kiss the ground and swear on the Koran that they would not betray or deceive or attack the sultan—an oath not always kept. The caliph, after having received tokens of royal favor, shook the sultan's hand and departed with the four justices. Robes of honor—more than twelve hundred at the accession in 1309 of Sultan Baybars II al-Jāshnagīr, according to Maqrīzī—were bestowed on the "men of the sword" and the "men of the pen," who then paraded, led by the new sultan, through the festively decorated streets of Cairo. The document of caliphal investiture, wrapped in a black silk pouch, was carried ahead of the vizier on the occasion. The day ended with a royal banquet for the amirs.

Generally, the sultans would spend the morning hours of each day, except during the month of Ramaḍān, attending to state business and administrative matters of a more or less routine nature. The daily morning report (*ruqʿat al-ṣabāḥ*) of the police chiefs of Old and New Cairo on fires, murders, and thefts during the past twenty-four hours would usually be the first item to require their attention. As a rule, the captain of the guard (*raʾs al-nawba*) on duty—there were four of them, one an amir of a hundred and three amirs of forty—would be the first person to see the sultan in the morning. He had direct access to the sultan at any time, day or night, and enjoyed the distinction of being addressed by the sovereign as "friend" (*yā akh*), rather than the usual *yā khūnd*, "lord."

Mondays and Thursdays (until the time of Barqūq, who changed the schedule to Sundays and Wednesdays, and later to Tuesdays and Saturdays, with Friday afternoons thrown in) were set aside for public audiences—initially held in the House of Justice (*dār al-ʿadl*), that is, the great portico of the Citadel, and at other times at the Courtyard of the Bench (*qāʿat al-dikka*), the viceroy's residence, or other places—to hear grievances (*qiṣaṣ, maẓālim*), a practice observed by the rulers of Egypt since the Tulunids. The sessions were convened in the very early morning hours, in winter sometimes by torchlight, and presented a veritable tableau of Mamluk protocol. On such occasions the sultan, since he was to act as neutral judge, sat on a stool placed below the imperial throne, or even on the ground, flanked on his right by the justices of the four rites, the Shafiʿite as the highest-ranking immediately next to the sultan, followed in descending order of rank by the Hanafite, the Malikite, and the Hanbalite representatives, and next, in succession, the secretary (*wakīl*) of the treasury and the superintendent of the prefecture of Cairo. On the sultan's left sat the head of the chancery, and opposite him the superintendent of the army (*nāẓir al-jaysh*), the superintendent of the privy purse (*nāẓir al-khāṣṣ*), the muftis of the four rites serving as legal experts, and a group of recording scribes (*kuttāb dast*), the whole forming a circle. If the vizier was one of the "men of the pen," he would sit between the sultan and the head of the chancery; but if he belonged to the "men of the sword," he would stand at some distance with the rest of the officers of the household, as did the viceroy—if there was one present, since the office was temporarily abolished in 1338 by al-Nāṣir Muḥammad. Behind the sultan, on the right and left, stood two rows of arms-bearers, masters of the wardrobe, and mamluks of the sultan's entourage (*khāṣṣagiyya*). At a distance of nine yards on the right and left sat the amirs of the royal council, and behind these stood the rest of the amirs positioned according to rank. Chamberlains and secretary-bailiffs (*dawādārs*) were stationed on the outside of the circle to sift and pass on the grievances and petitions.

The closest thing to a folksy appearance of the court in public was the annual celebration of the Prophet's birthday. Some three hundred to five hundred porters were needed to erect the gigantic tent on the Ḥōsh, consisting of four halls topped by a cupola with vents to let the light in. The sultan would be seated at the far end of the tent, together with the caliph, the four justices, the learned sheikhs, and the reciters of the Prophet's story in poetry and prose, as well as ranking members of the *awlād al-nās*, amirs, and various state functionaries. Leather tanks filled with sugar water were set up to provide refreshment for all comers, high and low. The celebration would begin in the late afternoon with readings from the Koran and the recital of poems and homilies appropriate to the occasion. After a joint sunset prayer, a meal and seasonal sweets would be served, and the recitals continued. Around nine o'clock, the various Sufi orders, with their emblems and banners, arrived and began their singing and swaying and dancing, which would last throughout the night. Money purses and other tokens of royal favor were bestowed as the night went on, for the Mamluks were much attracted to Sufism and their sultans were generous sponsors of its practitioners.

A frequent display of royal bounty was part of a sultan's duties and a way to stay in power: vanities had to be flattered, loyalties bought, jealousies assuaged. Not only did the medieval state feed and clothe its servitors, but the bestowal of robes of honor and generous money gifts, the donation of horses, and the extension of other royal favors accompanied almost every occasion on which the sultan officiated or even appeared in public. Robes of honor (*khilaʿ*), meticulously designed to fit the recipient's rank and station—red over yellow atlas, for instance, for senior amirs, white silk chenille for ranking members of the bureaucracy, white wool for judges and ulema—were so frequently and commonly bestowed (even slavers and horse traders were so rewarded) that their production kept an entire royal industry busy. Marks of signal distinction were the garments that came literally off the sultan's back, as when he bestowed the robe he wore during the Little Bairam prayer on one of the attending senior amirs.

Aside from five regular meals served daily at the court, three in the morning and two in the evening, there were huge banquets (*asmiṭa, walā'im*) on special occasions. The master of the table (*khwān-salār*) supervised the preparation of the food in the royal kitchens, the majordomo-in-waiting (*ustādār al-ṣuḥba*) acted as a sort of maître d'hôtel, a swarm of cupbearers (*suqāh*) headed by the royal cupbearer (*sāqī'l-mulk, al-sāqī*) served food and drink and cleared the table afterward, and a staff of tasters under the command of the *jāshnagīr* (the *shishni* of colloquial Egyptian) stood by to sample food and drink for possible poison. Guests ate and drank from gold, silver, and porcelain vessels. Although forks and spoons were known, eating was usually done with the fingers, which were constantly rinsed with water poured from ewers into large fingerbowls. Truly gargantuan amounts of food might be served: at a banquet given by al-Ashraf Khalīl on the occasion of the completion of the Ashrafiyya Palace in 1293, for instance, the guests consumed 3,000 sheep, 600 cows, 500 slaughter horses, and countless chickens and geese, not to mention the almost 90,000 kilos of sugar that went into drinks and sweets.

This bash cost the sultan 300,000 gold dinars alone for food and drink, robes of honor, and other royal gifts and favors, such as embroidered material, saddles, dresses for the women, and the like. Several high-ranking amirs received, in addition, gifts of a thousand dinars, thirty of the royal guard (*khāṣṣagiyya*) received five hundred dinars each, and every amir was given a fully bridled and caparisoned horse. Besides, treasury officials scattered gold coins during the circumcision ceremony for the sultan's younger brother Muḥammad and his nephew Mūsā, which was celebrated on the same occasion, and the entertainer of the day, a singer named al-Bulaybil ("Little Nightingale"), was paid a thousand dinars for his labors. A few years later, when young Muḥammad himself sat on the throne, he outdid his brother in extravagance on a similar occasion. For a party he gave in 1314 to celebrate the completion of the Qaṣr al-Ablaq, he ran up a bill, if one can believe Maqrīzī, of 500,500,000 dirhams.

Horses were a mamluk's prized possession, and to give them as gifts was a favorite way for the sultan to show his pleasure and favor. There were numerous occasions for it—in the spring, for instance, when the sultan went out to the royal paddocks; at the conclusion of military and sporting events; at various ceremonial affairs; when the sultan rode out on the hunt—so that senior amirs and members of the royal entourage might each receive as many as a hundred horses, some with full accoutrements, in the course of a year. Al-Nāṣir Muḥammad, a hippophile of the first order, had 4,800 horses in his stables and is said to have spent one million dirhams in a single day toward the purchase of Arabian purebreds. As many as eight hundred functionaries—amirs of ten and an assortment of troopers, grooms, veterinarians, and the like—worked in the royal stables. In charge of them was an amir of a hundred, the *amīr-ākhūr*, or equerry, while an amir of forty, the *sar-ākhūr*, was the official responsible for fodder. The sultan's horses, all branded with the royal *dāgh*, were not only walked and exercised daily, but occasionally displayed in horse shows—as in Fatimid times, before a royal procession, for instance. Moreover, there were the royal camel pens (*manākhāt*), where al-Nāṣir Muḥammad kept five thousand riding camels, and even stables for elephants.

Seven times in the spring, the sultan, accompanied by the mamluks of his retinue, the majordomo (*ustādār*), and an assortment of other functionaries, such as falconers, drivers, animal keepers, and physicians, members of his harem, and a train of amirs with their own mamluks, would go on hunting excursions—any one of which could easily last for a week. On such occasions he rode an unadorned horse; no banners and standards were carried over his head. If the procession passed through the fief of a senior amir, it was customary for the local feudatory to supply sheep, geese, chickens, sugarcane, and barley for the hunting party; the sultan, in turn, would bestow on him 4.2 kilos of gold, a robe of honor, and a fully bridled and equipped packhorse with a gold-embroidered housing (*kunbūsh*).

Royal hunting preserves stocked with game and wildfowl, and similar preserves of the ranking amirs, were the hunting grounds. When the hunting was done with falcons, the sultan would be accompanied by the master of the hunt, the *amīr-shikār*, who directed the falconers, or *bāzdāriyya*. Hunting dogs, decked out for the occasion in gold-embroidered silk and led by the dog-masters (*kilābziyya*), were used to hunt ostriches, antelopes, and gazelles, as were trained cheetahs, which had their own special keepers. Large game was hunted with javelins, arrows, or crossbows shooting lead, clay, or stone pellets (*qusiyy al-julāhiq*), birds usually with a blowgun (*zabṭāna*) and pellets called *bunduq*, which were carried in a sack by a special official, the *bunduqdār*. Even away from home and roughing it, the comforts of life were not forgotten: at the end of a day's hunt they could return to fully furnished and carpeted tents attended by a myriad of servants, enjoy the pleasure of a leisurely bath in wooden tubs, and eat well-prepared meals from lead camping dishes.

Numerous occasions throughout the year called for royal processions. Some were minutely designed to bring out the full panoply of royal and Mamluk splendor, such as the processions on the two highest Islamic festivals or during the annual parade of the *maḥmil* in the streets of Cairo in preparation for the pilgrimage; others were relatively low-key, as the weekly procession to Friday prayer or the procession on the occasion of the annual "anointing of the Nilometer" (*takhlīq al-miqyās*) and "breaking of the dam" (*kasr al-sadd*) to mark the opening of the irrigation season. A full-dress procession must have been a colorful spectacle indeed: ahead rode two files of *rikābdāriyya*, or stirrup holders, under the command of the *amīr-jandār*, the man responsible for the sultan's safety, to clear the road. They flanked others on foot who carried the gilded and gem-encrusted saddle cloth, the *ghāshiya*, which they waved from side to side. Behind them rode a horseman who sounded the royal trumpet (*shabbāba*), and then a pair of Mamluk squires, *al-jiftāh*, dressed identically in gold-bordered yellow silk tunics and mounted on identical white horses. Golden ribbons connected them with the sultan behind them, a safety device in case the sultan's horse stumbled or shied. Next came the sultan, riding a gray horse bedecked with a gold-embroidered neck caparison (*raqaba*) of yellow atlas—yellow being the color of Mamluk royalty—and a red atlas cloth, called *zunnārī*, over the croup. A senior amir riding by his side held the royal parasol (*jatar*) of yellow silk above the sultan's head, while halberdiers on foot, commanded by the *amīr-ṭabar*, surrounded him on all sides as bodyguards. By his side strode the *jumaqdār*, or mace-bearer, his eyes fixed on his lord, holding the gold-tipped mace aloft, and the *jūkāndār*, or polo master, carrying the royal curved dagger (*nimja*) and a steel buckler. At times, the chief chamberlain carrying a staff of office, or the treasurer (*khāzindār*) lugging a sack of money intended for charity would precede the sultan. Behind the sultan, a group of squires led royal horses covered with richly embroidered and gem-studded housings. Then followed the standard bearers, headed by the *ʿalamdār* who carried the great royal banner (*jālīsh*) of gold-embroidered yellow silk adorned with a tuft of horsehair, and behind them the armor bearers headed by the *ṣilāḥdār*. The amirs, on horseback or on foot, came next with their retinue of mamluks, in similar order and with hardly less pomp, and the tail end was brought up by the royal band, *al-ṭablkhāna al-sharīfa*, an ensemble more noisy than melodious, composed of four big drums, forty brass cymbals, four double-reed clarinets, and twenty small kettledrums.

It was Sultan al-Nāṣir Muḥammad who made polo games twice a week, at noon on Tuesdays and Saturdays, an obligatory part of Mamluk court ritual. The two teams were captained by the sultan and the commander-in-chief of the troops. At the end of the games, the sultan would reward the players as well as the polo master and his helpers with robes of honor. Horse races, not surprisingly, were a favorite pastime of the Mamluk elite. A hundred and fifty horses, or even more, at a time could be on the starting line. The race was between the sultan's horses and those of the amirs. The horses raced between two marble columns, the *ʿawāmīd al-sibāq*, erected on either end of the field, and were usually ridden by bedouin jockeys. The owners of the winners were rewarded with horses and robes of honor. As on other occasions, such as martial exercises or wrestling displays, betting was encouraged.

Despite the role they played as guardians of religious decency and sponsors of the Islamic establishment, the Mamluks rarely let religion interfere with their personal ambitions and pleasures. They did their drinking—except during Ramaḍān, of course—unabashedly in public: fermented mare's milk (*qimizz*), the drink of their Asian homeland; *būẓa*, a brew made from flour and fermented date juice; and *mizr*, a beerlike wheat or barley brew as old as Egypt. Although Baybars at one point cracked down on vice and immorality and had all breweries in Cairo destroyed, liquor concessions remained on the whole an important tax source. The Mamluks liked a good songfest in the Citadel and showered lavish rewards on the top entertainers, just as they enjoyed the performance and company of belly dancers, most of them Jewish and Armenian girls, some of whom they even brought into their retinues. And at celebrations like weddings and circumcisions, the royal mamluks and their amirs did not mind joining the fun and doing a bit of dancing themselves.

With all their general aloofness and isolation

from the indigenous population, there were times at which the court and the great feudal lords showed generosity to their Muslim and non-Muslim subjects, as when they provided free public meals on the two great Muslim holidays, the ʿĪd al-Fiṭr and the ʿĪd al-Aḍḥā, or contributed food and money when their Coptic employees celebrated their New Year (*nawrūz*) in early September. Until the public celebration of the latter was banned by Sultan Barqūq in 1385, the court would even put a state representative, the *amīr al-nawrūz*, in charge of the festivities, which sometimes were attended by the sultan himself. But such tokens of Mamluk benevolence and interreligious harmony had already been seriously threatened by the time of Barqūq. Thirty-one years earlier, Sultan Ṣalāḥ al-Dīn Ṣāliḥ (1351–54), amid a wave of anti-Christian sentiment, had altogether abolished a festival that used to bring non-Muslims and Muslims together: the traditional Coptic Feast of the Martyr, celebrated for three days beginning on 18 or 19 May. The immersion of a box containing a martyr's finger in the Nile in anticipation of the river's annual rise was deemed pagan and offensive; besides, the people had the habit of drinking themselves silly on the occasion. And four years later, his brother al-Ḥasan, much in the same vein, had put a ban on the public celebration of Coptic Christmas on 7 January.

UNIVERSITY OF MARYLAND
COLLEGE PARK

NOTE

The sources on which this chapter is based are al-Maqrīzī (Taqīy al-Dīn Abū 'l-ʿAbbās Aḥmad b. ʿAlī), *Al-Mawāʿiẓ wa-'l-iʿtibār fī dhikr al-khiṭaṭ wa-'l-āthār* (Būlāq, 1270/1853) and *Kitāb al-sulūk li-maʿrifat duwal al-mulūk*, ed. Ziyāda/ʿĀshūr (Cairo, 1956–73); al-Qalqashandī (Abū 'l-ʿAbbās Aḥmad b. ʿAlī), *Ṣubḥ al-aʿshā fī ṣināʿat al-inshā* (Cairo, 1383/1963); Ibn Ṭaghrībirdī (Jamāl al-Dīn Abū 'l-Maḥāsin Yūsuf), *Al-Nujūm al-zāhira fī mulūk Miṣr wa-'l-Qāhira* (Cairo, 1383–92/1963–72); Ibn Iyās (Muḥammad b. Aḥmad), *Badāʾiʿ al-zuhūr fī waqāʾiʿ al-duhūr*, ed. Mostafa (Cairo, 1960–75); Ibn Shāhīn (Ghars al-Dīn Khalīl), *Zubdat kashf al-mamālik wa-bayān al-ṭuruq wa-'l-masālik*, ed. Ravaisse (Paris, 1891); and al-ʿUmarī (Shihāb al-Dīn Aḥmad b. Yaḥyā b. Faḍl-Allāh), *Al-Taʿrīf bi-'l-muṣṭalaḥ al-sharīf* (Cairo, 1312/1894).

ANDRÉ RAYMOND

Cairo's Area and Population in the Early Fifteenth Century

The first precise data we have about the size and population of Cairo are those in the *Description de l'Egypte* compiled in 1798, and it was not until the last years of the eighteenth century that an exact and detailed map of Cairo could be drawn and population estimates established with any certainty. For earlier centuries there is almost no demographic information, but there are at least some indications—and sometimes quite complete ones—to help us reconstruct the topography of Cairo and formulate some hypotheses about its population. The works of Maqrīzī, especially his *Khiṭaṭ*, written between 1415 and 1424, are an almost inexhaustible mine of information, and it is regrettable that they have been so neglected from that point of view. Had they not been, a map of Cairo in the Mamluk period based on Maqrīzī's information might already have been drawn.[1] Using Maqrīzī's work, one could draw up a list of monuments, streets, districts, and so on, that would enable us to map the town and estimate the number of its inhabitants at the beginning of the fifteenth century. A comparison of those data with the precise and detailed information available for the end of the eighteenth century would then allow us to draw significant conclusions and make some hypotheses about the evolution of the town's structure, economic life, and population from Mamluk times to the end of the Ottoman period.

Difficulties will be encountered in such an effort, however, because Maqrīzī's description is not exhaustive, and his silence can in no way be considered as a negative proof, but only as a presumption of nonexistence. In addition, it is somewhat risky to compare data that are separated by a gap of almost four centuries, even if the relative stability of the social and economic basis of urban life from the fifteenth to the eighteenth century may tempt us to do so.[2] These pages represent a preliminary reflection, an occasional investigation of Cairo in the Mamluk period by an Ottoman historian,[3] and not an exhaustive study of this fundamental problem of urban history. They are meant to be provocative and an incentive to further discussion.

All the ideas usually ventured about the size and population of Cairo[4] seem to me equally unsatisfactory. No precise or reliable map is available for the city in the Mamluk period, although William Popper's sketches in his work on Ṭaghrī Birdī[5] are good examples of what could easily be accomplished from Maqrīzī's books if the innumerable topographical indications found there were to be systematically indexed and noted on a map. In a recent and excellent book about Cairo, Janet Abu-Lughod, referring to Popper's maps, unfortunately suggests that they represent "the built-up area of Cairo ca. 1460."[6] That is not the case. Although Popper used the map of the *Description de l'Egypte* as a *fond de carte*, he certainly did not claim that Cairo had the same area in 1460 as it had in 1798. A careful examination of his sketches shows that such an interpretation would be particularly misleading for the western part of the town beyond the Khalīj, where almost no toponym is mentioned.[7] The sixteenth-century scenograph of Dalle Greche, recently studied by Viktoria Meinecke-Berg, is interesting and relatively precise, but it is not entirely reliable as a map of Cairo.[8]

Because they are based neither on an exact cartography nor on precise data, population estimates for Cairo at any time remain in the area of hypothesis; they are almost as arbitrary as the reckonings of the travelers whose occasional convergences are more often attributable to chance or reliance on the same source than to any accurate accounting. To illustrate how useless it is to rely on the figures proposed by European observers, compare the numbers given by two such perspicacious and well-informed contemporaries as Digeon and Volney. Digeon put the population of Cairo at 600,000 inhabitants in 1778 and Volney at 250,000 in 1783; a few years later, in July 1798, and only a day apart, one member of the French expedition to Egypt proposed a figure of 400,000 (Boyer, 10 Thermidor an VI) and the other, 600,000 (Dupuis, 11 Thermidor).[9]

Although less erratic, modern estimates are based on not much firmer ground. Cairo historians credit the town with a population of from 500,000 to 600,000 inhabitants under the reign of Sultan Nāṣir Muḥammad ibn Qalā'ūn, around 1340. Clerget speaks of 600,000 inhabitants at least, and Abu-Lughod of a half-million; Dols suggests 451,008, but he admits that the estimates of Clerget and Abu-Lughod, though higher than his, "are not at all unlikely." Although it is impossible to give an exact number, the plague of 1348 and circumstances in Egypt at the beginning of the fifteenth century account for a significant drop in the population of Cairo, which probably reached its nadir in Maqrīzī's time. It recovered later in the fifteenth century, rising to 385,000 inhabitants around 1550, again according to Clerget. Dols mentions this figure, but basing his own calculations on Leo Africanus's reference to 23,000 households (*"feux"*) he suggests a much lower figure for the beginning of the sixteenth century, between 177,500 and 213,000 for the whole town.[10] In the absence of hard facts these figures must be considered mere conjectures.

TABLE 1. Number and Location of Marketplaces (*Sūq* and *Suwayqa*) and Caravanserais (*Qaysāriyya, Khān, Funduq, Wikāla*)

	According to Maqrīzī		*Ottoman Period*	
	Number	*Percent*	*Number*	*Percent*
Marketplaces				
Ḥusayniyya	9	10.3	7	4.9
Qāhira	57	65.5	68	47.2
Southern region	13	14.9	44	30.5
Western region	8	9.2	25	17.4
Total	87	99.9	144	100.0
Caravanserais				
Ḥusayniyya	1	1.7	12	3.5
Qāhira	47	82.5	244	70.1
Southern region	6	10.5	60	17.2
Western region	3	5.2	32	9.2
Total	57	99.9	348	100.0

NOTE: See figures 2, 3, and 4.

In the sketch to be drawn here for the topography of Cairo, I will extract from the *Khiṭaṭ* some rough data about commercial centers, haras, hammams, mosques, and madrasas. By analyzing their location and comparing those findings with similar elements for the Ottoman period we should be able to make a rough estimate of the size of Cairo in Maqrīzī's time.

On the location of markets and caravanserais, the *Khiṭaṭ* gives us plentiful and relatively complete information, which is summarized in table 1.[11] As the figures there show, commercial activity in Maqrīzī's time was concentrated in Fatimid Qāhira, and, more precisely, along the central part of the Qaṣaba. In the zone stretching between the Ṣāgha (fig. 1, I–6) and the Ka'akiyyīn (fig. 1, L–5) and covering an area 400 meters long and 200 wide, twenty-three suqs could be found (26.4 percent of the total) and twenty-three caravanserais (38.6 percent). Commercial centers were also fairly numerous in the southern part of Cairo, especially along the Shāri' al-A'ẓam, around the mosque of Ibn Ṭūlūn, and near Bāb Zuwayla. Most of the marketplaces beyond the Khalīj were nonspecialized *suwayqa* and, in the west, commerce was concentrated along the streets leading from Bāb al-Qanṭara and Bāb al-Kharq through Bāb al-Baḥr and Bāb al-Lūq.

Comparison with the Ottoman period confirms those conclusions. Although in 1798 Qāhira and the Qaṣaba remained the center of economic life and particularly of international trade, the markets of the southern and especially the western area had become both more numerous and more specialized, which seems to indicate an expansion of economic activity outside Qāhira, in areas still little developed in the fifteenth century. With respect to the western part of the city, the contrast with Maqrīzī's account is particularly striking and significant.

The location of the *ḥāra* gives us information that complements data derived from the study of markets and caravanserais about what we might call the urbanized areas, since Maqrīzī's own definition of the word *ḥāra* is "a place where houses cluster together" (*kull maḥalla danat manāziluhā*).[12] In Maqrīzī's time (table 2) most of the *ḥāra* were in Qāhira, in a zone that formed a sort of belt around the area where the economic life of the city was concentrated. The nine *ḥāra* of the southern region of the town stretched immediately south of Bāb Zuwayla. In the west Maqrīzī mentions just one single *ḥāra*, located near Bāb al-Qanṭara. By the eighteenth century, however, the markets inside

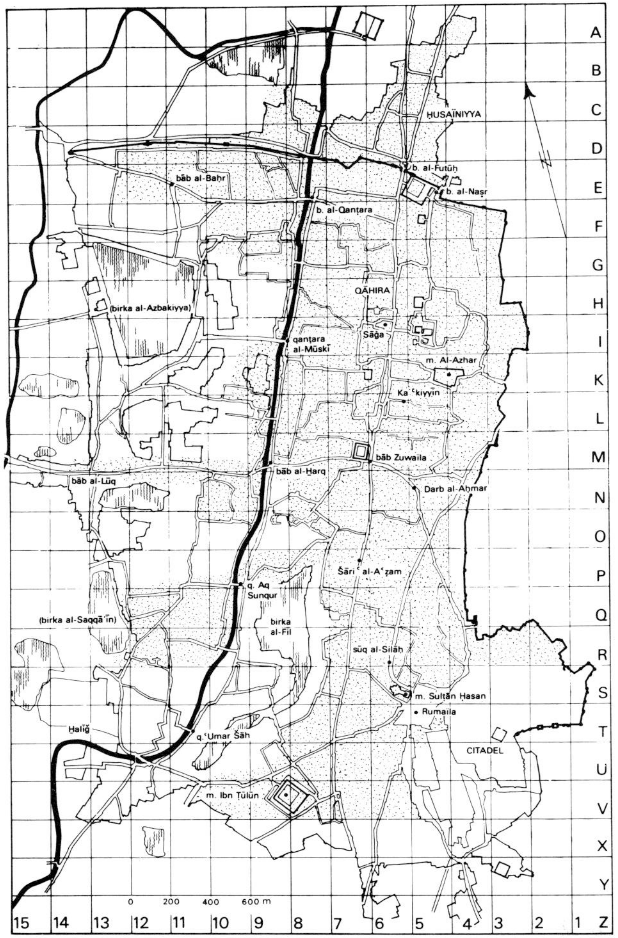

FIGURE 1. Extent of the built-up area of Cairo in Maqrīzī's time (dotted areas). Reproduced from A. Raymond, "Le Caire sous les Ottomans," in *Palais et maisons du Caire*, vol. 2, *Epoque ottomane* (Paris, 1983).

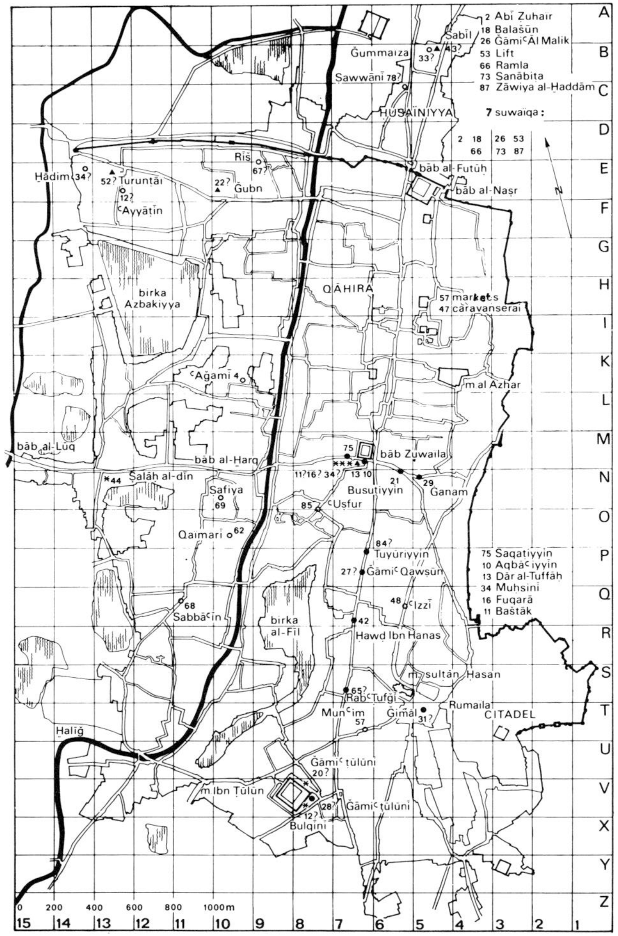

FIGURE 2. Location of marketplaces and caravanserais outside Qāhira, according to Maqrīzī. Reproduced from A. Raymond and G. Wiet, *Les marchés du Caire* (Cairo, 1979).

● *sūq*   * *qaysāriyya*

○ *suwayqa*   ▲ *khān, funduq, wikāla*

NOTE: Marketplaces and caravanserais within Qāhira are too numerous to include. Maqrīzī records 57 marketplaces and 47 caravanserais in this area.

Qāhira had so expanded that they had pushed the residential areas to the southern and western regions and turned them into residential areas for people working in Qāhira. A comparison of figures 5 and 6 will show the extent of the built-up area at the time of Maqrīzī and the considerable expansion of Cairo under the Ottomans, which is also notable for the increase in the number of *ḥāra* from thirty-eight to seventy-one.

Elsewhere I have tried to show for modern Arab cities how closely the number and location of public baths are related to the number of inhabitants and their distribution. This same relationship probably prevailed in remoter times as well.[13] Maqrīzī's precise information on this point is therefore particularly welcome (table 3).[14] The location of the public baths in use in Maqrīzī's time reflects the strong concentration of population in Qāhira (figs. 7, 8). All the baths mentioned for the southern region are concentrated along the Shāriʿ al-Aʿẓam, between Bāb Zuwayla and the mosque of Ibn Ṭūlūn. In the western region one bath apparently existed near the Khalīj (in I–9), but it was no longer in use in Maqrı-zī's time. Here again a comparison with the location of the baths in the Ottoman period is enlightening. Their large number (seventy-seven, as opposed to fifty-eight and thirty-one) and their even distribution seem to reveal a general increase in population, particularly in the southern and western parts of the town.

In contrast to the public baths and *sabīl*, or fountains, mosques do not seem to be totally reliable indicators of population distribution, but their presence at least indicates the existence of a settled population in a given area. The distribution of the mosques mentioned in the *Description de l'Egypte* among the four main regions of Cairo therefore corresponded more or less to the built-up areas, if not to the actual number of people living in them.[15] It is useful once again to compare those data with the location of the mosques mentioned in the *Khiṭaṭ* (table 4).[16]

Significantly, the number of mosques in Qāhira remained almost unchanged at sixty-nine and sixty-seven, respectively, from the fifteenth to the eighteenth century, indicating that Qāhira was already heavily populated under the Mamluks and that the number of inhabitants did not vary much from one period to the other (figs. 9, 10). In the fifteenth century, mosques were much less numerous in the southern area than in Qāhira, and some blanks appear on the map around the Birkat al-Fīl and on the southern limits of the town. The mosques mentioned by Maqrīzī are even fewer in the western part of the city, especially compared with their number in the *Description de l'Egypte*, and they are concentrated in three limited areas in the north, center, and south. Again these figures indicate a strong increase in population in the southern and western regions.

The topographic information available in Maqrīzī's *Khiṭaṭ*, supplemented by the *Description de l'Egypte*, enables us to draw a picture of Cairo's urban structure at the beginning of the fifteenth century, and the most striking point that emerges from it is the outstanding place Qāhira occupied in

TABLE 2. Number and Location of *Ḥāra*

	According to Maqrīzī		*Ottoman Period*	
Ḥāra	*Number*	*Percent*	*Number*	*Percent*
Ḥusayniyya	1	2.6	—	—
Qāhira	27	71.1	17	23.9
Southern region	9	23.7	19	26.8
Western region	1	2.6	35	49.3
Total	38	100.0	71	100.0

NOTE: See figures 5 and 6.

TABLE 3. Number and Location of Hammams

	In Maqrīzī's Time				
	Total Number	*Still in Use*		*Ottoman Period*	
Hammams	*Mentioned*	*Number*	*Percent*	*Number*	*Percent*
Ḥusayniyya	—	—	—	2	2.6
Qāhira	48	27	87.1	28	36.4
Southern region	9	4	12.9	30	39.0
Western region	1	—	—	17	22.0
Total	58	31	100.0	77	100.0

NOTE: See figures 7 and 8.

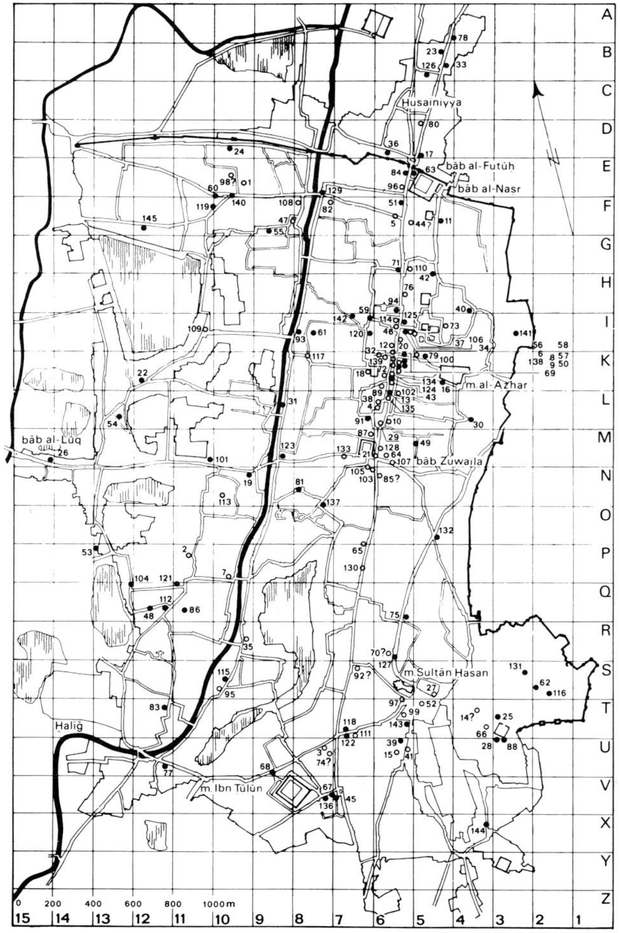

FIGURE 3. Location of marketplaces in the Ottoman period. Reproduced from Raymond and Wiet, *Les marchés du Caire.*

● mentioned in the *Description de l'Egypte*

○ not mentioned in the *Description*

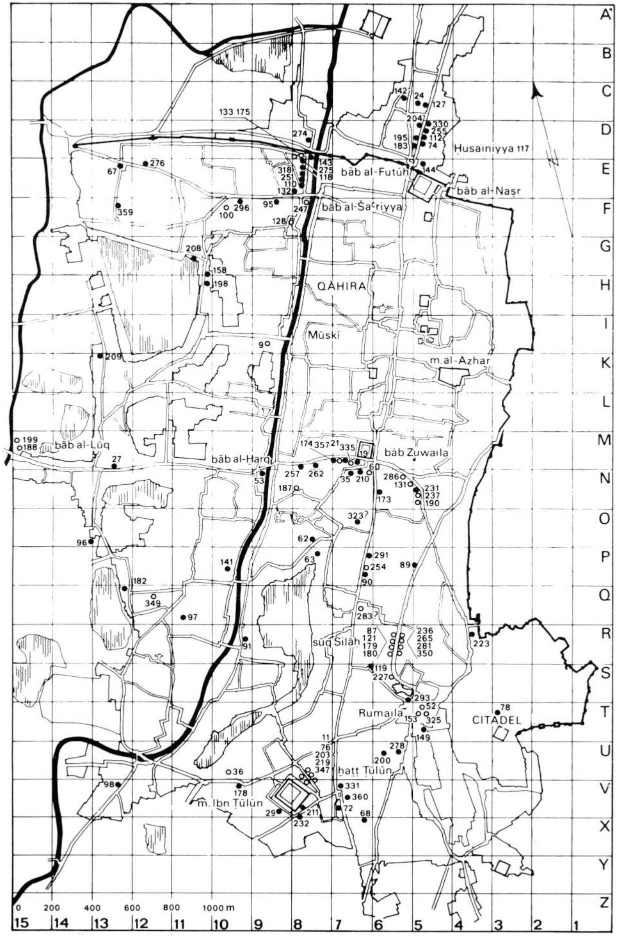

FIGURE 4. Location of *khān* and *wikāla* outside Qāhira in the Ottoman period. Reproduced from Raymond and Wiet, *Les marchés du Caire.*

● mentioned in the *Description de l'Egypte*

○ not mentioned in the *Description*

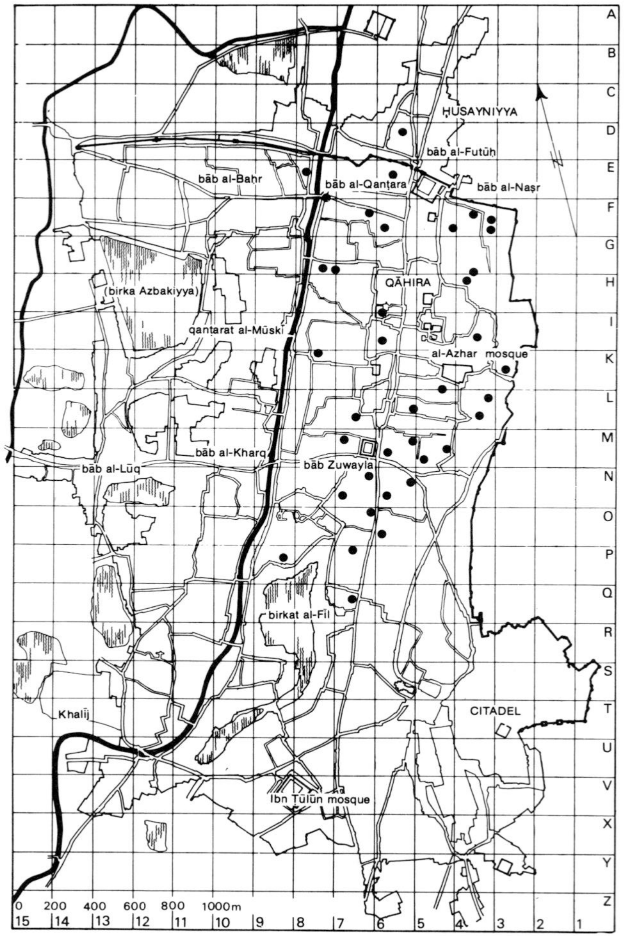

FIGURE 5. Location of *ḥāra*, according to Maqrīzī.

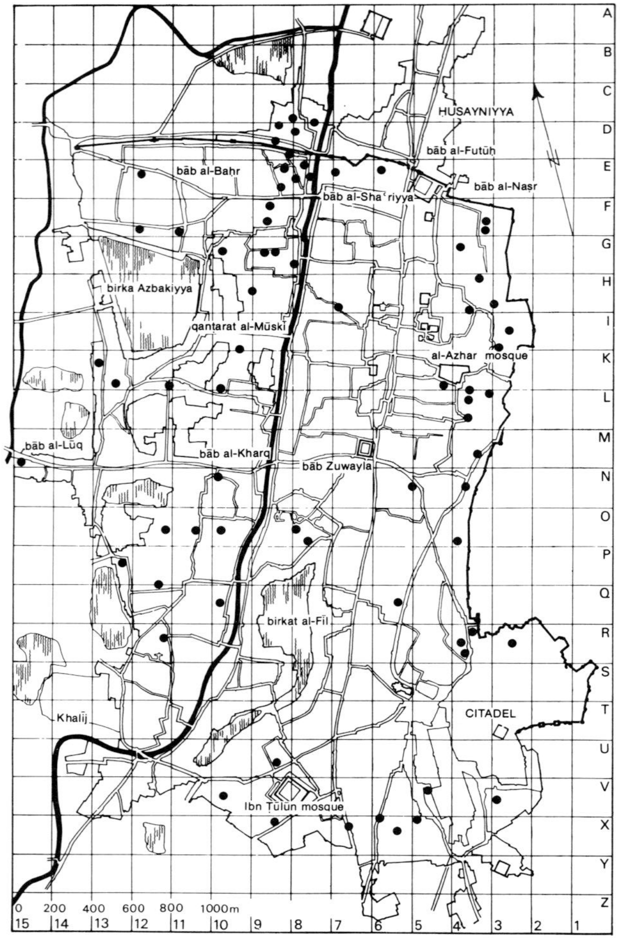

FIGURE 6. Location of *ḥāra* in the Ottoman period.

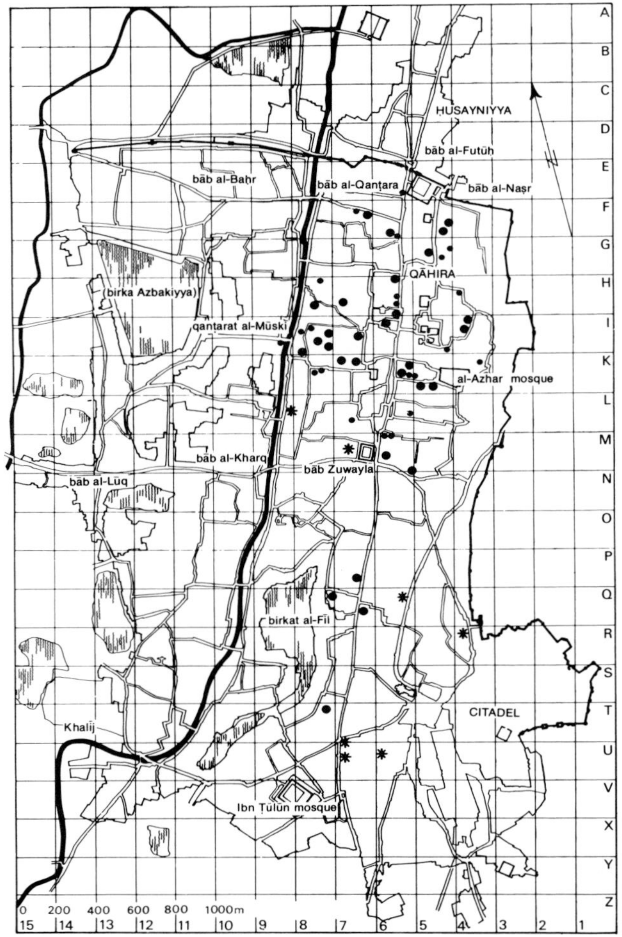

FIGURE 7. Location of hammams in Maqrīzī's time.
- ● still in use, according to Maqrīzī
- • no longer in use, according to Maqrīzī
- * not mentioned by Maqrīzī

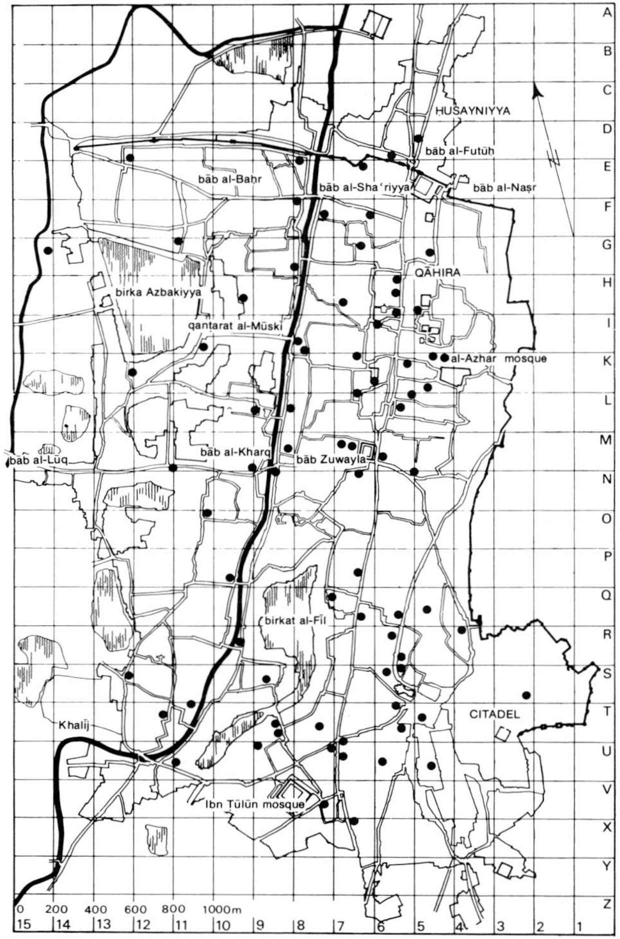

FIGURE 8. Location of hammams in the Ottoman period.

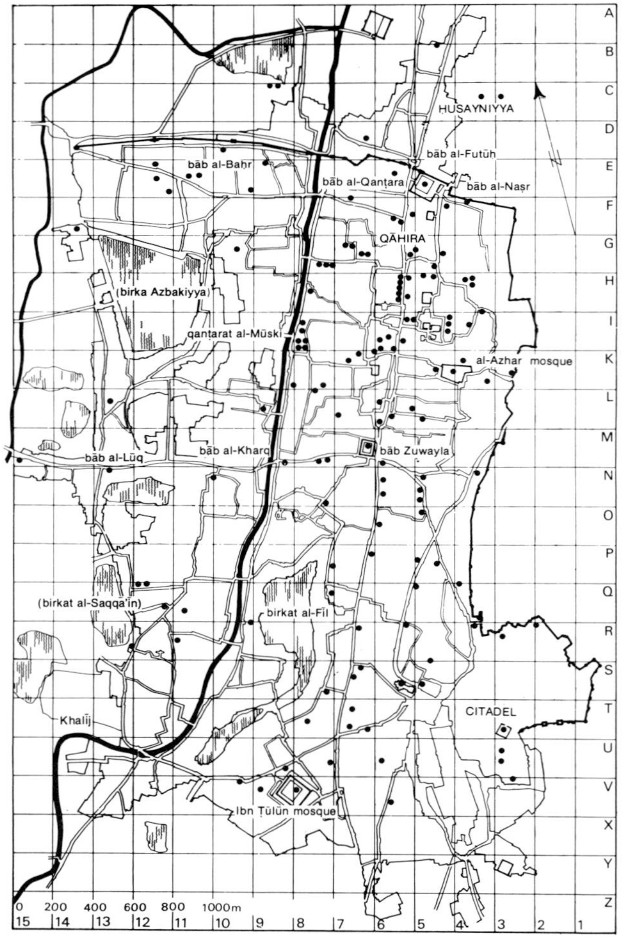

FIGURE 9. Location of mosques in Maqrīzī's time.

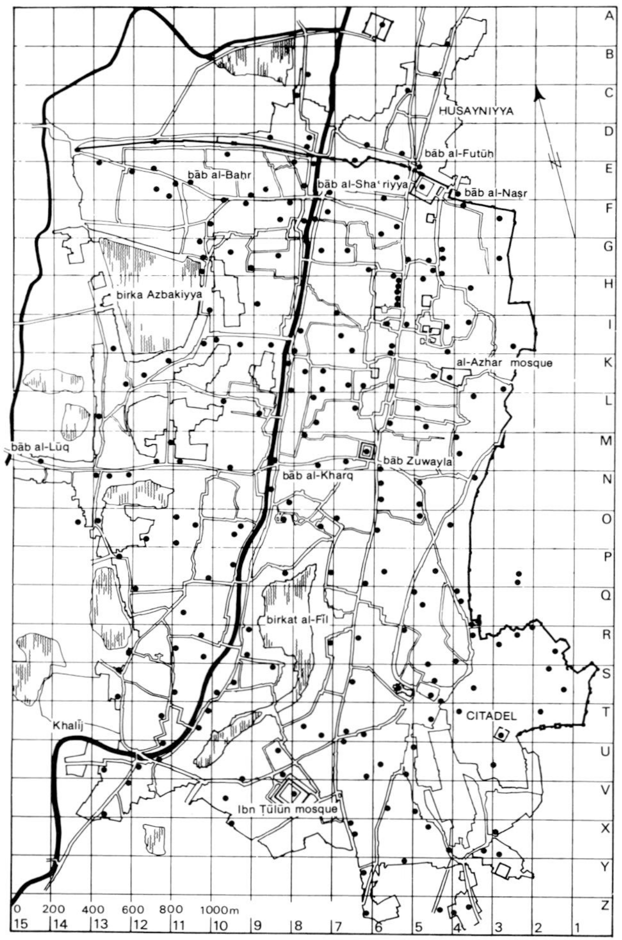

FIGURE 10. Location of mosques mentioned in the *Description de l'Egypte.*

TABLE 4. Number and Location of Mosques

Mosques	In Maqrīzī's Time		Description	
	Number	*Percent*	*Number*	*Percent*
Ḥusayniyya	5	3.4	9	3.7
Qāhira	69	47.3	67	27.6
Southern region	49	33.6	93	38.3
Western region	23	15.7	74	30.4
Total	146	100.0	243	100.0

NOTE: See figures 9 and 10.

Mamluk Cairo. Two-thirds of the markets of Cairo and four-fifths of its caravanserais were located there, along with 71 percent of the *ḥāra* mentioned by Maqrīzī, 87 percent of the hammams, and nearly half the mosques. The density of the population in Qāhira in Maqrīzī's time seems to have been about the same as in the eighteenth century: hence the relative stability of the number of hammams and mosques from one period to another (twenty-seven and twenty-eight hammams, respectively, and sixty-nine and sixty-seven mosques). The extension of commercial activities in the Ottoman period, as shown by the increase in the number of caravanserais, encroached upon the residential districts, and the surplus population had to spread outside the Fatimid limits.

It is likely that in Maqrīzī's time vacant areas still existed in the southern part of the city. A comparison between the locations of residential and commercial areas in the fifteenth and eighteenth centuries is quite revealing. A period of active mosque building in the fourteenth century reflects the expansion of Cairo in the southern area along the main north-south thoroughfares from Bāb Zuwayla to the Citadel through the Darb al-Aḥmar, or southward through the Shāriʿ al-Aʿẓam and from east to west from Bāb Zuwayla to Bāb al-Kharq and from Rumaīla to Ibn Ṭūlūn and the Khalīj. But the locations of the commercial centers and the *ḥāra*, hammams, and mosques show that, except for those thickly populated areas, settlement was sparse around the Birkat al-Fīl, along the Khalīj, and in the southern part of town.

The only scattered commercial zones beyond the Khalīj, the rather small number of the mosques, and the almost complete silence of the *Khiṭaṭ* concerning the existence there of *ḥāra* and hammams converge in the conclusion that the western region was only partly urbanized at the beginning of the fifteenth century, except for some limited sections. The most important settled zones were in the north, in an area spreading along the street beginning at Bāb al-Qanṭara and leading westward; in the center, in a stretch of land on both sides of the street leading from Bāb al-Kharq to Bāb al-Lūq; and in the south, in the area stretching between the Khalīj and the Birkat al-Saqqā'īn. Here again a comparison with the eighteenth century, when about one-sixth of the marketplaces, one-tenth of the caravanserais, one-fifth of the public baths, and one-third of the mosques were located in the west (as against one-tenth, one-twentieth, none, and one-sixth, respectively, in Maqrīzī's time), is significant.

Transferring all these elements onto a map allows us to propose a topography for the urbanization of the various parts of Cairo in the fifteenth century which differs notably from the one in the *Description de l'Egypte* (see fig. 1). Although the development of the streets, the expansion of the commercial centers, and the distribution of public and private buildings all suggest that in the eighteenth century the town was spread more or less evenly over all the area delineated by the French map, it is quite clear that in the fifteenth century the built-up zone occupied only a part of it. Popper's maps give a picture of the town in 1460 that is not markedly different from the one formed from Maqrīzī's descriptions. They show a striking abundance of toponyms in the region of Qāhira, though there are areas either sparsely populated or completely uninhabited to the south; the near-emptiness of the western zone away from the main streets is obvious. In spite of Cairo's slow recovery in the course of the fifteenth century, the main characteristics of the structure we have described probably remained intact up to the beginning of the Ottoman period. In 1518 the well-informed observer Leo Africanus estimated the population of the western region to be only 13 percent of the total population of the town.[17]

Dalle Greche's survey was published in 1549, but it is obviously based on earlier information and is the first reliable representation of Cairo. However, it still cannot reasonably be used as evidence that the town, in about 1517, occupied the total area extending on the map of 1798 between its northern, eastern, and southern limits and the Khalīj al-Nāṣirī in the west—that is to say, over roughly 800 hectares, as opposed to 660 in 1798.[18] The general structure of the town, particularly the network of the main streets, is drawn with great accuracy, especially when we consider that the map was executed in Italy from data collected in Egypt; but there is every reason to believe that whenever the mapmaker found an empty area he conscientiously filled in the space he had at his disposal with houses, whether there were actually any buildings there or not, in decorative rather than cartographic fashion. This is quite obvious in the southern zone, where a feature as important as the Birkat al-Fīl is ignored, and in the western zone, where no construction is recognizable, and where, except for the Azbakiyya, ponds and open spaces are not shown on the map. Even if, for its time, Dalle Greche's map gives a remarkably accurate picture of the general layout of the city, it is not reliable in its indications of built-up areas. To form a hypothesis about them we must turn back once more to Maqrīzī.

By comparing the information we have gleaned from Maqrīzī's account with the extent of the town in 1798, we can hypothesize that the built-up areas in Ḥusayniyya and Qāhira were not very different in size in the fifteenth century and in the eighteenth century—in both cases about 180 hectares (in 1798, 26 plus 153 hectares). The southern region must have extended over fewer than 200 hectares in the fifteenth century, as opposed to 266 in 1798, and the western region comprised 100 hectares at most, as opposed to 215 in 1798. The total built-up area could therefore not have been more than 450 hectares in the fifteenth century, as opposed to 660 in 1798.

Based on an average density of 400 inhabitants per hectare (a maximum number for the great Arab cities of the time, and the actual density of the population of Cairo in the Ottoman period), we arrive at a figure of between 150,000 and 200,000 inhabitants for Maqrīzī's Cairo, about half of whom lived in Qāhira, nearly as many as in 1798. The increase in population of Cairo during the Ottoman period is attributable mainly to the development of the regions south and west of the Fatimid nucleus of the town.

There is every reason to believe that before the great population drop in 1348 and the difficulties at the beginning of the fifteenth century, the population of Cairo was considerably larger. Maqrīzī makes numerous references to the effects of those disasters on the topography of the town. The rate of natural increase in population was so low in those centuries that demographic recovery was very slow, which explains why the effects of that crisis were still so apparent more than fifty years later.[19] Extrapolating from the diminution in the number of public baths in use—thirty-one out of fifty-eight (table 3)—we are led to the conclusion that the town might have lost some 40 percent of its inhabitants in 1348, a loss that was far from having been regained a hundred years later.[20] But judging from the probable extent of the built-up areas, even at its height toward the end of Nāṣir Muḥammad's reign, the town could not have had more than between 200,000 and 250,000 inhabitants in the midfourteenth century.

Cairo probably recovered somewhat in the fifteenth century, but its structure did not change fundamentally until the beginning of the sixteenth. The population around 1517 cannot have amounted to more than 200,000, since Popper's topographical work, coupled with the figures mentioned by Leo Africanus, shows that the western region was still sparsely settled a short time after the Ottoman invasion. The *intra muros* town of Qāhira was then supposed to have had 8,000 households, the suburb of Bāb Zuwayla (which seems to correspond to our southern region) about 12,000 households, and the suburb of Bāb al-Lūq (probably the western region, beyond the Khalīj) only about 3,000 households. It was only much later that the western region was completely settled, a process that was finished by the time of the French expedition in Egypt, although even then the empty spaces (*birka*, gardens, graveyards) were still extensive west of the Khalīj.

These estimates seem to correspond to what emerges from a study of the topography of Cairo based on Maqrīzī's information. But they will remain conjectures until a systematic study of Maqrīzī's work, as well as of the main historical sources of the Mamluk period, is undertaken. The estimates of 200,000–250,000 inhabitants in 1348 and 150,000–200,000 in 1420 seem low only when compared with the overly optimistic figures that have been proposed without any reference to the actual topography of the town. They will be seen in a more reasonable light if we remember that in the Western world at that time only Constantinople could boast of anything like that number of people. In 1328 Paris had only 80,000 inhabitants in a built-up area of 437 hectares, and in 1377 London is supposed to have had 60,000 in an area of 288 hectares.[21] Neither in numbers nor in density of population could those capitals of already powerful and populated states compete with the capital of the Mamluk empire.[22]

University of Provence
Aix-en-Provence

NOTES

1. When the index of the *Khiṭaṭ* of Maqrīzī undertaken by the Institut Français d'Archéologie Orientale in Cairo has been completed, it will throw new light on the history of Cairo during the Mamluk period.

2. The remarkable persistence of the main urban features, particularly the street network, from Maqrīzī to the *Description de l'Egypte* is one of the most striking manifestations of this stability.

3. On the occasion of the preparation of the publication of *Les marchés du Caire* (Cairo, 1979), with the late Gaston Wiet.

4. I will not deal here with the important problem of the satellite towns of Cairo (Old Cairo, Būlāq), nor with the extensions of the city. I will take into account only the central area that was later to become Ottoman Cairo and still later to be described by the French in 1798–1801.

5. William Popper, *Egypt and Syria under the Circassian Sultans: Systematic Notes to Ibn Ṭaghrī Birdī's Chronicles of Egypt* (Berkeley, Calif., 1955), maps 6–12.

6. Janet Abu-Lughod, *Cairo: 1001 Years of the City Victorious* (Princeton, N.J., 1971), map 10, p. 45.

7. I shall call "Qāhira" the Fatimid town extending from Bāb al-Futūḥ to Bāb Zuwayla and from the Khalīj to the eastern wall of the city *intra muros*; the term "southern region" will refer to the part south of Bāb Zuwayla and east of the Khalīj; the term "western region" designates the zone stretching westward beyond the Khalīj.

8. Viktoria Meinecke-Berg, "Eine Stadtansicht des mamlukischen Kairo aus dem 16. Jahrhundert," in *Mitteilungen des Deutschen Archäologischen Instituts: Abteilung Kairo*, vol. 32 (1976).

9. Archives Nationales, Paris, CC, Le Caire, B 1 336, 27 mai 1778 (Digeon); Volney, *Voyage en Egypte et en Syrie* (1822), 1:193; *Correspondance de l'armée française en Egypte*, vol. 7 (Paris, 1799), pp. 180, 186.

10. Marcel Clerget, *Le Caire*, 2 vols. (Cairo, 1934), 1:240–41; Abu-Lughod, *Cairo*, p. 37; Michael W. Dols, *The Black Death in the Middle East* (Princeton, N.J., 1977), pp. 196, 202.

11. André Raymond and Gaston Wiet, *Les marchés du Caire*, appendixes 3 and 5. We have been able to locate 57 of the 58 caravanserais of Maqrīzī's time. For the Ottoman period, 144 of 145 suqs and *suwayqa* have been located, and 348 of 360 *wikāla* and khans.

12. Maqrīzī, *Khiṭaṭ*, 2:2. Maqrīzī gives a list of 38 *ḥāra* (pp. 2–23). My map supplements the indications given by Abu-Lughod, *Cairo*, pp. 42–43. For the Ottoman period, see André Raymond, "La géographie des *ḥāra* du Caire au XVIIIème siècle," *Livre du centenaire de l'IFAO, Mémoires de l'Institut Français d'Archéologie Orientale*, vol. 104 (1980).

13. André Raymond, "Signes urbains et étude de la population des grandes villes arabes à l'époque ottomane," *Bulletin des Études Orientales* 28 (1975); "La localisation des bains publics au Caire au XVème siècle," ibid., vol. 30 (1978).

14. Maqrīzī mentions a total of 52 public baths, 51 of which have been located; 29 of them were still in use in his time. If we take into consideration some public baths whose existence is certain, but which are not mentioned by Maqrīzī, the total reaches 58, 31 of which were still in use (see Raymond, "La localisation des bains publics").

15. The figures established from the *Description de l'Egypte* are as follows: in Ḥusayniyya, 9 mosques in a built-up area of 26 hectares (1 mosque per 2.9 ha); in Qāhira, 67 mosques in a built-up area of 153 ha (1 mosque per 2.3 ha); in the southern region, 93 mosques in a built-up area of 266 ha (1 mosque per 2.9 ha); in the western region, 74 mosques in a built-up area of 215 ha (1 mosque per 2.9 ha). The relation between the number of mosques and the extent of the built-up area seems quite obvious. The figures are remarkably consistent (1 mosque per 2.9 ha), except in Qāhira, but it seems logical that in this central area the number of mosques would have been above average.

16. I have gone through the lists of the *jāmi'*, *madrasa*, and *masjid* given by Maqrīzī in the *Khiṭaṭ* (2:244–331, 362–405, 408–13). I have, moreover, taken into account the mosques mentioned in the list of the classified monuments of Cairo, some of which are not found in Maqrīzī's text, through 1432 (Barsbāy's mosque, no. 121, *Index to Mohammedan Monuments*). The *Description* makes no distinction among the various types of mosque; they are all referred to as "*jāmi'*."

17. Léon l'Africain (Leo Africanus), *Description de l'Afrique* (Paris, 1956), 2:503–7.

18. Dalle Greche's map is studied by Meinecke-Berg (see n. 8).

19. According to Daniel Panzac, "Endémies, épidémies et population en Egypte au XIXème siècle" (in *L'Egypte au XIXe siècle*, R. Mantran, ed. [Paris, 1982], pp. 83–100), the normal rate of increase of the population of Cairo before the beginning of the nineteenth century amounted to only 5 per 1,000. Relying on natural increase alone, it would have taken eighty-two years to compensate for the loss of one-third of the population.

20. See Dols, *Black Death*, pp. 212–18.

21. J. C. Russell, *Medieval Regions and Their Cities* (Bloomington, Ind., 1972), pp. 124, 150.

22. No modifications have been made to this paper since it was first presented at the symposium in Washington in May 1981. The views expressed here have, however, been taken up again in my contribution ("Le Caire sous les Ottomans") for the collective volume *Palais et maisons du Caire*, vol. 2, *Epoque ottomane*, published by the CNRS in 1983.

JOHN ALDEN WILLIAMS

Urbanization and Monument Construction in Mamluk Cairo

By the fourteenth century Islamic civilization, shaken to its roots by the destruction during the thirteenth century of both the Abbasid caliphate in the east and the Almohad caliphate in the west, was experiencing a general renaissance from Spain to Central Asia and India. The city of the age, indeed of the world, was Cairo. The keenest observer of the period, the polymath Ibn Khaldūn, writing at the castle of Ibn Salāma near Oran in 1375–79, had not yet seen Cairo, but he was well aware of its unique position:

When the cities of the Persians in Iraq, Khurasan, and Transoxania fell into ruins, and sedentary culture—which God devised for the attainment of learning and crafts—left them, learning departed from the Persians. . . . Today no city has a more abundant sedentary learning than Cairo; she is the Mother of the World, the iwan of Islam, the wellspring of learning and the crafts. Some sedentary culture survived in Transoxania because of the dynasty there, so those cities also have a portion of learning and the crafts that cannot be denied.[1]

Although the great cities which were once the mines of learning are now in ruins, such as Baghdad, Basra, and Kufa, yet God (exalted be He) has replaced them with cities still greater, while learning was transferred from them to . . . Khurasan and Transoxania in the east and to Cairo and adjacent regions in the west. These cities remained in the midst of abundance, with a continuous civilization, and the tradition of instruction there was maintained. The people of [Cairo and] the east in general are more firmly rooted than others in the art of instruction and in all other crafts, to the point that many from North Africa who have traveled eastward seeking learning have supposed that the minds of the easterners were more perfect than those of people from the Maghrib, and that they were of firmer intelligence and greater discrimination by their inborn disposition . . . but this is not so.[2]

In connection with instruction in crafts, we have heard of attainments by the people of Egypt which are not to be matched, such as teaching tame donkeys and dumb animals and birds words and acts whose rarity is to be wondered at, and which people of the Maghrib cannot comprehend.[3]

In this age, we observe that learning and instruction are found as nowhere else in Cairo, because its civilization is developed and its sedentary culture has been thoroughly established for thousands of years. Hence the crafts are also thoroughly established there and well diversified.[4]

The legalist secretary of Sultan Abū 'Inān [the Marinid, of Fez] was asked about Cairo when he returned from a journey to Egypt while delivering a [royal] message to the tomb of the Prophet [in Medina] in the year 756[1355] [and replied] "Briefly, I can express it this way. All that one may imagine in advance he observes to fall short of the image he imagined, owing to the greater reach of the imagination over what is perceived by the senses, except for Cairo: she is greater than all that one may imagine about her."[5]

The rulers of Cairo, this city that so astonished the world of the fourteenth century, were a self-perpetuating corporation of military slaves, a legacy from the last Ayyubid sultan of Egypt. They had supplanted his relatives, but had been tolerated by the Abbasid caliph in Baghdad, by the ulema, and by other Muslim rulers because they seemed to offer Egypt the best hope of security in the chaos of the thirteenth century. By nature and function they were military custodians, conservative in all their ways. They set their stamp on everything they touched: the government, the arts of war, the learning and culture, the arts, crafts, and architecture that they patronized were all highly conservative. In this they were neither the cause nor the effect: they were offered leadership by a culture and an age that feared to lose its heritage.

The Mamluks could offer their subjects security from everyone but themselves, by the fourteenth century. The institution cost a great deal to maintain, financially, morally, and politically. Its factions and officers intrigued incessantly against each other and fought open battles whenever the leadership was in doubt. At such times, the Mamluk soldiery would run wild, attacking the civilians, plundering their shops, and carrying off their wives and children. Advancement in the corps occurred through a mixture of merit and ruthlessness, and to secure the complaisance of the ulema and sheikhs, who were the real leaders of the people, the Mamluk amirs multiplied pious bequests and outward marks of deference to the law of Islam and its scholars. The most characteristic Mamluk structure is the tomb complex: a madrasa, mosque, or khanqah (in some cases a combination of all three), often with a Koran school and a *sabīl* (a dispensary of free drinking water), and sometimes even a charity hospital, attached to the donor's tomb.

There is a strong element of paradox in a mausoleum complex in Islam, where even monumental tombs arrived only in the third century (ninth century A.D.). In early practice many of the dead were buried in their residences, as the Prophet had been. There are probably genuine hadiths that inveigh against building tombs higher than the level of the ground or using them as places of prayer. Fundamentalists have always criticized monuments that glorified the dead, so the creation of a charitable endowment helped justify the building of a handsome domed tomb. However, in Cairo there was a tradition of mausoleum shrines for Shiite saints from the twelfth century.[6] This had been accepted in Sunni practice under the Ayyubids, with the creation of a madrasa and a great domed mausoleum *mazār* at the grave of the Sunni imam al-Shāfiʿī, perhaps the first tomb complex of the city. One should also remember that the mosque and tomb of the Prophet at Medina had by this time grown into a conspicuous and internationally revered example of the mausoleum complex.

Still, it is quite clear that the chief model for the Mamluks was the Ṣāliḥiyya madrasa complex on the site of the palace of the Fatimid imams in the heart of the royal quarter of Qāhira. This site, the area known as Bayn al-Qaṣrayn, was to see a series of remarkable monuments in Cairene architecture. Sultan Ṣāliḥ's madrasa had been built in 1243, and not until his death in 1249 was his tomb constructed on the northeast side of his madrasa complex, the first ever built in Egypt to accommodate all four Sunni *madhhab*s.

Whether by accident or design, this last great Ayyubid monument served in different ways as a legitimizing monument for the Bahri Mamluks. The corps had been created by Sultan Ṣāliḥ, and when his mamluk Baybars I had stopped the Mongol advance, created a Mamluk empire, chastened the Franks, and restored the Abbasid caliphate in Cairo, he built his own madrasa to the northeast of his master's tomb, still on the site of the palace of the imams. If he had not died and been buried in Syria, he would have been interred there. Qalā'ūn, who consolidated Baybars's work and founded a dynasty, then built his own tomb complex (a madrasa and hospital) directly opposite, symbolically on the site of the Fatimid heirs to the throne. Barqūq, the first of the Burji Mamluk sultans, then built his own khanqah-madrasa and a

PLATE 1. Bayn al-Qaṣrayn, former site of the eastern and western Fatimid palaces. At the left are the fragmentary remains of the madrasa of Baybars I, the mausoleum of Sultan Ṣāliḥ Najm al-Dīn Ayyūb (1250), and the Ottoman *sabīl-kuttāb* of Hüsrev Pasha (1535); above is the finial of the minaret at the door of Sultan Ṣāliḥ's madrasa (1243). The madrasa of Sultan Qalā'ūn and the entrance to the māristān (1285) are at the right.

PLATE 2. Early and late mausolea. The dome of al-Sawābī (1285) is in the foreground; the mausoleum of Sūdūn Amir Majlis (1505) is behind.

tomb to the north of Qalā'ūn's. In the sixteenth century, an Ottoman viceroy built a *sabīl-kuttab* between the tomb of Ṣāliḥ Ayyūb and the door of his madrasa. All these constructions can be viewed as political statements by patrons who knew exactly what they wanted to say.

Only senior mamluks were allowed to marry, and a mamluk's son was not allowed to inherit his father's position. A mamluk's wealth was lent to him by the state, and was returnable at death. Even the Mamluk sultans realized how frail were their hopes that their sons would sit in their place. A monument was an investment in stability in a hasty world, and if it included a charitable establishment and stipends for prayers and Koran recitations for the donor's soul, it might offer him some comfort in the world of his permanent sojourn.

The first Mamluk monuments conservatively followed the style of the Ayyubids, who in Cairo patronized architecture very like that of the late Fatimid period.[7] The Qalā'ūn complex at Bayn al-Qaṣrayn was the first really innovative building of Mamluk times, incorporating influences from Syrian, North African, and Gothic architecture. Mamluk architecture is bracketed by two great periods: the third reign of Qalā'ūn's son al-Nāṣir, when he was firmly in control of the corps, some thirty years from 1310 to 1340; and another period of about thirty years from 1468 to 1496, the reign of Sultan Qāytbāy.

The city the Mamluks had inherited from the Ayyubids included the historically important Fatimid walled city and a southern portion that was developing between its southern gate, the Bāb Zuwayla, and the new royal city built by Ṣalāḥ al-Dīn. The older city of Fustat to the south had been burned by the Fatimid government in 1168 to keep it from falling into the hands of invading Crusaders. However, a part of it survived, chiefly as a river port, around the old mosque of ʿAmr ibn al-ʿAṣ and the Byzantine fortress of Babylon, and was known as the Old Miṣr (garrison-capital). Opposite it, on the isle of Rawḍa, the Ayyubid sultans had a second stronghold, the River (*baḥrī*) Citadel, where the Bahri mamluks were stationed in Ṣāliḥ Ayyūb's reign.

All this meant that the city was being pulled to develop toward the southwest. Baybars I briefly arrested this trend by developing an area to the north of Fatimid Cairo, part of Ẓāhir al-Qāhira ("Outside Cairo"), a name that echoed his own regnal title of *al-malik al-ẓāhir* ("the ascendant king"). The suburb around the great congregational mosque and a palace he built before 1270 was also called Ḥusayniyya. The creation of new royal quarters or suburbs was always a highly lucrative affair for Muslim monarchs: the land was bought cheap and sold dear, and new royal markets brought in high revenues as merchants and notables moved to the desirable new area.

However, the most phenomenal growth of the Mamluk city occurred in the decades of the third reign of al-Nāṣir ibn Qalā'ūn, south of Bāb Zuwayla, and many new monuments were created in this zone by the amirs at the instigation of the sultan. These included a number of splendid new mosques. Until about 1318, the law that there should be only one jamiʿ for the Friday prayer seems to have been more or less observed.[8] Qāhira had one jamiʿ, Old Miṣr another, the ninth-century mosque of Ibn Ṭūlūn had been renovated in 696/1296 by Sultan Lājīn for the area south of Bāb Zuwayla, the Citadel had a congregational mosque built by al-Nāṣir, and the quarter of Ḥusayniyya had the mosque of Baybars I. Between 1329 and 1340, four new congregational mosques were constructed between the southern walls and the Citadel: that of Ilmās, or Yilmāz (1329–30); of the sultan's son-in-law Qawṣūn (1329–30); of Bashtāk (1335), opposite his khanqah,[9] now disappeared; and of another son-in-law, Alṭunbughā al-Māridānī (1339), the most splendid of all and without a tomb. After al-Nāṣir's death in 1341, three more congregational mosques were built in this zone, those of Aṣlam al-Silāḥdār (1344–45), Aqsunqur (1346–47), and Shaykhū al-ʿUmarī (1349), whose mausoleum in a khanqah was built directly opposite the mosque.

Presumably the decision to permit a plurality of jamiʿs was arrived at by consideration of *maṣlaḥa*, the general interest of the Muslim community. Once applied, the decision was to have a continuous effect on the development of Cairo's quarters and neighborhoods. The sultan actively subsidized the public constructions of the great amirs that made his southern development a more desirable place to live, and it was probably a profitable investment, since the palaces and mansions of the powerful and rich quickly followed, along with markets and armorers' shops.

The growth of the southern area checked development in Ḥusayniyya, and after the Black Death (1347–49) the northern suburb seems to have been deserted, and by 1403, abandoned. Even the great plague did not stop the construction of monuments in the southern zone: as we have seen, the mosque of Shaykhū was built at exactly this time.

In 1325, al-Nāṣir completed the construction of a new canal, the Nāṣirī Khalīj, to the west of the city, to drain the new land that had been created by the eastward shift of the riverbed, bringing water from the Nile as far north as the Birkat al-Raṭlī and then joining the much older Miṣrī Khalīj, to provide water and a channel for water transport all the way north to the sultan's great khanqah and his new country seat at Siryāqūs (see map). This was a royal enterprise, made possible by the corvée of thousands of peasants. The area between the Miṣrī Khalīj and the Nāṣirī, with its several large ponds or *birka*s, was quickly laid out with orchards,

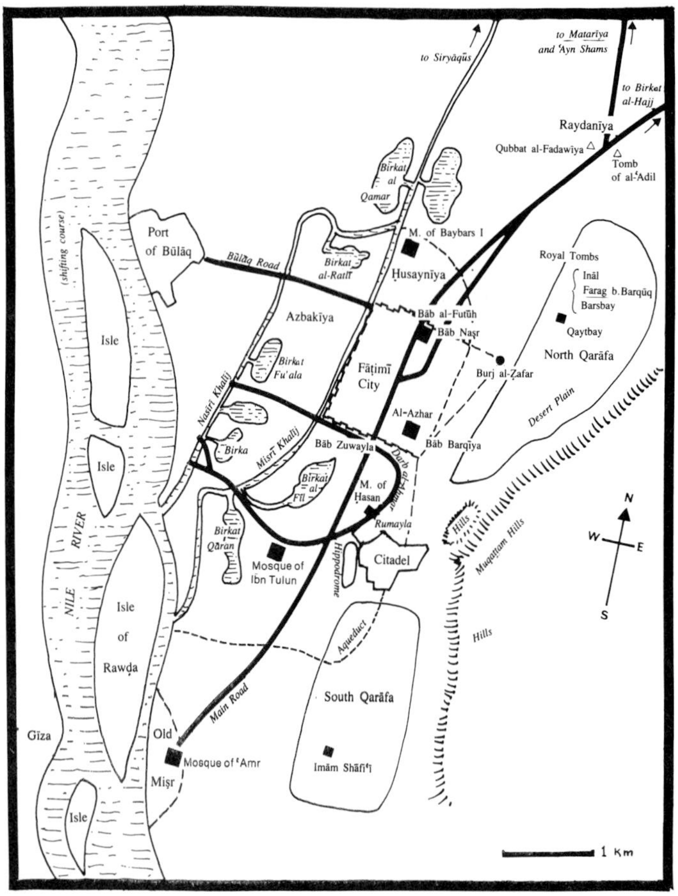

FIGURE 1. Sketch map of Mamluk Cairo.

PLATE 3. Mosque of Assanbughā, 1370. Note the mixed use of land: a paneled, polychrome mosque façade stands next to a townhouse with mashrabiyya belvedere. One of the two ground-floor shops was probably originally the mosque *sabīl*.

gardens, and villas, as well as new residential streets. They retained their delightful character even into the Ottoman period.

Al-Nāṣir also developed the riverbank area between Miṣr and Bulaq. North of Miṣr, he constructed al-Jāmiʿ al-Jadīd. In the area called Zarībat al-Sulṭān he erected a royal commercial warehouse (*dār wikāla*) and two large lodging complexes (*rabʿ*s); the Amir Baktimur al-Sāqī added two hammams (one perhaps for women); the Amir Ṭaybars built a mosque and khanqah. Another similar quarter was the Zarībat Qawṣūn. There were other mosques, madrasas, lodging complexes, and mills, belvederes overlooking the Nile, gardens, mansions, and markets all along the riverside as far north as Bulaq. By the early fifteenth century, however, all of them had been abandoned or destroyed.[10]

At Bulaq, "the important people began to build in 713[1313], owing to the sultan's passion for construction,"[11] and in 737/1336 the Amir Aydumur al-Khaṭīrī built a splendid jamiʿ with a Shafiʿite madrasa in it for the neighborhood.

These years of al-Nāṣir's third reign were Cairo's greatest days of glory. The city stretched from Ḥusayniyya in the north along the Nāṣirī Khalīj in the west, to approximately the line of the sultan's aqueduct in the south, where it joined the southern cemetery, the Qarāfa, in which dwellings for the living had always mingled with tombs for the dead.

The indomitable Moroccan traveler Ibn Baṭṭūṭa, who visited Cairo at this time (726/1326), states that "Cairo surges as the waves of the sea with her throngs of folk, and can scarce contain them for all the capacity of her situation and staying power,"[12] but the Qarāfa apparently left the strongest impression. "At Old Cairo is al-Qarāfa, a place of vast repute for blessed power, whose special virtue is mentioned in a tradition related by al-Qurṭubī. . . . people build there beautiful domed chapels and surround them by walls, and they construct chambers in them. . . . Some build a religious house or a madrasa by the side of the mausoleum."[13]

The Citadel, to the north of the Qarāfa, was a city in itself, described as follows in the fifteenth century by al-Ẓāhirī:

> The royal residence . . . is surrounded by ramparts, moats, towers, and numerous iron gates which make it impregnable. It would take too long to give a detailed description of the palaces, stables, mosques, schools, markets, and baths which are found in the [Citadel]; we must limit ourselves to pointing out the most remarkable things and those which can best give an idea of the greatness of the Empire. The Multicolored Palace [Qaṣr al-Ablaq, built by al-Nāṣir] is composed of three main buildings used for official ceremonies. They are covered with marble of different colors, and the ceilings are painted in gold and blue and decorated with various paintings. The Great Hall has nothing in the world to equal it; it stands alone and is separated from al-Qaṣr al-Ablaq; it is surmounted by a very high, beautiful green dome. That is where the royal throne is kept. This dome, which is of the most beautiful architecture inside and out, rests on marble columns. The Great Mosque of the Citadel [that of al-Nāṣir] is equally wondrous; I am assured that it can hold five thousand faithful. Columns of tremendous size [Ptolemaic in origin] are seen within. It is flanked by two minarets of striking architecture. In this Castle are found little apartments for the sulṭān's gatherings; they are of astonishing elegance and richness. A certain number of mansions house the sulṭān's wives. The Mamlūk barracks are twelve in number; each of them is almost as long as a street and can hold up to a thousand Mamlūks. The interior court of the citadel is of enormous size; in it are a vast garden and a little pond. The stables in which the monarch's horses are kept are also very vast, and great in number.[14]

In stating that the fortifications were "impregnable," al-Ẓāhirī was echoing the judgment of the twelfth century, when they were built. In the early sixteenth century, however, the expert opinion of the Venetian ambassador Trevisano was that "Cairo has a citadel which is not very strong. . . . It dominates the entire city. . . . This citadel would not be called a fortress back home; it would be called a magnificent palace."[15] The two quotations encapsulate Mamluk military history. Invincible in the thirteenth century, the corps was merely quaint in the sixteenth.

It was also in the period of al-Nāṣir that the northern Qarāfa, north and east of the old Fatimid city, began to develop, although the expansion which would turn this into a separate suburb had not yet occurred, and its great development as a cemetery would come with the plague.

To the south of Cairo, the separate city of Miṣr still flourished as a port and satellite center of learning and the crafts. It had not yet been devastated by the plague or cut off from prosperity by the northern river port of Bulaq.

The time of al-Nāṣir was also the period of the finest metalwork, enameled glass, miniature painting, and textiles. The population is estimated to have reached over half a million,[16] and this made it the greatest city west of China, the city of the Arabian Nights.

Despite the remarkable growth of Cairo's suburbs and satellites, and the sultan's incitement of the amirs to build monuments and mansions in the new areas, the most desirable location for a residence or a monument remained the densely populated area of the walled Fatimid city, particularly on the *qaṣaba*, the main street, from Bāb Zuwayla to Bāb al-Futūḥ. In practice, however, this was available only to the rulers, for a sultan's tomb complex or a very great amir's palace. Baybars II, while still a great amir, had built in 706–09/1306–10 the greatest khanqah in the city as his complex, opposite the Ayyubid khanqah of Sa'īd al-Su'adā' and on the site of the old Fatimid palace of the viziers, south of Bāb al-Naṣr. This was analogous to building a madrasa near the Ṣāliḥiyya, and in every sense ambitious. Al-Nāṣir suppressed the khanqah for sixteen years when he returned to rule the third time. Al-Nāṣir had also taken over the madrasa of the usurper Kitbughā, a mamluk of Qalā'ūn who had been regent for al-Nāṣir, and then exiled him to the castle of Karak in Transjordan. This mausoleum complex, the first four-iwan, four-*madhhab* madrasa in the city, with a marble Gothic portal from Acre, had been placed next to Qalā'ūn's tomb complex at Bayn al-Qaṣrayn in 695/1295, in an obvious attempt to advertise Kitbughā as Qalā'ūn's true political heir. Just as obviously, al-Nāṣir could not allow this, and when he returned the second time to the throne in 1298, he took over the madrasa (which was not yet functioning), installed the four chief qadis there to teach, and moved his mother's body to the empty tomb. Later his son Anūk was buried there as well. Although it has often been stated that al-Nāṣir planned to be buried in this madrasa, the waqfiyya of his khanqah at Siryāqūs proves that he planned to be buried in the khanqah.[17] In fact, however, he was buried hastily in his father's tomb.

The amirs could build monuments along the winding side streets of the old city, and did so all

PLATE 4. Courtyard and iwans, khanqah of Baybars II al-Jāshnagīr, 1306–09. Some ruined residential rooms are visible to the left and rear. The structure is indistinguishable from that of a two-iwan madrasa. Note use of wooden beams in brick courses, an earthquake precaution.

PLATE 5. Mosque-madrasa of Amir Ṭaghrībirdī, 1440. This is an example of the adaptation of a monument to its site: the façade and mausoleum are on the street side, at the right, and the four-iwan court must be approached by a winding passage.

through the Mamluk period, but the available sites usually presented a problem. A madrasa, khanqah, mosque, or mausoleum had to face Mecca, to the southeast of Cairo. The streets were already laid out and could not be altered, and the façades of the monuments had to be aligned with them. Since the reason for building a monument in the first place was usually to shelter its founder's tomb, it had to appear prominently on the street side. Monuments were visible symbols and sources of power. Their individuality was expressed in the arrangement of the mausoleum dome, the minaret, and the portal, which were so disposed as to dominate the view and assert control of the public space of the street. There is an *arriviste* element in this architecture created for an elite whose sons could not inherit.

The sites, often those of residences which had been purchased and torn down, might be almost any shape, but that was a problem with which Cairo architects were familiar, given a situation in which the streets preceded the monuments. The first religious structure of the city to be built on a Mecca axis differing from the street-entrance axis had been the Fatimid mosque of al-Aqmar, built in 519/1125. This problem was rather easily solved by making the façade thick on one side and thin on the other, inserting a series of diminishing chambers, and skewing the mosque courtyard to the southeast. Monuments in the old city had to solve three often differing needs—to be imposing, to face the street, and to face Mecca—and some often ingenious plans were developed to fit them to their sites. Similar needs were often apparent in the southern and western areas outside the walls, proving that here, as well, the streets usually preceded the foundations. It is no exaggeration to say that the Cairo architects could build Mecca-oriented monuments almost anywhere, and that in no other Islamic city were so many adjustments of monument to site necessary: it is one of the distinctive features of Cairo architecture. In the process,

PLATE 6. Complex of Amir Qijmās al-Isḥāqī, 1480, Qāytbāy period. Note the innovative use of this site: the complex is built on a wedgelike traffic island, with the *sabīl-kuttāb*, dependents' house, and ablution court across the street, to the left.

the older courtyard-and-hypostyle type of mosque was frequently abandoned. The mosque of Aṣlam al-Silāḥdār (745–46/1344–45) foreshadows a later, frequently recurring type of Mamluk mosque with a plan reminiscent of a four-iwan madrasa with a covered central court, though in this case the southeast and northwest iwans are replaced by small hypostyle halls.

During this fertile period of Cairo's greatest security and splendor, a number of important architectural innovations occurred which served as precedents for the builders of the Circassian period (1382–1517). It was during this time that the neighborhood religious center evolved which was at the same time a jamiʿ, a madrasa, and a khanqah. Another innovation of the Nāṣirī period was a new form of minaret. Early Bahri minarets were almost always square towers with rounded or octagonal upper stories, surmounted by a fluted dome—a legacy of the North African antecedents of the Fatimids. In the mosque of Alṭunbughā al-Māridānī, the square base is little more than a transition between the building and two receding octagonal stories, which are then surmounted by a circle of slender colonnettes with a bulbous stone finial. The elegant and distinctive result is sometimes called the "Circassian" minaret, but it is the creation of al-Nāṣir's architects.

The Mamluks built monuments not only for piety or self-glorification but also for a strong economic motive, since by tying up a sizable part of their property in waqfs they could provide for their descendants. The waqfiyya of Baybars II provided good livings for four hundred sufis and one hundred soldiers and children of mamluks.[18] Ibn Khaldūn, writing in the Circassian period, describes clearly how monuments were used for this purpose:

> One of the crafts is instruction in learning. This has been strengthened and preserved . . . because the Turkish amirs under Turkish rule were fearful that the ruler might turn against their descendants whom they left as heirs, because he had claims against them as his slaves or freedmen, and because dangers and misfortunes from a king are always to be dreaded. Thus they sought to build many madrasas, *zāwiyas*, and ribats, and endowed them with waqfs which yielded income, giving a share of this to their descendants either as supervisors of the endowment or as beneficiaries, as well as from a general wish to do good and receive recompense for their good intentions and good deeds. Thus endowments grew in number, and the income and profits from them became huge. Students and teachers multiplied because of the number of stipends available, and people traveled to Cairo in search of learning from Iraq and the Maghrib. Trade in the sciences grew brisk, and the seas of learning boiled. "God creates what He desires" [Koran 3.47].[19]

Al-Nāṣir had been a skilled politician, maintaining a balance of power among the great amirs. Once he was dead and his restraint removed, they plotted against each other, and their factions made and unmade weak sultans from among his minor sons and grandsons until the end of the Bahri period.[20] Despite many violent disturbances, the city continued to build in the areas developed by al-Nāṣir until the Black Death and after.

Even though between a fourth and a third of the population died in the Black Death of 1347–49, once the disease abated in February 1349 the city recovered rapidly. It was not the last visitation; the plague struck again in 1374–75, 1379–81, 1403–04, 1410–11, 1429–30, 1437, 1448–49, 1459–60, and 1476.[21] Nonetheless, Friar Felix Fabri in 1483 could still exclaim, "One would not find today any city vaster or grander under heaven; none equals it for size, population, power and riches, buildings and temples. It is an admirable thing that so great a number of people, made up of such different folk from all over the world, of all sects, so opposed, can be governed."[22] It is clear that Cairo continued to act as an urban magnet, drawing fresh population to itself despite the ravages of epidemics and a frequently oppressive and unstable government.

As quarters were depopulated, they quickly went to ruin. This is particularly known to have happened in Ḥusayniyya, in Miṣr, and along the river, but it was a general phenomenon. To quote Fabri again, "They construct with cubes of mud, sun-baked, so that if ever it rained for two whole days in Cairo as it happens to do with us, and even up to six days, all the city would commence to melt like a candle. This country lacks wood, and except for temples and palaces, all is built of earth."[23]

Abandoned houses were liable to be plundered of their wooden beams, doors, and shutters, and mud-brick construction deteriorates rapidly when not maintained. This would help account for the ruined neighborhoods on which so many travelers comment in the late fourteenth century and after. Monuments and mansions were customarily built of ashlar or fired brick, and these usually endured much longer. The mansions of the Mamluk amirs or of rich merchants were vulnerable, however, in the recurrent factional strife. This in turn accelerated the division of the city into many units—neighborhoods with doors barring the streets which could be locked at night, each with its own mosque.

Even the misfortunes of the city seem to have stimulated monument building. The mamluk corps apparently had less resistance to the plague than did the indigenous population, and were very hard hit. In the rapidly growing cemeteries at this time are not only many simple domed tombs, but also some great tomb foundations.

Khanqahs, madrasas, mosques, and other foundations, including palaces, were built in the southern zone for great amirs and for princesses of the reigning family. In the commercial city of Miṣr, a family of Kārimī merchants[24] named Kharrūbī built a madrasa. It is strikingly apparent that work was able to continue and that skilled artisans were available for such projects during the epidemic and immediately after. Eclipsing all of these was the greatest funerary complex of the Bahri Mamluk period, the immense cruciform jamiʿ with four madrasas of Sultan Ḥasan ibn Muḥammad al-Nāṣir, built in 757–64/1356–62. It is the highest achievement of Mamluk architecture, and writers from Maqrīzī to Gaston Wiet have exhausted superlatives in describing it.[25] The enormous expenditures it required had apparently been made possible by confiscating the lands of the Coptic Church and by the plague. Since the Shariʿa made the sultan the heir of anyone who died without legal heirs, the epidemic put huge sums in the sultan's hand, as well as allowing him to make unheard-of endowments. A green-domed hall (*qubba khaḍrā*) had been associated with supreme rule since Umayyad times. Ḥasan's domed tomb chamber is on an imperial scale, and one wonders if the original dome color was green or turquoise. Apart from the four madrasas (each with an interior court and one or two iwans), there were kitchens, baths, a watertower, a *qayṣāriyya*, shops, and probably also a hospital.

When Ibn Khaldūn arrived in Cairo in 1384, he "beheld the city of the universe, the orchard of the world, the thronging-place of the nations and anthill of the human race; the iwan of Islam and throne of empire, embellished with palaces and pavilions, ornamented with khanqahs and madrasas, illumined by the moons and stars of its learned men. . . . I wandered the streets of the city filled with passing throngs, its markets crammed with good things, and we continued to remark upon this metropolis, its far stretches of flourishing constructions and its expansive condition."[26] Impressed he must have been; every visitor was. The Italian Frescobaldi in 1384 observed that "In this city of Cairo there are more people than in the whole of Tuscany, and in [one] street there are more people than in Florence."[27]

In fact, an upswing in the city's fortunes had begun, and a strong sultan, Ibn Khaldūn's patron Barqūq, the first of the Circassians, had emerged in 1382. He had begun work on a tomb complex in Bayn al-Qaṣrayn, completed in 788/1386, which is variously described by Ibn Khaldūn's student Maqrīzī as a jamiʿ, madrasa, and khanqah.[28] In fact, it was all three, and its position had, as we observed above, a high symbolic value. Although Barqūq allowed himself to be buried in the mausoleum, he stipulated that his final resting place should be built in the northern Qarāfa near the tomb of his father, Ānaṣ, whom he had had brought to Cairo from Circassia after he became sultan. This was where certain revered Sufi sheikhs had been buried.[29] A new mausoleum, khanqah, and jamiʿ, which was also a madrasa because it included *dars* for the Sufis, was then built in the northern Qarāfa by his son, Sultan Faraj, from 1399 to 1410, and Barqūq's body was moved to it. It has two domes, perhaps the finest stone domes of the period. The first monument had been built for reasons of state and prestige; the second reflects the sultan's inner convictions and personal preferences.

Although a wife of al-Nāṣir, Khuwānd Ṭughāy, had built a mausoleum-khanqah in the northern Qarāfa in 749/1348, it was under the Circassian sultans that the northern Qarāfa became a royal cemetery. The khanqah-madrasa-*zāwiya* of Sultan Barsbāy (829/1425), the tomb, khanqah, and ribat of Sultan Ināl (855–60/1451–56), and the exquisite mausoleum and madrasa of Sultan Qāytbāy (877–79/1472–74), with a belvedere and a lodging complex (*rabʿ*) as part of the waqf, were built in this area, as well as the tomb and khanqah of the Amir Kabīr Qurqumās (Kırkmaz) (911–13/1506–07), which is on a royal scale. Moreover, a shift in fifteenth-century trade routes aided development of this cemetery as a suburb.

Cairo was near the nadir of its fortunes under Faraj ibn Barqūq. Tīmūr devastated Syria in 1400, and locusts added to the famine there. Low Nile floods and famine occurred in Egypt, and the plague came again in 1403–04. The greatest period of internal conflict in the Mamluk state fell between 1400 and 1422. Maqrīzī states that "more than half of Cairo, its estates and environs, were ruined; two-thirds of the population of Miṣr died of famine and plague, and innumerable others were killed in insurrections in this reign."[30]

As Janet Abu-Lughod points out, "the blight which had hitherto been confined to the suburban ring now spread into the very heart of the central city. Once-bustling markets were abandoned. The luxury markets closed for lack of customers. Cairo retrenched toward the portions settled before the expansive era of al-Nāṣir b. Qalāwūn."[31] André Raymond estimates that the population in 1410–20 fell as low as 150,000–200,000.[32]

Yet after Faraj, Sultan Mu'ayyad, a former mamluk of Barqūq, built a great tomb complex-mausoleum, jami', khanqah, and madrasa for Sufis on the *qaṣaba*, just inside Bāb Zuwayla, between 1416 and 1420. The minarets were placed on top of the two Fatimid gate-towers of 1092, and there was a hammam, residence, kitchen, and library for the Sufis, as well as a cistern for storing water from the Nile and a *sabīl* for distributing it to passers-by.[33] Nothing was lacking. Mu'ayyad also built a fine hospital (*māristān*) near the Citadel. Urban decline meant no lack of new foundations, though older ones were often closed or curtailed when sultans diverted their waqfs to their own foundations.

Under another former mamluk of Barqūq, Sultan Barsbāy (1422–38), regulations for the Eastern spice trade (which was now Cairo's most important source of foreign revenue) were adopted, and these had profound results for the urbanization of Cairo and its satellites. Up to that point, goods from the Indian Ocean had been transshipped at Aden for the ports of Aydhab and Quṣayr in Egypt. They were then sent by caravan to Qūṣ in Upper Egypt and by Nile shipping to Miṣr.[34] Because of interference with his merchants by the ruler of Aden, Barsbāy ordered the ships to go directly to Jedda, which he could control. Goods were there taxed, sent by land and sea to Ṭūr and Qulzum (Suez) in Egypt, and thence by caravan to Bulaq, north of Cairo, where some were selected for resale to European merchants through Alexandria and Damietta.[35] Bulaq's importance was now assured, and Miṣr was reduced to handling only commerce from Upper Egypt. The mills, the arsenal, the sugar industry, and the wood and leather trades all moved to Bulaq in the fifteenth century.[36] By 1483, a Flemish visitor could observe that "Bulaq is much larger than Babylon [Miṣr]... one sees beautiful and rich houses full of every possible and imaginable merchandise, for here is found the principal entrepôt of merchandise brought to Cairo. It is such a remarkable spectacle that one cannot describe it."[37]

Barsbāy had built a mausoleum with a khanqah-madrasa on the *qaṣaba*, south of the old Ṣāliḥiyya madrasa and on the west side of the street in 1425, but when plague struck Egypt again in 1429, he began a new complex in the northern Qarāfa, completed in 835/1432. This contained a tomb, khanqah-madrasa-jamiʿ, with kitchens, residence, apartments for sheikhs, a living unit (*riwāq*) for his own descendants, and two *zāwiyas*, places for Sufi observances: one for all Muslims, the other for dervishes of the Aḥmadī Rifāʿī *tarīqa*. The *zāwiyas* were opposite the khanqah-madrasa, and have today disappeared, except for a dome that was part of the dervish *zāwiya*.[38]

Under Sultan Qāytbāy (1468–96), Cairo experienced a new time of splendor. Like al-Nāṣir, this greatest of Circassian patrons encouraged his amirs to build. He himself sponsored the construction of bridges, fortresses, commercial houses, canals, and religious foundations, not only in Cairo, Alexandria, and Jerusalem, but in the provincial towns of Syria and Egypt as well. He also campaigned several times in northern Syria. It is not clear where the money was coming from: there were constant complaints from the Europeans that taxes on commerce were too high (though their merchants continued to make excellent profits); financial crises were continual; and the chronicler Ibn Iyās states that the sultan resorted frequently to *muṣādarāt* (confiscations and extortions) in dealing with the rich. The agricultural productivity of the empire appears to have fallen; peasants were oppressed. The Indian Ocean trade, more important than ever, virtually ceased in 1498, owing to the new capability of Portuguese ships to circumnavigate Africa. Yet Cairo must have grown in population at this time; there was new urbanization in the northeast, and directly to the west of the Fatimid city, between the Miṣrī Khalīj and the Nāṣirī Canal, there was renewal. Here the Amir Azbak reclaimed an area that had been abandoned after 1403,[39] and in the early 1470s built a palace on an artificial lake, or *birka*, and a madrasa. Other amirs then built mansions in this area, known as Azbakiyya, and it became a popular resort. Leo Africanus, who was in Cairo in 1517 when the Ottomans took the city and again in 1520, says,

> Hither after Muhammadan sermons and devotions the common people of Cairo, together with the bawds and harlots, do usually resort, and many stage players also, and such as teach camels, asses, and dogs to dance; a thing very delightful to behold. Others keep certain little birds in cages, and whoever desireth to know his fortune must give the bird a coin, which she taking in her bill carries to a little box, and then coming forth brings a little scroll containing either his good or evil success in times to come; and others sing songs of battles and ballads to the people.[40]

Azbakiyya was north of Bāb al-Lūq, which Leo describes as a separate suburb with about three thousand families.

To the northeast of Cairo, a new development was taking place in the eastern part of what had once been Ḥusayniyya. Here a suburb stretched along the road from Bāb al-Naṣr as far north as Raydāniyya, where the road forked. The Raydāniyya area had been a favorite resort of the Mamluks all through the fifteenth century, with a famous place for falconry known as *maṭʿam al-ṭayr*, "bird-feeding ground."[41]

The Raydāniyya area now became a pleasance for the Mamluk court, and Ibn Iyās, the chronicler of the late fifteenth century, reports many court outings and processions which passed that way, at this time built up with mansions of amirs decorated for the occasion, on their way to parade through the *qaṣaba* and up to the Citadel.[42] A hippodrome and reviewing stand were built there.

At Raydāniyya, one road led eastward to Birkat al-Ḥajj, the first stage on the fifteenth-century pilgrim road. The other led northward to the village of Maṭariyya, with its spring and tree associated with the Virgin and Christ Child, and its famous garden of balsam trees, which both Muslims and Christians seem to have regarded as miraculous.[43]

Just to the south of Maṭariyya, the Amir Yashbak min Mahdī, grand *dawādār* or major-domo, and most powerful amir under Qāytbāy, built a palace and *muntaza*, or pleasance, with a khanqah-madrasa, which Felix Fabri visited and described as an earthly paradise. Joos van Ghistele, a gentleman of Ghent who visited in 1483, says, "It is an extraordinarily beautiful summer house, with a garden which is among the most beautiful and well ordered that one may find on earth; the house is very richly decorated in all sorts of colors, gold, silver, and blue, with rich stone floors and walls inside and out. It is so beautiful, rich, and strange that it is difficult to describe."[44]

All that remains today of this residence of the grand *dawādār*—where sultans were entertained—is a part of his pleasure-dome, the Qubba. Directly opposite is King Farūq's favorite residence, Qubba Palace, today a republican palace where the former Shah of Iran was housed at the end of his life, and the whole quarter is still known by the name al-Qubba.

At Raydāniyya, the *dawādā*r Yashbak in 1479–81 built an even larger pleasure-dome, with appurtenances. The dome, which writers formerly mistook for a gigantic mausoleum, has been known since the nineteenth century as the Qubbat al-Fadāwiyya, but has been identified by Doris Behrens-Abouseif as the creation of Yashbak min Mahdī.[45]

In 906/1501, Sultan al-ʿAdil Ṭūmānbāy built his mausoleum at Raydāniyya, on the other side of the caravan road from the pleasance of Yashbak. It was at Raydāniyya as well that the Mamluks chose to make their unsuccessful stand against the army of the Ottoman sultan Selim Yavuz.

Under the last ruling Mamluk sultan, Qānṣūh al-Ghawrī (1501–16), the Mamluk capital had its days of Indian summer. His tomb complex, a madrasa-jamiʿ with appurtenances fronting a mausoleum-khanqah, was built in the market for spice and silk on the *qaṣaba* and still gives its name, the Ghūriyya, to this part of the old Fatimid city. It was on a grand scale for the Circassian period, which from the time of Qāytbāy had tended to the elegant and charming rather than the overwhelming, but it is also rather tasteless, one of the "poor imitations surviving from an inspired period [that of Qāytbāy]," as Wiet says.[46]

By the early sixteenth century Venetian visitors to Cairo were beginning to sniff at the city's great name: "She is in all respects a city inferior to her reputation. It is true nonetheless that she is very rich and that money is very abundant. It is believed that the population is one and a half million, but it is not half so much, and the greater part of it are common people and poor folk."[47] The Fleming van Ghistele furnishes us with a more sympathetic Renaissance view, in the last quarter of the fifteenth century, under the relatively benign rule of Qāytbāy:

> Cairo is certainly the greatest city in the world that we know. . . . It does not touch the Nile on all sides, but only at its two extremities. One extremity joins another inhabited place called Babylon [Miṣr], and the other extremity stretches to another inhabited place called Bulaq. . . . In the interior of the city, there are so many people that three or four families live in the same house. It is not even possible to lodge all the population in the city. One sees many folk lodging all outside the city in tents, pavilions, holes, and pits. These people, for lack of habitation, cannot lodge in the city. The streets are so narrow that in some it is difficult to walk three abreast, and in some places they are so dark that the bats fly in the day as if it were night. . . . At the Grand Bazaars there are so many people passing that it is difficult to cross them at certain hours of the day. Most of the shops in the houses of this street sell food, such as bread, cooked meats, fish, and all sorts of delicious fruits. . . . The mosques are very beautiful and quite sumptuous, with a tower surmounted by a gilded crescent.[48]

Although the streets which lead from Cairo to Babylon to Bulaq, and from Bulaq to Cairo are in part bordered with habitations, there are nonetheless in the space between these three a great number of promenades, gardens and orchards. . . . One sees pretty little houses of pleasure, all sorts of delicate and sweet-smelling plants, and every sort of fruit so that it is wonderful to see, and truly resembles a terrestrial paradise.[49]

The lords, notables and merchants pass their leisure time in these orchards and gardens; sometimes ten or twelve days without leaving . . . one sees women coming and going and paying visits to their folk. . . . In truth, they live there as though in paradise.[50]

UNIVERSITY OF TEXAS
AUSTIN, TEXAS

NOTES

1. Ibn Khaldūn, *The Muqaddima*, text from *Ta'rīkh al-ʿAllama Ibn Khaldūn* (Beirut, 1955–59), 1:1023.

2. Ibid., pp. 781–82.

3. Ibid., p. 872.

4. Ibid., p. 785.

5. *Al-Taʿrīf*, text from ibid., 7:1060.

6. See Caroline Williams, "The Cult of ʿAlid Saints in the Fatimid Monuments of Cairo," part 1, *Muqarnas* 1 (1983).

7. See, for example, the madrasa of Sultan Ṣāliḥ, as described in K. A. C. Creswell, *Muslim Architecture of Egypt*, 2 vols. (Oxford, 1959), 2:94–103. Slides and notes on many Cairo monuments can be found in John A. Williams and Caroline Williams, *Art and Architecture of Cairo* (published by Visual Education, 1977), sets 3–10.

8. Maqrīzī states that in the Bahri Mamluk period Friday prayers were said in more than a hundred mosques in Greater Cairo, and by the early fifteenth century the number had increased to a hundred and thirty; see *Kitāb al-Mawāʿiẓ wa'l-Iʿtibār fī Dhikr al-Khiṭaṭ wa'l-Athār*, (Bulaq, 1270/1853), 2:245. Some of these were, of course, quite small buildings.

9. Ibid., p. 309. The mausoleum would probably have been in the khanqah, a favored site for Mamluk tombs. Qawṣūn's mausoleum was in his khanqah underneath the Citadel, which faced another jamiʿ he had built (see ibid., p. 425).

10. Ibid., 2:117, 131–32, 304.

11. Ibid., p. 131.

12. *The Travels of Ibn Baṭṭūṭah*, trans. H. A. R. Gibb (Cambridge, 1956), 2:41.

13. Ibid., pp. 45–46.

14. Translated in Gaston Wiet, *Cairo, City of Art and Commerce* (Norman, Okla., 1964), pp. 142–43.

15. Also translated in ibid., p. 144. For a twelfth-century verdict, see Ibn Jubayr, *Rihlat Ibn Jubayr* (Beirut, 1959), p. 25: *qalʿa manaʿa*, "unapproachable."

16. Some of the best population estimates can be found in Michael W. Dols, *The Black Death in the Middle East* (Princeton, N.J., 1977), pp. 218ff.

17. I am grateful to Dr. Leonor Fernandes for drawing my attention to the waqfiyya in the Citadel archives. I have discussed al-Nāṣir's khanqah and the provisions of the waqfiyya in "The Khanqah of Siryaqus: a Mamluk Royal Religious Foundation," in *Towards an Islamic Humanism: Studies in Memory of Mohamed el-Nowaihi* (Cairo, 1984). The story of his unceremonious burial is in Maqrīzī, *Khiṭaṭ* 2:304–05. It was apparently done to allow the new regime to consolidate its new position and to avoid the mass gatherings that a public funeral would occasion.

18. Maqrīzī, *Khiṭaṭ*, 2:417.

19. Ibn Khaldūn, *Muqaddima*, 1:786.

20. Maqrīzī gives a colorful picture of the times in discussing the careers of Qawṣūn and Alṭunbughā. It is worth quoting for its *Arabian Nights* character, and shows how the popular literature of the time paralleled historical realities:

> Qawṣūn came from the land of Berke Khān [the Golden Horde] in the following of the Khuwānd Bint Uzbek, wife of al-Nāṣir, on the 13th Rabīʿ II, 720 [1320]. He had with him some few whips and quirts and such worth about 500 dirhams to trade with, and would peddle them in the markets and under the Citadel and inside it. It happened one day that he entered the royal stables to sell what he had, and one of the equerries fell in love with him, since he was a beautiful tall boy of about eighteen years of age. He would come and visit the equerry, until one day the sultan saw him and liked what he saw. He inquired about him, and was informed that he came to sell what he had and that one of the equerries had grown fond of him. He ordered him to be brought to him, and purchased him from himself to enroll him among the royal mamluks. He made him one of the *sāqīs* [cupbearers], and conceived a great passion for him. He made him an amir of ten, then an amir of forty, then an amir of one hundred at the head of a thousand, and promoted him until he reached the highest rank. Then he sent to his country and fetched his brethren, Sawsūn and others of his kin, and ennobled them all. The sultan was so partial to him that no one ever obtained from him what Qawṣūn obtained. He gave his daughter to him in marriage, and married his sister, and when he felt death near, he made him the guardian of his sons. Al-Nāṣir's son Abū Bakr had been designated heir to the throne and received the kingdom at his death. Qawṣūn took hold of the reins of the monarchy, and deposed Abū Bakr in two months' time, sent him away to the city of Qūṣ in Upper Egypt, and then killed him. Then he took Kuçuk, the son of al-Nāṣir, who was five years old, and titled him *al-malik al-ashraf* [the nobler king]. Qawṣūn then became the sultan's viceroy for the land of Egypt. He made amirs of sixty or more of his own followers and rela-

tives, gave great gifts, spent money lavishly, and all the affairs of the state were in his hand. When Abū Bakr Manṣūr was sultan, Alṭunbughā al-Māridānī traduced him to Qawṣūn and said, "He is resolved to seize you." At that Qawṣūn plotted and deposed Abū Bakr and slew him at Qūṣ, and this although Alṭunbughā had received greater honor from Abū Bakr than he had from his father. Then when the mamluks raged and the Amir Qutlubughā came with an army from Damascus and the amirs all turned against Qawṣūn, Alṭunbughā was at the root of it all. [*Khiṭaṭ*, 2:307–8]

21. These dates are taken from Dols, *Black Death*, p. 211, except the last, which is taken from Felix Fabri, *Voyage en Egypte de Felix Fabri* (Cairo, 1975), p. 572.

22. The first quotation is from Fabri, *Voyage en Egypte*, pp. 525–26; the second from p. 573.

23. Ibid., p. 530.

24. The *Kārim* was the great sea caravan by which spices were conveyed from India to Egypt; see *Encyclopaedia of Islam*, 2d ed., s.v. "Kārimī," for discussion and bibliography.

25. See, for example, Maqrīzī's *Khiṭaṭ*, 2:316: "It was built on the grandest scale in the finest harmony and stateliest form; no temple of the Muslims in all their lands is its equal; for three years work on it did not stop for a single day; construction cost was 20,000 dirhams or nearly 1,000 mithqals of gold per day; on the centering for the great iwan alone a hundred thousand dirhams were spent and then the centering was thrown out as rubbish; it is said to be greater by five cubits than the iwan of Kisra at Ctesiphon; the great dome has no peer in Egypt, Syria, Iraq, North Africa, or Yemen; among the builders' marvels are the matchless marble minbar, the enormous portal, and the four colleges around the level of the jamiʿ hall; when one of the minarets fell in 762 [1360] it killed some three hundred orphans who were in the Qur'ān school underneath; the sultan had endowed it with immense waqfs of which only a small part remains; most of them were distributed as fiefs to amirs and others by his successors." Gaston Wiet, in *The Mosques of Cairo* (Paris, 1966), pp. 107–08, writes of "the unforgettable edifice, impregnable, rising skyward with imperial calm, the very symbol of Islam envisaged in all its majesty; the noble and vigorous idea of the architect which produced . . . delicate execution, . . . eloquence totally lacking in bombast, . . . profusion of light, dizzy heights, . . . breathtaking beauty, and royal majesty."

26. Ibn Khaldūn, *Tā'rīkh al-ʿAllāma*, 7:1058–59.

27. Leonardo Frescobaldi, *Visit to the Holy Places of Egypt, Sinai, Palestine and Syria in 1384* (Jerusalem, 1948), p. 49; a translation of *Viaggi in Terra Santa di Leonardo Frescobaldi e d'altri del secolo XIV*. The populous street is probably that between Bāb al-Futūḥ and Bāb Zuwayla.

28. Maqrīzī, *Khiṭaṭ*, vol. 2: on p. 235 he calls it jamiʿ and madrasa, and on p. 418, khanqah.

29. Ibn Ṭaghrī Birdī, trans. William Popper as *History of Egypt, 1382–1469 A.D.*, University of California Publications in Semitic Philology, 13, 14, 17–19, 22, 23 (Berkeley, Calif., 1954–60), pt. 2, p. 171.

30. Quoted in ibid., p. 198.

31. Abu-Lughod, *Cairo*, pp. 39–40.

32. André Raymond, "La population du Caire, de Maqrīzī à la *Description de l'Egypte*," *Bulletin des Études Orientales*, 28 (1975):205; see above, p. 30.

33. I am indebted for this information to Dr. Leonor Fernandes, who has studied the waqfiyya and discusses its provisions in "Evolution of the Khānqāh Institution in Mamluk Egypt" (Ph.D. diss., Princeton University, 1980).

34. See Jean-Claude Garcin, *Un centre musulmane de la Haute Egypte médiévale: Qūs* (Cairo, 1976), pp. 208–27.

35. See *Encyclopaedia of Islam*, 2d ed., s.v. "Barsbāy." Details of his reign may be found in Ahmad Darrag, *L'Egypte sous le règne de Barsbāy* (Damascus, 1961); see, for example, pp. 204–22.

36. See Nelly Boulos Hanna, "The Wikālas of Būlāq" (Master's thesis, American University in Cairo, 1981), pp. 26–27.

37. Joos van Ghistele, *Voyage en Egypte*, French translation by Renée Bauwens-Preaux (Cairo, 1975), p. 57.

38. Leonor E. Fernandes, "Three Sufi Foundations in a Fifteenth-Century Waqfiya," *Annales Islamologiques* 17 (1981):141–56.

39. According to Maqrīzī, *Khiṭaṭ*, 2:313, speaking of the area around the former jamiʿ of al-Jākī.

40. John Leo Africanus, Hakluyt Series (London, 1896), vol. 2, pp. 874–76 (here transposed in orthography).

41. See William Popper, *Egypt and Syria under the Circassian Sultans: Systematic Notes to Ibn Ṭaghrī Birdī's Chronicles of Egypt* (Berkeley, Calif., 1955), passim and map 6.

42. Ibn Iyās, *Chronicles*, 2:390, 425ff., and elsewhere.

43. See, for example, Fabri, *Voyage en Egypte*, pp. 377ff., as well as most of the later travelers. Maṭariyya is still revered by Eastern and Western Christians for its associations with the Holy Family.

44. Van Ghistele, *Voyage en Egypte*, p. 154.

45. The best source of information on the *qubba* of Maṭariyya and that at Raydāniyya is Doris Behrens-Abouseif, "The North-Eastern Extension of Cairo under the Mamluks," *Annales islamologiques* 17 (1981):172–78.

46. Wiet, *Cairo, City of Art and Commerce*, p. 99.

47. Domenico Trevisano in *Le Voyage d'Outremer*, ed. Ch. Schefer (Paris, 1884), pp. 207–08.

48. Van Ghistele, *Voyage en Egypte*, pp. 17–19.

49. Ibid., p. 154.

50. Ibid., p. 160.

LAILA ʿALI IBRAHIM

Residential Architecture in Mamluk Cairo

The most striking feature of medieval architecture in Egypt, whether in religious, commercial, or residential constructions, is its verticality. Buildings are high and designed to emphasize their height, a feature also found in pre-Islamic architecture, examples of which can still be seen around the Red Sea area. Vertical recesses, narrow openings, monumental portals, which stretch upward but rarely rise higher than the top of the façade, add to the impression of loftiness. Interiors are given the same treatment. Living units expand vertically rather than horizontally; multiunit constructions (*rab*ʿs) consist of one or two stories of duplexes or triplexes built above commercial spaces.

The prototype for this architecture was probably pharaonic Egypt, or so Alexandre Lézine believed[1] when he compared, with justification, the tall, multistoried houses of Islamic Egypt with drawings of multistoried Old Kingdom houses from Birsha, which he called *maisons tours* or tower houses (fig. 1). Other studies done on the pharaonic house show that its concepts were very similar to Egyptian Islamic houses in other aspects as well.[2]

The principles that lay behind the design of living units in medieval Cairo were virtually identical for large and small, rich and poor; the only differences lay in scale and decoration. They had the following characteristics in common:

1. A living room or hall (*qāʿa*) was the main constituent of the house, with various dependencies attached to it to form a unit. The word *qāʿa* originally meant a flat surface, and was first used to designate the courtyard of the house.[3] Later, it was applied to the reception hall which, whether partly open or entirely covered, was fully incorporated into the structure. The central areas in the *qāʿa*s uncovered in Fustat were either unroofed, partly roofed, or simply covered by a tent (*surādiq*). Palaces consisted of several such units connected together. The hall was made as large as allotted land and available roofing material and techniques allowed—in fact, plans were usually developed in terms of the roofing possibilities available.

2. Privacy was achieved for both men and women by the use of bent entrances, vestibules, and perforated wooden screens on windows in the men's quarters as well as in the harem.

3. Compared with that of many Islamic countries, residential architecture in Egypt was rather extraverted and, wherever feasible, provided a view onto the street. In the palace of Amir Bashtāk,[4] for

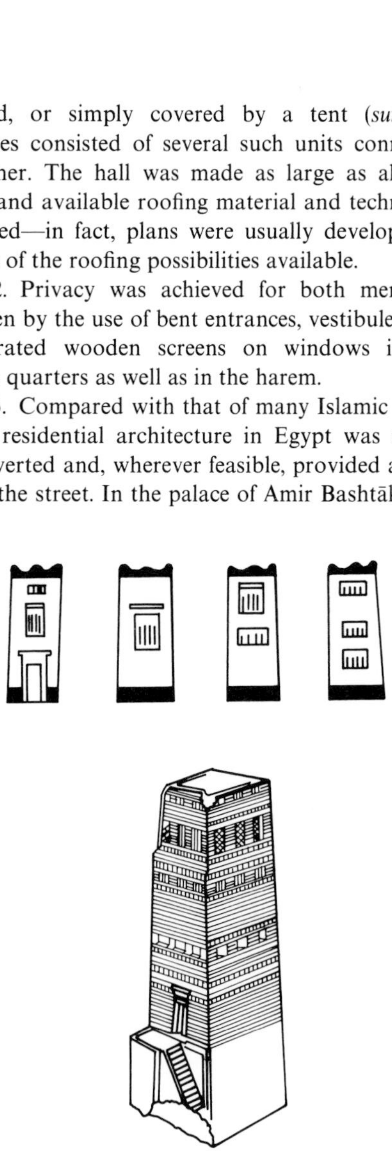

FIGURE 1. Pharaonic houses. (Drawings from Birsha; reconstruction by Alexandre Lézine.)

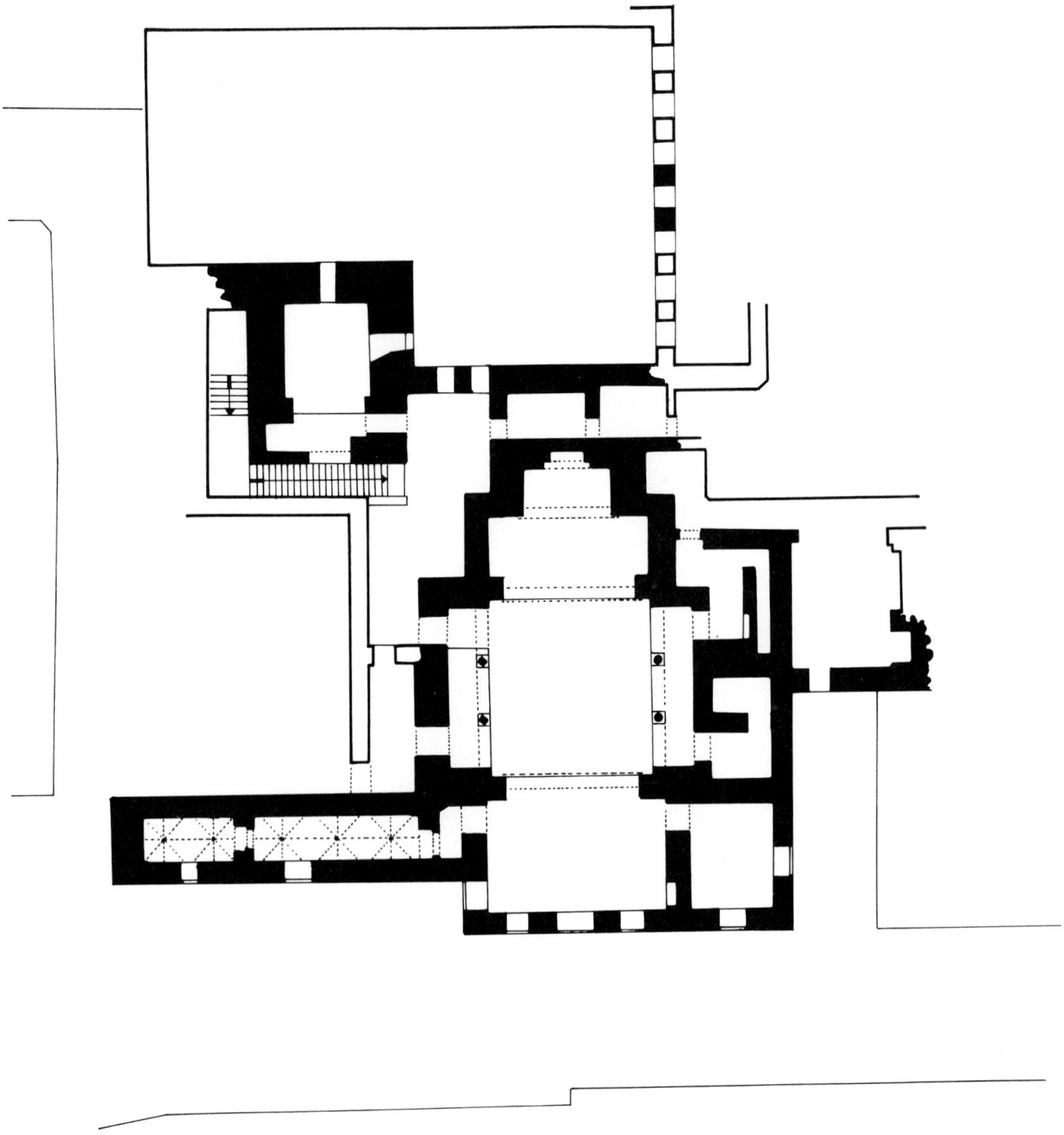

FIGURE 2. Palace of Amir Bashtāk, plan of first floor. (Drawing by J. Revault and B. Maury.)

PLATE 1. Palace of Amir Bashtāk, façade, showing the corridor along the street side. *Index*, no. 34 (1334–39).

example, his private apartment included a main iwan in the reception hall, a private salon or bedroom, and a long corridor with windows occupying the entire façade, all of them overlooking the Bayn al-Qaṣrayn, the main *qaṣaba* of Cairo, and not the courtyard (fig. 2; plate 1). When a house had an exterior view, that detail was always mentioned in waqf documents. The rental units in the multiunit construction or *wikālat* built by Sultan al-Ghawrī,[5] for example, had only one street façade, and the units on the three interior sides overlooked the courtyard. The corridor for the street-side units, however, ran along the courtyard, giving those units a street view (plate 2). Probably they also commanded higher rents (fig. 3).

4. Except for curtains, furnishing was sparse, and most of it, such as cupboards, sideboards, and sofas, fitted into walls or recesses. That left free the maximum space possible inside the *qāʿa* for sitting and for circulation. To save space, staircases were typically narrow and steep.

5. The medieval, like the pharaonic, house had no dining room. Food was served in the *qāʿa* on trays placed in stands that were stored away when not in use.

6. An enclosed outside space was provided for domestic activities. In a private house both the courtyard and the roof were used; in multiunit constructions, a separate, walled-off space on the roof was supplied for each living unit. Although courtyards are given little attention in waqf documents and were rarely even paved, comparing the built area to the street on the map of the *Description de l'Egypte*[6] shows clearly that inner courtyards were very much needed for light and air. Travelers' accounts and medieval historical descriptions testify that the capital of Egypt was then, as now, very compact and densely populated.

Fustat (and later Qāhira) was a great commercial center, and for centuries it dominated all East-West trade. Land in the city was extremely valuable, and lack of space not only forced the buildings upward, but created another feature peculiar to Egypt; all buildings followed the street alignment so as to use every inch of land. Because of the scarcity and price of land, the streets were narrow considering the size of the population they served and the height of the houses along them, but no narrower than those of other medieval cities. Projections on the walls added to the impression of narrowness: each successive story was built on brackets projecting out from the story below

PLATE 2. Side street in medieval Cairo, near the Bāb Zuwayla

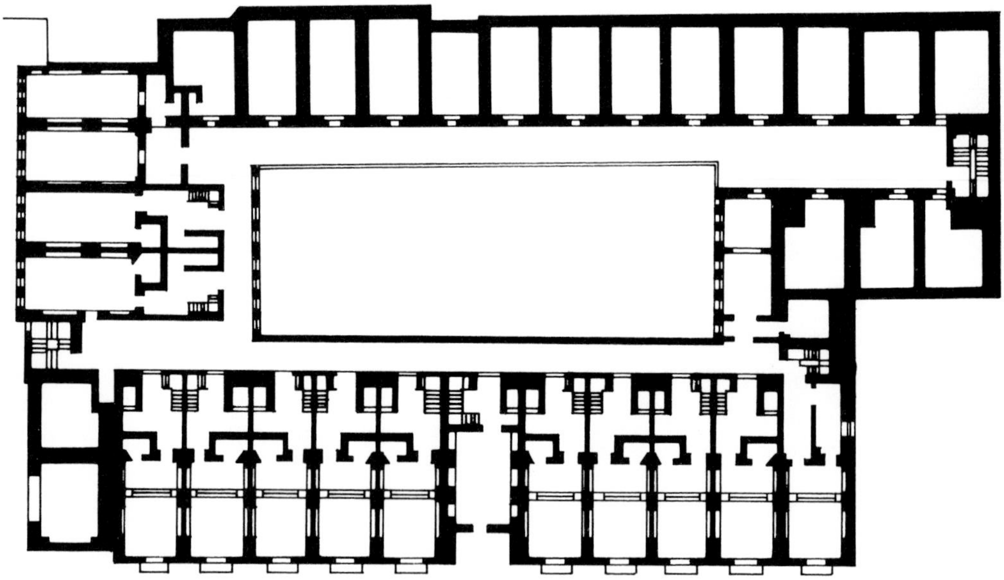

FIGURE 3. *Wikāla* of Qāytbāy, multiunit construction plan. *Index*, no. 9 (1480). (Courtesy of the Center of Documentation, Organization of Antiquities, Cairo.)

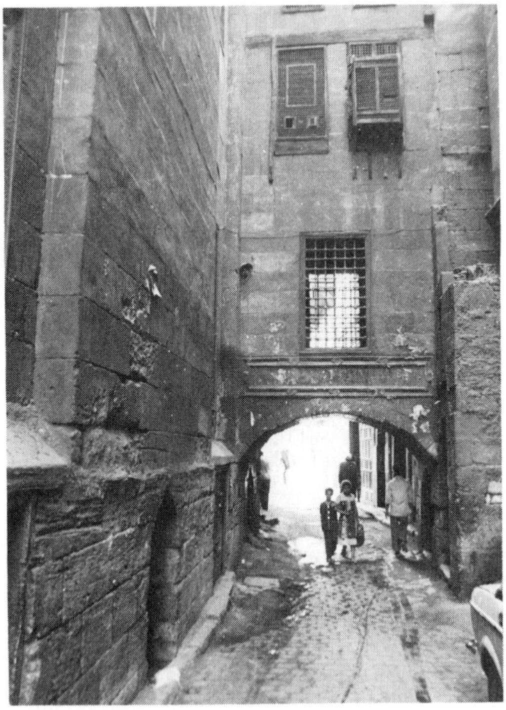

PLATE 3. Bridge across a street, adjacent to the mosque of Qijmās al-Isḥāqī. *Index*, no. 114 (1480–81).

(fig. 4). People also built on *saqā'if* (sing. *saqīfa*) or bridges laid across the side streets (plate 3). These and the projections had, however, to be constructed strictly according to regulations given in *ḥisba* books.[7]

Some travelers also mention the dark color of Fustat's houses. Unlike domes and cemetery structures, which were plastered from an early date (writing in the first half of the ninth century, al-Kindī remarks that, "on approaching the cemetery with its domes and enclosures, it appears to be a white city"),[8] exterior walls were not plastered, but simply covered with Nile silt. Not a single house in Fustat has been found with an exterior plaster revetment. Exteriors of palaces—the Dār al-Bayḍā or "White House," for example—and mosques were, however, plastered.[9] But by late Ayyubid times, Ibn Sa'īd,[10] describing the palaces in Qāhira, writes, "I saw on the walls of their palaces numerous openings [*ṭāqāt*] made of lime [*kils*] and gypsum [*jibs*], and I was told that these openings were replastered [probably whitewashed] yearly." The Fustat houses must have looked very like the old houses that still exist in Yemen and southern Arabia today, since styles, while they usually originate in the great centers of civilization, tend to persist the longest, sometimes for centuries, in the remote areas where change of any sort is slow.

Ibn Sa'īd also tells us that the citadel at Rawḍa was plastered,[11] and certainly by the

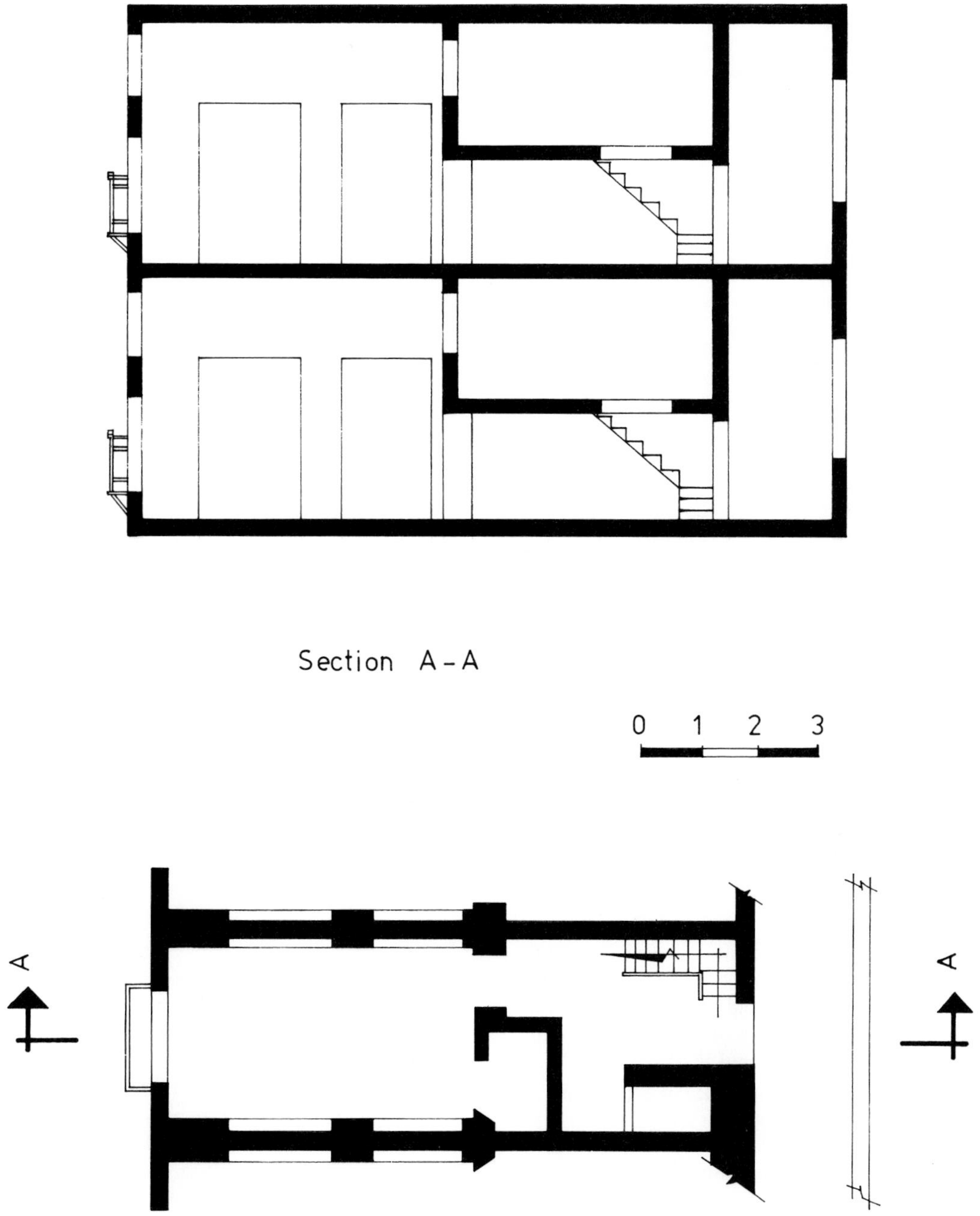

FIGURE 4. *Wikāla* of Qāytbāy, section of living units. *Index*, no. 9 (1480). (Courtesy of the Center of Documentation, Organization of Antiquities, Cairo.)

Mamluk period all the grand residences were plastered, if not partly faced with dressed stone. In Barqūq's reign, when the sultan returned from a campaign or the Hajj, all the buildings along his entry path through the city were replastered—or, more probably, whitewashed.[12] Except for portals, they remained undecorated, however: even palaces had no exterior decoration, though royal constructions such as khans and *wikālat*—for example, the *wikālat* of Qāytbāy at al-Azhar and at the Bāb al-Naṣr[13]—were very elaborately decorated on the exterior.

ROYAL PALACES

Not a single royal palace has survived from the medieval period, and the only extant frescoes are those found in the debris of a hammam north of Fustat ascribed to the Fatimid period (they are now in the Museum of Islamic Art in Cairo).[14] One therefore has to rely on whatever information can be gleaned from the historical sources to figure out their general layout and interior decoration. Such sources are particularly scarce, probably because few historians or travelers would have been in a position to gain entrance to a royal palace. We are told, however, that Khumārawayh (884–95), son of Ibn Ṭūlūn, had a hall in his palace decorated with life-size representations showing him surrounded by his concubines, dancers, and musicians. The figures were made of painted wood covered with jewels and gold.[15] This tradition of wall painting seems to have continued into the Fatimid period: according to Nāṣir Khusraw the *maṣtaba* or platform of the Fatimid caliph was decorated with hunt and tournament scenes.[16] The Fatimid vizier al-Yāzūrī called a painter from Baghdad and another from Cairo to paint a dancer in trompe-l'oeil in a recess in his palace.[17] In the Mamluk period, Sultan Qalā'ūn had the walls of his state hall decorated with views of all the citadels and fortresses he had conquered.[18] His son al-Ashraf Khalīl had his amirs and *khāṣṣakī*s represented on the walls of a projection (*rufruf*) he built on the Citadel overlooking the city.[19]

The Great Iwan, the Mamluk state hall in the Citadel (plate 4), was a square, domed structure with colonnades on three sides.[20] According to Nāṣir Khusraw, the twelve units of the Fatimid palace were also square; and the caliphs' state hall also had a dome.[21] Undoubtedly this domed form was considered a mark of status, but in many cases it was also the only technique available for roofing a large square area without using columns, and once again the roofing chosen determined the floor plan. Wood for roofing was imported, and the beams never exceeded eleven meters: this is why, for example, the iwan of the mosque of the Sultan Ḥasan, which measured more than 25 by 20 meters, could not have been flat-roofed.[22]

The Qaṣr al-Ablaq, another state hall built in the Mamluk period, had a hall with a raised iwan at each end. The sultan's private residence at the Citadel consisted of three palaces or *quṣūr*[23] and a *kharja*, or projection, all of which overlooked the city. The sultan slept in one of the palaces inside a wooden tower or *burj*, with the royal guard standing watch.[24]

The women's quarters (*ḥarīm*) consisted of seven *qāʿa*s: one for each of the sultan's four wives, her children, and her retinue; two for receptions; and one for the sultan's concubines. The grand *qāʿa*, built in the Ayyubid period, was called the *qāʿat al-ʿawāmīd*, or hall of the columns. Although, as its name suggests, it probably had columns, beginning in the midfourteenth century columns and piers tend to disappear from *qāʿa*s and *qāʿa*-plan madrasas and mosques. Another *qāʿa* in the Citadel was called the *muʿallaqa*, which meant that it was built on an upper story;[25] such *qaʿa*s on upper stories were introduced quite early.

The royal household dependencies or *buyūt*, such as the kitchens (*ṭablkhāna, ṭishtkhāna, sharābkhāna, farshkhāna*), were housed in separate buildings and served all the royal palaces.

AMIRAL RESIDENCES

Only parts of amiral palaces dating from the Mamluk period have reached us, and what survive are usually the main *qāʿa* and the entrance unit. Nevertheless, descriptions of royal palaces provide insight into the construction of these residences as well, since the amirs imitated the sultan in every way they could, and the rich bourgeoisie imitated the amirs.

The houses of Fustat were probably of an early type, Tulunid or even pre-Tulunid, for they were built directly on the rock. Their irregular boundary lines suggest that they were probably built when the *khiṭṭa*s (settlements on unused land) and the *dār*s were divided among various tenants. The successive layers of floor paving show that they were used for a long time, probably until Fustat was destroyed toward the end of the Fatimid period. It remained abandoned until, in 1240–41, Najm al-Dīn Ayyūb moved into the fortress he had built on Rawḍa Island, and many

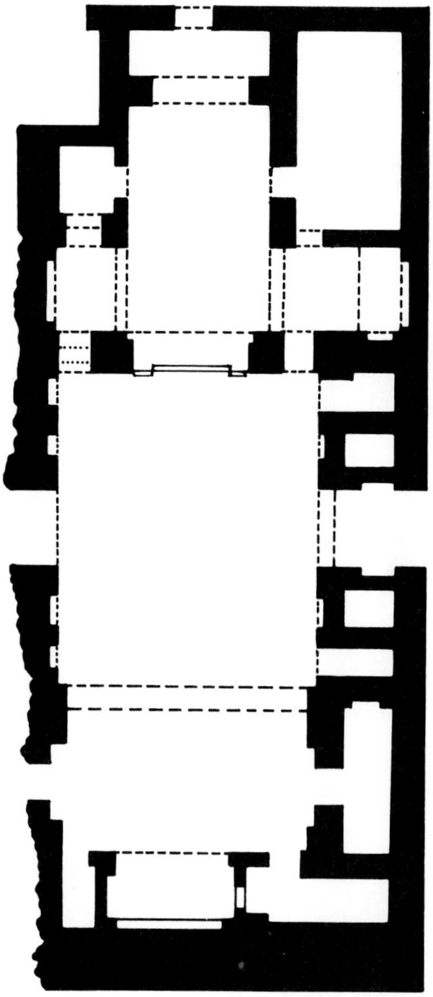

FIGURE 5. Saint George Monastery, Dayr al-Banāt, plan of ground floor. (Drawing by Alexandre Lézine.)

amirs moved from Cairo to Fustat, which was just opposite. They probably restored or reused what was left of these earlier constructions along the Nile.[26] The hall of what is now the Saint George Monastery for women in Old Cairo, known as Dayr al-Banāt (fig. 5),[27] for example, was most probably the *qāʿa* of a palace rebuilt by an Ayyubid amir on the foundations of an earlier one, for its plan is identical to the early *qāʿa*s of Fustat. By the late Ayyubid period the plan of the Mamluk *qāʿa*, that is, the elongated hall with two raised iwans at either end and a central area either open or with a high ceiling, had certainly taken shape.

It is unfortunate that no Fatimid or Ayyubid houses have survived, for these were built in areas where great change took place during the Mamluk period. The two iwans with the *salsabīl*s, or fountains, in the māristān of Qalā'ūn,[28] believed to be the remains of a western Fatimid palace, and the *Description de l'Egypte* plan of the state hall built by Najm al-Dīn Ayyūb in the citadel at Rawḍa[29] were both parts of what had originally been royal constructions, and perhaps had special plans. The hall at Rawḍa, however, may be considered a transitional plan between the Fustat house plan and the Mamluk *qāʿa*. Pauty draws attention to its striking similarity in plan to House VI in Fustat (fig. 6).[30] The *qāʿa* of Ahmad Kohia, dated 710/1310, also still bears a resemblance to the houses of Fustat. The *qāʿa* of al-Dardīr,[31] however, is almost certainly wrongly dated as Fatimid, for both its plan and its architecture cannot be earlier than the late Ayyubid or early Mamluk period.

The *qāʿa*s of Fustat had a triple-arched *riwāq*, or loggia, at one end with three rooms behind it, the central one larger than the other two.[32] The *riwāq* and the three rooms probably comprised the

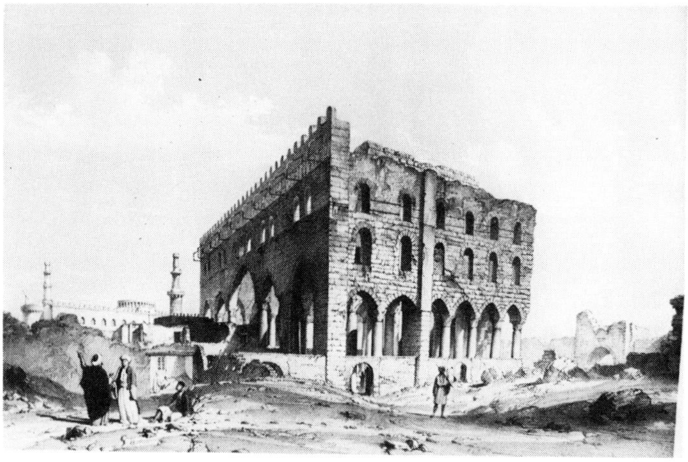

PLATE 4. The Great Iwan at the Citadel.

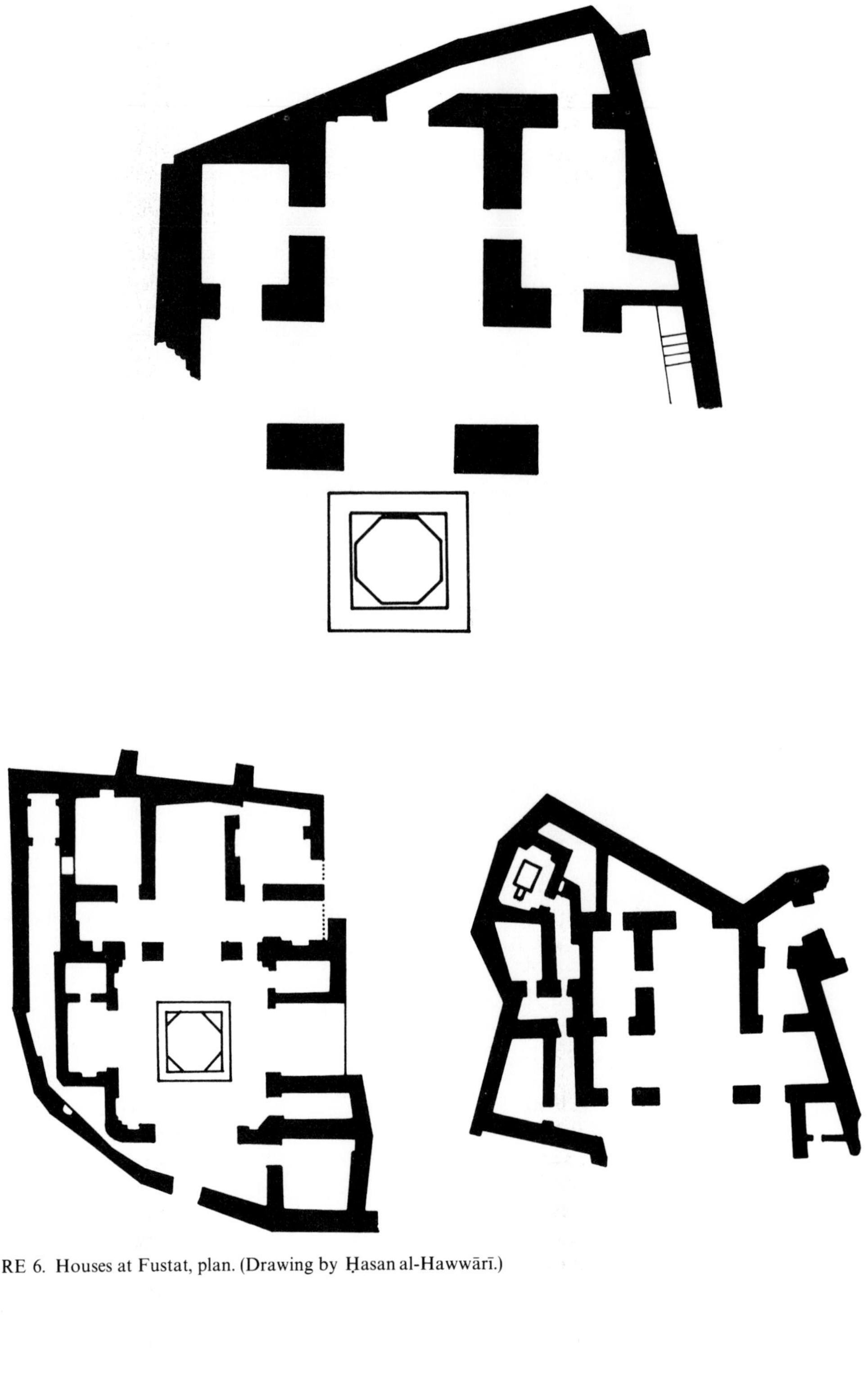

FIGURE 6. Houses at Fustat, plan. (Drawing by Ḥasan al-Hawwārī.)

private apartment of the master of the house, and a certain ceremonial significance seems to have been attached to its tripartite arrangement. Some *qāʿas* in Fustat had a narrow passage that ran from one of the side rooms to an opening in the rear wall of the central room (fig. 6), suggesting that the master of the house appeared to the assembly from that opening. In a Mamluk *qāʿa*, at least one room, the *khazāna nawmiya*, or bedroom, was attached to the main iwan reserved for the master of the house and from which he appeared to his guests. The important *qāʿas* of Fustat were usually built above street level, though ground-floor *qāʿas* existed. In 1964 the late Gamal Mehrez[33] uncovered parts of a *qāʿa* with a fountain and flowerbeds in Fustat that was on a second story. Nāṣir Khusraw mentions roof gardens in Fustat in the Fatimid period.[34] When the *qāʿa* was above the ground, the ground floor below was partly solid construction and partly vaulted corridor.

Another grand residence built in part on vaulted corridors was uncovered in 1932 during the excavations north of Fustat conducted by the Museum of Islamic Art in Cairo.[35] Like the other *qāʿa*, it has behind it the first steps of a staircase that probably led either to an upper story or to the roof. According to al-Iṣṭakhrī,[36] the houses in the area north of Fustat were more spread out and lower than the houses inside the city, but these two houses were at least three stories high. The latter house has not been published, but the architect ʿĀdil Yāsīn and I made a survey of the hammam next to it and have surveyed the house itself.[37] The area was built mostly by Tulunid amirs and inhabited by the Ikhshīdids and later by the Fatimids. It was abandoned during the plague and crisis of 1066. Attached to the house is a gallery which probably had shops, as did other houses in Fustat. Cairo has always been a commercial city, and all buildings included shops. Even the Mamluk amirs had shops installed beneath their palaces, as, for example, in the palaces of Ṭāz and Bashtāk (plate 5).[38]

There are only four extant grand *qāʿas*, all from amiral palaces dating from the Mamluk period—Ālīn Āq, Bashtāk, Yashbak (that is, the Isṭabl of Amir Qawṣūn), and Ṭāz;[39] all four are second-story constructions. Six others, less grand in scale, are on the ground floor, and all but one of these belonged to high officials from the bourgeois class.[40] All these grand residences date from the Bahri Mamluk period. The extant residences dating from the Circassian Mamluk period are on a much smaller scale. Grand residences had more than one

PLATE 5. Shops beneath the palace of Amir Bashtāk. *Index*, no. 34 (1334–39).

qāʿa. For example, we know from Sultan Barsbāy's waqf that the palace of Amir Salār had both an upper and lower *qāʿa*.[41] In grand residences, both upper and lower *qāʿas* had mashrabiyya-screened upper galleries called *aghānī*, usually reached from the central area of the *qāʿa* by a small staircase. There sat the musicians whose duty it was to wake the sultans and amirs with music in the morning and to put them to sleep with music every night (plate 6).

PORTALS AND VESTIBULES

Only the elite had the right to have grand portals. Each portal indicated the rank of the amir by the blazon painted on it,[42] and during the Bahri Mamluk period amirs were allowed to hang painted war weapons there until Sultan Barqūq forbade the practice.[43] Traditionally, weapons were also displayed on the Citadel gates and city gates. Amirs of a certain rank could also have *ṭablakhāna* played at their gates. The *ṭablakhāna* unit was usually housed next to the street gate.

Vestibules were luxuriously decorated because, as al-Khafājī says,[44] special attention had to be

PLATE 6. Upper gallery for musicians, *qā'a* of Amir Tashtamur, made a madrasa by Khushqadam al-Aḥmadī. *Index*, no. 153 (1366–77).

given them, for "that is where the visitor is received and where the guest waits until admitted inside the house and where the amir's mamluks sit all day."

Grand residences had several entrances, but only two portals, one on the street and another in the courtyard. An amir did not dismount in the street; he usually rode through the stable entrance to the inner gate before dismounting, and this was also true of important visitors. Al-Jawharī relates that when Sultan Barqūq sent word to a sick amir that he intended to visit, the amir ordered the entire distance from the stable entrance to his bedroom spread with silk, which indicates that even a sultan entered from the stable gate if he came on horseback.[45]

COUNTRY HOUSES

City and country houses differed very little in style. A *manẓara*, a royal or amiral residence outside the city, sited as the name suggests for a view to the outside (just as a city house looked onto the street), was apparently almost identical to any urban house with an upper *qā'a*. No free-standing *manẓara* has survived in Egypt, but we have detailed descriptions of more than one in the waqf documents.[46] The same was true for the royal or amiral houses along the Nile. A grand residence known as the Barābikhiyya in Bulaq (a suburb north of Cairo), as we learn from its description in the waqf of Sultan Qānṣūh al-Ghawrī,[47] resembled a town house except that, like all houses looking out onto the Nile, a canal, or a pond, it had a *qayṭūn* (a room or loggia) giving directly onto the water.[48]

CEMETERIES

Cemeteries in Egypt have always been inhabited. In the Mamluk period, suqs, hammams, mills, and bakeries could all be found in them, and in addition to permanent dwellers they had many visitors, for people enjoyed going there. Even amirs spent their weekends, feasts, and holidays in the cemetery.

The sultans and the amirs both built great funerary complexes, either tomb-madrasas or tomb-khanqahs. Maqrīzī tells us that the amirs built *quṣūr* (sing. *qaṣr*) which they called *turab* (sing. *turba*) or tombs. In the waqf document of the Amir Qurqumās,[49] the residential section attached to his tomb-madrasa complex is also called a *qaṣr*, and there are several other examples of living accommodations attached to funerary complexes. The waqfiyya of Amir al-Aqūsh[50] states that the living quarters adjoining the *turba* were built for the founder's family if they wished to live there, or for rental if they did not. There were multiunit *irba'* and other rental property in the cemeteries as well.

The living quarters attached to the funerary complex where the sultan or the amir and his family stayed are usually referred to as *maq'ad* (literally, "a place for sitting"). There were also *maq'ads* in palaces, which usually opened onto the courtyard. The *maq'ad* differs in plan from the *qā'a*. It is a raised, elongated hall reached by a staircase, and has either an arcade along the longer side to be used as a loggia or windows instead of arcades, in which case it is called *maq'ad qibṭī* (that is, Coptic). A *maq'ad* might have a raised sofa at one end (plate 7).[51]

MIDDLE-CLASS HOUSING

Middle-class dwellings ranged all the way from luxurious residences to ordinary family houses, either built by the tenant or rented. Rich families often rented the grand residences that were sometimes included in waqfs. The upper middle class or bour-

PLATE 7. *Maqʿad* of Amir Māmāy. *Index*, no. 51 (1496).

geoisie, mainly high officials, pen-bearers, and rich merchants, imitated the amirs' way of life except that they were not permitted a fanfare or a display of arms on their entry gates. Some of the middle-class houses were very luxurious. In the mid-fourteenth century a qadi named Ibn Zanbūr built a house with seven *qāʿa*s so richly decorated with beautifully carved marble that Amir Sirgatmish did everything he could to have this wealth confiscated so he could lay hands on the marble—he eventually succeeded.[52]

Those who could not afford to build a house rented an apartment in a multiunit building called a *rabʿ* (pl. *irbaʿ*). These were built as investments by rich people, amirs, and sultans, usually above a shop, khan, *wikāla*, or *qayṣāriyya*. The commercial space was restricted to the ground floor, and occasionally the floor above was used for storage. There was no internal connection between the commercial space and the living units.[53] Waqf documents refer to the three types of rental units as *qāʿa*, *riwāq*, and *ṭabaqa* (pl. *ṭibāq*). Except for bathing facilities—going to the public bath was a popular pastime—each unit had its own facilities. No rental *qāʿa*s have survived from the medieval period, but from waqf documents we know they were usually on the ground floor, because they are rarely mentioned as *muʿallaqa*, that is, on an upper story. Ibn Duqmāq mentions a *qāʿa* in Fustat which was rented out for weddings,[54] and there is still a Mamluk *qāʿa* in Old Cairo, Qāʿat al-ʿIrsān, that was once used for that purpose. From Ibn Muyassir we know that in 518/1125 Vizier Ma'mūn al-Baṭā'iḥī built a *dār* to rent out during the festivities of the opening of the canal in the reign of Caliph al-Āmir.[55]

*Riwāq*s to be rented out were usually on an upper story; one gathers from waqf documents that they were architecturally almost identical to the *ṭibāq*. *Ṭibāq* were usually duplexes, rarely triplexes, each unit consisting of a small entrance, a recess for water jars, a latrine, and a small storeroom placed so as to screen the main room from the entrance. A small staircase led to a mezzanine overlooking the main room, which was double the height of the mezzanine. It had a raised iwan for sitting and a set each of upper and lower windows to provide ventilation to the entire unit.

VENTILATION AND LATRINES

Ventilation was a main concern in the medieval period, and latrines and drainage were also given special attention. There were latrines on each story and attached to every unit. The latrines on the upper stories had small perforated domes for ventilation and those on lower stories had flues behind the seats that reached to the roof.[56] In palaces, seats were made of marble and latrines even had marble mosaic floors.[57]

This very rapid and general survey of residential architecture in Cairo from early Islamic to Mamluk times demonstrates that, in spite of the drastic changes on the political scene wrought by successive dynasties, domestic architecture throughout the period changed very little.

AMERICAN UNIVERSITY IN CAIRO
CAIRO, EGYPT

NOTES

1. Alexandre Lézine, "Persistance de traditions préislamiques dans l'architecture domestique de l'Egypte musulmane," *Annales islamologiques* 11 (1972): 1–22, plate 1. See also the drawings from the Neb-Amon tomb, XIX dynasty.

2. M. S. Sa'īd, "The Evolution of the Houses and the Palaces in Pharaonic Egypt" (Master's thesis, Cairo University, 1981). Houses also had fountains before the Arab conquest of Egypt. See Ibrāhīm ibn Muḥammad ibn Aydamur al-'Alā'ī, known as Ibn Duqmāq, *Kitāb al-Intiṣār li-Wāsiṭat 'Iqd al-Amṣār (Description de l'Egypte d'Ibn Duqmāq)*, ed. Karl Vollers (Paris, 1893), 4:5.

3. Majd al-Dīn Muḥammad ibn Ya'qūb al-Fayrūzabādī, *Al-Qāmūs al-Muḥīt*, 2d ed. (Cairo, 1371/1952), 3:79.

4. The palace of the Amir Bashtāk appears in the *Index to Mohammedan Monuments in Cairo* on the special 1 : 5000 scale maps of Cairo, Survey of Egypt, 1951 (hereafter cited as *Index*), no. 34 (735–40/1334–39).

5. Wikālat Qānṣūh al-Ghawrī, a khan-and-rab' multiunit construction, *Index*, no. 64 (909–10/1504–05).

6. Commission des Monuments d'Egypte, *Description de l'Egypte, ou Recueil des observations et des recherches* . . . , 6 vols. (Paris, 1809–28), vol. 1, pl. 26, "Le Kaire."

7. Ibn al-Rāmī, *Kitāb al-Bayān fī Aḥkām al-Binyān*, MS al-Khāzana al-'Āmama, Tunis no. A 8⁰, 2834.

8. 'Umar ibn Muhammad ibn Yusuf al-Kindī, *Faḍā'il Miṣr* (Cairo, 1391/1971), p. 65. Ibn Duqmāq, *Kitāb al-Intiṣār*, 4:10, quoting Ibn Yūnus, says that the first plastered tomb in Egypt was that of Ibrāhīm ibn Ṣāliḥ ibn 'Ali ibn 'Abd-Allah ibn 'Abbās, built around 165/782.

9. Ibn Duqmāq, *Kitāb al-Intiṣār*, 4:5.

10. Ibn Sa'īd al-Maghribī, *Al-Mughrib fī Ḥuly al-Maghrib, "Kitāb al-Nujūm al-Zāhira fī Ḥuly Ḥaḍrat al-Qāhira"* (Cairo, 1970), p. 24.

11. Ibn Sa'īd al-Maghribī, *Al-Mughrib fī Ḥuly al-Maghrib, "Kitab al-Ightibāṭ fī Ḥuly al-Fusṭaṭ"* (Cairo, 1953), pp. 8–9. Ibn Duqmāq, *Kitāb al-Intiṣār*, 4:110.

12. 'Ali ibn Dāwūd al-Ṣayrafī al-Jawharī, known as al-Khaṭīb, *Nuzhat al-Nufūs wa'l-Abdān fī Tawārīkh al-Zamān* (Cairo, 1970), 1:341, 338.

13. At al-Azhar, *Index*, no. 75 (882/1477), and at Bāb al-Naṣr, *Index*, no. 9 (885/1480).

14. Fragments of stucco alveoles, inv. nos. 12881, 12882, 12883, 12884, 12885.

15. Taqī al-Dīn Aḥmad al-Maqrīzī, *Kitāb al-Mawā'iẓ wa'l-I'tibār fī Dhikr al-Khiṭaṭ wa'l-Āthār* (Bulaq, 1270/1853), 1:316–17.

16. Nāṣir Khusraw, *Safarnāma*, trans. Y. al-Khashshāb (Cairo, 1364/1945), p. 63.

17. Maqrīzī, *Khiṭaṭ*, 2:318; the two painters were al-Quṣayr and Ibn 'Azīz. Another picture in a trompe-l'oeil depicted Joseph in the well; it was painted by al-Kutāmī in the house of Ibn al-Nu'mān in the cemetery. There is also a stalactite painted in a trompe-l'oeil in the Jami' al-Qarāfa.

18. Ibn 'Abd al-Zāhirī, *Tashrīf al-Ayyām wa'l-'Uṣūr fī Sīrat al-Malik al-Manṣūr* (Cairo, 1961), p. 139.

19. Maqrīzī, *Khiṭaṭ*, 2:212–13.

20. Robert Hay, *Illustrations of Cairo* (London, 1840), pl. 19.

21. Nāṣir Khusraw, *Safarnāma*, p. 63. These were 100 cubits square, and the state hall was 60 cubits square. For the description of the state hall, see Maqrīzī, *Khiṭaṭ*, 1:388.

22. Ibn Faḍl Allah al-'Umarī, *Masālik al-Abṣār*, vol. 5, fol. 69, MS Dār al-Kutub, Ma'ārif 'āma, no. 8. *L'Egypte au commencement du quinzième siècle d'après le traité d'Emmanuel Piloti de Crète* (incipit 1420), introd. P. H. Dopp. (Cairo, 1950), p. 24. The qibla iwan of the mosque of Sultan Barqūq has the largest flat roof (*Index*, no. 187 [786–88/1384–86]), about 11 m; the span between the columns is 10 m. The qibla iwan of the mosque of Sultan Ḥasan (*Index*, no. 133 [757–64/1356–62]) is 26.5 by 21.0 m, and the other three iwans are each 14.5 by 14.0 m.

23. Maqrīzī, *Khiṭaṭ*, 2:209–10; two palaces were reached by staircases. Khalīl ibn Shāhīn al-Zāhirī, *Kitāb Zubdat Kashf al-Mamālik wa Bayān al-Ṭuruq wa'l-Masālik*, ed. Paul Ravaisse (Paris, 1893), p. 26.

24. Maqrīzī, *Khiṭaṭ*, 2:212. Shihāb al-Dīn Aḥmad ibn Ḥajar al-'Asqalānī, *Al-Durar al-Kāmina fī A'yān al-Mi'a al-Thāmina*, 2d ed. (1385/1966), 2:19 (Baktimur, no. 1308).

25. Zāhirī, *Tashrīf al-Ayyām*, pp. 26–27.

26. Maghribī, *Al-Mughrib fī Ḥuly al-Maghrib, "Kitāb al-Ightibāṭ fī Ḥuly al-Fusṭāṭ"* (Cairo, 1953), p. 11; Maqrīzī, *Khiṭāṭ*, 1:342.

27. Alexandre Lézine, "Les salles nobles des palais mameloukе," *Annales islamologiques* 10 (1972): 72–74, pls. 5–7. The ground level of this *qā'a* is particularly low.

28. K. A. C. Creswell, *The Muslim Architecture of Egypt* (New York, 1978; hereafter cited as *MAE*), 2:207; plan drawn by Hertz in 1913.

29. Ibid., 2:86, fig. 38. *Description de l'Egypte*, 2:159, pl. 33.

30. Edmond Pauty, *Les palais et les maisons de l'époque musulmane du Caire* (Cairo, 1933), p. 34.

31. Qāʿat al-Dardīr, *Index*, no. 488 (12th century). It owes its name to Sheikh Aḥmad al-Dardīr (d. 1201/1787); Creswell, *MAE*, 1:261–63, fig. 159, dates it in Fatimid times.

32. The origin of this plan, which came to be known as the "Samarra" plan, is said to be as follows: Masʿūdī (d. 346/958) relates that the Abbasid caliph al-Mutawakkil (847–62) introduced a new type of construction at Samarra which became known as *al-ḥīrī*, or the *riwāq* and *kumayn*, that is, the loggia and two sleeves. One evening one of the caliph's courtiers told him that a king of al-Ḥīra (of the Nuʿmāniyya of Banī Naṣr) had introduced that plan because it was like an army formation in war (*ḥarb*), and the king was a warrior and wanted to be reminded of war at all times. The king sat at the center (*ṣadr*) of the *riwāq* with the two sleeves (*kumayn*) to his right and left. In those two recesses (*baytayn*) sat his amirs and dignitaries (*khawāṣṣ*). To the right was the *khazāna* (room) for the *kiswa* (dress or covers) and to the left the *khazāna* for drinks (*sharāb*). The *riwāq* covered the *ṣadr* and the two sleeves, and the three doors gave onto the *riwāq*. This plan became very common as ordinary people adopted it. Maçoudi, *Les prairies d'or*, ed. and trans. C. Barbier de Meynard and Pavet de Courteille (Paris, 1873), 7:192–93.

33. Gamal Mehrez, "Manāzil al-Fusṭāṭ," *Abḥāth al-Nadwa li Tārīkh al-Qāhira*, March–April 1969 (Cairo, 1970), pp. 323–51, figs. 1–13. Summary in French, "Les habitations d'al-Fustat," *Colloque international sur l'histoire du Caire, 27 mars–5 avril 1969*, Ministry of Culture, pp. 321–22.

34. Nāṣir Khusraw, *Safarnāma*, pp. 50, 70.

35. The excavations were carried out under the supervision of the late Ḥasan al-Hawwārī on the site of al-ʿAskar, known today as Sīdī Abū'l-Sāʿūd. He published one house only, the so-called Dār al-ʿImāra, in "Une maison de l'époque toulounide," *Bulletin de l'Institut d'Egypte*, vol. 15 (1932–33):79–87, pls. 1–10.

36. Abū Isḥāq al-Fārisī, known as al-Iṣṭakhrī, *Kitāb al-Aqālīm, Liber Climatum, Abu Ishac el-Faresi Vulgo el-Ifsthachri, e Codice Gothano*, ed. J. H. Moeller (Gotha, 1839), p. 26.

37. To appear in a forthcoming issue of *Kunst des Orients*.

38. Aly Bahgat and A. Gabriel, *Fouilles d'al-Fustat* (Paris, 1921), houses I–II; Mamluk palaces, Bashtāk, *Index*, no. 34 (735–40/1334–39); Ṭāz, *Index*, no. 267 (753/1352).

39. Waqf of Sultan Barsbāy, Ministry of Waqfs, no. 880.

40. Palaces of Ālīn Āq, *Index*, no. 249 (693/1293); for Bashtāk and Ṭāz, see above, n. 38); for the Iṣṭabl of Amir Qawṣūn, known as the palace of Yashbak, see *Index*, no. 266 (c. 738/1337).

41. *Qāʿa* of Aḥmad Kohia, *Index*, no. 521 (710/1310); *qaʿa* of Sharaf al-Dīn, *Index*, no. 176 (717–38/1317–37); *qaʿa* of Muḥibb al-Dīn, *Index*, no. 50 (751/1350); *qaʿa* of Tashtamur, known as Khushqadam al-Ahmadī, *Index*, no. 153 (768–78/1366–77); *qaʿa* of Shakir ibn al-Ghanam, *Index*, no. 96 (774/1372–73); and *qaʿa* of al-Dardīr (see above n. 31).

42. Abū ʿAbbās Aḥmad ibn ʿAli al-Qalqashandī, *Subḥ al-Aʿshāfī Ṣināʿat al-Inshā* (Cairo, 1913), 4:61–62.

43. Maqrīzī, *Khiṭaṭ*, 2:118, 198, 54. Al-Qalqashandī, *Subḥ al-Aʿshā*, 3:374; ʿAbd al-Raḥman al-Jabartī, *ʿAjāʾib al-Āthār fī'l-Tarājim wa'l-Akhbār* (Cairo, 1322/1904), 3:21.

44. Shihāb al-Dīn Aḥmad al-Khafājī, *Shifāʾ al-Ghalīl Fīmā fī Kalām al-ʿArab min al-Dakhīl* (Cairo, 1371/1952), p. 124.

45. Al-Jawharī, *Nuzhat al-Nufūs wa'l-Abdān fī Tawārīkh al-Zamān*, 1:94; Sultan Barqūq visiting the sick amir al-Jūbanī.

46. Waqf of Amir Itmish al-Bajāsī, Ministry of Waqfs, no. 1143 (798/1396). Waqf of Qadi Yaḥyā Zayn al-Dīn, Dār al-Wathāʾiq, no. 110/17 (855/1452).

47. Waqf of Sultan Qānṣūh al-Ghawrī, Ministry of Waqfs, no. 882.

48. Muḥammad ibn Abī al-Surūr al-Ṣiddīqī al-Shāfiʿ Qayṭūn, *Al-Qawl al-Muqtaḍab fīmā Wāfaqa Lughāt Ahl Miṣr min Lughāt al-ʿArab* (Cairo, 1962), p. 156.

49. Waqf of the Amir Qurqumās, Ministry of Waqfs, no. 901 (dated 1517), p. 61. Maqrīzī, *Khiṭaṭ*, 2:443–45.

50. Waqf of Amir Sayf al-Dīn al-Aqūsh, Ministry of Waqfs, no. 610 (698/1299).

51. The only remaining *maqʿad* adjoining a palace dating from the Mamluk period is that of Amir Māmāy, *Index*, no. 51 (901/1496); the palace has disappeared. The *maqʿad* attached to the palace of the Amir Ṭāz is a later addition; the two extant *maqʿads* adjoining the funerary complex are that of Sultan Qāytbāy in the cemetery (*Index*, no. 101 [879/1474]), and that of Sultan Qānṣūh al-Ghawrī in the city (*Index*, no. 66 [909–10/1504–05]), termed in his waqf (see above, n. 47) *"qibṭī,"* that is, a Coptic type.

52. Maqrīzī, *Khiṭaṭ*, 2:59–62.

53. Waqf of Sultan Qāytbāy, Ministry of Waqfs, no. 886 (879–912/1475–1507); Wikālat Qāytbāy at al-Azhar, *Index*, no. 75 (882/1477); Sultan Qānṣūh al-Ghawrī's waqf, Ministry of Waqfs, no. 882 (916/1511); Wikālat al-Ghawrī, *Index*, no. 64 (909–10/1504–05).

54. Ibn Duqmāq, *Kitāb al-Intiṣar*, 4:13.

55. Ibn Muyassir, *Akhbār*, p. 64.

56. For the flues reaching to the roof and the perforated dome, see the funerary complex of Amir Qurqumās, *Index*, no. 162 (911–13/1506–07). Perforated domes are found at an early date; see the waqf of Urdukīn, daughter of al-Sayfī Baktamur, Dār al-Wathāʾiq, no. 16/5 (717/1317).

57. Waqf of Sultan Barsbāy, Ministry of Waqfs, no. 880 (841/1438), palace of Amir Salār.

DONALD P. LITTLE

The Ḥaram Documents as Sources for the Arts and Architecture of the Mamluk Period

Although, for reasons which are not clear to me, few documents or records of any kind—let alone archives—have survived from the Islamic Middle Ages, a number of collections of considerable interest have recently been uncovered in Cairo,[1] in Ardebil,[2] and in Jerusalem.[3] Of these, only those discovered within the precincts of the Dome of the Rock and the Aqṣā Mosque in Jerusalem, the so-called Ḥaram documents, will be discussed here.

As is evident to any reader of the history of Jerusalem written at the end of the fifteenth century by Mujīr al-Dīn al-ʿUlaymī, documents dating from as early as the twelfth century were available in the city to scholars of Mujīr al-Dīn's day. Both in his descriptions of the Islamic monuments of Jerusalem and in his biographies of its scholars, Mujīr al-Dīn frequently refers to legal records (*mustandāt sharʿiyya*) and endowment deeds (*waqfiyyāt*) that he had consulted for the data they contained and complains on occasion that he cannot locate a particular document that he needs.[4] There are indications that such records were known to exist in Jerusalem into our own century, some five hundred years later: Max van Berchem does not identify his informant, but he does tell us that medieval Islamic archives were said to be extant at the citadel of Jerusalem as late as 1914.[5] Van Berchem chose not to follow up this lead, and therefore we may never know what, if anything, we may have missed, unless those same archives turn up in some neglected corner. In the meantime, we shall have to be content with the almost nine hundred fourteenth-century documents discovered in 1974 and 1976 by Amal Abul-Hajj, at that time director of the Islamic Museum in the Ḥaram al-Sharīf, who found them stuffed into locked drawers of display cabinets belonging to the museum. Recognizing the importance of her find, Abul-Hajj took active measures, in cooperation with a team from the McGill Institute of Islamic Studies, to conserve and photograph the documents so as to ensure their preservation and their availability to scholars. Its state of preservation and variety establish the collection as a discovery of major importance for the study of medieval Islamic history in general and the history of Jerusalem under the Mamluks in particular.[6]

Most of the documents are in Arabic, but twenty-seven are written in Persian. The latter apparently have nothing whatsoever to do with Jerusalem or the Mamluks; they deal with business and legal transactions involving persons and property in Azerbaijan. How these documents happened to be in Jerusalem I do not know, but I favor the explanation that a family of Azerbaijani origin settled in that city sometime in the fourteenth century, bringing the documents with them as records of transactions they conducted in their homeland. Names and dates in the documents indicate that they may emanate from the Jalāyirids, a family prominent in the Mongol dynasty, who ruled western Iran and the Caucasus from 1336 to 1432. Whatever their provenance, the Persian papers are extremely interesting and important, being among the earliest specimens we have of Islamic documents written in Persian.

The Arabic documents pose problems of identification if only because they are so numerous and so varied in type. They consist of roughly 875 pieces of paper or parchment containing various kinds of records and deeds. A few, no more than 14, are so closely related to the Persian documents in form and content that I feel justified in calling them Persianate and in believing that they were deposited in Jerusalem by the same Azerbaijani family who brought the Persian documents there. The remaining 861 papers are different. Their dates provide a clue to their nature: approximately 80 percent of those that are dated fall between the years 1393 and 1397. A second clue is the recurrence of the same name on so many of them. That name is al-Qāḍī Sharaf al-Dīn ʿĪsā ibn Abī'l-Rūḥ ibn Ghānim al-Anṣārī al-Khazrajī al-Shāfiʿī, whom we know from a brief biographical reference in Mujīr al-Dīn's history to have been a Shāfiʿī judge in Jerusalem at exactly the time indicated by the dates on most of the documents.[7] I am reasonably sure, therefore, that most of the Arabic documents constitute records of this particular judge, copies of documents that were authorized by him, or documents that were addressed to him, usually in his capacity of chief Shāfiʿī judge of Jerusalem. However, he also served in other capacities in the city, and those functions are equally, if not more, important for our purposes. He was in charge of two institutions founded in Jerusalem by Ṣalāḥ al-Dīn—the Khanqah al-Ṣalāḥiyya and the Māristān al-Ṣalāḥī—as well as supervisor of the pious endowments of the city (Nāẓir al-Awqāf al-Mabrūra fī'l-Quds al-Sharīf).[8] Accordingly, many of the documents are related to his activities as administrator of waqfs. Although a large number—the ledger accounts, for example—bear neither a date nor Qadi Sharaf al-Dīn's name, some provide clues indicating that they could be records connected with pious endowments that he administered. The presence in the collection of documents which either predate or postdate the qadi's lifetime suggests that his papers may have formed part of a large collection belonging to the Shāfiʿī court of Jerusalem, and that the papers of Sharaf al-Dīn accidentally survived in disproportionate numbers. This hypothesis also accommodates the presence of the Persian and Persianate documents, most of which are legal records that for some reason or other could have been filed in the Jerusalem court by an Azerbaijani family resident there. If the Ḥaram collection does represent the remnants of an archive, one might speculate that these may be a part or the whole of that archive referred to by van Berchem as being in the Jerusalem citadel some eighty years ago.[9] I prefer, however, to think that the citadel collection was even larger and richer and may still emerge more or less intact. Certainly none of the extant Ḥaram documents is among those cited by Mujīr al-Dīn.

I have discussed elsewhere what I consider to be the significance of the Ḥaram collection for the study of Muslim diplomatics, the relationship between the theory and practice of Islamic law, and the history of Jerusalem, especially the history of the common men and women of Jerusalem who were not important or famous enough to be mentioned in a chronicle or a biographical dictionary.[10] The importance of this group of documents lies mainly in its significance for the social and economic history of Jerusalem under the Mamluks. Here, however, I shall limit the discussion to a residual asset, as it were—that is, their importance as a resource for students of the arts of Mamluk Jerusalem, by which I mean the arts in the most general sense. At this point, however, I can only discuss the collection from this perspective as a means of indicating possibilities for future research. First, I shall briefly consider the documents as specimens of calligraphy; second, as sources of information about monuments and other buildings in late fourteenth-century Jerusalem; and finally, as sources for data regarding material objects.

From the calligraphic point of view, it is extremely difficult to say much about the scripts in which the documents are written because of the lack of advanced scholarship on chancery and notarial scripts in Arabic and Persian. The several important works on Islamic calligraphy that have appeared in recent years are mainly devoted to books, inscriptions, or displays of calligraphic virtuosity.[11] Thus, while it might be said that virtually all of the Ḥaram documents are written in some form or another of *naskh*, *riqāʿ*, *taʿlīq*, *dīwānī*, *tawqīʿ*, or *nastaʿlīq*, given the great range of observable variations within those types, that does not say anything very significant. In fact, at this stage, problems of legibility are more pertinent than questions of style, and in this respect the documents range from studied clarity to careless scrawls. The range can be illustrated by a royal decree (plate 1) and a death inventory (plate 2).

Plate 1 shows three lines from a decree prepared for and signed by the Bahri Mamluk Sultan al-Malik al-Nāṣir Muḥammad ibn Qalāʾūn, dated 3 Rajab 701 (4 March 1302). It provides an example of what I venture to call *riqāʿ*, and is a model of refined handbook clarity written by a master scribe of the Mamluk chancery in Cairo. In contrast is the clumsy, unornamented, almost undotted scrawl of a notary attached to the Shāfiʿī court in Jerusalem, used for an estate inventory (plate 2). It is dated 12 Dhū'l-Ḥijja 793 (11 October 1391) and was prepared for a poor woman of Maghribi extraction, whose estate was possibly not sufficient to pay a skilled scribe—certainly other court documents from the Ḥaram prove that notaries could write clearly when they wanted to. On

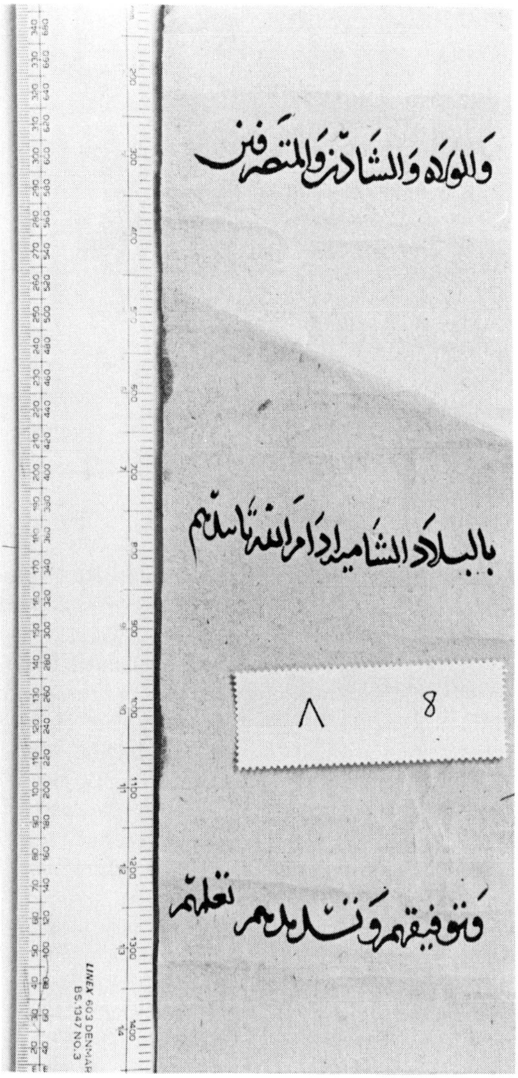

PLATE 1. Royal decree.

the other hand, although we might be tempted to assume that legibility was related to the competence of the scribe, this was not necessarily the case. Plate 3, for example, depicts another royal decree, this one signed by the Burji Sultan al-Malik al-Ẓāhir Jaqmaq on 18 Dhū'l-Qa'da 844 (10 April 1441), in a script which looks like a cross between *dīwānī* and *ijāza*. Though the chancery scribe who wrote it was obviously skilled in his art, his primary concern, in this instance at least, could not have been legibility: the script is sufficiently cursive to cause considerable difficulty.

Occasionally documents were written in a script that virtually defies decipherment. Such is the case with document 78 (plate 4), otherwise notable for its impressive seal, a red *tamgha*, usually associated with Mongol documents;[12] this is one of the Persianate group, written in Arabic but having no discernible connection with Jerusalem. It is a bill of sale for a slave purchased in the year 784/1382. The presence of the *tamgha* and the bold endorsements written in the right margin are enough to establish it as having emanated from a rich source, so that again the choice to write in a "difficult" script must have been deliberate.

Document 875 (plate 5), written in Persian *ta'līq* is equally troublesome. From its format alone—a wide right margin, few words to a line, and lines rising toward the left with wide spaces between them—this document, like document 8 (plate 1), is identifiable as a decree. Thanks largely

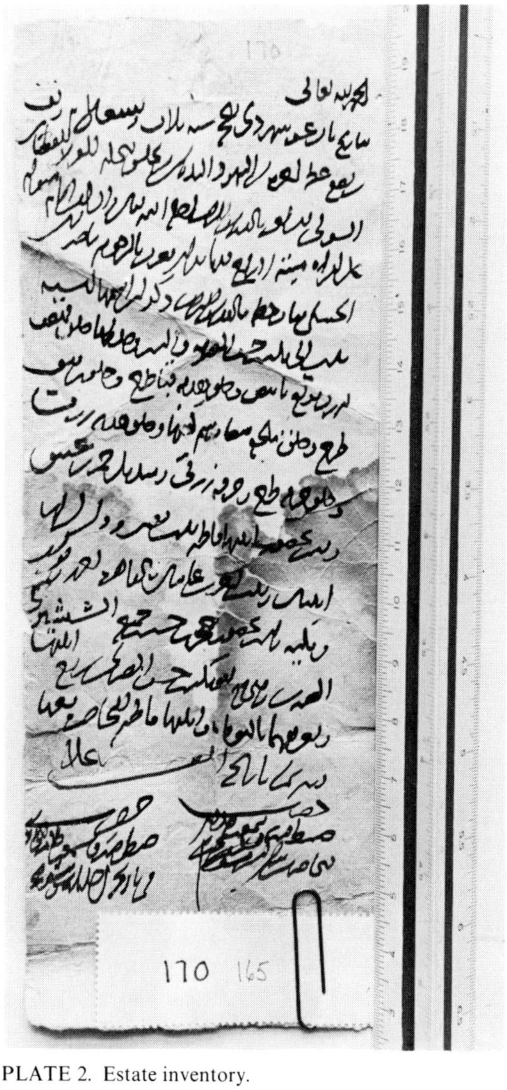

PLATE 2. Estate inventory.

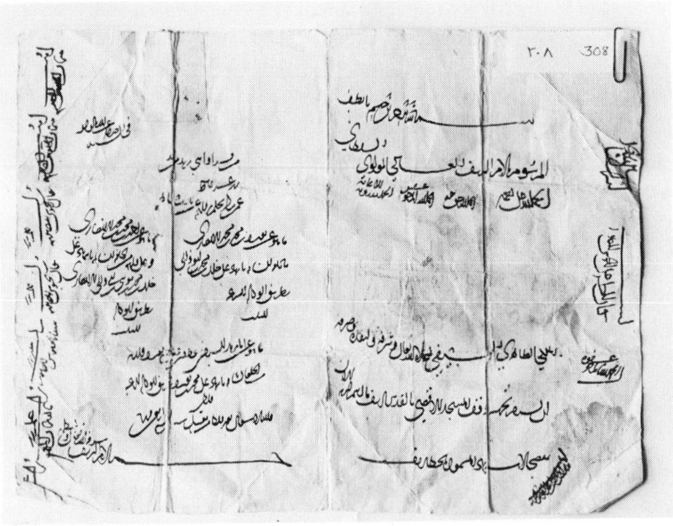

PLATE 3. Royal *murabba'a* decree.

to the research of S. M. Stern we know that this format was used for Islamic decrees from at least Fatimid times by high-ranking officers of state.[13] In fact, this document is so similar in appearance to a Jalāyirid firman recently published[14] that it can almost certainly be identified as a Jalāyirid decree, especially since the date, 9 Jumādā II 754 (12 July 1353) fits. Notice the line of Mongolian in Uigur script written near the bottom, between lines 7 and 8. Several of the Persian documents contain passages written in Uigur Mongolian as well as Armenian, which is not as strange as it might seem if, indeed, these documents did originate in Azerbaijan, where Arabic, Persian, Mongolian, and Armenian, among other languages, flourished simultaneously.

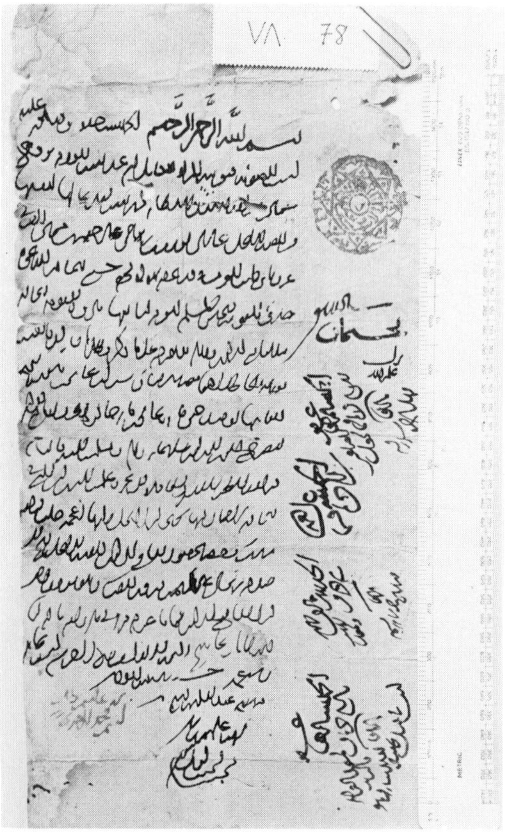

PLATE 4. "Persianate" purchase deed for a slave.

Two more examples of calligraphy illustrate the similarity of many of the Persian documents to the Persianate ones written in Arabic. Number 832 (plate 6), which contains an acknowledgment of a debt and is dated 27 Ṣafar 723 (7 March 1323), is written in Arabic; number 861 (plate 7), an acknowledgment of the receipt of a loan, is in Persian, with an Arabic heading and date, 30 Jumādā I 716 (20 August 1316). The similarities in the format and script (*tawqī'*) of the two documents are greater than the differences and point to what I believe is the continuity and mutual influence exercised by the Arabic and Persian diplomatic traditions in the thirteenth and fourteenth centuries. Without some basic research on chancery and notarial calligraphy, however, one can only take refuge in Stern's still valid advice that we avoid "the question of the script of the [chancery] documents, since our knowledge of the development of Arabic writing is still rudimentary."[15] Careful analysis of the Ḥaram documents will no doubt advance our knowledge of calligraphy if considered along with the detailed discussion of chancery scripts provided by the Mamluk encyclopedist al-Qalqashandī,[16] but that is a project of some magnitude.

A second category of documents contains data on buildings in Jerusalem. Of these by far the most

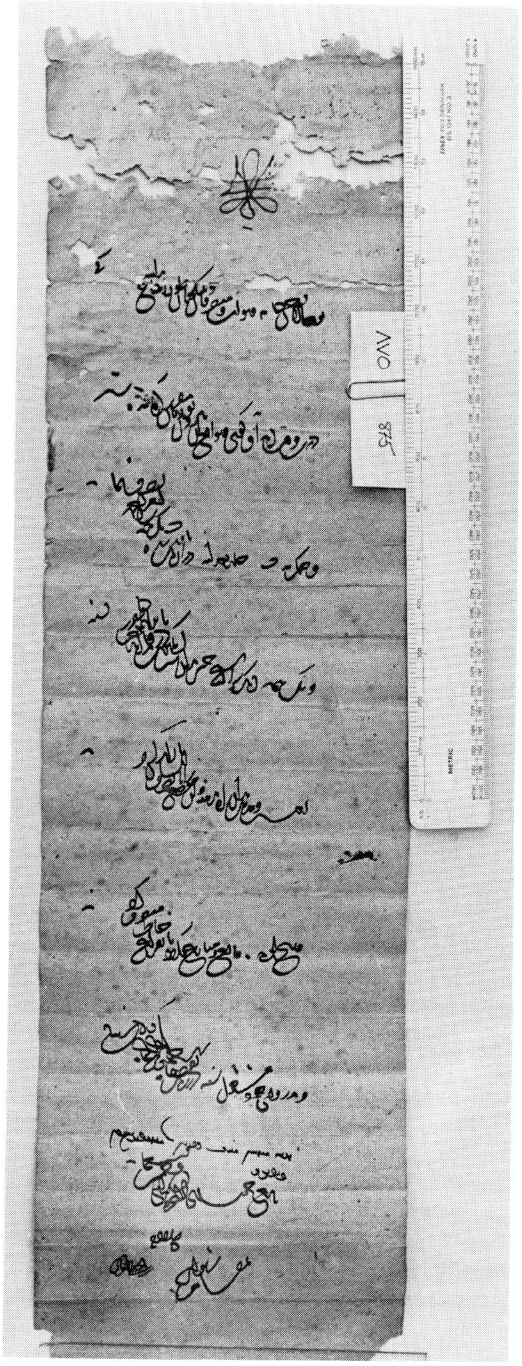

PLATE 5. Jalāyirid decree.

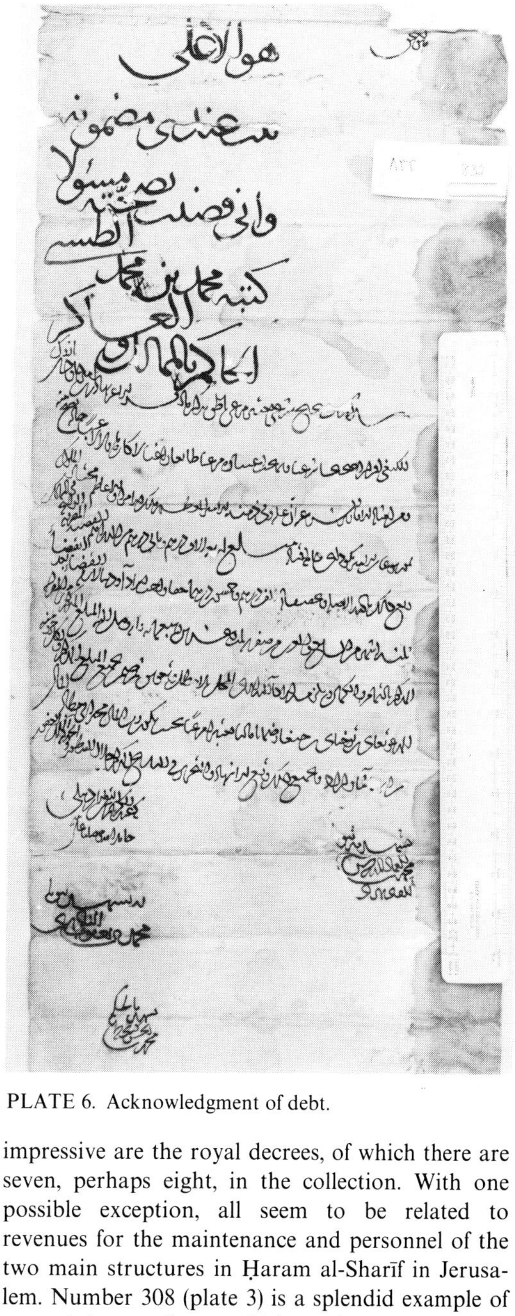

PLATE 6. Acknowledgment of debt.

impressive are the royal decrees, of which there are seven, perhaps eight, in the collection. With one possible exception, all seem to be related to revenues for the maintenance and personnel of the two main structures in Ḥaram al-Sharīf in Jerusalem. Number 308 (plate 3) is a splendid example of a royal decree of a type hitherto known only from chancery and notarial manuals. Signed by Sultan Jaqmaq, it is called a *murabbaʿa* by dint of its division into four pages. The main text accompanied by registration notations is on the recto; the date, summary, signature, and more registration notations appear on the two pages of the verso. Its contents provide endowment income for the Aqṣā Mosque and thus corroborate the evidence in liter-

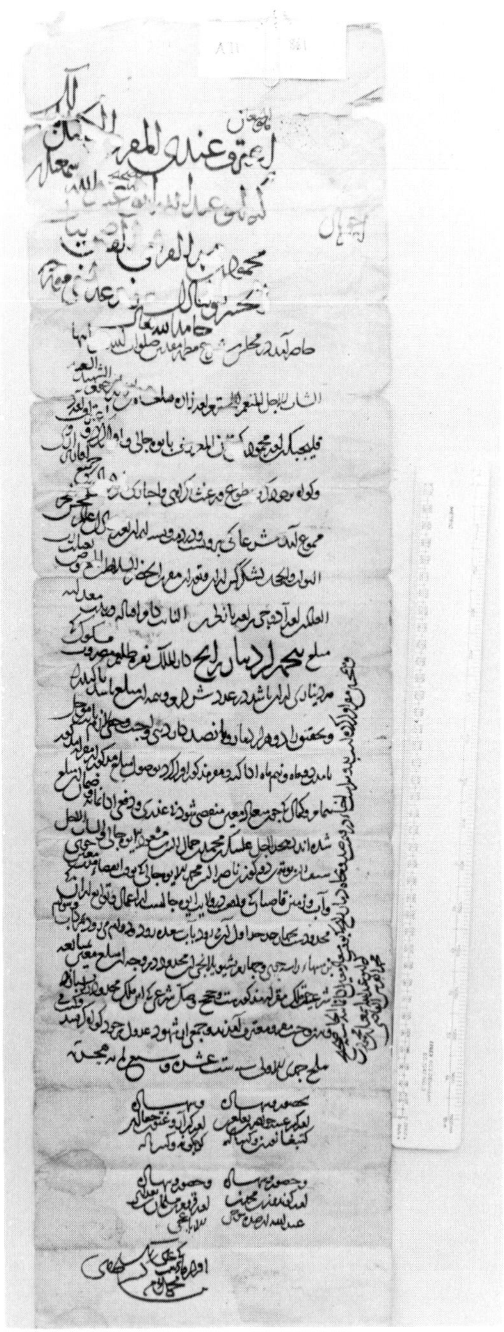

PLATE 7. Acknowledgment of a loan.

ary sources and inscriptions that the Mamluk sultans were interested in providing funds for the buildings and staff of the sacred structures of Islam.

In addition to the royal decrees issued for the benefit of al-Aqṣā and the Dome of the Rock, there are numerous lesser decrees issued by Mamluk amirs and judges for the benefit of lesser religious institutions in the city. Document 14, for example, is another *murabbaʿa*, or squared decree. Though much less pretentious in script and format than Jaqmaq's decree, its form is essentially the same, with the text written on the recto and the date and authorization on the verso, along with the signature of the authorizing amir written in the form of a motto or *ʿalāma*. This document, dated 17 Ṣafar 785 (21 April 1383), is a decree issued by a Mamluk amir, the supervisor of the waqf for the tomb and madrasa of Amir Ṭāz, built in 763/1361–62,[17] appointing a sheikh, one Burhān al-Dīn Ibrāhīm al-Nāṣirī, to recite the Koran and hadith at the tomb for a salary of fifteen dirhams per month.

Number 10 is a similar document, but contains a petition written on the recto with the response written in the form of a decree on the verso. This petition has the same format as all the petitions familiar to us from the research of Stern,[18] with a wide right margin containing the *tarjama*, or name of the petitioner, in this case al-Shaykh Burhān al-Dīn, the same sheikh whose name appears on the previous decree. In the stereotyped formula, *yuqabbil al-arḍ wa-yunhī*, Burhān al-Dīn asks permission to be domiciled in a Jerusalem madrasa headed by a qadi. On the verso appears the response of the judge in the form of a decree, dated 20 Ṣafar 780 (18 June 1378), couched in typically bureaucratic language, promising to assign Burhān al-Dīn lodgings in the ribat of this institution, unless it is already full, in which case he is to be placed on the waiting list.

Besides decrees, several other types of documents contain data on buildings in Jerusalem. For example, number 774 (plate 8), entitled a *waraqa* (literally "a leaf"), is written on a standard-sized sheet of paper called a *daftar*, which has been folded in half to form four pages; it contains two holes for a still visible piece of string used to tie it together with related documents. This *waraqa* contains an itemization of revenues for the year 791/1388–89 in favor of the Khanqah al-Ṣalāḥiyya, the Sufi convent founded by Ṣalāḥ al-Dīn and headed by the Shāfiʿī judge, Sharaf al-Dīn. Essentially it is an itemization of rental income, arranged in columns, from a bath (*ḥammām*), roofed stalls (*muṣaqqafāt*), shops (*ḥawānīt*), a mill (*ṭāḥūn*), and other establishments for the benefit of the khanqah. Beneath each entry the amount of rent is recorded, interestingly enough, in the *siyāqa* script which is, of course, the script best known from the Ottoman archives, though it was used as early as Abbasid times by scribes of financial bureaus for accounting

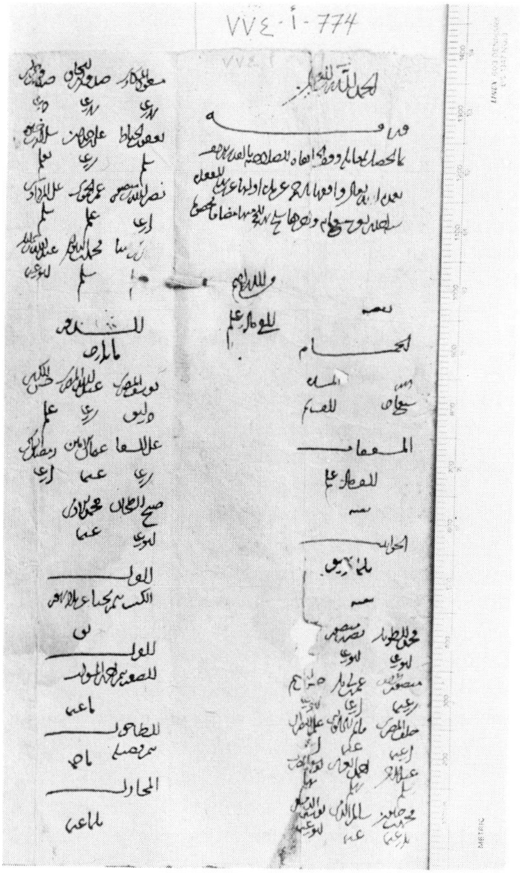

PLATE 8. Itemization of waqf revenues.

purposes.[19] This is among the first evidence we have that *siyāqa* was used by accountants of the Mamluk period. The total revenues, along with a summary of the document, are written on the verso.

Document 773-A is also a *waraqa*, very similar in format to number 774. It contains an itemization of expenses incurred in 795/1392 for *ʿamāʾir*—repairs, or perhaps construction—of a bath (*al-ḥammām al-mubārak*), included in the waqf of the Khanqah al-Ṣalāḥiyya. Various materials are listed—lime (*kils*), stone (*ḥijāra*), salt (*milḥ*), sand (*ramla*), oil (*zayt*), and a receptacle for ashes (*iqmīm*)—with the cost of each recorded again in *siyāqa* script.

The last type of document connected with buildings is the deed, of which three types are represented: purchase deeds, leases, and endowment deeds. But since the data on buildings to be found in all three types tend to be similar, one example should suffice. Document 353 (plate 9) is a purchase deed written on parchment for a house (*dār*) located in the neighborhood of a mill, Ṭāḥūn al-Bāsiṭī, in Jerusalem. The house was bought for 450 dirhams on 15 Ṣafar 777/16 July 1375 by a man named al-Ḥājj Muḥammad ibn al-Marḥūm al-Ḥājj Aḥmad ibn ʿAlīʾl-Ṣayʿīrī, who was a resident of Jerusalem, from a woman called al-Ḥājja Ṭayyiba bint al-Ḥājj Muḥammad ibn ʿAbd Allāh al-Miṣriyya, zawjat al-Ḥājj Abū Bakr ibn Muḥammad ibn Jaʿfar al-Miṣrī. The deed specifies that the entire house, not just a part, was sold for this amount, and its components are spelled out in detail: an apartment (*bayt wāḥid*), the roof (*saṭḥ*), a latrine (*murtafqa*), and a courtyard (*sāḥa*) with a gate (*bāb*).

The deed also specifies the exact boundaries of the house in terms of the four points of the compass, beginning at the south, because that was the direction of the qibla. On the south the house was bounded by a waqf house belonging to Ibn Fāʾid; on the east by a passable lane (*darb maslūk*); on the north by a garden called the Ḥākūrat al-Bāsiṭī; and on the west by the mill. This deed is accompanied by two ancillary documents. One, written beneath the deed, attests the transfer of the property from the public treasury (*bayt al-māl*); the other, on the back, is a certification of the deed by the Shāfiʿī court in Jerusalem.

Obviously, these data are of considerable interest to students of Mamluk Jerusalem, especially when correlated with other documents and sources. From the *nisba*s of the parties named in

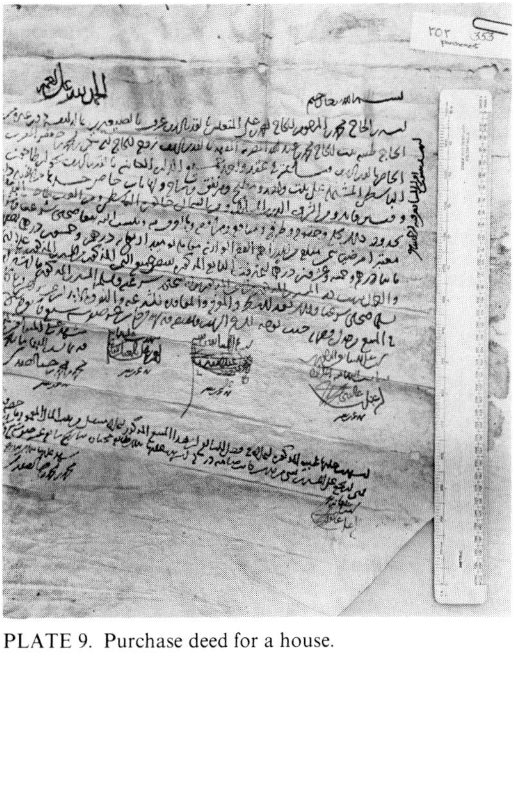

PLATE 9. Purchase deed for a house.

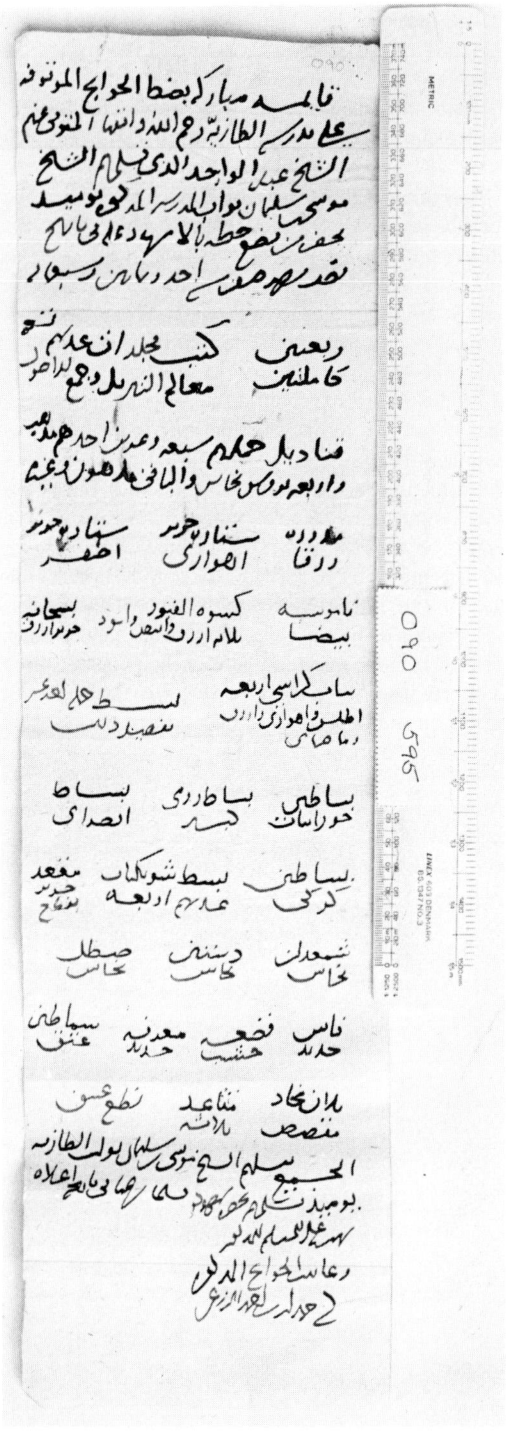

PLATE 10. List of objects left to the Madrasa al-Ṭāziyya.

legal transactions, for example, it might be possible to deduce information about the ethnic composition of various neighborhoods and quarters. Although the price paid for the house does not mean much in itself, when correlated with prices paid for other properties and objects recorded in other documents and in literary sources it could become significant. For scholars interested in medieval urban housing, the itemization of the components of the building and the definition of its environment are of evident value. Finally, from a different point of view, this document is valuable *qua* document, providing, as it does, evidence of the continuity of an Islamic legal and notarial tradition for sales which stretches back to Abbasid times and forward to the Ottoman period.[20]

Some of the Ḥaram documents yield important data on the use to which buildings were put. A copy of the waqfiyya (number 643) for the tomb and *zāwiya* built for Muḥammad Bāk Zakariyyā in 751/1350–51[21] includes, for example, a list of the persons who lived in the building and used its facilities, along with the functions they were supposed to perform and the stipends they were paid. Unfortunately, this is the only document of that particular sort in the collection, but many others contain incidental information on the use of Jerusalem's buildings, ranging from its noblest edifices to the humblest houses and apartments.[22]

Something can also be learned from these documents about moveable objects, and our knowledge of the Mamluk minor arts can thereby be augmented. In the Ḥaram there are many lists; in fact, the major part of the collection consists of inventories of one kind or another. Some of these inventories were compiled regularly; others were drawn up only once. Number 595 (plate 10) is an example of the latter; labeled a *qā'ima mubāraka* ("blessed list"), it enumerates the objects placed in endowment for the Madrasa al-Ṭāziyya by a decreased sheikh, ʿAbd al-Wāḥid, in Ṣafar 781/ June–July 1379. It is mercifully legible, so that a good idea of objects deposited and used in a madrasa can be gained, beginning, of course, with books—both the Koran itself (*rabʿatayn kāmilitayn*) and Koranic commentary (*Maʿālim al-Tanzīl*) and tradition (*Jamʿ al-Uṣūl*). Candlesticks are listed, some gilded (*mudhdhahab*) and some made of cheaper materials. Perhaps of chief interest are the carpets, which are identified by the place in which they were woven: both imported varieties, such as Rūmī (Anatolian) and Aq Ṣarā'ī, and domestic, or of Palestinian origin, from Ḥawrān, Karak, and Shawbak, are represented.

Document 76 is a similar list, dated 26 Dhū'l-Ḥijja 790 (26 December 1388), but it is couched in the form of a waqfiyya in which a lady named Sufrā Khātūn endowed objects for the madrasa and *turba* which we know from Mujīr al-Dīn she had established in the city in 768/1367.[23] Like the previous inventory, this one lists a variety of things—household objects, such as copper pots, trays, and wash basins, some of which are designated by weight and material. Carpets that Sufrā Khātūn donated to the building are identified, again, as Rūmī, Aq Ṣarā'ī, and Shawbakī, but they are also designated by numerical terms, *rubā'ī* (fourfold), *suḍāsī* (sixfold), *'ushārī* (tenfold), which probably refer to dimensions.

Of related interest in the field of textiles and costume under the Mamluks is the inventory of a clothing shop (number 611) owned by a merchant from Ḥama located in the Sūq al-Khila' (literally, the "Garments Market"). His stock is listed by fabric, color, origin, and sometimes style, and should constitute a valuable source for the study of clothing and fabrics.[24]

The approximately 450 specimens of estate or death inventories (plate 2), the most numerous type of document in the collection, are also valuable for the study of the clothing of common people. They were compiled on a systematic and regular basis with the authorization of the Shāfi'ī court in conjunction with the public treasury and the viceroy of

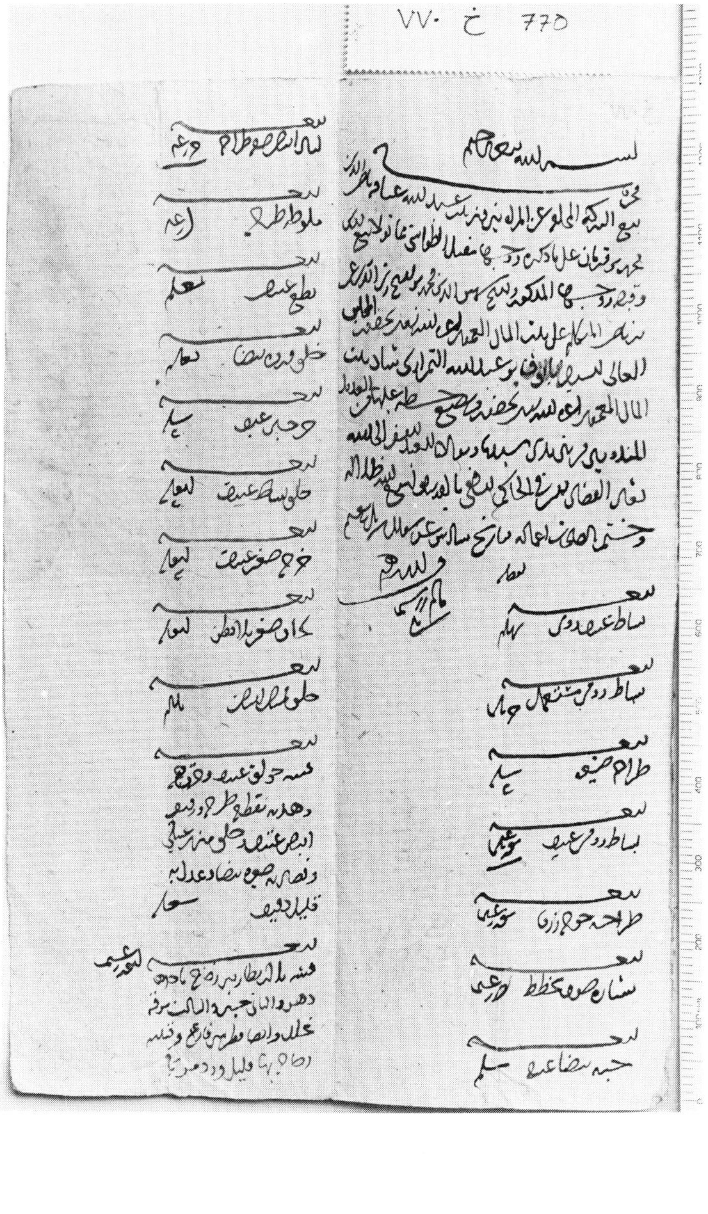

PLATE 11. A *makhzūma*.

Jerusalem,[25] and were made when a person was either already dead or terminally ill. Such an accounting was intended to ensure that the estate would be divided according to the strictures of Islamic law and to guarantee that the state would obtain its legal share of residual estates. The place of residence is often specified: in number 89, for example, a dead woman named Fāṭima bint ʿAbd Allāh al-ʿAjamiyya was found in a hostel called the Ribāṭ al-Malik at Bāb al-Duwaydāriyya. Frequently, however, the person's house was described as being located in a particular quarter or in relation to a public building. Such is the case with Āsiya bint Abī Bakr ibn Ḥasan al-Miṣrīyya, whose effects, enumerated in document 165 (plate 2), dated 12 Dhū'l-Ḥijja 793 (13 October 1391), were found in a house known as Dār al-Marḥūm Nāṣir al-Dīn al-Ḥanbalī at Bāb Ḥiṭṭa.

The inventory mentions all a person's possessions: if the person was poor, or perhaps a visitor, it might consist solely of the clothes (*thiyāb badanihi*) the person was wearing, which is of course a handy indication of what common people in late fourteenth-century Jerusalem did wear. The enumeration often includes fabric and color; sometimes even style is specified. The inventory for a person of considerable means and a permanent resident of the city can include household effects and precious objects—furnishings and cooking utensils, jewelry, cosmetic aids, tools, and the like. Unfortunately these inventories do not include the values assigned to these objects, but public sales of the effects of deceased persons were frequently conducted for the benefit of the heirs by agents of the Shāfiʿī court. Accordingly, records, called *makhzūmāt*, of these sales were kept. They include the price paid for each object, written in *siyāqa* script. Number 770 kh (plate 11), for example, the record

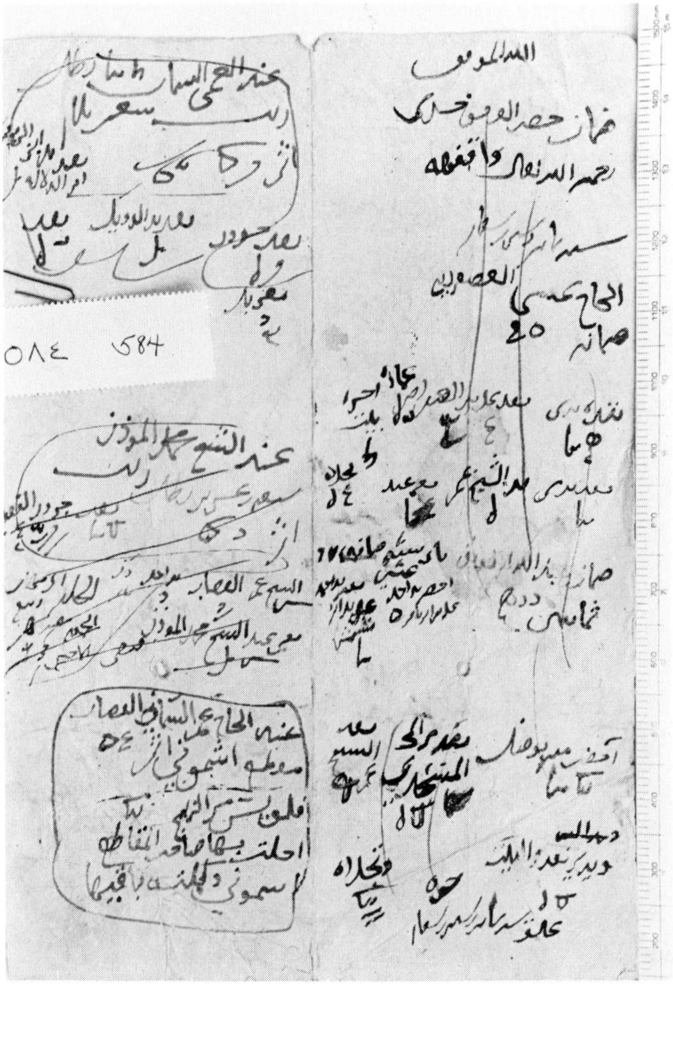

PLATE 12. Account notations.

of sale of the effects of a freedwoman, Nayrūz bint 'Abd Allāh, *'ataqāt* Nāṣir al-Dīn Muḥammad ibn Qaramān, zawjat Muqbil(?) al-Ṭawāshī, includes an old Rūmī carpet sold for eight dirhams, a used Rūmī carpet for five dirhams, a striped woolen curtain for twenty-one dirhams, an old white jubba for six dirhams, and so forth. The inventory continues on the verso, with an itemization of the expenses of the sale and signatures of the witnesses.

Another *makhzūma*, number 768, in exactly the same format, was made for a person whose substantial wealth was in the form of Egyptian, Syrian, and Italian gold; he turns out to have been the Sufi sheikh of Zāwiyat Muḥammad Bāk. A fascinating list (number 61) of a similar type consists almost entirely of books sold for the same Sheikh Burhān al-Dīn mentioned in some of the other Ḥaram documents and gives an idea of the types of books in circulation at the time, the prices they fetched, and, since the names of the purchasers are given, the sort of persons who bought them.[26]

Finally, the Ḥaram collection includes documents which, though they have defied analysis so far, may well prove significant. Some are rough accounts (plate 12), many of which contain entries consisting of persons' names, each name preceded by the word *'inda* (meaning a debit, an amount owed) with a numerical amount and/or the name of a commodity. Occasionally, one of these pages has a heading with a date. They are probably accounts in favor of waqf properties and commodities in Jerusalem administered by the Qadi Sharaf al-Dīn. I do not yet know what their ultimate significance may be, but they may have some bearing on the management of buildings in the city.

Nor can I foresee, for that matter, the ultimate significance of the Ḥaram collection as a whole. Suffice it to say that almost all the Arabic documents—some 860—contain some data bearing on buildings and possessions in late fourteenth-century Jerusalem, and that they constitute a mine of information for students of Mamluk art and architecture. Their nature does pose substantial difficulties, however, since they constitute not a complete archive but only random records with scraps of information that must be retrieved, organized, and analyzed before they can make much sense. Nevertheless, the Ḥaram collection is unique: with the possible exception of the Egyptian papyri, no collection of medieval Islamic documents equals it.

INSTITUTE OF ISLAMIC STUDIES
MCGILL UNIVERSITY
MONTREAL

NOTES

1. Four hundred fifty-nine Mamluk documents were discovered in the Ministry of Pious Endowments in 1967, and an additional 97 documents of the same period came to light in 1978. See Muḥammad Muḥammad Amīn, *Al-Awqāf wa'l-Ḥayāt al-Ijtimā'iyya fī Miṣr 648–923/1250–1517* (Cairo, 1980), pp. 2–3.

2. More than 800 Persian documents were discovered in 1970 in the shrine of Sheikh Ṣafī' l-Dīn in Ardabil. See Bert G. Fragner, "Das Ardabīler Heiligtum in den Urkunden," *Wiener Zeitschrift für die Kunde des Morgenländes* 67 (1975) : 171–73.

3. For an account of the discovery of documents in the Ḥaram al-Sharīf, see my "Significance of the Ḥaram Documents for the Study of Mediaeval Islamic History," *Der Islam* 57, no. 2 (1980) : 189–219.

4. Mujīr al-Dīn al-'Ulaymī, *Al-Uns al-Jalīl bi-Ta'rīkh al-Quds wa'l-Khalīl*, 2 vols. ('Ammān, 1973), 2:42, 46, 53, 118, 119, 126, 129, 130, 131, 144, 146, 151, 182, 219, 220, 221, 235, 244, 245, 260, 269, 271.

5. Max van Berchem, *Matériaux pour un Corpus Inscriptionum Arabicarum*, part 2, *Syrie du Sud: Jerusalem*, 3 vols., vol. 2, *Ḥaram* (Cairo, 1925, 1927), pp. 10–11, n. 3.

6. Linda S. Northrup and Amal A. Abul-Hajj, "A Collection of Medieval Documents in the Islamic Museum at the Ḥaram al-Sharīf," *Arabica* 25 (1978) : 282–91.

7. Mujīr al-Dīn, *Al-Uns*, 2:127.

8. Ḥaram documents 25 and 615.

9. See n. 5, above.

10. In addition to my "Significance of the Ḥaram Documents," see my *Catalogue of the Islamic Documents from al-Ḥaram aš-Šarīf in Jerusalem* (Beirut, forthcoming).

11. E.g., Nājī Zayn al-Dīn, *Muṣawwar al-Khaṭṭ al-'Arabī* (Baghdad, 1968); Annemarie Schimmel, *Islamic Calligraphy* (Leiden, 1970); Yasin Hamid Safadi, *Islamic Calligraphy* (London, 1978); Anthony Welch, *Calligraphy in the Arts of the Muslim World* (Austin, Tex., 1979); Priscilla P. Soucek, "The Arts of Calligraphy," in *The Arts of the Book in Central Asia, 14th–16th Centuries*, ed. Basil Gray (London, 1979), pp. 7–34; Mohamed U. Zakariya, *The Calligraphy of Islam: Reflections on the State of the Art* (Washington, D.C., 1979).

12. See Jan Reychman and Ananiasz Zajackowski, *Handbook of Ottoman-Turkish Diplomatics*, rev. and trans. Andrew S. Ehrenkreutz (The Hague, 1968), pp. 166–67.

13. S. M. Stern, *Fatimid Decrees: Original Decrees from the Fatimid Chancery* (London, 1964), pp. 103–10.

14. Soucek, "Arts of Calligraphy," p. 13, illus. 6.

15. Stern, *Fatimid Decrees*, p. 104.

16. Aḥmad ibn 'Alī al-Qalqashandī, *Ṣubḥ al-A'shā fī Ṣinā'at al-Inshā'*, 14 vols. (Cairo, 1913–19), 3:1–222.

17. Mujīr al-Dīn, *Al-Uns*, 2:45.

18. Stern, *Fatimid Decrees*, pp. 91–102.

19. Lajos Fekete, *Die Siyāqat-Schrift in der türkischen Finanzverwaltung*, 2 vols. (Budapest, 1955), 1:13–33. Cf. Walther Hinz, "Das Rechnungswesen

orientalischer Reichsfinanzämter im Mittelalter," *Der Islam* 29 (1950) : 6–9.

20. See Jeanette A. Wakin, *The Function of Documents in Islamic Law: The Chapter on Sales from Ṭaḥāwī's Kitāb al-Shurūṭ al-Kabīr* (Albany, N.Y., 1972), pp. 37–70; R. Y. Ebied and M. J. L. Young, *Some Arabic Legal Documents of the Ottoman Period* (Leiden, 1976), pp. 2–6.

21. Mujīr al-Dīn, *Al-Uns*, 2:44.

22. For the use of Islamic documents as sources of information on Mamluk buildings, see ʿAbd al-Laṭīf Ibrāhīm, "Al-Wathā'iq fī Khidmat al-Āthār: al-ʿAṣr al-Mamlūkī," in *Kitāb al-Mu'tamar al-Thānī li'l-Āthār fī 'l-Bilād al-ʿArabiyya* (Cairo, 1958), 205–87; Ṣāliḥ Lamʿī Muṣṭafā, *Al-Wathā'iq wa'l-ʿImāra: Dirāsa fī'l-ʿImāra al-Islāmiyya fī'l-ʿAṣr al-Mamlūkī'l-Jarkasī*," (Beirut, 1980).

23. Mujīr al-Dīn, *Al-Uns*, 2:43–44.

24. For data on clothing in the Mamluk period, see L. A. Mayer, *Mamluk Costume* (Geneva, 1952). Also helpful is Yedida Kalfon Stillman, *Palestinian Costume and Jewelry* (Albuquerque, N. M., 1979).

25. An estate inventory is being published by Hoda Lotfy, "A Documentary Source for the Study of Material Life: A Specimen of the Ḥaram Estate Inventories from al-Quds in 1393 A.D.," *Journal of the Economic and Social History of the Orient* (forthcoming).

26. This document is being published by Ulrich Haarmann, "The Library of a Fourteenth-Century Scholar," *Proceedings of the Third International Conference on the History of Bilād al-Shām* (forthcoming).

DAVID A. KING

The Astronomy of the Mamluks: A Brief Overview

In the eighth and ninth centuries the Muslims assimilated with remarkable facility the sophisticated traditions of mathematical astronomy that they had inherited from Greek, Persian, and Indian sources. In the ninth century the center of this activity was first in Baghdad and later in Iran. Soon thereafter, Syrian and Egyptian astronomers began to rival their contemporaries in those earlier centers in the quality of their scientific work. Rakka in the early tenth century and Cairo in the late tenth century were among the leading centers of astronomy in the world. The celebrated astronomer al-Battānī, whose works were to be so influential in Europe in later centuries, worked in Rakka; the great astronomer Ibn Yūnus worked for the Fatimid caliphs al-ʿAzīz and al-Ḥākim[1] in Fustat. The study of astronomy in both Syria and Egypt then continued without a break through the Mamluk and Ottoman periods.

When considering astronomy in Egypt and Syria under the Mamluks, it is easy to pay insufficient attention to the main trends of the five centuries of Islamic astronomy that had preceded it, but when the Mamluks came to power in the midthirteenth century, both Cairo and Damascus had already been active centers of astronomy for a very long time. The transfer of two astronomers—Mu'ayyad al-Dīn al-ʿUrḍī and Muḥīy al-Dīn al-Maghribī—to the observational program at the Ilkhanid observatory in Maragha apparently made Cairo the more important of the two, and it seems to have maintained that preeminence until the early fourteenth century, for in those years Syrian astronomers came to Cairo to study astronomy. In the midfourteenth century the provincial capital of Damascus usurped its place for a time, not only in the Mamluk empire, but in the Islamic world as a whole, as the school of astronomers associated with the Umayyad Mosque far surpassed those working in Cairo or anywhere else. When Tīmūr devastated Damascus in 1401, however, the center again returned to Cairo, where some of its leading astronomers were associated with the Azhar Mosque. There it remained until the end of the sixteenth century, when the center of Islamic astronomy shifted once more, this time to Istanbul.

Although the major Mamluk astronomers were often *muwaqqit*s, employed by mosques and madrasas to determine the astronomically defined times of prayer, many were apparently not associated with religious institutions at all. Nor do we know of any Mamluk sultans or high government officials who were particularly interested in astronomy or who sponsored specific astronomers, in sharp contrast with Rasulid Yemen, where, in an astronomical tradition closely related to that of the Mamluks, the leading astronomers were associated with the sultans and were often even sultans themselves.

The main sources for the study of Mamluk astronomy are manuscripts, the richest collections of which, for Mamluk texts and Ottoman copies, are to be found in Cairo, Damascus, Istanbul, Berlin, Oxford, Paris, and Princeton, and in the Chester Beatty Library in Dublin. Except for those in the Süleymaniye Library in Istanbul, they are

This paper is a slightly modified version of that presented at the Mamluk symposium recorded in this volume. A more detailed survey of Mamluk astronomy, with a more extensive bibliography, appeared in *Isis* 74 (1983):531–55. George Saliba of Columbia University kindly read a preliminary draft, and his comments have been incorporated. I also thank Renée Bernhard, Irene Gilman, Michael Heberger, and Kathy Young for their assistance.

now cataloged. In all, several hundred of them are available, but virtually none of even the most important ones are yet published.

Another important source of our knowledge of Mamluk astronomy is, of course, Mamluk instruments for observation and calculation (and Ottoman instruments based on Mamluk design). The two major instrument collections are in Oxford and Istanbul.

The historical and biographical Mamluk sources are disappointing. They provide little information on the astronomers who compiled the treatises and tables or the craftsmen (usually astronomers as well) who made the instruments. The scientific texts and the instruments themselves remain, then, our most dependable sources.

There are extant Mamluk treatises for all five fields of medieval astronomy.[2] The first field, *'ilm al-hay'a*, or theoretical astronomy, studies geometrical models to reproduce the motions and distances of the sun, moon, and five naked-eye planets, as well as models of the planetary system as a whole. The solar, lunar, and planetary models which the Muslims took over from the *Almagest* of Ptolemy are described in Mamluk texts, but in a radically modified form. The second field, *'ilm al-zījāt*, or mathematical astronomy, studies the determination of the planets' positions from their geometric models. Tables were compiled in the so-called *zījs*, or astronomical handbooks, for the computation of solar, lunar, and planetary positions for any given time. Some two hundred *zījs*, several of which were compiled in Mamluk Egypt and Syria, are known from the medieval period. The most important Mamluk *zījs* are the midthirteenth-century Egyptian *Muṣṭalaḥ Zīj* and the *zīj* of Ibn al-Shāṭir compiled in Damascus a century later. The *zīj* called *Tāj al-azyāj* by the astronomer Muḥīy al-Dīn al-Maghribī was compiled in Damascus also in the midthirteenth century, but was apparently not widely used. The *zīj* called *al-Lum'a*, compiled by the fifteenth-century Cairo astronomer al-Kawm al-Rīshī, was based on the *zīj* of Ibn al-Shāṭir; other fifteenth-century Egyptian and Syrian *zījs* were based on the contemporary *Sulṭānī zīj* of Ulugh Beg of Samarqand and on the earlier *Īlkhānī zīj* of the astronomers of Maragha. Ephemerides displaying positions of the sun, moon, and planets for each day of the year were also compiled annually. Unfortunately, no Mamluk examples survive, but presumably they were similar to the Rasulid Yemeni ephemerides as well as the later Ottoman ones, which do survive.

Third, also part of the *'ilm al-zījāt*, was spherical astronomy that studied the apparent daily rotation of the sun and stars about the observer. Its most important practical application was *'ilm al-mīqāt*, the science of astronomical timekeeping by the sun and stars which determined the time of day or night by applying trigonometric formulas to data derived from the observation of an instantaneous position of the sun or of a given star. The relevant trigonometric formulas dated from the eighth and ninth centuries and were well known to the Mamluks, and trigonometric tables were available to facilitate calculations. From them, the Mamluk astronomers compiled very impressive tables for timekeeping and for regulating the astronomically defined times of prayer.

The fourth field, *'ilm al-ālāt*, was the science of instruments for representing the apparent daily rotation of the heavens about the observer—the celestial sphere and astrolabe, for example—and for calculating and computing—the trigonometric grids on quadrants, for instance. The most common astronomical instruments had been the astrolabe and quadrant, but Mamluk astronomers developed the latter to the point where it replaced the astrolabe as a favored instrument in all areas of the Islamic world except Iran and India.

The fifth and final field, *'ilm aḥkām al-nujūm* or *'ilm al-tanjīm*, that is, astrology, was widely practiced throughout the Islamic world in medieval times, but surprisingly little Mamluk astrological material survives.

Discoveries made in the past few years through careful study of the primary sources completely dispel the notion that astronomers associated with mosques and madrasas did not contribute much to the development of science. The picture that we now have of Mamluk astronomy is impressive from every aspect and is so specifically Islamic as to be of exceptional historical and cultural interest.

IBN AL-SHĀṬIR'S PLANETARY THEORY AND IBN AL-SARRĀJ'S ASTROLABE

About twenty-five years ago, my colleague E. S. Kennedy was working on some treatises on theoretical astronomy compiled by the scholars associated with the observatory of Maragha in northwestern Iran in the midthirteenth century. Until then, it had been thought that the Muslims had done little to modify or improve upon the models of Ptolemy described in the *Almagest*, but Kennedy noticed that the illustrations of the plan-

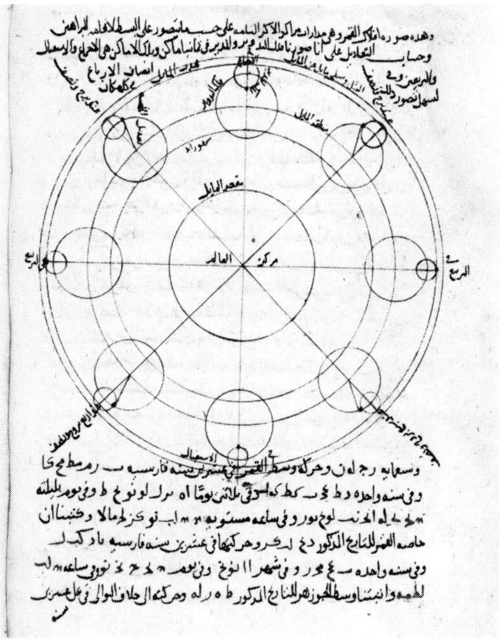

PLATE 1. Illustration of the new model for the moon in the treatise on theoretical astronomy by Ibn al-Shāṭir. Bodleian Library, Oxford, MS Marsh 139.

etary models in those treatises differed from Ptolemy's. By investigating the accompanying texts, he was able to establish that these new models improved upon the Ptolemaic ones by removing their inherent weaknesses. Further investigation revealed that a treatise by Ibn al-Shāṭir, the chief *muwaqqit* of the Umayyad Mosque in Damascus in the middle of the fourteenth century, contained even more fully developed models (plate 1). These were later shown to be mathematically identical to those of Copernicus, who worked in Poland a century and a half later.[3] Although there is no hint of a heliocentric planetary system in Ibn al-Shāṭir's writings, his other geometric modifications of Ptolemy's models are the same as those of Copernicus. The relation between the two has been investigated by a number of scholars in recent years, and a direct link between Copernicus and his Muslim predecessors, though not yet proved, remains a distinct possibility.

In Ptolemy's geometric models for the sun, moon, and planets, the celestial body moves on an epicycle whose center, representing the mean position of the planet, turns around a circle called the deferent. The motion of the epicycle center on the deferent is uniform, not about the observer at the center of the universe, but about a point "in space" called the equant. (Thus the ancient models reproduce the elliptical orbits of the solar system.) The essence of Ibn al-Shāṭir's planetary theory and the theories of several of his predecessors is the apparent replacement of the eccentric deferent and equant of the Ptolemaic models by secondary epicycles. The reasons behind this development were philosophical as well as scientific: the ultimate aim was to produce a planetary theory composed of uniform motions in circular orbits and at the same time to solve the major problem of Ptolemy's lunar model, which, while it adequately reproduced the lunar motion on the ecliptic, did not properly reproduce the variations in the distance of the moon from the earth. In Ptolemy's model the maximum apparent size of the disc of the moon appears considerably larger than its minimum apparent size, a situation clearly in conflict with observation. Ibn al-Shāṭir's new lunar model to some extent corrected the major defect of the Ptolemaic lunar model by considerably reducing the variation in the lunar distance. In the case of the sun, no apparent advantage was gained by the additional epicycle. For the five planets, the relative sizes of the primary and secondary epicycles were chosen so that the models would remain mathematically equivalent to those of Ptolemy, but the details of these planetary models are extremely complicated.

A more accessible example of the sophistication of Mamluk astronomy is an astrolabe made in Aleppo in the early fourteenth century. The astrolabe, inherited by the Muslims from the Greeks, was widely used in the first centuries of Islamic astronomy.[4] It is a two-dimensional representation of the three-dimensional universe—a model of the universe that one can hold in one's hands. On the front of the astrolabe, the rete (*ʿankabūt*), fitted with pointers representing the brightest stars and a circle representing the ecliptic (the apparent path of the sun among the stars), can be made to rotate over a series of plates (*ṣafāʾiḥ*), each engraved with a horizon and a meridian and other astronomically significant curves for a particular latitude. The apparent daily rotation of the sun and stars about the observer and his horizon can thus be simulated. Each side of each plate serves a particular terrestrial latitude, and the typical medieval astrolabe contained a series of plates to serve different latitudes.

In 1975, while cataloging scientific manuscripts in Cairo, I came across a manuscript of a treatise on the astrolabe by the early fourteenth-century Syrian astronomer Ibn al-Sarrāj, about whom little is known except that he worked in

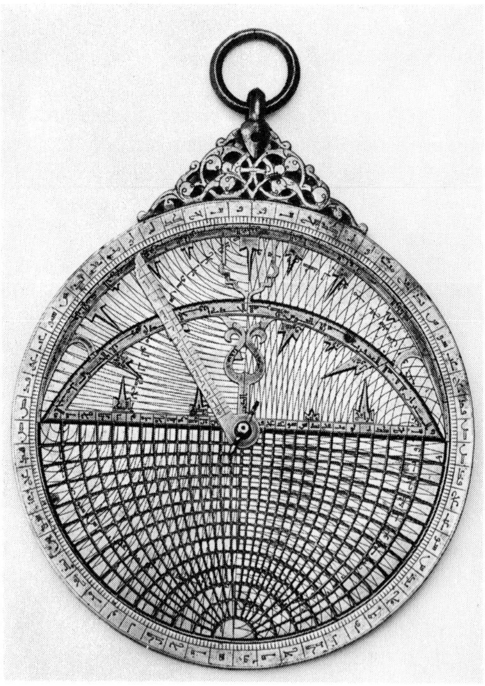

PLATE 2. Front of the universal astrolabe of Ibn al-Sarrāj. Benaki Museum, Athens.

Aleppo and does not seem to have been attached to any religious or academic institution. The treatise describes a universal astrolabe, that is, one that can perform all operations by using a special rete and a single universal plate. A similar instrument had already been invented by ʿAlī ibn Khalaf in Andalusia in the eleventh century, but Ibn al-Sarrāj claims to have invented it himself. We realize why when we turn to an unusual instrument that was actually made by Ibn al-Sarrāj and is preserved in the Benaki Museum in Athens. It is indeed a universal astrolabe, but considerably more complicated than the one he describes in his treatise. This instrument is clearly a subsequent and more elaborate version of his prototype, with a series of plates inside and an unusual grid on the back (plate 2).

Why should a universal astrolabe be fitted with a set of plates, and what was the function of the grid? In 1977, I found in the Chester Beatty Library in Dublin a treatise on this very instrument by ʿIzz al-Dīn al-Wafāʾī, who was the *muwaqqit* at the mosque of al-Muʾayyad in Cairo about the year 1450. Al-Wafāʾī, whose name is inscribed on the rim of the Benaki astrolabe as one of its owners, complains in the introduction to his treatise that Ibn al-Sarrāj had left no instructions on the use of this very unusual instrument and then proceeds to write some himself. His treatise deals with every aspect of the Benaki astrolabe and its functions, and from it we learn that Ibn al-Sarrāj's instrument is in fact a quintuply universal astrolabe. It works for any latitude in five different ways, using any one of the five main components of the instrument.

Ibn al-Sarrāj's astrolabe is surely the most ingenious instrument from the entire medieval period but hardly the most practical; it is really a mathematical toy. The average astronomer of the time did not need a quintuply universal astrolabe; what he needed was a quadrant engraved for a specific latitude, which was both cheaper to construct and easier to use. Ibn al-Sarrāj himself devised a quadrant of that sort, an example of which, made by a fourteenth-century astronomer, is also now in the Benaki Museum. It is cunningly wrought in ivory and inscribed with markings for both Cairo and Damascus (plate 3). Incidentally, the excellence of the construction found in these masterpieces of decorated metalwork and ivory is undeniable, and it is a pity they were not represented in the *Art of the Mamluks* exhibition.

One last remark on Ibn al-Sarrāj's astrolabe: the front part is identical to the so-called Mathematical Jewel of John Blagrave, an English astronomer who published a book on the instrument in 1585, but the precise relation between the Syrian and English instruments and the universal astrolabe and plate invented in eleventh-century Andalusia is still under investigation.

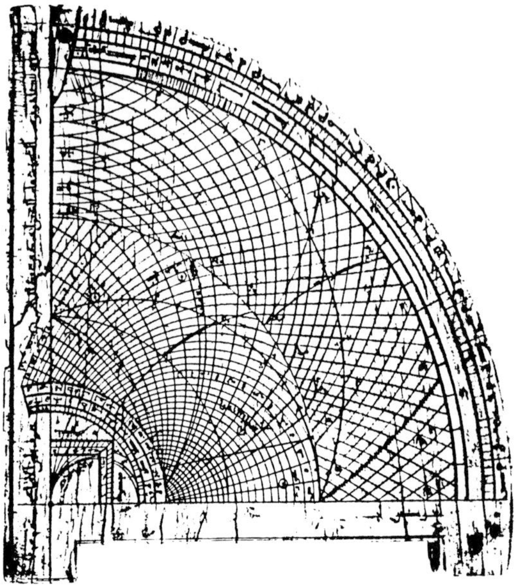

PLATE 3. Ivory quadrant with markings for both Damascus and Cairo, based on a design by Ibn al-Sarrāj. Benaki Museum, Athens.

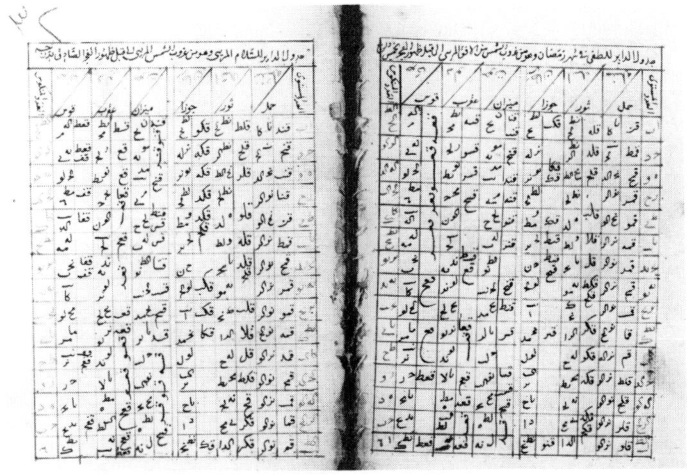

PLATE 4. Two of the approximately one hundred pages of tables in the corpus used for timekeeping and regulating the times of prayer in medieval Cairo. Egyptian National Library, Cairo.

ASTRONOMICAL TIMEKEEPING

The Mamluk *muwaqqit*s used sophisticated astronomical tables and instruments to regulate the times of the five daily prayers; because the Islamic calendar is lunar, these begin in the evening: the *maghrib* at sunset, the *ʿishā'* at nightfall, the *fajr* at daybreak, the *ẓuhr* shortly after midday, and the *ʿaṣr* at midafternoon. With their tables and instruments the *muwaqqit*s could correctly determine to the nearest minute or so the appropriate times, which vary from day to day throughout the year. The Mamluk tables were not the first to have been compiled for that purpose, but apparently it was only in Mamluk times that they were commonly used by *muwaqqit*s. They continued in use both in their original forms and in various modified versions until the nineteenth century. The tables used for this purpose in Islamic countries nowadays, printed in newspapers, pocket diaries, and wall calendars, owe their inspiration to the Mamluk tables.

Until the early 1970s, none of these Mamluk tables for timekeeping was known to exist. Now, however, two extensive manuscript corpuses of tables for timekeeping are known, for both Cairo and Damascus.[5] Each corpus contains over a hundred pages of tables with more than thirty thousand entries. We also have smaller sets for Aleppo, Tripoli, Jerusalem, and Mecca, and even a set for regulating prayer times for each degree of latitude from Mecca to Istanbul.

The medieval tables are considerably more interesting than the modern ones. Some of those in the Cairo corpus give, for example, the time that elapses between sunset and the moment exactly twenty minutes before dawn when the lamps that lit the minarets during the nights of Ramaḍān should be extinguished (plate 4). The correct times are tabulated for each day of the year and are computed specifically for Cairo. The tables shown in plate 5, part of the corpus used in Mamluk and Ottoman Damascus, were computed by the midfourteenth-century *muwaqqit* al-Khalīlī, a col-

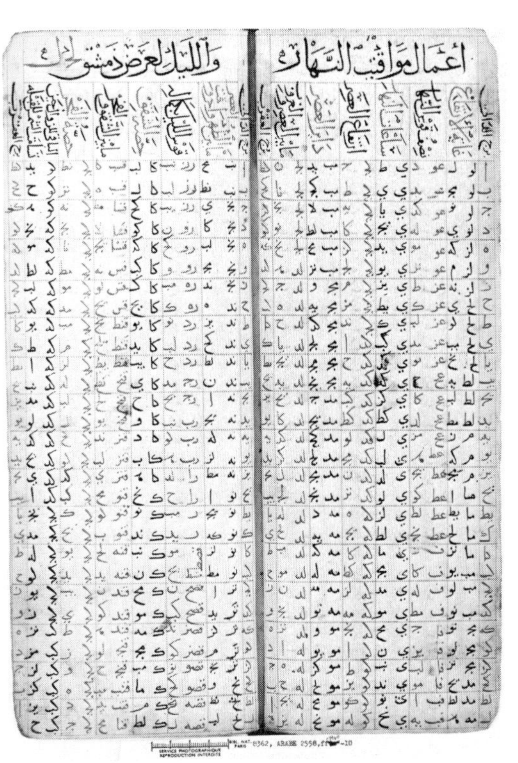

PLATE 5. Two of the approximately one hundred pages of tables in the corpus used for timekeeping and regulating the times of prayer in medieval Damascus. Bibliothèque Nationale, Paris, MS ar. 2558.

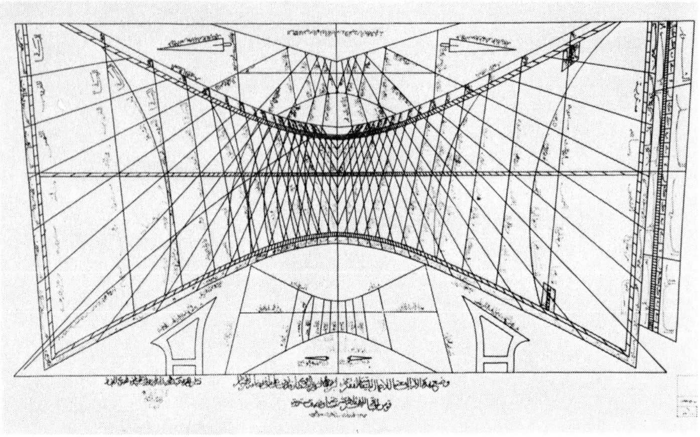

PLATE 6. Nineteenth-century copy of the sundial made by Ibn al-Shāṭir for the main minaret of the Umayyad Mosque in Damascus. (Courtesy of M. Alain Brieux, Paris.)

league of Ibn al-Shāṭir. They have a different format from the Cairo tables: for each day of the year, read vertically, various important times are tabulated in columns across the double page. To use the tables one must also have at hand an astrolabe or quadrant to ascertain when the times displayed in the tables have actually arrived, just as modern tables cannot be used without a clock.

The times for the daylight prayers of Islam are defined in terms of shadow lengths: the *ẓuhr* begins shortly after midday, when the shadow is observed to have increased; the *ʿaṣr* begins when the increase is equal to the length of the object casting the shadow and ends when it is twice the length of the object. The precise determination of the prayer times, based on these definitions, is facilitated by using a sundial, a device inherited by the Muslims from the Greeks. To watch a shadow move across a sundial is clearly easier than to read tables along with some kind of observational instrument. The Muslims contributed considerably to sundial theory from the ninth century onward.

In Mamluk and Ottoman times, a sundial was featured in most mosques.[6] Ibn al-Shāṭir constructed a magnificent one, set up on a platform on the main minaret of the Umayyad Mosque. Its remaining fragments are now on display in the garden of the Archaeological Museum in Damascus. The shadow is cast by a gnomon, set up on the meridian, and the markings on the sundial display the hours of day in various systems, as well as the times for the daytime prayers. An exact replica of Ibn al-Shāṭir's sundial, made by a Syrian *muwaqqit* in the late nineteenth century, is still *in situ* on the minaret. It was described for the first time in the modern literature in 1972 and is shown in plate 6. We know a great deal more about Mamluk sundial construction now that we have identified some Mamluk texts that describe precisely how to make them. Ibn al-Shāṭir also invented a small universal sundial containing a magnetic compass, which could be set up in the cardinal directions and made functional for any of a series of latitudes in the Mamluk world.

A large sundial constructed in 1296 was a feature of the mosque of Ibn Ṭūlūn in Cairo until the eighteenth century, when the scholars who went with Napoleon's expedition to Egypt found its fragments in the mosque, put them together as best they could, and made a hand copy of the ensemble. The fragments then disappeared and have never been recovered, but a drawing was published in the *Description de l'Egypte*. The Ibn Ṭūlūn sundial is different from the one in Damascus, but it is also of a type described in Mamluk texts on sundial construction. Recent investigations of the curves on its fragments have led to the interesting conclusion that it was probably destroyed by an irate *muwaqqit* when he realized that because of a basic flaw it did not, and indeed could not, correctly indicate the time for the afternoon prayer. A third recently published Mamluk sundial is a vertical one on the wall of the madrasa of Qāytbāy in Jerusalem, and others are described in Mamluk texts. Most of the Mamluk and Ottoman sundials still *in situ* are in bad shape: their gnomons have been bent to support telephone wires or drainpipes, when they have not been entirely lost.

THE QIBLA AND THE ORIENTATION OF ARCHITECTURE IN EGYPT AND SYRIA

Another task for Muslim astronomers was determining the qibla, or local direction of Mecca, for any given locality by calculating it from the geo-

PLATE 7. Section of al-Khalīlī's table showing the qibla as an angle to the meridian given in degrees and minutes, expressed as a function of terrestrial latitude (entered horizontally) and longitude (entered vertically). Bibliothèque Nationale, Paris, MS ar. 2558.

graphical coordinates of the locality and of Mecca: the complicated trigonometric formulas giving the qibla in terms of the latitudes and longitudes were derived by Muslim astronomers in Iraq in the ninth century.[7] Several pre-Mamluk astronomers had tried their hands at compiling tables that would display the qibla as an angle to the local meridian or north-south line for each degree of latitude and longitude, within certain limits, but because of the complexity of the exact trigonometric formula, they used approximations to compile them. It was left for the Mamluk astronomer al-Khalīlī to compute the first accurate qibla table. To use it the terrestrial latitude and longitude are fed in and the qibla simply read off (plate 7). The entries in this remarkable table number more than three thousand; they are given in degrees and minutes and are computed with remarkable accuracy—in error by, at most, one or two minutes. This we know by comparing al-Khalīlī's values with the accurate values given by an electronic computer. Al-Khalīlī's table was discovered in 1970 in a manuscript in the Bibliothèque Nationale in Paris, and only two other copies have since been identified. The table was apparently not widely used, but it is nevertheless the most sophisticated trigonometric table known to me from the entire medieval period.

One of the tables in the Cairo corpus that was used for timekeeping in Mamluk and Ottoman Cairo displays the altitude of the sun for each day of the year when it is in the direction of a ventilator (*bādahanj*). From it we learn that a ventilator is supposed to be set up so that its back is aligned with the direction of winter sunrise, some 27 degrees south of east in Cairo and Fustat. Clearly this description has nothing to do with the winds in Cairo, or so one might be forgiven for thinking. We know from medieval travelers' accounts, from the *Description de l'Egypte*, and from nineteenth-century photographs that most private houses built in Cairo in the medieval period, some of which were several stories high, were fitted with ventilators. The imposing ventilator on the Ottoman Musāfirkhane which survives to this day is indeed aligned in accordance with the Mamluk table.

The mosque of ʿAmr in Fustat, the first mosque built in Egypt, is also aligned to face the winter sunrise. The direction of the rising sun at midwinter has, of course, nothing whatsoever to do with the actual direction of Mecca, but it was taken as the qibla by the first Muslims in Egypt. When in the tenth century the Fatimids built the new city of al-Qāhira alongside the pharaonic Red Sea Canal, it turned out that the canal was exactly perpendicular to the qibla of the mosque of ʿAmr in Fustat. That was of course fortuitous—the direction of the canal was dictated solely by the local topography—but as a result the largely orthogonal street plan of Fatimid Cairo was aligned in the qibla of the *ṣaḥāba*.

We now know that the ventilators of medieval Cairo were aligned with the major axis of the city, perpendicular to the qibla of the *ṣaḥāba* and parallel to the canal. The medieval Egyptian term for ventilator was *bādahanj*, a word of Persian origin (the modern term *malqaf*, for windcatcher, is not attested before the eighteenth century). This then raises the question whether this distinctive feature of the vernacular architecture of medieval Cairo was a direct descendant of the ventilators of ancient Egypt or imported from Iran and Iraq, as the Persian name would indicate. A Mamluk astronomical text by a fourteenth-century Egyptian legal scholar suggests that the second possibility is the more likely. In it, a treatise on the use of a

PLATE 8. Section from a fourteenth-century treatise on the almuantar quadrant by the Egyptian legal scholar Ibn al-Qāṣiḥ dealing with the orientation of ventilators. Egyptian National Library, Cairo, MS DM 26.

particular variety of quadrant, one kind of Cairene ventilator is called *al-furātī*, a word clearly related to the Euphrates (plate 8). But the early history of the *bādahanj* in Cairo is still by no means clear.

Even the shape and design of the Cairene ventilators were dictated by astronomical alignments. The astronomical texts tell us that one diagonal of the base of the ventilator had to be east-west, and that the west side had to be open to the winds. But the ventilators were aligned in this fashion not only for aesthetic reasons. The medieval Egyptian folklore of the winds as recorded, for example, by al-Qalqashandī, who wrote in Cairo about 1400, confirms that the limits of the favorable *shamāl*, or north wind, and the favorable *ṣabā*, or east wind, are the cardinal directions. Thus, the *shamāl* blows from between due north and due west, and so on. The medieval ventilators were designed to receive both the *shamāl* and *ṣabā* winds. The splendid ventilator of the Musāfirkhane, one of the few surviving specimens, is indeed open on its western side as well as in the front, and its shape—it is roughly twice as wide as it is deep—accords precisely with the information on ventilators given in Mamluk astronomical texts (see fig. 1). The painting by J. L. Gérôme reproduced in plate 9 shows two crude ventilators on Cairo rooftops, but these are incorrectly oriented in relation to the direction in which the Egyptians are praying nearby.

Although the Fatimid city of al-Qāhira was fortuitously oriented in the qibla of the *ṣaḥāba*, the Fatimids did not appreciate their good fortune. Ibn Yūnus, the astronomer of the caliphs al-ʿAzīz and al-Ḥākim, had determined the qibla for them by mathematical means as 37 degrees south of east, rather than 27 degrees south of east, so the earliest mosques in al-Qāhira—al-Azhar and al-Ḥākim—were erected skew to the street pattern by some ten degrees. Many later Mamluk mosques and madrasas built in the old city have exteriors aligned with the street plan and interiors twisted by

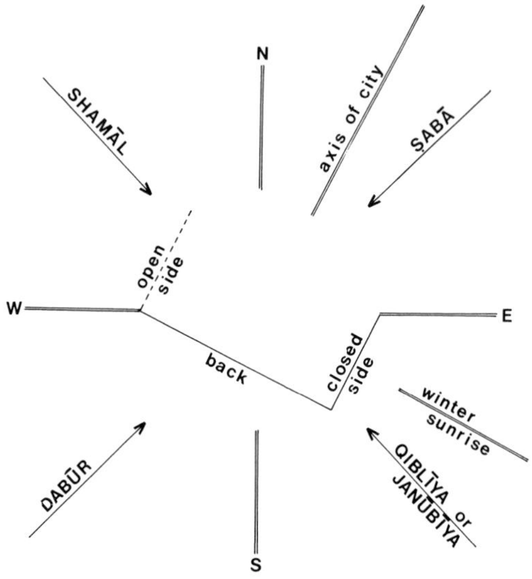

FIGURE 1. Orientation and plan of the ventilators in medieval Cairo, together with the directions of provenance of the winds according to medieval Egyptian folklore.

PLATE 9. J. L. Gérôme's painting *Prayer on the Rooftops* shows two small ventilators. Their orientation, however, is incorrect; if the ventilators are facing slightly east of north, then the Egyptians are praying roughly due north. Clearly the artist has superimposed two visual images: that of the Cairo rooftops, and that of the Egyptians at prayer. Kunsthalle, Hamburg.

some ten degrees so that they face the qibla of the astronomers. Of course, the main thoroughfare of Fatimid Cairo is not precisely parallel to the canal, but the mosques and madrasas on that thoroughfare are aligned with the canal (or the perpendicular *qiblat al-ṣaḥāba*), which accounts for the numerous kinks in it.

The curious orientations found in other religious architecture in Cairo are less easily explained. Christel Kessler was the first to show how the plans of those mosques are adapted to the street plan and the qibla, but the key to a fuller understanding of the situation is provided by the fifteenth-century scholar al-Maqrīzī, who discussed the different orientations of mosques in Cairo, and indeed all over Egypt (fig. 2).[8]

The Mamluk City of the Dead was deliberately built at 10 degrees to the axis of the Fatimid city. The mausolea there are aligned externally and internally with the new street plan, which is in the qibla of the astronomers. Even the crescents on the domes are aligned so that, when looking at them face on, one is facing the qibla. The tombs inside these Mamluk mausolea are, of course, also aligned in the qibla, so that the bodies lying on their sides are facing Mecca. The true qibla for Cairo is 45 degrees south of east, differing from the Mamluk value by another eight degrees, so modern mosques and graves are oriented slightly differently. The reason the Mamluk value is eight degrees off the true qibla is simply that medieval measurements of longitudes were generally rather inaccurate, and even the correct formula will not yield the correct qibla if the data are imprecise.

In Syria a very different situation prevailed. The qibla of the *ṣaḥāba* was due south, and the

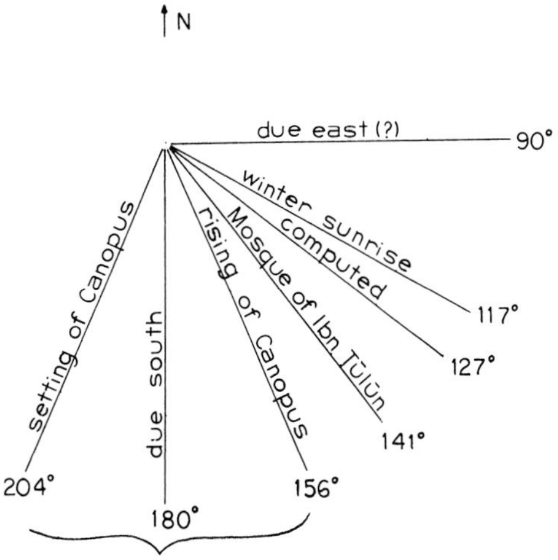

FIGURE 2. Qiblas used in Egypt, according to al-Maqrīzī.

PLATE 10. A list of localities, mainly in Syria and Palestine, giving their latitudes, longitudes, and qiblas, the latter computed by al-Khalīlī. On the left side is a list of pilgrim stations and their latitudes on the road from Damascus to Mecca. Bibliothèque Nationale, Paris, MS ar. 2558.

qiblas advocated by the astronomers, some 45 degrees east of south for Jerusalem, 30 degrees east of south for Damascus, and 20 degrees east of south for Aleppo, were seldom used for mosque orientation (plate 10). Even in the new Mamluk city of Tripoli, for which the qibla given in Mamluk astronomical sources is about 30 degrees east of south, the mosque orientations vary from about 15 degrees east of south to about 10 degrees west of south. We learn from Michael Meinecke that some of these mosques are modeled on mosques in Aleppo and Hama,[9] and I suspect that the orientations of some of the Tripoli monuments may simply reflect the orientations of the buildings on which they were modeled.

A whole corpus of medieval Islamic literature on folk astronomy, a popular tradition independent of the sophisticated discipline of mathematical astronomy, tells how to determine the qibla using the sun, moon, stars, and even the winds.[10] This literature, only recently investigated, also provides a kind of sacred geography quite distinct from the tradition of mathematical geography that the Muslims inherited from the Greeks; according to it the world is divided into sectors about the Kaaba. In the Mamluk illustration shown in plate 11, each of the twelve sectors of the world is associated with a particular side or corner of the Kaaba, and the qibla in each sector is defined by an astronomical direction. The Muslims who built the mosque of ʿAmr facing the winter sunrise did so, I believe, because they wanted it to face the northwest wall of the Kaaba, that is, they wanted the qibla wall of the mosque to be parallel to that particular wall of the Kaaba, which is, as we now know, itself astronomically aligned.

ASTROLOGY

It is safe to assume that the Mamluk sultans had considerable interest in astrology even though there are few surviving texts to prove it.[11] The historian Ibn Abi'l-Faḍā'il records that when Sultan al-Nāṣir Muḥammad ibn Qalā'ūn became ill with diarrhea, astrologers and geomancers, as well as his doctors, were consulted. Sultan al-Nāṣir Aḥmad had in his service an astrologer named Ibrāhim al-Ḥāsib al-Malikī al-Nāṣirī, who assembled an enormous astrological compendium, extant in a unique manuscript in the British Library. A *malḥama*, or book of prognostications for each month of the Syrian year, dedicated to Sultan Qāytbāy, is preserved in a single manuscript in the Chester Beatty Library. The prognostications are based on such criteria as the physical appearance of the lunar crescents at the beginning of Muslim months, comets, thunder, lightning, earthquakes, and the like, and apparently derived mainly from hermetic material. No doubt other such treatises are yet to be found. Of course, astrology was frowned upon by the religious authorities. The fourteenth-century Hanbali theologian Ibn Qayyim al-Jawzīya of Damascus wrote a polemic against astrology.[12] Further investigation of the texts and of the available historical sources is necessary before we can talk intelligently about the role of astrology in Mamluk society.

The Ottomans were heirs to the entire Mamluk Egyptian and Syrian traditions as well as to the Iranian-Transoxanian tradition in astronomy. Their astronomical activity was centered in Istanbul, but it does not concern us here. In this brief overview I have attempted to convey something of the sophistication of Mamluk astronomy and to illustrate some of its most inher-

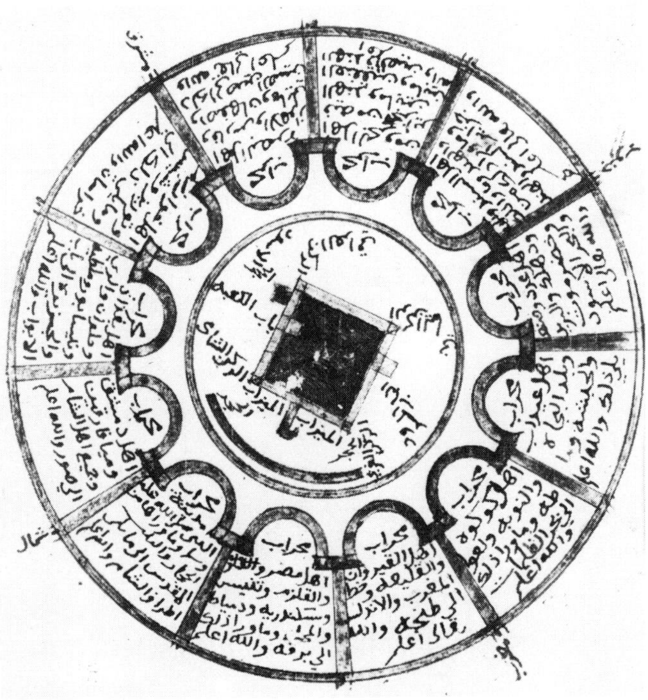

PLATE 11. Diagram of the world divided into sectors about the Kaaba, from a fourteenth-century Egyptian astronomical manuscript. Egyptian National Library, Cairo, MS DM 637.

ently interesting aspects, which are not restricted to the history of science. The Mamluks left behind them a scientific heritage as impressive as any in the Islamic world, whose scientific age was drawing to a close, or in Europe, where a new scientific age was just beginning.

HAGOP KEVORKIAN CENTER FOR NEAR EASTERN STUDIES
NEW YORK UNIVERSITY
NEW YORK

NOTES

1. See the articles "al-Battānī" and "Ibn Yūnus" in the *Dictionary of Scientific Biography.*

2. For an overview, see D. A. King, "The Exact Sciences in Medieval Islam: Some Remarks on the Present State of Research," *Middle East Studies Association Bulletin* 14 (1980):10–26.

3. On Ibn al-Shāṭir and his achievements, see E. S. Kennedy and I. Ghanem, eds., *The Life and Work of Ibn al-Shāṭir, an Arab Astronomer of the Fourteenth Century* (Aleppo, 1976). See also the article "Ibn al-Shāṭir" in the *Dictionary of Scientific Biography.* Both Ibn al-Shāṭir's treatise on theoretical astronomy and a treatise by his predecessor al-ʿUrḍī are currently being investigated by George Saliba of Columbia University.

4. On the astrolabe, see *Encyclopaedia of Islam,* 2d ed., s.v. "*Asṭurlāb,*" by W. Hartner. On the various instruments invented by Ibn al-Sarrāj, see D. A. King, *The Astronomical Instruments of Ibn al-Sarrāj,* to be published by the Benaki Museum.

5. On astronomical timekeeping in medieval Cairo and Damascus, see D. A. King, "Ibn Yūnus' *Very Useful Tables* for Reckoning Time by the Sun," *Archives for the History of Exact Sciences* 10 (1973):342–94, and "Astronomical Timekeeping in Fourteenth-Century Syria," *Proceedings of the First International Symposium on the History of Arabic Science* (Aleppo, 1976), 2:75–84. See also the articles "Ibn Yūnus" and "al-Khalīlī" in the *Dictionary of Scientific Biography.*

6. On some Mamluk sundials, see L. Janin, "Le cadran solaire de la Mosquée Umayyade à Damas," *Centaurus* 16 (1972):285–98; L. Janin and D. A. King, "Ibn al-Shāṭir's *Ṣandūq al-Yawāqīt*: An Astronomical Compendium," *Journal for the History of Arabic Science* 1 (1977):187–256; Janin and King, "Le cadran solaire de la mosquée d'Ibn Ṭūlūn au Caire," ibid. 2 (1978):331–57; D. A. King and A. G. Walls, "The Sundial on the West Wall of the Madrasa of Sultan Qāytbāy in Jerusalem," *Art and Architecture Research Papers* 15 (July 1979):16–21.

7. On the qibla problem in general, see the *Encyclopaedia of Islam,* 2d ed., s.v. "Ḳibla," and also the references cited below, nn. 8 and 10. For al-Khalīlī's table, see D. A. King, "Al-Khalīlī's Qibla Table," *Journal of Near Eastern Studies* 35 (1975):81–122.

8. On orientations in medieval Cairo, see Christel Kessler, "Mecca-oriented Architecture within the City: Reflections on a Singular Building Practice of Medieval Cairo," to appear in a memorial volume for Professor Nuwayhi to be published by the American University in

Cairo, and my study "Architecture and Astronomy: On the Ventilators of Medieval Cairo and Their Secrets," *Journal of the American Oriental Society* 104 (forthcoming).

9. Michael Meinecke, "Regional Architectural Traditions: Evolution and Interrelations," a paper presented at The Renaissance of Islam: The Art of the Mamluks, National Gallery of Art, Washington, D.C., May 13–16, 1981.

10. On this, see D. A. King, "Astronomical Alignments in Medieval Islamic Religious Architecture," *Annals of the New York Academy of Sciences* 385 (1982):303–12, and "The Sacred Geography of Medieval Islam," *Islamic Art* 3 (forthcoming). See also Gerald S. Hawkins and D. A. King, "On the Orientation of the Ka'ba," *Journal for the History of Astronomy* 13 (1982):102–09.

11. On Islamic astrology, see the article "Astrology/Astronomy, Islamic" by George Saliba in *Dictionary of the Middle Ages* (forthcoming), and idem, "The Astrologers in Medieval Islamic Society," a paper presented at the Second International Symposium for the History of Arabic Science, Aleppo, 1979.

12. John W. Livingston, "Ibn Qayyim al-Jawziyyah: A Fourteenth-Century Defense against Astrological Divination and Alchemical Transmutation," *Journal of the American Oriental Society* 91 (1971):96–103.

JAMES W. ALLAN

Sha'bān, Barqūq, and the Decline of the Mamluk Metalworking Industry

It is generally agreed that the overthrow of the Bahri and the establishment of the Burji Mamluks coincided with major changes in Mamluk culture as a whole, though the changes involved and the reasons for them are all too rarely analyzed. My aim here is to examine the Mamluk metalworking industry in the period around A.D. 1400, to try to discover, first, what was actually happening to the industry and, second, the reasons for it.

A study of Mamluk metalwork in the period between about 1360 and the accession of Barqūq in 1382 suggests that the metalworking industry suffered decline, but in quantity rather than quality. As evidence of the continuing quality one may cite a magnificent inlaid tray in the name of al-Malik al-Manṣūr, who must be al-Manṣūr Muḥammad (1361–63) or al-Manṣūr 'Alī (1376–82) (plate 1);[1] an inlaid ewer in the name of the Rasulid Sultan al-Malik al-Afḍal Dirghām al-Dīn al-'Abbās (1363–77) (plate 2);[2] the inlaid box of Aydamur, governor of Aleppo in 1371–72;[3] and a group of objects that were probably made during the reigns of al-Ashraf Sha'bān (1363–76) and al-Manṣūr 'Alī (1376–82), including a basin of Qutlubughā[4] and an anonymous bowl in the Bibliothèque Nationale bearing a European coat-of-arms (plate 3).[5] The decoration of these latter pieces may be compared to that on mosque lamps dedicated to al-Ashraf Sha'bān.[6]

PLATE 1. Brass tray inlaid with silver and gold, c. 1361–82; diameter c. 80 cm. Victoria and Albert Museum, London, no. 420–1854. (Photo courtesy of Victoria and Albert Museum.)

PLATE 2. Brass ewer inlaid with silver and gold, c. 1363–77; height 53 cm. Museo Nazionale del Bargello, Florence, no. 357C. (Photo courtesy of Bargello.)

For the period from the accession of Barqūq until the midfifteenth century, very few pieces of Mamluk metalwork seem to have survived. From Barqūq's reign there is a silver inlaid bronze key from the Kaaba dated 795/1393,[7] and a silver inlaid fragment of a larger object, probably a mosque lamp, bearing Barqūq's titles was sold in Paris in 1981 (plate 4).[8] Among surviving objects of his successors are a lock in Istanbul[9] and a key in the Louvre,[10] both significantly of iron inlaid with gold, dating from Faraj's reign, a chandelier of beaten copper dating from the end of al-Mu'ayyad Shaikh's reign,[11] two mirrors[12] and a beaten brass stand from Barsbāy's reign[13] (1422–37) (plate 5), a beaten brass bowl for incense from Jaqmaq's reign (1438–53),[14] and a beaten brass basin probably also attributable to Jaqmaq's reign.[15] It is true that the sheet-metal objects bear stippling, which is the normal sign of original inlay; the stippling is so light and traces of inlay so completely absent, however, that one has the impression that the objects were never intended to receive it. This fact, plus the general dearth of surviving objects, points to a decline both in the quality and the quantity of brasses from the early Burji period onward.

A study of door fittings reveals a similar decline. From Ayyubid times and after we have evidence for the use of cast bronze or brass plaques as decoration for doors of important buildings. The extant doors in the mosque of Sultan Ḥasan (1356–61) are in this tradition and are magnificent examples (plate 6).[16] So too are the portal doors of the complex of Barqūq (1384–86), which both in their main designs and in their inscriptions are inlaid with silver.[17] However, also in the complex of Barqūq, in the northern, western, and southern walls of the *saḥn*, are six other bronze-plated doors in a very different style: openwork metal revetments in the form of a central medallion divided into six equal parts with large trefoil finials and quarter corner pieces.[18] Some doors now in the Islamic Museum in Cairo[19] suggest that this style may well go back to earlier Mamluk times, but it was to become characteristic of Burji door designs, and one of its obvious advantages is that it

PLATE 3. Brass bowl inlaid with silver, c. 1363–82; diameter 21.3 cm. Bibliothèque Nationale, Cabinet des Medailles, no. 5621. (Photo by Kalus.)

PLATE 4. Mosque lamp neck, brass inlaid with silver, c. 1382–99; diameter 25 cm, height 12.5 cm. (Photo by Cornette de Saint-Cyr.)

uses far less metal than the typical Bahri style. Where the design comes from is difficult to say, though a direct and intriguing parallel occurs in the same complex in another medium—a pair of wooden doors, whose design is very reminiscent of bookbinding decoration.

Ten years later, in 1395, the madrasa of Maḥmūd al-Kurdī was given a door with a basic design similar to Barqūq's *ṣaḥn* examples, The quantity of metal used, because of the overall layout, is about halfway between the typical Bahri and Burji styles. The next extant doors are to be found in the mosque of al-Mu'ayyad Shaikh and were placed in position in 1416. However, we know from al-Maqrīzī and Ibn Iyās that al-Mu'ayyad took them from Sultan Ḥasan's mosque and that they therefore date from 1356–61.[20] The two doors inside the vestibule of his mosque, on the other hand, have decoration of the typical Circassian type. Then we come to the doors of the mosque-madrasa of al-Fakhrī, built in 1418 (plate 7). The door leaves are covered by sheets of brass onto which the cast bronze plaques are nailed, and there is no inscription on the doors to confirm their dating. Our knowledge that, two years earlier, the sultan had taken doors from another building for use in his own and the fact that stylistically the doors of al-Fakhrī are more like those of Ayyubid

PLATE 5. Brass stand, c. 1422–37; height 26 cm. Victoria and Albert Museum, no. 934–1884. (Photo courtesy of Victoria and Albert Museum.)

PLATE 6. Bronze door revetments on east side of qibla iwan of the mosque of Sultan Ḥasan, Cairo, 1356–63; 250 × 120 cm.

PLATE 7. Bronze door revetments of the mosque of al-Fakhrī, Cairo, 1418; 330 × 180 cm.

and early Mamluk times raise certain doubts about their date and suggest that they too come from an earlier building.

The typical Burji door-facing style continues, for example, in the doors of the mosque-madrasa of al-Ashraf Barsbāy (1423–24) (plate 8), until the reign of al-Ghawrī, when the earlier style reappears in his madrasa of 1503–04. From these Cairene doors one can thus see a second, less luxurious design emerging from obscurity in the 1380s to dominate door styles from the 1390s.

Damascus doors suggest a similar decline in metal quantity and luxuriousness, although most of the evidence has been destroyed. The doors of the māristān of Nūr al-Dīn (1154) (plate 9) point to a midtwelfth-century geometric door revetment style. This style finds a more developed if eccentric form in the great iron doors of the Aleppo citadel (plate 10), dating from the reign of al-Malik al-Ẓāhir Ghāzī in 1211,[21] and in the superb bronze door revetments of the mausoleum of Imam Awn al-Dīn at Mosul, dating from 1248.[22] Given the history of door revetments in fourteenth-century Cairo we may postulate a similar development during the Bahri period in Syria, a development of which, however, we know nothing, presumably owing to the removal of all door fittings by the governor Baydamur on the orders of al-Ashraf Shaʿbān in 1374, for reuse in the Mamluk capital.[23]

The next surviving group of Damascus doors are those of the Umayyad Mosque. The great east door was erected in 808/1405 by Amir Shaikh al-Khāṣṣakī, the future Sultan al-Mu'ayyad Shaikh, and in the following year Nawrūz al-Ḥāfiẓī erected the north doors (plate 11). The side doors of the west entrance were hung in 819/1416, and in the following year the northern pair of side doors of the east entrance were put in position, probably by Īnāl, formerly *dawādār* of Amir Nawrūz al-Ḥāfiẓī, who had been executed three years earlier.[24] In all these cases there is a strong impression of meanness about the work compared with that of earlier

PLATE 8. Bronze door revetments of the mosque-madrasa of al-Ashraf Barsbāy, Cairo, 1423–24; 210 × 150 cm.

PLATE 9. Detail of the bronze door revetments of the māristān of Nūr al-Dīn, Damascus, 1154.

PLATE 11. Bronze revetments of the north doors of the Umayyad Mosque at Damascus, dated A.H. 809 (A.D. 1406).

times—small sheets of thin, embossed sheet metal nailed up side by side. A scarcity of money or metal, or both, seems again to be indicated.

The objects reviewed so far suggest the following points. First, between about 1360 and the accession of Barqūq in 1382, there was a decline in the quantity of metal objects produced; second, from late in the fourteenth century until (approximately) the accession of Qāytbāy there was a very striking reduction in the quantity of objects produced and in the luxuriousness of the brass working; third, the Cairene doors suggest a shortage of money and/or metal from the last decade of the fourteenth century onward, a point supported

PLATE 10. Iron doors of the gateway at the head of the bridge of the Aleppo citadel, dated A.H. 608 (A.D. 1211).

in a limited way by the Damascus evidence. The question now is to what extent the literary evidence supports and explains this situation.

The first point that may be drawn from the literature is that throughout the late fourteenth century the metalworking industry in Damascus at least was prospering. In 1374, according to Ibn Sasra,[25] Baydamur received a second order from al-Ashraf Shaʿbān, this time for brocade and embroidery, housings and robes. Ibn Sasra continues:

The viceregal palace became a workshop, and there was no room for anyone to place his foot because of the craftsmen; men making brocade, people sewing and others moulding gold, men working with furnaces, people packing and others weighing. One who supervised the work in the viceregal palace told me that among all the work there were 700 pieces of brocade, each piece containing from 300–500 mithqāls. There were made also gold needles with pearl heads—2,000 of them; silver needles with gold heads for the slave girls—3,000 of them; 1,200 pairs of Yalbughāwī embroidery, likewise saddlecloths and saddlebags of brocaded satin—120 saddlebags; 300 camel saddles dressed with gold and silver, 60 stirrups of gold and silver, chains and halters for the camels—a large amount.

Although Ibn Sasra adds the ominous words, "No vice-roy was able to do this after Baydamur," other literary evidence points to a continuing industry for the next twenty years. The Italian traveler Simono Sigoli visited Damascus in 1384–85[26] and records large numbers of brass basins and ewers inlaid with figures, leaves, and other subtle designs in silver. Fifteen years later, in 1400–01, the *Vita Tamerlani*[27] mentions master craftsmen working in copper and brass, as well as in gold, silver, and iron, in that city.

Of the metalworking industry in the capital during the late fourteenth century we know little directly from literary sources. However, Maqrīzī's descriptions of the suqs as they were in his day, in the second and third decades of the fifteenth century, indirectly make some important points. Thus of the market of the inlayers he writes, "In our time inlaid copper has become little used by people, and it is very rare to find it. There are some people who for several years have applied themselves to buying such of it as is available on the market, and the removal of inlay from it is pursued for material gain. A small remnant of metalworkers remain in this market to the present day."[28] Of the market of the spurmakers he writes:

I knew a time when people used spurs of pure gold, both *qālib* and *saqṭ*, or of pure silver. It was only the very pious who did not, and used *qālib*s of iron, overlaid with gold or silver, and *saqṭ*s of silver. People were compelled to abandon this practice: you can rarely find anyone whose spur *saqṭ* is silver, and today one almost never finds a golden spur. They used to sell in this market complete silver gear for horses' bridles, sometimes in enameled silver, sometimes in silver gilt: the weight of what was in this gear could reach as much as five hundred silver dirhams. All this has disappeared. . . . Here they also used to sell inkstands and objects of price, such as penknives and so forth, in which were silver and gold.[29]

In his descriptions of the markets of the beltmakers and the bridlemakers Maqrīzī gives useful indications of when the decline happened. He writes: "The amirs and *khāṣṣakiyya* in the days of al-Nāṣir and later used gold belts, certain of them even encrusted with precious stones. Each year the sultan distributed to the Mamluks a considerable quantity of gold and silver belts, and this continued until the accession of al-Nāṣir Faraj; but it was very rare during the reign of al-Malik al-Mu'ayyad Shaikh."[30] In his description of the bridlemakers' bazaar Maqrīzī goes further:

There they used to sell all the accessories of bridles, made of leather. In this suq equally were found an appreciable number of gilders and specialists in *kuft* [plating], used for bridles, stirrups and spurs, etc., and of makers of saddlepads and pommels. . . . I have seen saddles used by troops and secretaries in the pommels of which there were six collars of silver gilt decorated in relief, and silver circlets. Hardly anyone ever rode with a plain saddle, except a qadi, shaikh, or divine. After the accession of Barqūq all the military used very luxurious saddles, whose pommels were of gold or silver, plated or pure metal. This became so prevalent that virtually every army horseman used the saddle we have described; *musaqqat* saddles ceased to be used. After the events of the year 806 poverty hit the people, and disorders got worse. Gold and silver saddles became rare, and only a small number are found today: they are used by the principal amirs and leading Mamluks.[31]

Maqrīzī's comments read as considered and rational observations, rather than simply as regrets for "the good old days," and his indications of when the situation deteriorated are particularly important: the key reign appears to have been that of al-Nāṣir Faraj (1399–1412).

Maqrīzī also gives important pointers to the reasons for the decline of the industry. "After the events of the year 806 [1403] poverty hit the people," he writes, and he is here referring to what appears to have been the worst year of inflation recorded in Egypt in the late fourteenth and early fifteenth centuries. It was not, however, the only one, for 1394–95, 1398, and 1415–16 are also recorded in the texts as disastrous years for price rises.[32] In periods of high inflation living standards drop, and it may be assumed that this economic situation had a marked effect on the metalworking industry.

"Disorders got worse," continues Maqrīzī, and it is clear that the continuous civil wars of the early Burji period were another major factor in industrial decline. Damascus in 1389, 1391, 1392, 1396, and 1398 witnessed warfare between rival Mamluk factions and a series of major conflagrations which destroyed, among others things, the markets of the smiths and armorers.[33] For Damascus another disaster was Tamerlane's conquest: although the amount of damage done may not have been as great as the fifteenth-century historians allege, Tīmūr sent from the city to Samarqand the official master craftsmen of the city, who must have included not only the armorers specified by de Clavijo, but also gold- and silversmiths, coppersmiths, and blacksmiths.[34]

A third reason for the industry's decline is suggested elsewhere by Maqrīzī. In his *Treatise on Famines* he writes: "As for the . . . artisans, wage workers, porters, servants, grooms, weavers, laborers and their like, their wages multiplied many times over. However, not many of them remain, for most of them died. A worker of this type is not to be found except after strenuous searching."[35] Here he is ascribing a leading role in industrial decline to the Black Death. Plague certainly had a major impact on the Mamluk empire, bringing a steady decline in population, and metalworkers would have suffered as much as any other indigenous group in Egypt or Syria. Support for its relevance in this context is seen in the quantity of surviving metalwork between the 1350s and 1380s, for the first outbreak of plague was in 1347, with regular recurrences thereafter.

Perhaps the most significant factor in the decline of the metalworking industry, however, was the shortage of metal itself, in particular of silver and copper.[36] The initial shortage of silver is shown by the lack of surviving dirhams from Barqūq's reign. Only two types are known from his first reign (784–91/1382–89)—a Cairo group dated A.H. 789 and a Syrian group from Aleppo and Hama, one of which is dated A.H. 784. No silver issues are known from his second reign (792–801/1390–99). Silver coins remained scarce throughout Faraj's reign and copper *fulūs*, which had become more and more common in the second half of the fourteenth century, now took over: in 805/1403 the exchange rate system of dinar: dirham became dinar: trade-dirham, and transactions were made either in gold or copper.

Silver became more widespread from 815/1412 when first al-Musta'īn Billāh and then al-Mu'ayyad Shaikh issued silver dirhams—the *nawrūzī* and the *mu'ayyadī*. However, Maqrīzī asserts that the dirham did not really reappear in circulation in Cairo until 817/1414,[37] when al-Mu'ayyad Sheikh returned from his successful campaign in Syria against Nawrūz with large quantities of nawrūzī and bunduqī (Venetian) dirhams. European, and possibly Central Asian,[38] silver had evidently accumulated in Syria despite the shortage in Cairo. Even so, silver was an uncertain commodity, and al-Mu'ayyad Sheikh's announcement of the dirham as the standard currency of the empire in 821/1419 could not be enforced owing to the inadequate supply of that precious metal.

The crisis continued intermittently, for in his *Kitāb al-Sulūk* under the year 839/1435 Maqrīzī wrote that the people in Cairo were prevented from making vessels and instruments of silver, the silver being carried to the mint for minting dirhams,[39] and there must have been other occasions when the silver available was grabbed by the government at the expense of the artisans.

There was also a shortage of copper. Copper had been minted in increasing quantities from the reign of al-Nāṣir Muḥammad and took over from the dirham in 1403. The historians accuse Jamāl al-Dīn Maḥmūd al-Ustādār (d. 1397) of flooding the Egyptian market with copper and selling silver to the Europeans, but Bacharach has suggested that Jamāl al-Dīn merely expanded the production of copper *fulūs*, probably by exporting silver to Europe at a high price, buying copper at a low cost, and minting it as quickly as possible in order to make a profit on the minting fee.[40]

A shortage of copper is first recorded in the sources in 808/1405,[41] and scarcity appears to have continued to the end of Jaqmaq's reign (1453). A numismatic solution was to debase copper coins or to use substitute metals, and from 1410 are found references to *raṭl*s of copper, iron, worked copper, iron tools, and horseshoes, while in 1421 Maqrīzī wrote that *fulūs* had become so corrupted that copper coins were mixed with broken iron nails, iron horseshoes, and pieces of copper and lead, and that in a *qinṭār* (100 *raṭl*) of *fulūs* one would find that less than a quarter of them were copper coins; the rest would be copper, iron, and lead.[42]

Such comments vividly portray the problems of a copper shortage, as do certain comments in the sources having to do with the conflicting demands for copper for the making of coins and the manufacture of objects. Thus al-Jawharī writes of the year 826/1423, "In this year new *fulūs* were very rare, and the reason was the moving of them over the sea to the land of Yemen, and the making of them in workshops into vessels, dishes, cups, etc."[43] Maqrīzī gives a similar story in much more detail:

On the 28th [of Ramaḍān in the year 826/1423] the sultan gathered the merchants and money changers because of the *fulūs*. For from the time when it was agreed that the minted *fulūs* were worth seven dirhams per *raṭl*, and pieces five dirhams per *raṭl*, they became rare, so that they could scarcely be found. The reason for that was that the merchants did much trading in it and a *qinṭār* of *fulūs* having reached eight hundred dirhams made up many loads of pure *fulūs* and sent them to the Hejaz, the Yemen, India, and the Maghrib in immeasurable quantities, because of the chance of profit this presented. Others made from them copper vessels, such as cooking pots, and sold them for thirty dirhams a *raṭl*. A group applied themselves to acquiring bits of iron, copper, lead, and tin; they separated each group of metal and made something suitable from it, and made much profit. Furthermore, whoever had some of these [*fulūs*] was miserly about using them in commercial transactions. A group applied itself to gathering them and so they became rare so that one could not obtain them. Commerce came to a halt because of the lack of *fulūs*. When the people gathered in the presence of the sultan opinion was firm that pure *fulūs* were worth nine dirhams a *raṭl*, and that no one was to trade with any pieces of copper, iron, lead, or tin. This was proclaimed, and anyone who disobeyed and left the country with any of these was threatened with dire punishment.[44]

This description gives fascinating insight into the conflicts between government, artisans, and traders that the shortage of metal must have inspired throughout the first quarter of the fifteenth century. It was surely significant that the shortages of metal occurred in a period of continuous civil war, when the government was endlessly in desperate need of ready cash to pay its troops, and at a time when the plague continued to reduce the mamluk population at an alarming rate, requiring yet more ready cash for the purchase of replacements. The indirect effect of civil unrest and the plague, whose direct influence we have already mentioned, must also therefore be taken into account.

The period around 1400 is therefore a very important and a very intriguing one in the history of Mamluk metalwork. For once, the surviving metal objects and the literature complement each other, and a reasonably rounded picture emerges. The archaeological evidence points to a decline in production and to the introduction of techniques using less metal, beginning possibly in the reign of Barqūq and certainly in the reign of Faraj. The literary evidence indicates a flourishing industry until the turn of the century and offers a convincing set of circumstances that would have produced the decline—a population being reduced by plague; a period of inflation with critical years of price rises, which brought disastrous drops in the standard of living; a political situation that was unstable at best and brought highly destructive civil war at worst, especially in Damascus; a government requiring abundant cash to meet the cost of the numerous military expeditions needed to put down rivals and to continue the purchase of new mamluks in a time when the plague and civil war combined to reduce them at unprecedented speed; and a shortage of silver and copper, which affected the whole nation and must have had a major impact on the luxury metalworking industry.

Yet, black as the situation was, it was not the end of the story for the Mamluk metalworking industry. During the reign of Qāytbāy inlaid brasses were given a new lease on life, and the quality of repoussé work reached hitherto unknown heights. Whether this revival, like the earlier decline, rested on economic and social factors, or whether it was due to the initiative and patronage of Qāytbāy himself, is a question which cannot be answered here, but one that will certainly repay detailed study in the future.

Ashmolean Museum
Oxford

NOTES

1. Victoria and Albert Museum, no. 420–1854. Sheet bronze or brass tray, inlaid with silver and gold; diameter c. 80 cm, height 5 cm. The monumental inscription reads: *'izz li mawlānā al-sulṭān a * al-malik al-'ālim al-'ā * mil al-'ādil al-ghāzī 'azza naṣruhu*, "Glory to our lord the sultan, the king, the knowing, the diligent, the just, the conqueror, may his victory be glorified."

The central inscription reads the same, except that it omits *'azza naṣruhu* and adds *al-mujāhid*, "the holy warrior"; the other three circular inscriptions read as the latter, but after *al-mujāhid* add the further titles *al-murābiṭ al-muthāghir*, "the defender, the protector of the frontiers." Around the central area is a three-part inscription reading: *'izz li mawlānā al-sulṭān al-malik al-'ālim al-'āmil * al-'ādil al-ghāzī al-mujāhid al-murābiṭ al-muthāghir * al-mu'ayyad al-manṣūr sulṭān al-islām wa'l-muslimīn 'azza naṣruhu*, "Glory to our lord the sultan, the king, the knowing, the diligent, the just, the conqueror, the holy warrior, the defender, the protector of the frontiers, the fortified by God, the victorious, sultan of Islam and the Muslims, may his victory be glorified." In the roundels are the words *'izz li mawlānā al-sulṭān*, "Glory to our lord the sultan."

Around the outside of the tray's rim is the inscription: *'izz li mawlānā al-sulṭān al-nāṣir al-'ālim al-'āmil al-'ādil * al-ghāzī al-mujāhid al-murābiṭ al-muthāghir al-mu'ayyad al-manṣūr nāṣir al-dunyā wa'l-d * īn qātil al-kufara wa'l-mushrikīn muḥyī al-'adl fī 'l-'ālam[īn] abū 'l-fuqar[ā] * wa'l-masākīn al-sulṭān al-Malik al-Manṣūr nāṣir al-dunyā wa'l-dīn*, "Glory to our lord, the sultan, the victor, the knowing, the diligent, the just, the conqueror, the holy warrior, the defender, the protector of frontiers, the fortified by God, the victorious, victor of the world and religion, slayer of the infidels and polytheists, reviver of justice in the worlds, father of the indigent and the poor, Sultan al-Malik al-Manṣūr, victor of the world and religion." In the roundels on the outside of the rim are the words *'izz li mawlānā al-sulṭān.*

2. Museo Nazionale del Bargello, Florence, no. 357C; Hayward Gallery, *The Arts of Islam* (London, 1976), no. 216.

3. Louvre, no. 7438; L. A. Mayer, *Saracenic Heraldry* (Oxford, 1933), p. 86; Orangerie des Tuileries, *Arts de l'Islam des origines à 1700 dans collections publiques françaises* (Paris, 1971), no. 169.

4. Museum of Islamic Art, Cairo, from the Harari Collection, published in Mayer, *Saracenic Heraldry*, pp. 193–94 and pl. 34.1.

5. Bibliothèque Nationale, Cabinet des Medailles, inv. no. 5621, diameter 21.3 cm. See H. Lavoix, "De l'ornementation arabe dans les oeuvres des maîtres italiens," *Gazette des Beaux-Arts* 17 (1877): 27–28. Lavoix maintains that the coat-of-arms is that of the archbishop of Monreale in 1379, Paulus de Urbe, though because of the lack of color other possibilities abound. I am grateful to Dr. Ludvik Kalus for details of this bowl and the photograph of it.

6. Gaston Wiet, *Lampes et bouteilles en verre émaillé* (Cairo, 1929), pls. 59–61.

7. Janine Sourdel-Thomine, "Clefs et serrures de la Ka'ba," *Revue des études islamiques* 39 (1971): 72–73, no. 12 and pl. 7a.

8. Nouveau Drouot, salle 6, mardi, le 26 mai 1981, *Art islamique*, lot no. 89.

9. Sourdel-Thomine, "Clefs et serrures," pp. 74–75, no. 13 and pl. 7.

10. G. Migeon, *L'Orient musulman* (Paris, 1922), vol. 2, no. 48, pl. 17.

11. Gaston Wiet, *Objets en cuivre* (Cairo, 1932), pl. 14.

12. One is in the Museum of Islamic Art, Cairo, no. 15246; *Islamic Art in Egypt, 969–1517* (Cairo, 1969), no. 81. The other is in Izmir; R. M. Riefstahl, *Turkish Architecture in Southwestern Anatolia* (Cambridge, 1931), p. 116, fig. 228.

13. Victoria and Albert Museum, no. 934–1884, sheet brass, height 26 cm., diameter of top 19.3 cm. The inscriptions are published in Mayer, *Saracenic Heraldry*, p. 106, Bayāzīd. The blazon gives the clue to the dating. See Michael Meinecke, "Zur mamlukischen Heraldik," *Mitteilungen des Deutschen Archäologischen Instituts, Abteilung Kairo*, vol. 28, pt. 2 (1972), pp. 265–67.

14. Museum of Islamic Art, Cairo, no. 3335; Wiet, *Objets en cuivre*, pl. 27 and pp. 82–84.

15. In Ghana; I owe this information to Ray Silverman, who will publish the piece.

16. For a detailed study of Cairene doors, see Hoda Batanouni, "Catalogue of Mamlūk Doors with Metal Revetments" (Master's thesis, American University of Cairo, 1975).

17. Ministry of Waqfs, *The Mosques of Egypt* (Giza, 1949), vol. 2, pl. 95.

18. Ibid., pl. 96a.

19. Museum of Islamic Art, Cairo, no. 2389; Batanouni, "Catalogue of Mamlūk Doors," pp. 149–51.

20. Ministry of Waqfs, *Mosques of Egypt*, vol. 1, pl. 81; Batanouni, "Catalogue of Mamlūk Doors," pp. 88–93.

21. For the doors of the māristān of Nūr al-Dīn, see Jean Sauvaget, "Notes sur quelques monuments musulmans de Syrie," *Syria* 24 (1944–45), pl. 17. For the Aleppo citadel doors, see Ernst Herzfeld, *Matériaux pour un Corpus Inscriptionum Arabicarum*, pt. 2, *Syrie du Nord: Inscriptions et monuments d'Alep* (Cairo, 1955), pp. 86–88 and pl. 36b.

22. F. Sarre and Ernst Herzfeld, *Archäologische Reise im Euphrat- und Tigris-gebiet* (Berlin, 1911), vol. 2, pp. 268–70, pl. 8b. Ibn al-Razzāz al-Jazarī, in *The Book of Knowledge of Ingenious Mechanical Devices*, trans. and annotated by D. R. Hill (Dordrecht, 1974), pp. 191–95, written in 1206, gives a detailed description of how such door revetments were made.

23. W. M. Brinner, *A Chronicle of Damascus 1389–1397* (Berkeley, Calif., 1963), vol. 1, pp. 249–50; vol. 2, p. 188.

24. For the great east door, see G. Migeon, *Manuel d'art musulman, II. Les arts plastiques et industriels* (Paris, 1907), fig. 194, now in the National Museum, Damascus; the text is published in Mayer, *Saracenic Heraldry*, p. 201, and by A. Rihaoui, "Notes d'épigraphie arabe," *Bulletin des Études Orientales* 20 (1967): 210–11. For the inscriptions on the north doors, see Mayer, *Saracenic Heraldry*, p. 173. One of the side doors of the east entrance was published by K. Wulzinger and C. Watzinger, *Damaskus, die islamische Stadt* (Leipzig, 1924), pl. 3c, and is also published in a slightly renovated state by Meinecke, "Zur mamlukischen Heraldik," pl. 66a, who (p. 262, n. 306) suggests the identification of the blazon as that of Īnāl. The dating for the side doors of the western entrance and for the northern side door of the eastern entrance is provided by 'Abd al-Bāsiṭ, quoting Ibn Kathīr: see H. Sauvaire, "Description de Damas," *Journal Asiatique*, 9 ser., vol. 7, p. 220. As yet no precise date seems to have come to light for the southern side door of the eastern entrance (though it would appear to be contemporary with the northern one) or for the great west door.

25. Brinner, *Chronicle of Damascus*, 1:250–51; 2:189.

26. Simono Sigoli, *I viaggi in Terra Santa* (Parma, 1865), pp. 61–62.

27. W. J. Fischel, "*Vita Tamerlani*—A New Latin Source on Tamerlane's Conquest of Damascus," *Oriens* 9 (1956): 226.

28. Aḥmad al-Maqrīzī, *Al-Mawā'iz wa'l-I'tibar bi Dhikr al-Khiṭaṭ wa'l-Āthār* (Bulaq, 1854), 2:105.

29. Ibid., pp. 97–98; André Raymond and Gaston Wiet, in *Les marchés du Caire* (Cairo, 1979), translate *qālib* as *collier*, or "neck," and *saqṭ* as *molette*, or "rowel." The basis for this translation is unclear, and I know of no surviving Mamluk spurs to prove the use of rowels.

30. Maqrīzī, *Khiṭaṭ*, 2:99.

31. Maqrīzī, *Khiṭaṭ* 2:98. *Kuft* is a problematic word, which has been discussed by Quatremère, *Histoire des sultans mamlouks d'Egypte* (Paris, 1837–45), vol. 2, pt. 1, pp. 114–15, and received further comment from D. S. Rice, "Studies in Islamic Metalwork 5," *Bulletin of the School of Oriental and African Studies* 17, pt. 2 (1955): 228–29, n. 5. While it certainly means the inlaying of one metal with another, it must also mean a plate of metal used to adorn wood or textile, as, for example, when Maqrīzī talks of *kuft* in connection with bridles, or when Abu'l-Fidā' talks of saddles and bridles as *mukaffata* (quoted by Quatremère).

32. Jere Bacharach, "A Study of the Correlation between Textual Sources and Numismatic Evidence for Mamluk Egypt and Syria A.H. 784–872/A.D. 1382–1468" (Ph.D. diss., University of Michigan, 1967), pp. 45–46.

33. Ira R. Lapidus, *Muslim Cities in the Later Middle Ages* (Cambridge, Mass., 1967), pp. 27–28; p. 250, n. 42.

34. The amount of damage done is contested by Lapidus in ibid. The list compiled by Lapidus of artisans taken by Tīmūr (p. 252, n. 48) includes engravers and coppersmiths, but I failed to find any mention of them in the texts he cited. However, the *Vita Tamerlani* lists the official master craftsmen at the time of Tīmūr's conquest as workers in "gold, silver, iron, cotton, linen, glass, copper, brass, and almost every craft under the sun" (Fischel, "*Vita Tamerlani*—A New Latin Source," p. 226), and later records that Tīmūr took with him "the official craftsmen, of whom Damascus had a great number" (ibid., p. 229), who presumably therefore included these metalworkers. On the other hand, Ibn 'Arabshāh (*Kitāb 'Ajā'ib al-Maqdūr fī Akhbār Tīmūr* [n.p., 1841], p. 239), although he gives a list of the groups of craftsmen Tīmūr sent to Samarqand, does not mention any metalworkers among them.

35. Maqrīzī, *Ighāthat al-Umma bi-Kashf al-Ghumma*, ed. M. M. Ziyāda and J. M. al-Shaiyāl (Cairo, 1940), p. 75; Gaston Wiet, "Le traité des famines de Maqrīzī," *Journal of the Economic and Social History of the Orient* 5, pt. 1 (1962): 76. The nature of the plague and its impact have been studied by Michael W. Dols in his book *The Black Death in the Middle East* (Princeton, N.J., 1977).

36. In this discussion I must acknowledge the debt I owe to the thesis of Jere Bacharach mentioned above, especially pp. 218–33, from which most of the information comes.

37. Maqrīzī, *Kitāb al-Sulūk li Ma'rifat Duwal al-Mulūk*, ed. S. Ashūr (Cairo, 1972), vol. 4, pt. 1, pp. 287–88.

38. E. Ashtor, *Les métaux précieux, et la balance des payements du Proche-Orient à la basse époque* (Paris, 1971), p. 44.

39. Maqrīzī, *Sulūk*, vol. 4, pt. 2, p. 977.

40. Bacharach, "Textual Sources and Numismatic Evidence," pp. 200–01, 244.

41. Ibid., pp. 239–69, discusses in detail Mamluk copper coinage and the copper shortage.

42. Maqrīzī, *Sulūk*, vol. 4, pt. 1, p. 549.

43. Jawharī, *Nuzhat al-Nufūs wa'l-Abdān fī Ta'rīkh al-Zamān*, ed. H. Habashi (Cairo, 1974), p. 23.

44. Maqrīzī, *Sulūk*, vol. 4, pt. 2, pp. 641–42.

MARILYN JENKINS

Mamluk Underglaze-Painted Pottery: Foundations for Future Study

When Mamluk pottery is mentioned, the type most often conjured up is the very well known so-called Mamluk sgraffito ware, which is discussed in this volume by George Scanlon. However, there is another large and important category of pottery from this period, an underglaze-painted ware, painted in black, turquoise, and cobalt in various combinations or alone under a transparent clear or turquoise glaze.

In spite of the importance and size of this category, the history of Islamic ceramics can, up to now, boast of no single class of Mamluk underglaze-painted pottery the profile of which has been fully drawn including its source or sources of inspiration, the dates of its production, and the country or countries of its manufacture. Such essential information has always been a matter of speculation or mystery.[1]

As nothing conclusive has so far been put forth regarding this large category of pottery, it is my intention to lay a series of foundations on which others, as well as I myself, can build. These foundations will consist solely of "materials" that are totally verifiable by either neutron-activation analysis, actual dates on objects, *in-situ* evidence, or contemporary texts. There will be no speculation or interpretation in the presentation that might contaminate otherwise pure foundations which can and, I hope, will serve as the basis on which to build a history of this little-known but vast category, containing relatively few complete pieces but an immense number of fragments.[2]

Eighty-seven whole or fragmentary objects from the Metropolitan Museum of Art and the Madina Collection were subjected to neutron-activation analysis,[3] and fifty-one from among these, which form three separate and distinct groups, are of interest here (fig. 1).

The first group has been code-named "Syria" as no further precision is possible at this point in our knowledge (plates 1–8b). This group is by far the largest formed by those objects subjected to neutron-activation analysis, and it makes such a tightly knit group—that is, the concentration levels of the trace elements tested are found to be so similar in each object—that on the basis of the testing one can state not only that all the members of the group must come from the same area in Syria but that they must have been made from a common clay source. Therefore, all of the objects in

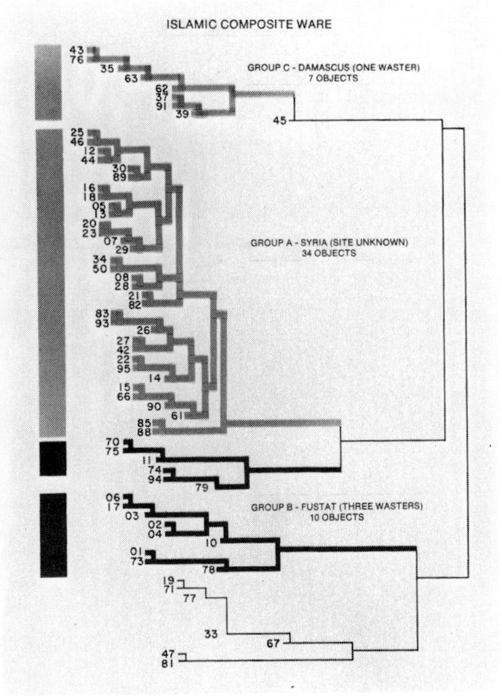

FIGURE 1. Islamic composite ware.

a

b

c

PLATE 1. "SYRIA" GROUP. Underglaze-painted bowl fragments: *a*, Metropolitan Museum of Art, New York, Rogers Fund, 1913, 13.190.138; *b*, Metropolitan Museum of Art, New York, Rogers Fund, 1908, 08.256.138; *c*, Metropolitan Museum of Art, New York, gift of Ginsberg and Levy, 1921, 21.52.12.

a

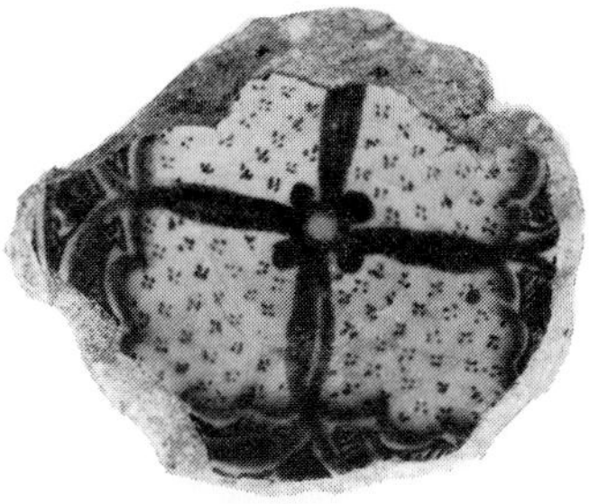

b

c

d

PLATE 2. "SYRIA" GROUP. Underglaze-painted tile panel and bowl fragments: *a*, Metropolitan Museum of Art, New York, Rogers Fund, 1923, 23.12.2a-f; *b*, Metropolitan Museum of Art, New York, Rogers Fund, 1908, 08.256.212; *c*, Metropolitan Museum of Art, New York, Rogers Fund, 1908, 08.184.54; *d*, Metropolitan Museum of Art, New York, Rogers Fund, 1907, 07.238.58.

a

b

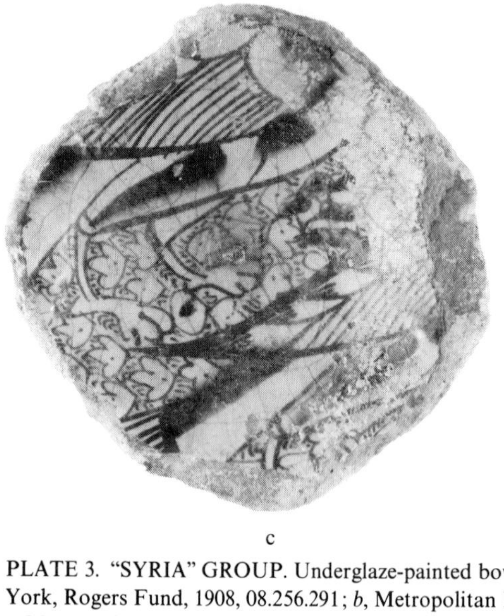

c

d

PLATE 3. "SYRIA" GROUP. Underglaze-painted bowl and albarello fragments: *a*, Metropolitan Museum of Art, New York, Rogers Fund, 1908, 08.256.291; *b*, Metropolitan Museum of Art, New York, Rogers Fund, 1908, 08.184.44; *c*, Metropolitan Museum of Art, New York, Rogers Fund, 1913, 13.190.15; *d*, Metropolitan Museum of Art, New York, Rogers Fund, 1907, 07.238.40.

a

b

c

d

PLATE 4. "SYRIA" GROUP. Underglaze-painted bowl fragments and oil lamp: *a*, Metropolitan Museum of Art, New York, Rogers Fund, 1913, 13.190.27; *b*, Metropolitan Museum of Art, New York, gift of Jack A. Josephson, 1973, 1973.79.62; *c*, The Madina Collection, New York; *d*, Metropolitan Museum of Art, New York, Rogers Fund, 1907, 07.238.35.

a

b

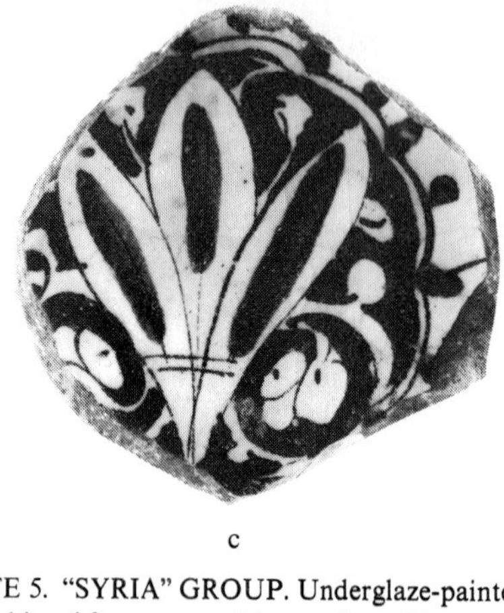

c

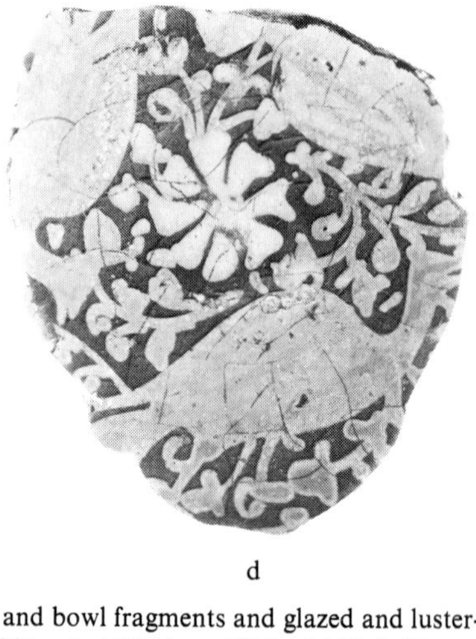

d

PLATE 5. "SYRIA" GROUP. Underglaze-painted fragmentary albarello and bowl fragments and glazed and luster-painted bowl fragment: *a*, Metropolitan Museum of Art, New York, gift of Kouchakji Frères, 1910, 10.105; *b*, Metropolitan Museum of Art, New York, X365; *c*, Metropolitan Museum of Art, New York, Rogers Fund, 1913, 13.190.177; *d*, Metropolitan Museum of Art, New York, gift of Rafael Guastavino, 1928, 28.89.2.

a

b

c

d

PLATE 6. "SYRIA" GROUP. Underglaze-painted bowl fragments and tile panel: *a*, Metropolitan Museum of Art, New York, Rogers Fund, 1913, 13.190.154; *b*, Metropolitan Museum of Art, New York, Rogers Fund, 1913, 13.190.134; *c*, Metropolitan Museum of Art, New York, Rogers Fund, 1922, 22.185.12; *d*, Metropolitan Museum of Art, New York, Rogers Fund, 1908, 08.256.135.

a

b

c

d

PLATE 7. "SYRIA" GROUP. Underglaze-painted bowl fragment, dish, tile, and small vase: *a*, Metropolitan Museum of Art, New York, Rogers Fund, 1908, 08.256.275; *b*, The Madina Collection, New York; *c*, The Madina Collection, New York; *d*, The Madina Collection, New York.

a

b

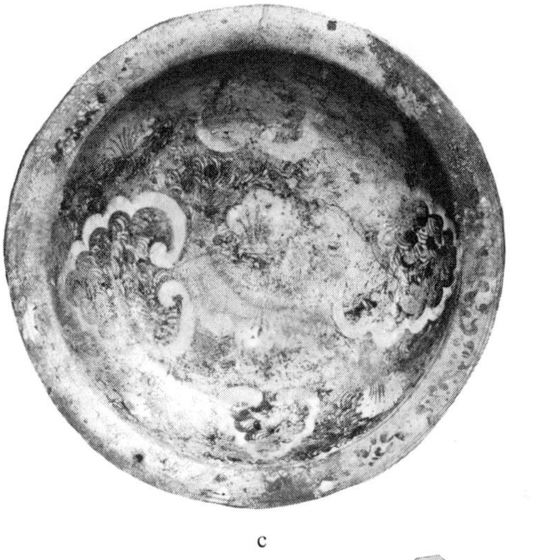

c

d

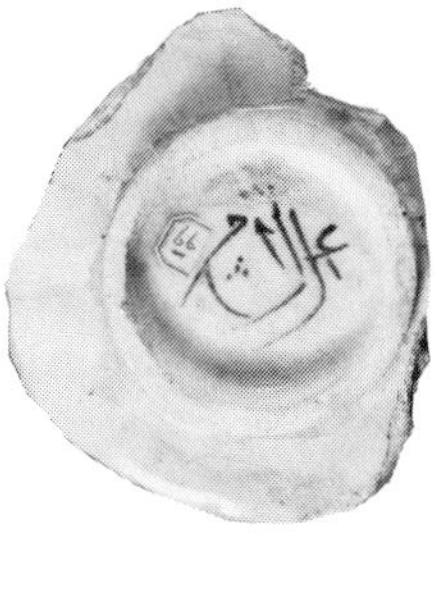

e

PLATE 8. "SYRIA" GROUP. Underglaze-painted bowl fragment and glazed and luster-painted bowl fragment: *a*, Metropolitan Museum of Art, New York, Rogers Fund, 1908, 08.256.357; *b*, Metropolitan Museum of Art, New York, gift of Rafael Guastavino, 1928, 28.89.3. "DAMASCUS" GROUP. Underglaze-painted bowl and bowl fragment: *c*, Metropolitan Museum of Art, New York, gift of Fahim Kouchakji, 1965, 65.76.7; *d*, *e*, Metropolitan Museum of Art, New York, gift of Jack A. Josephson, 1973, 1973.79.24.

this group were made in the same center. That Damascus is the place of manufacture is suggested by the fact that the group includes two bowl fragments luster-painted on a cobalt-blue glaze (plates 5d and 8b) which are of the same type as the complete vase in the Kuwait National Museum which bears two inscriptions stating that it was made in Damascus for Asad al-Iskandarānī.[4] In addition, another, complete object in the group, a tile in the Madina Collection (plate 7c), is of a type that is found gracing the *ṣaḥn* walls in the Darwishiyye Mosque in Damascus.[5] However, as a Damascus attribution has not been verified by the neutron-activation analysis undertaken in connection with this paper, I will simply call the group "Syria" for now. The fact that the tests did not determine that these objects belong to the group to be discussed next—which is definitely of Damascus manufacture—does not preclude the "Syria" group's having been made in Damascus. It could simply have been made from a different clay source.[6]

The second group (plates 8c–10b)[7] has been named "Damascus," since one of its members is a waster in the Metropolitan's collection (plate 9c, d) that was "found in an old cemetery on the outskirts of Damascus."[8]

The third group[9] is called "Fustat" (plates 10c–13e), so named because three of its members are wasters from that site (plates 11a; 12c, d, e, f), two generously provided for my research by George Scanlon, the other forming part of the Metropolitan's collection.

Using whole or fragmentary objects from among each of the groups discussed and illustrated above, I will attempt to draw the profiles of the three classes of objects. Each of these is quite precisely datable and has a well-defined provenance and a definable prototype; therefore these profiles can, I hope, serve as firm bases on which ultimately to build the history of the whole category of Mamluk underglaze-painted pottery.

There is a class of objects within the "Syria" group that bears a radiating interior design, the individual sections of which are decorated with a series of dots (usually arranged in groups of four), vine scrolls on a hatched ground, and actual or pseudoinscriptions on a dotted ground. The same designs may also be present within a freer layout.[10] This class can be dated because a fragment with both a radiating design and the same decoration within the compartments exists in the Islamic Museum in Cairo; it bears in the central interior roundel the phrase *sanat khamsa wa-arbaʿīn*, that is, the year A.H. 45.[11] As the word representing the hundreds is lacking, speculation as to the century could ensue, were it not for an albarello in the Museo di Capodimonte in Naples which fits very well into this class and which is dated, in numerals, 717/1317.[12]

In view of the date on the albarello, the Cairo fragment must be dated 745/1345 or twenty-eight hijra years after the albarello. Thus, we are in the presence of a class of underglaze-painted pottery that was produced somewhere in Syria during the first half of the fourteenth century. The prototype for this class is Iranian. We know from neutron-activation analysis that the bowl in plate 14 as well as another in the Metropolitan[13] were both made from the same clay source and that therefore the one in plate 14 was made in exactly the same center as that illustrated by Dimand, which all Islamic art historians would or could call "Sultanabad."[14]

Let us now move approximately one hundred years later in Syria and consider our "Damascus" group. One of the pieces in this group is a hexagonal tile in the Madina Collection (plate 9b),[15] which is very similar to the most common type decorating the tomb and mosque of Ghars al-Dīn Khalīl al-Tawrīzī al-Dasārī in Damascus.[16] Thus, our neutron-activation analysis securely places the execution of the tile decoration of the complex in Damascus, and the similarity of the tested tile to those *in situ* allows us also to be quite sure of when the manufacture took place.

We know according to the chronicle of al-Asadī that Ghars al-Dīn died in 826/1424 and that his complex was completed the previous year; in June of that year the first prayer was performed in the mosque.[17] Thus, we can safely state that the decoration of this complex was executed in the second or third decade of the fifteenth century.

The designs on these tiles bear no resemblance whatever to those on the century-earlier class previously discussed, and therefore we must look elsewhere for the source of their inspiration. The clue to this source has lain hidden in this long-famous tomb and mosque for half a millennium. Among the tiles in the mosque area of the complex is a rectangular panel[18] composed of six tiles decorated with a mosque lamp suspended in a lobed niche above a rahle holding a book. To the right of this stand is the artist's signature, ʿAmal Ghaybī Tawrīzī.

This inscription (the reading of which is mine)[19] allows us to place Ghaybī in Damascus in the second or third decade of the fifteenth century. It is quite probable that he was at the head of the

a

b

c

d

PLATE 9. "DAMASCUS" GROUP. Underglaze-painted fragmentary tile, hexagonal tile, and waster: *a*, The Madina Collection, New York; *b*, The Madina Collection, New York; *c*, *d*, Metropolitan Museum of Art, New York, Rogers Fund, 1911, 11.61.1.

a

b

c

d

PLATE 10. "DAMASCUS" GROUP. Underglaze-painted tile and bowl: *a*, Metropolitan Museum of Art, New York, bequest of Edward C. Moore, 1891, 91.1.103; *b*, Metropolitan Museum of Art, New York, bequest of William Milne Grinnell, 1920, 20.120.237. "FUSTAT" GROUP. Underglaze-painted bowl fragment: *c*, *d*, Metropolitan Museum of Art, New York, gift of Jack A. Josephson, 1973, 1973.79.6.

a

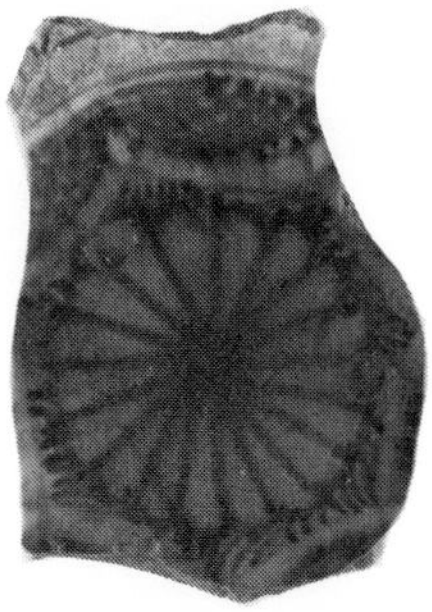

b

c

d

PLATE 11. "FUSTAT" GROUP. Underglaze-painted fragmentary waster and bowl fragments: *a*, Metropolitan Museum of Art, New York, gift of S. C. Bosch-Reitz, 1923, 23.205.3; *b*, Metropolitan Museum of Art, New York, Rogers Fund, 1908, 08.256.280; *c*, Metropolitan Museum of Art, New York, Fletcher Fund, 1975, 1975.31.4; *d*, Metropolitan Museum of Art, New York, Rogers Fund, 1913, 13.190.187.

a

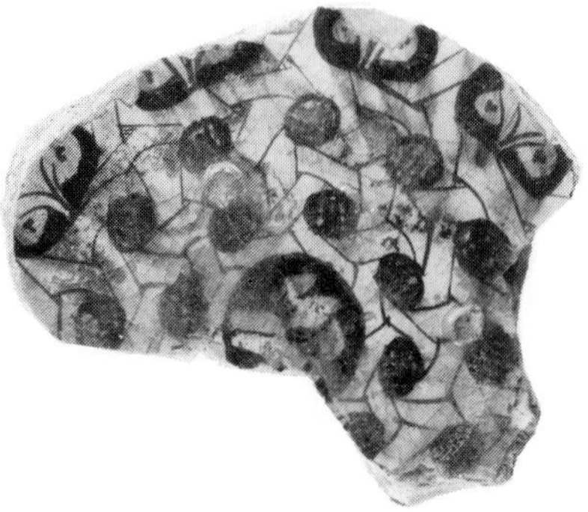

b

c

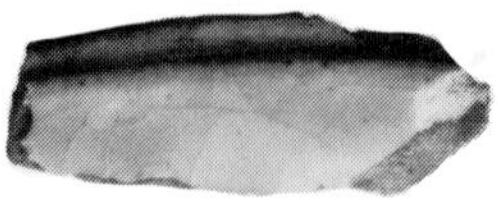

d

e

f

PLATE 12. "FUSTAT" GROUP. Underglaze-painted bowl fragments and waster fragments: *a*, Metropolitan Museum of Art, New York, Rogers Fund, 1907, 07.238.13; *b*, Metropolitan Museum of Art, New York, Rogers Fund, 1908, 08.256.77; *c*, *d*, provided by George T. Scanlon; *e*, *f*, provided by George T. Scanlon.

a

b

c

d

e

PLATE 13. "FUSTAT" GROUP. Underglaze-painted bowl fragments: *a*, Metropolitan Museum of Art, New York, Rogers Fund, 1908, 08.256.101; *b*, *c*, Metropolitan Museum of Art, New York, gift of Jack A. Josephson, 1973, 1973.79.9; *d*, *e*, Metropolitan Museum of Art, New York, gift of Jack A. Josephson, 1973, 1973.79.36.

PLATE 14. Underglaze-painted bowl. Metropolitan Museum of Art, New York, Rogers Fund, 1910, 10.44.5.

atelier that executed the decoration of this complex for the Mamluk vizier of Damascus, since his is the only signature on the vast amount of ceramic architectural decoration in the complex. In addition, his signature specifically informs us that he belonged to or was connected with Tabriz.[20]

An analogous situation is to be found in contemporary Turkey. Not long after the completion of the Ghars al-Dīn complex in Damascus, artisans from Tabriz completed and signed the Yeshīl Jāmiʿ in Bursa: "made [by] the masters from Tabriz."[21] Although the technique is different, one is struck by the similarities of the niche contour and the lamp shape in a panel from the Yeshīl Turbeh in Bursa[22] and the same features on the panel from the Ghars al-Dīn mosque.

The other rectangular, but now quite garbled, tile panel in the mosque area of the Ghars al-Dīn complex[23] bears close affinities to the waster in our "Damascus" group (plate 9c, d). The two teardrop-shaped configurations with a basket-weave pattern on the panel relate closely to the pattern on the two larger bowls of the waster set, thus placing the waster also in the second or third decade of the fifteenth century. John Carswell, who first published both of the rectangular panels in this mosque, has already presented the iconography of the 1,362 hexagonal tiles in the complex that fit securely in this class, therefore obviating the need to do so again.

Thus, we are here in the presence of a class of underglaze-painted pottery that was produced in Damascus during the second or third decade of the fifteenth century and whose most immediate prototype appears to have been a not yet identified Persian one (perhaps from the Tabriz area).

Let us finally consider the Fustat group. First of all this group contains a fragment signed Ghaybī (plate 10c, d) and one signed Ghaybī al-Shāmī (plate 13b, c). Thus neutron-activation analysis has provided concrete proof of a second foreign sojourn of this illustrious potter, this time in Fustat. A corollary to this fact is that these objects must have been made after 1423, but presumably not much later. Ghaybī's fame in Damascus is proven by his use of the *nisba* al-Shāmī when working in Fustat. However, a square tile in the Islamic Museum in Cairo, which was brought there from the mosque of al-Sayyida Nafīsa, bearing the signature Ibn Ghaybī al-Tawrīzī,[24] shows that

a

b

c

d

e

f

PLATE 15. Underglaze-painted bowl fragments: *a*, *b*, Metropolitan Museum of Art, New York, gift of Jack A. Josephson, 1973, 1973.79.20; *c*, *d*, Metropolitan Museum of Art, New York, gift of Jack A. Josephson, 1973, 1973.79.28; *e*, *f*, Metropolitan Museum of Art, New York, gift of Jack A. Josephson, 1973, 1973.79.59.

Ghaybī's Tabriz origins were still important in fifteenth-century Cairo. That at least some of the work by Ghaybī and his son was contemporary is proved by a fragment in the Metropolitan's collection (plate 15a, b) that bears in an interior cartouche the inscription ʿAmal ibn Ghaybī and on the bottom a countersignature Ghaybī,[25] which is incidentally also indicative of an atelier headed by Ghaybī.

There is a fragment in the Islamic Museum in Cairo which makes it possible to broaden this class of objects considerably.[26] It is the bottom of a bowl signed Ghaybī and decorated with a radial design emanating from a roundel. There were originally six sections, separated by hatched rays bordered by plain areas, containing three different designs: a fretwork composed of a series of *Y* shapes, a floral scroll on a dotted ground, and a stylized palmette design also on a dotted ground. This design must be a refinement of, as well as the successor to, that on the popular Syrian class of the first half of the fourteenth century already discussed.

This identical design is also found on objects signed by al-Ustādh al-Miṣrī,[27] Ghazzāl (plate 15c, d) or al-Ghazzālī, and al-Barrānī (plate 15e, f). Thus all the bowls signed by these artists as well as by Ghaybī or Ghaybī's son must form part of this Fustat class dating to the second quarter of the fifteenth century or slightly later.[28]

The square tile signed Ibn Ghaybī al-Tawrīzī illustrates Syrian stylistic influence on Fustat production at this time in the manner in which a white design outlined in black is silhouetted on a blue ground, as seen on the rectangular tile with teardrop-shaped configurations in the Ghars al-Dīn complex. An example of iconographic influence moving in the same direction can be seen in the adaptation of the basket-weave design first seen on the latter tile to a shard in the Fustat group (plate 12b).

Thus we are here in the presence of a class of underglaze-painted pottery that was produced in Fustat during the second quarter of the fifteenth century or slightly later by ceramists, at least one of whom emigrated from Damascus, who used earlier as well as contemporary Syrian designs as prototypes.

Finally, as a postscript, let us turn now to five tiles or groups of tiles that we were unable to test but that are datable, by means of the inscriptions they bear or the buildings they decorated, to the very end of the Mamluk period and that, in addition, continue traditions first seen in the square tile signed Ibn Ghaybī al-Tawrīzī. Two of these are round tiles, each bearing the name Qāytbāy (r. 1468–96), one being in the Islamic Museum in Cairo and the other in the Kuwait National Museum.[29] Each of these has a white inscription, outlined in black, silhouetted on a blue ground, and is thus related stylistically to the field of the Ibn Ghaybī tile. A third object, in the form of a lunette consisting of five tiles, bears the name of the same sultan and was taken from a *sabīl* built by him in 1495–96.[30] Another very similar lunette bearing the name of Sultan Jānbalāt (1500–01) was taken from his madrasa.[31] Both of the latter are now in the Islamic Museum in Cairo and are blue underglaze-painted on a white ground and are thus stylistically related to the border of the Ibn Ghaybī tile. These and the large inscriptional tiles that originally encircled the dome of the tomb of Sultan Qānṣūh al-Ghawrī, which was completed in 1503–04, consist of white letters with a thin black border on a blue ground.[32]

May these foundations, as well as the incomplete picture given of the end of the period, serve as the bases on which ultimately to build a history of this little known but important category of Mamluk pottery.

METROPOLITAN MUSEUM OF ART
NEW YORK

NOTES

1. A typical statement is that of the late Arthur Lane: "In Syria fragments of the blue-and-black class have been found in the site of the potter's quarter at Damascus, at Baalbek and at Hama; but they are also very well represented at Fustat, where [it is] almost impossible to distinguish between local Egyptian wares and those imported from Syria . . . and their general finish is more careless than that of the contemporary Persian 'Sultanabad types' from which they evidently derived" (*Later Islamic Pottery* [London, 1957], pp. 17–18).

2. I would like to thank my collaborators, Dr. Pieter Meyers and Mrs. Lore Holmes of the Metropolitan Museum's research laboratory, as well as those private collectors, directors and curators of public collections, and scholars here and abroad who made their objects or their photographic archives available. I am especially grateful to Muhammad Kholy, Dr. Michael Rogers, Dr. Oliver Watson, and Dr. ʿAbd al-Raʾūf ʿAlī Yūsuf for allowing me to photograph objects and to Professor Maan Madina for allowing samples to be taken from objects in the Madina Collection.

3. Neutron-activation analysis provides the elemental composition of the tested material. Statistical treatment of the analytical data gives indication only of provenance and not of age. Therefore, those within the

groups discussed are not necessarily contemporary, nor were they originally thought to be.

4. *Islamic Art in the Kuwait National Museum*, the al-Sabah Collection, ed. Marilyn Jenkins (London, 1983), p. 84.

5. Karl Wulzinger and Carl Watzinger, *Damaskus, die islamische Stadt* (Berlin, 1924), pl. 38a.

6. Listed in the order in which they occur on the dendogram of the neutron-activation analysis in fig. 1, the complete or fragmentary objects falling into the "Syria" group are as follows: nos. 25, 46, plate 1a; no. 12, plate 1b; no. 44, Metropolitan Museum of Art 91.1.130, Ernst Kühnel, *Islamic Arts* (London, 1970), fig. 89; no. 30, plate 1c; no. 89, plate 2a; no. 16, plate 2b; no. 18, plate 2c; no. 5, plate 2d; no. 13, plate 3a; no. 20, plate 3b; no. 23, plate 3c; no. 7, plate 3d; no. 29, plate 4a; no. 34, plate 4b; no. 60, mistakenly numbered 50 on dendogram, plate 4c; no. 8, plate 4d; no. 28, plate 2c; no. 21, plate 5a; no. 82, plate 5b; no. 83, plate 5c; no. 93, plate 5d; no. 26, plate 6a; no. 27, plate 6b; no. 42, Metropolitan Museum of Art 41.165.45, Marilyn Jenkins, J. Meech-Pekarik, and S. Valenstein, *Oriental Ceramics: The World's Great Collections, vol. 12, The Metropolitan Museum of Art* (Tokyo, 1977), pl. 263; no. 22, plate 3c; no. 95, plate 6c; no. 14, plate 6d; no. 15, plate 7a; no. 66, plate 7b; no. 90, plate 7c; no. 61, plate 7d; no. 85, plate 8a; no. 88, plate 8b.

Three additional facts further corroborate a Syrian, as opposed to an Egyptian, provenance for this group and suggest that objects of this type found in Egypt were imported: (1) George T. Scanlon's statistics for Fustat, as enumerated in his "Fustat Mounds: A Shard Count, 1968," *Archaeology* 24, no. 3 (June 1971): 225, show that between 1,200 and 1,400 black-and-blue underglaze-painted wares ranked fifth in popularity (his daily count yielding only 400 shards of this type versus 6,900 imitation celadon shards, 6,200 yellow-brown sgraffito shards, 1,700 green sgraffito shards, and 500 yellow-brown slip-painted shards); (2) the largest number of objects fitting into this group was found in Fustat, but none of the many such objects tested fit in our Fustat group; and (3) decoration found in this group was copied in the sgraffito technique in Egypt; see, for example, Ernst Grube, *Islamic Pottery of the Eighth to the Fifteenth Century in the Keir Collection* (London, 1976), no. 227.

7. Listed in the order in which they occur on the dendogram of the neutron-activation analysis in fig. 1, the complete or fragmentary objects falling into the Damascus group are as follows: no. 43, plate 8c; no. 76, plate 8d, e; no. 35, plate 9a; nos. 63, 62, plate 9b; no. 37, plate 9c, d; no. 91, plate 10a; no. 39, plate 10b.

8. Letter dated 26 January 1911 from the dealer J. Zado Noorian, New York, to the Metropolitan Museum of Art.

9. Listed in the order in which they occur on the dendogram of the neutron-activation analysis in fig. 1, the complete or fragmentary objects falling in the Fustat group are as follows: no. 70, plate 10c, d; no. 75, plate 11a; no. 11, plate 11b; no. 74, plate 11a; no. 94, plate 11c; no. 79, plate 11d; no. 6, plate 12a; no. 17, plate 12b; no. 3, plate 12e, f; no. 2, plate 12c, d; no. 4, plate 12e, f; no. 10, plate 13a; no. 1, plate 12c, d; no. 73, plate 13b, c; no. 78, plate 13d, e.

10. Priscilla P. Soucek, *Islamic Art from the University of Michigan Collections* (Ann Arbor, 1978), no. 20; and Esin Atıl, *Renaissance of Islam: Art of the Mamluks* (Washington, D.C., 1981), no. 81. Actual or pseudo-inscriptions on a dotted ground are frequently found on Syrian pottery of the Ayyubid period.

11. Aly Bey Bahgat and Felix Massoul, *La céramique musulmane de l'Egypte* (Cairo, 1930), pl. L, 86. Although other fragments bearing this phrase are known, this is the only one I know of combining the phrase with this particular radiating design.

12. Marco Spallanzani, *Ceramiche orientali a Firenze nel Rinascimento* (Florence, 1978), pl. 11. The part of its calligraphic decoration that can be seen in the illustration, as read by Professor Maan Z. Madina, Columbia University, may be either indicative of its use, or allegorical, or both: "If you squander musk in the land of camphor you will surely be ostracized."

13. Plate 14 is Metropolitan Museum of Art 10.44.5, Rogers Fund, 1910. The other bowl referred to is illustrated in M. S. Dimand, *Metropolitan Museum of Art: A Picture Book. Islamic Pottery of the Near East* (New York, 1936), fig. 14.

14. Bertold Spuler, *Die Goldene Horde* (Leipzig, 1943), p. 95. Nāṣir al-Dīn Muḥammad concluded peace with the Ilkhanids in 1323. It is not impossible that, after the conclusion of this peace treaty or during the breakdown of Ilkhanid rule, Persian potters moved to Syrian cities and continued their work there in a very similar style and/or trained local potters.

15. See also Atıl, *Renaissance*, no. 85.

16. John Carswell, "Six Tiles," in *Islamic Art in the Metropolitan Museum of Art*, ed. Richard Ettinghausen (New York, 1972), p. 115, pl. 6, D1.

17. Wulzinger and Watzinger, *Damaskus, die islamische Stadt*, p. 91. Michael Meinecke, in the lecture discussed in note 20, agrees with the inauguration date of the complex but further states on the authority of al-Nu'aimī's *Al-Dāris fī Tārīh al-Mādaris* that the mosque was endowed in 823/1420 when the mausoleum was already completed. Thus, one can place the production of the building's tile decoration in the second or third decade of the fifteenth century.

18. Carswell, "Six Tiles," p. 117, pl. 8, right.

19. Ibid., p. 100; and Atıl, *Renaissance*, p. 151.

20. A movement of artists from Iran to Syria, similar to that suggested in n. 14, seems also to have been taking place a hundred years later. Michael Meinecke, in a lecture at the World Conference on Arab-Islamic Civilization in Damascus in April 1981, suggested that Ghaybī and his workshop moved from Iran to Egypt and from there to Syria and then to Turkey. My contention that the movement was from Iran to Syria and from there to Egypt is confirmed by Ghaybī's use of the word *al-shāmī* after his name on a fragment we know that he made in Egypt (plate 13b, c). We know from the Ghars

al-Dīn complex that Ghaybī was from Tabriz; thus, unless he had worked in Syria and achieved fame there before emigrating to Egypt he would have had no reason to use the epithet *al-shāmī*. Dr. Meinecke kindly provided me with a copy of his lecture, in which he independently arrived at some of the conclusions presented here.

The situation in fifteenth-century Damascus, when a Tabrizi artisan was called to decorate a building for an important Mamluk official, was in fact parallel to that in Cairo a hundred years earlier. Maqrīzī discusses the Cairene commission regarding the building of the Friday Mosque of Amīr Qawṣūn in 730/1330: "the building of both minarets was entrusted to a man from the area of Tabriz who was brought by Amir Aitmish al-Muḥammadī from there. He built them according to the prototype of the minarets of Tabriz." Michael Meinecke, "Die mamlukischen Fayencemosaikdekorationen: Eine Werkstätte aus Tabriz in Kairo (1330–1350)," *Kunst des Orients* 11, nos. 1–2 (1976–77): 91. Dr. Meinecke has shown that this commission was the beginning of a series of works by this anonymous Tabrizi architect and his atelier, which continued until 1348, when they returned to Iran and continued to work in Kirman and Isfahan.

21. R. M. Riefstahl, "Early Turkish Tile Revetments in Edirne," *Ars Islamica* 4 (1937) : 252. Although the building was completed in 822/1419 or 1420, the tile cycle was not completed until some time later. J. D. Hoag, *Islamic Architecture* (New York, 1977), p. 312, gives the year 1424 for its completion, and Meinecke, in the above-mentioned lecture, suggests 1428.

22. Katerina Otto-Dorn, *Turkische Keramik* (Ankara, 1957), fig. 26.

23. Carswell, "Six Tiles," p. 117, pl. 8, left.

24. Riefstahl, "Early Turkish Tile Revetments," fig. 28. I think the previous reading of this signature as Ghaybī ibn al-Tawrīzī is incorrect, because the two upper squares should be read from bottom to top as are the two lower squares. No whole or fragmentary objects are known to me that mention Ghaybī in conjunction with his father.

25. Plate 15a, b is Metropolitan Museum of Art 1973.79.20, plate 15c, d is 1973.79.28, and plate 15e, f is 1973.79.59; all are gifts of Jack A. Josephson, 1973.

26. Bahgat and Massoul, *Céramique musulmane*, pl. K, 85 and 85 bis.

27. Armand Abel, *Ghaibī et les grands faïenciers égyptiens de l'époque mamlouke* (Cairo, 1930), pl. 1.

28. Riefstahl, "Early Turkish Tile Revetments," p. 276, says that faïence was unknown on Egyptian architecture between 1348 and 1495. Perhaps the tile signed by Ghaybī's son should be placed in the second half of the century at the earliest.

29. Gaston Wiet, *Album du musée arabe du Caire* (Cairo, 1930), pl. 69; and *Islamic Art in the Kuwait National Museum*, ed. Jenkins, p. 85.

30. Riefstahl, "Early Turkish Tile Revetments," fig. 26.

31. Bahgat and Massoul, *Céramique musulmane*, pl. O, 134.

32. Claude Proust, *Les revêtements céramiques dans les monuments musulmans de l'Egypte* (Cairo, 1916), pl. 4,2.

GEORGE T. SCANLON

Mamluk Pottery: More Evidence from Fustat

It has heretofore been accepted that among the arts of the Mamluk period ceramics have played the role of aesthetic stepsister. Though manufacture of ceramics was copious both in Egypt and Syria, and though the variety of shapes and decoration is impressive, it can hardly be argued that the artistic norms for pottery were as consistently high as those operative in the metalworking and glass ateliers, let alone those applied to architectural decoration for two and a half centuries. The motival and symbolic patterns were of course common to all metiers, allowing Mamluk art a visible consistency in both influence and variation; but somehow they were less "artful" in execution and effect when demonstrated through pottery vessels.

Two of my recent studies have attempted to redress this balance of opinion, though to reverse it would be impossible. In the first,[1] evidence was presented from certain unstratified mounds of Fustat to indicate the sheer mass of the material remains and to establish the broad technical and decorative categories.[2] The second[3] was particularly concerned with ceramic shapes and sought to prove that within just two of the aforementioned categories—Mamluk sgraffito and slip-painted wares based on red clays of varying composition and tightness of potting—a vigorous variety of options in size and shape can be ascertained. Further, this variety stemmed from a medley of influences (continuing Fatimid, Persia-through-Syria, Chinese, and Cypriot), paralleling those to be found enlivening the other minor arts of the time. Again the evidence came from the registered objects of the Fustat Expedition of the American Research Center in Egypt. To be sure, these articles represent only the most exploratory of efforts and are archaeological rather than art-historical in intent, but they succeed to the degree that together they put the problem of Mamluk ceramics in a tighter and more relevant focus.

Here I shall demonstrate how the contents of one pit corroborated the findings of my first article, thereby providing a more deeply proven insight into the ceramic tastes of the Mamluk period. Further, the contents pointed to a shift, perhaps a degradation, in that taste, and in one instance yielded a type of decoration hitherto unrecorded for the era. The pit and its contents are roughly described in the Preliminary Report of the season when it was discovered and the contents carefully analyzed; its position can be gleaned from figure 1 and plan I of the report.[4] It was the deepest pit (11.1 m) to be excavated in Fustat-*B*, and it demonstrated a two-period, widely spaced, reality: down to 9.5 m the contents were entirely Mamluk; beyond that point the excavation was more precise (25 cm rather than 50 cm layers), and the contents proved to be entirely of the pre-Fatimid period. Filter fragments all conformed to one or both chronological characteristics established for this period; for example, the filter was placed along the neck of the vessel rather than at the jointure of neck and shoulder, and all were concave in profile. Many had scratched pseudoepigraphical and rough floral motifs external.[5] The few glass fragments carrying any decorative detail were also of the same date, and so was the carved bone fragment to be seen in

The Foreign Currency Program of the Smithsonian Institution supported the Fustat Expedition through contractual arrangement with the American Research Center in Egypt. Hard currency sustenance for the 1968 season was provided by the Kelsey Museum of the University of Michigan and the Corning Museum of Glass. None of these institutions is responsible for the opinions herein expressed.

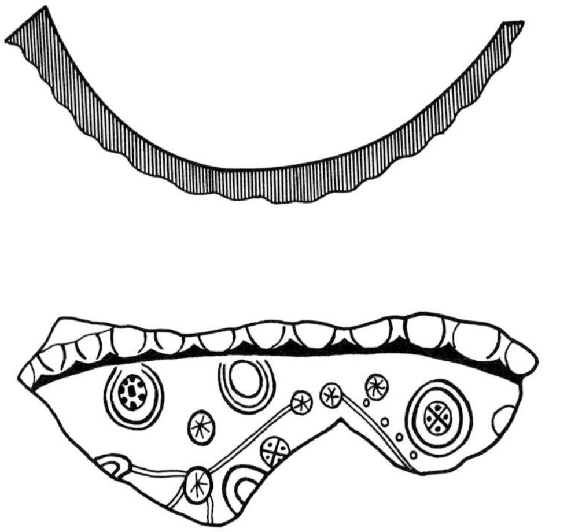

FIGURE 1. Large fragment of unglazed white–buff-ware bowl; lightly carved decoration, pinched scalloping at rim; 9th century. Kelsey Museum, University of Michigan, Fustat Exp. reg. no. 68-12-28.

PLATE 1. Fragments of unglazed white–buff-ware bowl; for decoration see fig. 1.

figure 2-a of the report.[6] Two fragments from the same unglazed white–buff-ware vessel (fig. 1; plate 1) carry a lightly carved decoration and a pinched scalloping about the rim. They were found in the muddy fill at the very base of the pit and therefore can again be considered definitely pre-Fatimid. Finally a more particular early ninth-century date may be hazarded because two copper coins of Maḥfūz, the finance director of Egypt in 186–87/802–03, came forth from the last 1.5 m of undisturbed fill.[7]

The contents of the upper 9.5 m proved to be completely Mamluk: no coins were found, but the ceramics cannot be considered to have come from any other period. Most particularly, the filter fragments are characteristically post-Fatimid, allowing a date later than c. 1200.[8] Thus it was obvious that the pit had been scavenged down to 9 m or so[9] and then refilled either from the tailings of the effort or from adjacent mounds. If the latter can be posited for pit A, then the contents should be analogous to those of the mounds analyzed in my previously mentioned article "Shard Count." In general this proved to be the case, in that no type listed in table 1 of that article was missing. Hence we are a little more certain which types have to be studied in depth before we obtain a complete picture of the Mamluk ceramic aesthetic.

The exact analogues can be studied first. The number of imported Lu'ang Ch'uan celadons (plate 2) was in proportion with the enormous output of local imitations (plates 3 and 4). Not only shapes but motifs were almost slavishly imitated: compare plate 2, far left and far right, with plate 3, lower right, and the carved fish in plate 2, center, with that less delicately obvious in plate 4, lower left. The small intact imitation celadon goblet in the upper middle of plate 3 is especially noteworthy. It is obvious from plate 4 that the Egyptian control of tonality and glaze rarely equaled the Chinese originals and that the incised patterns were often too heavy and never achieved (as they sometimes did in the Fatimid period, imitating S'ung celadon and porcelain models) the lightly "brushed" effect of Chinese incised wares.[10]

A similar truth obtains for blue-and-white imports and their local imitation. One small fragment (plate 16, lowest row, middle left) was probably part of a small cup, and the fuzziness of the underglaze drawing might lead one to assign the

PLATE 2. Selection of Lu'ang Ch'uan celadon shards found in pit A, c. 1250–1450.

PLATE 3. Selection of Egyptian imitations of Lu'ang Ch'uan celadons found in pit A, c. 1300–1450.

original vessel to the fifteenth century. It contrasts strongly with the finely painted bowl fragment found in the same season, though further to the south in the concession (plate 5),[11] but an equally fuzzy drawing at the base of another blue-and-white vessel was also found in the same season to the east in the concession (plate 6).[12] The most interesting of the imitation shards found in pit A formed part of a large bowl (plate 7), whose interior was covered with a fine all-over pattern of intermingled leaves, vines, and small flower clusters, and whose exterior carried a radial pattern of tapering triangular compartments outlined in blue. The blue is a trifle pale, but the drawing is precise enough to associate it with one of the master ceramists of the genre. The overall effect of the execution is unlike any of the published examples, but comparison with the latter allows us to assign the vessel to the fourteenth rather than the fifteenth century.[13]

All the imitation wares of the time were made

PLATE 4. Same as plate 3.

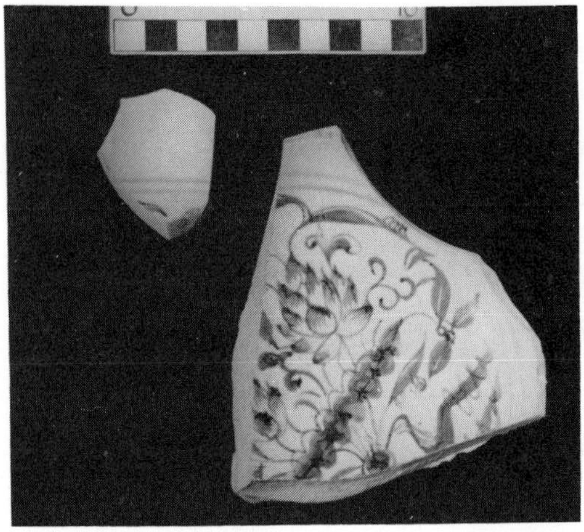

PLATE 5. Fragments of Chinese blue-and-white bowl, 14th century. Museum of Islamic Art, Cairo, Fustat Exp. reg. no. 68-9-8.

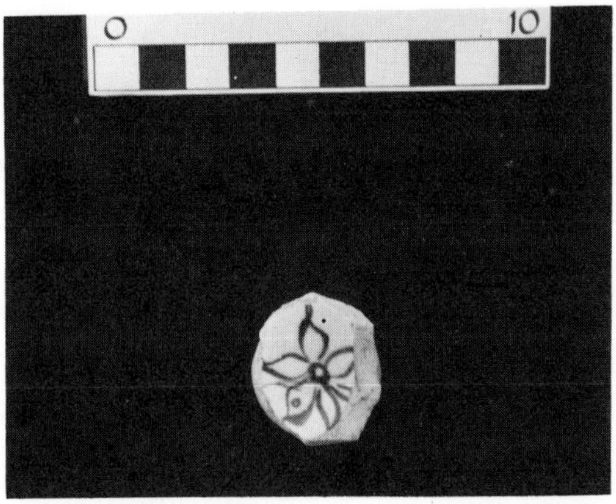

PLATE 6. Base of small Chinese blue-and-white bowl, 15th century. Kelsey Museum, University of Michigan, Fustat Exp. reg. no. 68-11-97.

from a basic white clay which sometimes turns slightly gray or buff in firing. Though black specks or air bubbling are sometimes found in the fired clay, it is generally tight and consistent; never, however, as tight and consistent as the Chinese originals.[14] The same holds true for two other ceramic wares whose decorative schema (one in blue and black against a white slip, all under a clear alkaline glaze; the other a silhouette of black design on a white slip under a transparent turquoise alkaline glaze) find their ultimate source, via Syria, in Persia. Marilyn Jenkins, in another article in this volume, groups both blue-and-white imitation wares (based on Chinese models) and blue-black-white wares (based on Persian models) into a single category and credits Syria as the primary source of production. I believe it wiser to keep them distinct, and allow Egypt parity of production in blue-and-white imitations, on the basis of the large number of wasters found at Fustat. The blue-black-white wares (quite often with touches of red) were imitated earlier and present a more complex problem.

Sometime during the late twelfth century the prototypes of these wares (blue-black-white and turquoise silhouette) arrived in Syria (more particularly in Rakka), where they were imitated throughout the thirteenth century. These imitations found their way into Egypt and were themselves imitated in Egypt, as can positively be shown by wasters

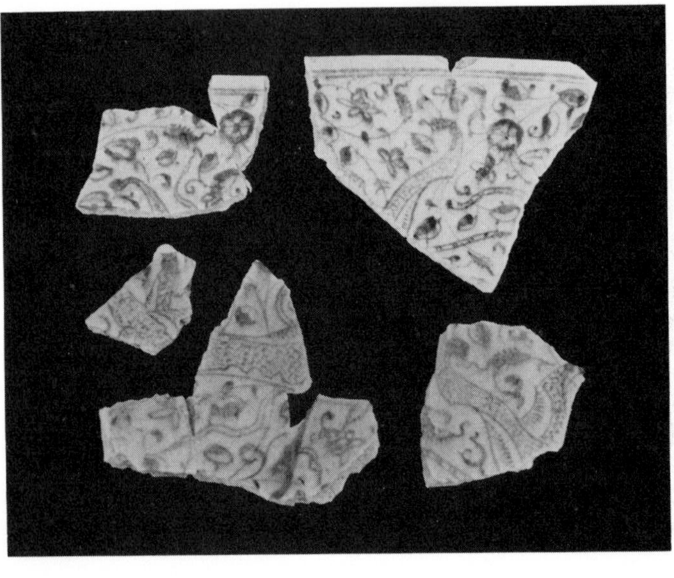

PLATE 7. Fragments of Egyptian imitation blue-and-white bowl found in pit A, 14th century.

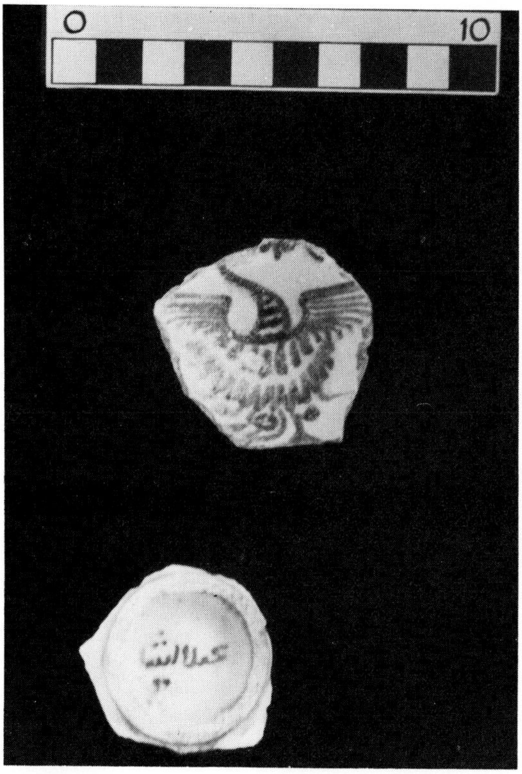

PLATE 8. Base of imitation blue-and-white bowl; potter's name, al-Shāmī, on underside (*shown at bottom*); 14th century. Museum of Islamic Art, Cairo, Fustat Exp. reg. no. 68-11-37.

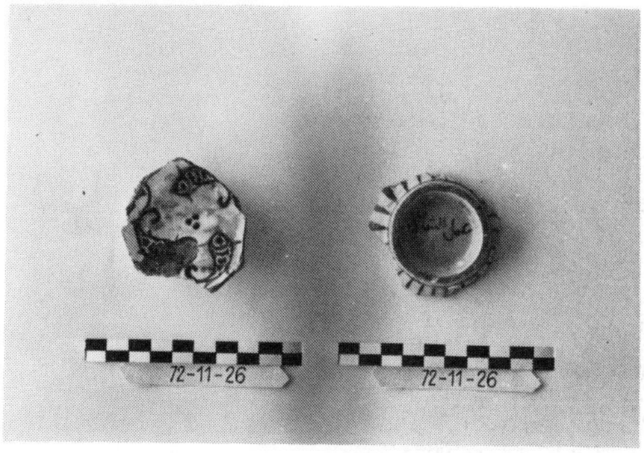

PLATE 9. Base of imitation blue-and-white bowl; potter's name, al-Shāmī, on underside (*shown at bottom*); 14th century. Museum of Islamic Art, Cairo, Fustat Exp. reg. no. 72-11-26.

whose motival components derive from Syrian examples. Attention to details provides sufficient evidence whereby the Syrian can be distinguished from the Egyptian imitation: the former is more finely potted, the clay is less coarse and generally whiter, the walls of the vessels are thinner and the overall contour more shapely, the painted motifs are sharper, the slips do not run beneath the glaze, and finally, the glaze itself is more evenly distributed on the interior and does not "pool."[15] There is a further complication: the Egyptian potter may have copied from Persian originals. Fragments of Kashan luster and Kashan silhouette wares have been found in the mounds of Fustat, and the frequent imitation of Sultanabad wares (particularly with inner surfaces in very low relief) requires a model that has yet to be reported from Syrian loci.[16]

The Mamluk levels in pit A provided a great deal of evidence for the imitation of blue-black-white wares, sustaining the statistical evidence from the mounds analyzed in "Shard Count," though there were none with the additional red slip.[17] The fragments assembled to form the bowl in figure 2 and plate 10 came from between 2.0 and 3.6 m. The design of the swirling entrelacs and hatched area is rather good, but the application of the blue slip was too hasty and its surrounding of the central hatches was never achieved. It is Egyptian, lacking utterly the finely controlled slip painting to be found in the bowl base reproduced in plate 3-a of "Shard Count." As there is no manganese under the glaze, one is wiser to assign the bowl from pit A to some time before 1400 rather than after.

It was argued in 1968 from the analysis of the mounds that the introduction of manganese as an underglaze color indicated on the one hand the debasement of blue-black-white wares and on the other a return to favor of a color that had dominated Egyptian taste throughout the Fatimid period.[18] A proportionate number of shards came from practically all the Mamluk levels in pit A to confirm the findings of "Shard Count." The radial pattern, so familiar from blue-black-white wares, dominated, but in all cases black had been replaced by manganese, and the drawing was more free

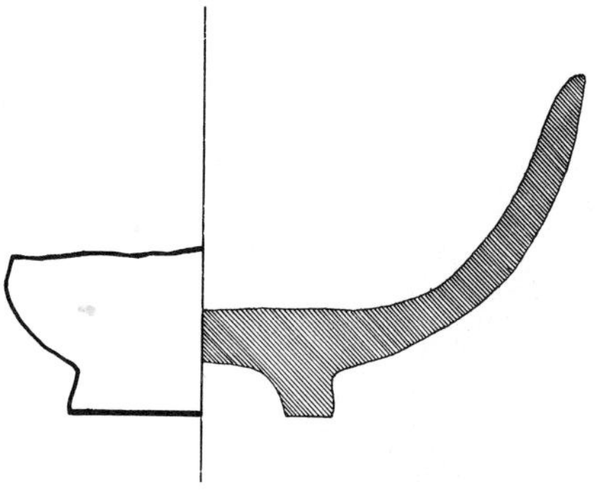

FIGURE 2. Profile of bowl in plate 10.

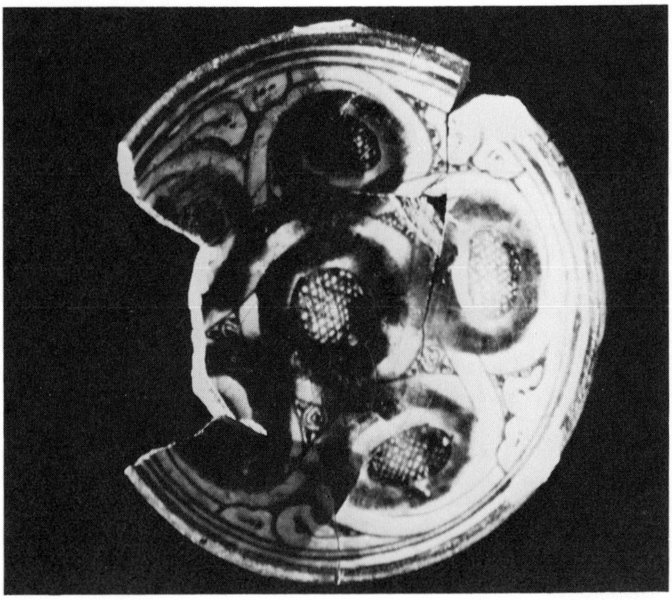

PLATE 10. Matching fragments of underglaze-painted bowl; grayish white clay, black and blue decoration on white; late 14th century. Kelsey Museum, University of Michigan, Fustat Exp. reg. no. 68-11-91.

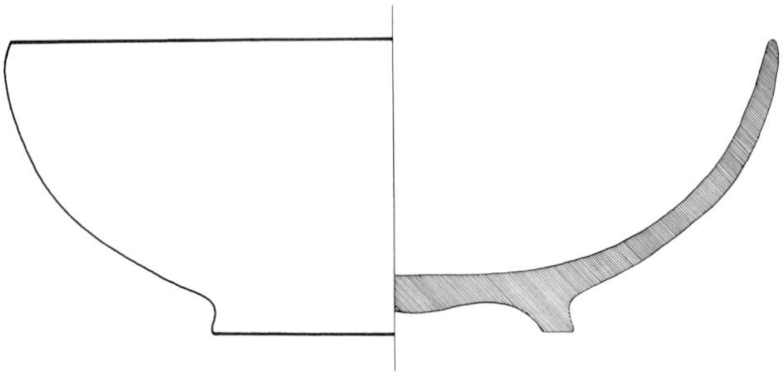

FIGURE 3. Profile of bowl in plate 11.

PLATE 11. Matching fragments of underglaze-painted bowl; grayish white clay, manganese and blue decoration on white; 15th century. Kelsey Museum, University of Michigan, Fustat Exp. reg. no. 68-12-59.

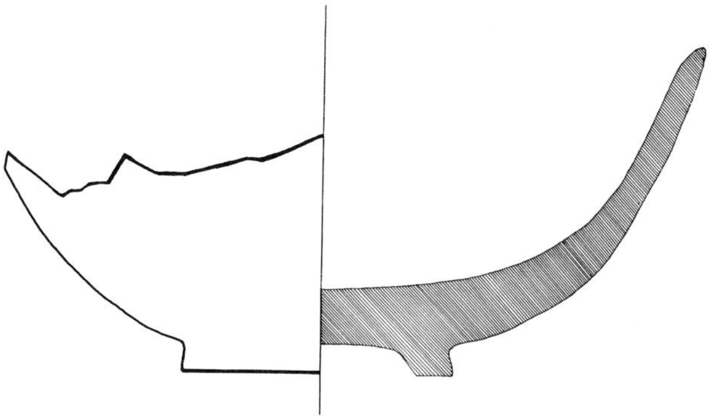

FIGURE 4. Profile of bowl in plate 12.

hand than geometrically and proportionately controlled, as in the fine example to be seen in plate 3-a of "Shard Count" or plates 1 and 2 of Abel's book. Its malproportionate asymmetry can be seen in the bowl of figure 3 and plate 11, which, in addition to the usual thickening radial lines and hatchwork wedges, contains the novel device of an abstract palm tree in three of the six wide panels.[19] This motif is represented in neither the original Persian range nor the Syrian imitation of underglazed painted wares. It is very familiar, however, in Egyptian ceramics, on glazed and unglazed vessels alike, from the very earliest Islamic period.

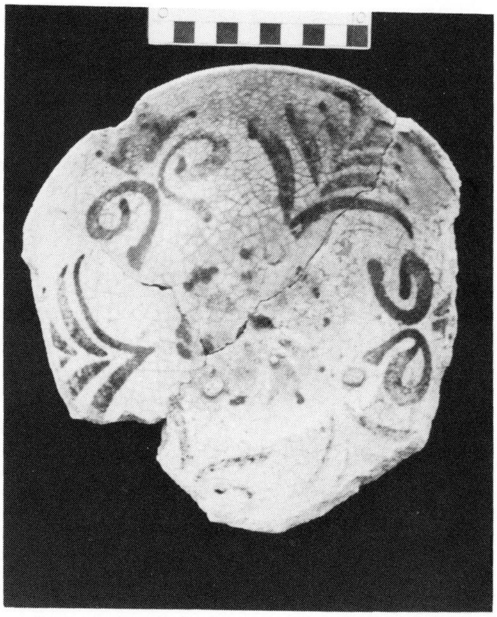

PLATE 12. Matching fragments of underglaze-painted bowl; granular buff-white clay, manganese decoration on white under greenish transparent glaze; 15th century. Kelsey Museum, University of Michigan, Fustat Exp. reg. no. 68-11-90.

Indeed one may add it to Grube's list of motival survivors from pharaonic times.[20] It is especially difficult to date the reappearance of such a motif, for the pieces which make up the bowl in figure 3 and plate 11 were found in exactly the same levels as those which formed figure 2 and plate 10. There seems to have been a qualitative decline in ceramic production in the fifteenth century, so we may hazard that century for all manganese substitutions for black in these imitative wares, though fully cognizant that the true blue-black-white may have been manufactured into the fifteenth century, as was the imitation blue-and-white.

This same palm-tree motif appears on another bowl composed from fragments found on either side of the 2.0 m level in pit A (fig. 4; plate 12). It is a most disappointing product of the Egyptian atelier. The original white clay is almost pure buff in color; and the vessel is weakly potted, owing to the granular consistency of the paste. The central rosette has simply disappeared in the firing; the palm trees and mirror swirls are so freely drawn and distributed that the overall effect is distressingly asymmetrical. But it is the overglaze which most disturbs: instead of being fully transparent, it is greenish in hue and unevenly distributed across the inner surface (the bowl has been reproduced in color in plate 4-a of "Shard Count"). It is clearly indicative of the decay of Mamluk ceramics: the potting is abysmal, the clay poorly composed, the drawing erratic, the two slips reduced to one with poor tonality after firing, and the glazing impure and badly distributed. The motival referents are simplistic, almost recidivist, completely unrelated to the broad conspectus of themes deriving (in white clay wares) from China, Persia, and Syria. Very few other shards of this poor glazed ware have been found in Fustat-B (no others in pit A); hence, although it signals some sort of nadir in the realm of Mamluk ceramics, it cannot signify wide-

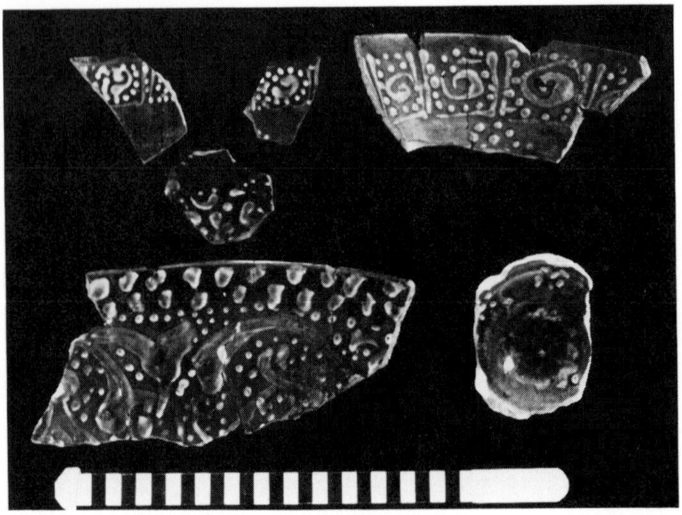

PLATE 13. Selection of thickened white-slip underglaze-painted ware; relief effect under transparent green glaze, white-buff clay; 15th century.

spread taste. Clearly it is from the middle to late fifteenth century.

No single shard of imitation Sultanabad ware (comparable to that of plate 3-k of "Shard Count") was found in the Mamluk levels of pit A, but the proportion of silhouette wares under a transparent green glaze relative to those under the more usual Persian-Syrian turquoise glaze (as noted in table 1 of "Shard Count") was maintained in the pit. The preference for green indicates a purely Egyptian taste, as very few green silhouette wares are reported from Persia and none from Syria. The deepening of the turquoise toward an almost cobalt hue (to be seen in plate 3-f of "Shard Count") may parallel the reappearance of manganese and be construed as a fifteenth-century phenomenon.[21]

Pit A did, however, provide an unusual variation within the white (and buffish white) clay wares relative to the finds from the mounds discussed in "Shard Count." This was an underglaze slip painting so thick as to be relief-like to the touch. The design was always of thickened white slip under a clear green glaze (plate 13 and the black-and-white photograph on p. 229 of "Shard Count"; all the shards therein also come from pit A). The type should be clearly distinguished from the more usual Mamluk slip wares based on red clays (discussed at length in my "Mamluk Ceramic Shapes" and amply illustrated in plate 6 of "Shard Count"). Numerically it outnumbered the shards of the latter in pit A and must therefore be considered as something of a gloss on the statistics of table 1 of "Shard Count." The designs are somewhat slapdash but echo those found in most other types of Mamluk decorated ceramics, the type of clay and decorative technique notwithstanding. There is even a throwback to Fatimid decoration in the stenographic "baraka" border design (plate 13, upper right).[22] We are left with the question of whether to consider this ware a "white" variant of silhouette wares or a version of imitation Sultanabad ware (many of whose motifs it discreetly copies) suitable for a poorer clientele. Though the shapes were standard Mamluk, the artistic quality was never very high. With present evidence it is difficult to date the initiation of its manufacture, but its slight aesthetic effect fits well with the pattern of decline in the fifteenth century.

A more puzzling vessel came forth intact from the layer between 7.7 and 8.2 m, well above the level at which the Mamluk evidence ceased. It is a chalicelike bowl on a flaring pedestal foot, which itself has a single ribbing at the adjointure to the body. The clay is a grainy buffish white, and its light green glaze seems to have been applied without any intermediate slip. On the outside of the incurving rim a festoon appliqued ornament of a looped vine and small doughnut-like shapes is affixed almost at random on either side. The glaze has all but disappeared (fig. 5; plate 14). The clay is not unlike that of the bowl in figure 4 and plate 12, though the object is more securely potted; and the shape in its separate parts can be paralleled in the smaller Mamluk sgraffito vessels.[23] But it is the mode of decoration—appliqued festooning—that makes for typological pause, since it is usually associated with the earliest types of lead-glazed pottery in Egypt.[24] It is unique in the published material, and may, if it is Mamluk, represent yet another aspect of the recidivism noted above:

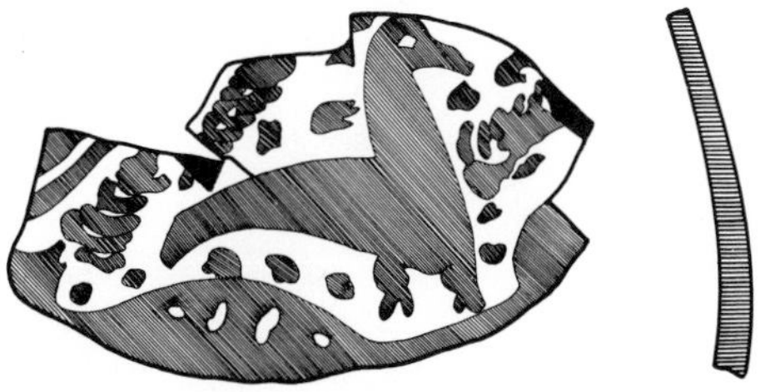

FIGURE 6. Matching fragments of unglazed vessel; rough, brown-red clay, black painted decoration on orange slip; 15th century(?). Kelsey Museum, University of Michigan, Fustat Exp. reg. no. 68-11-92.

added proof of the artistic poverty of fifteenth-century production.

This same trend is noticeable in four matching fragments from the curving wall of a vessel made from a rough, granular, brownish-red clay. It is covered by an orange slip on which has been painted a bird among disparate foliage in black slip. There is no covering glaze (fig. 6). The fragments were found just below 3.5 m and therefore well within the Mamluk fill. Very little unglazed slip-painted ware has been reported for this period, and none was found in the area analyzed in "Shard Count." Such wares were imported into Egypt from Nubia during the so-called classic Christian period (tenth–eleventh centuries);[25] and certain types of slip-painted unglazed wares of the Coptic-continuity types have been found at Fustat from loci of the ninth–tenth centuries.[26] However, the former are obvious from their superior potting and autochthonous motifs, which were never imitated in Egyptian production, and the latter were always of distinctive white clays. The example under discussion is both much less well painted and inferior in potting to either of these earlier genres. It seems doubtful that our vessel was meant to be glazed, for, with an orange slip, it falls outside the normal range of underglaze slip-painted glazed wares. We

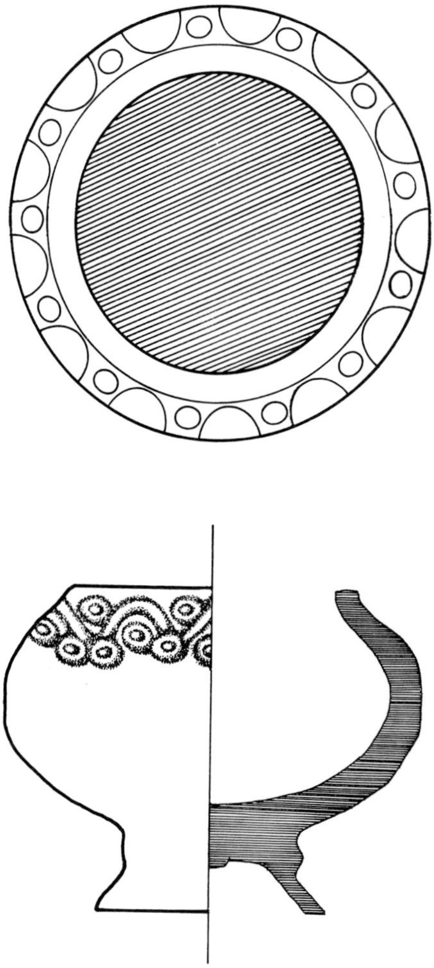

FIGURE 5. Profile of bowl in plate 14.

PLATE 14. Green glazed chalice-bowl found intact in pit A; appliqued decoration at external rim; 15th century(?). Kelsey Museum, University of Michigan, Fustat Exp. reg. no. 68-12-42.

PLATE 15. Selection of Mamluk sgraffito and slip-painted glazed wares found in pit A; red and brownish red clays; 14th–15th centuries.

are left with the alternative of conceiving it as yet another possible proof of the economic impoverishment of the fifteenth century, when glazed vessels were beyond the means of some of the customers of the Cairo ateliers.

Notwithstanding these variants and exemplars of a surprising recidivism, the overwhelming number of the shards in the upper 9.5 m of fill were of red and red-brown clays, covered internally and externally with variations of two standard colors: a range from honey-gold to chocolate-brown, and green. The underglaze decorations were incised (sgraffito) or painted, or combinations of both techniques appeared on the same vessel (plates 15 and 16). The percentages echo those recorded in "Shard Count" (an exception being noted for the white clay ware of plate 13), which would seem to indicate that these types of ceramics represent the mass taste of the Mamluk era, types which certainly existed well into the fifteenth century, though perhaps in reduced numbers. Further, most of the motival variety encountered in other publications[27] was duplicated in the pit under discussion. Thus if we conflate the evidence of our particular pit with that from the far larger area surveyed in "Shard Count," we achieve a more tightly focused picture of the production of the ateliers of Cairo from c. A.D. 1200–1500. Lingering tastes, imports, imitations, variations, and atypical responses to straitened economic circumstances we may now see in their purely archaeological setting. Future research must define the emergence, development, and decay (or better, etiolation) of separate decorative themes. Archaeology outside Fustat may supply a keener chronological edge in aid of such a process.

AMERICAN UNIVERSITY IN CAIRO
CAIRO, EGYPT

PLATE 16. Selection of Mamluk glazed wares found in pit A; 14th–15th centuries.

NOTES

1. George T. Scanlon, "The Fustat Mounds: A Shard Count 1968" (hereafter cited as "Shard Count"), *Archaeology* 24, no. 3 (June 1971) : 220–33.

2. The analysis of the mounds in 1968, though original, pales before that carried out on more than a million shards accruing to the Antiquities Service from the excavations of Aly Bahgat and those undertaken by the Service after his death. This work was directed by Mr. Abd al-Rahman Abd al-Tawwab, late Director-General of Coptic and Islamic Antiquities. When the results are published, the tentativeness of our studies will be shown in sharp relief.

3. George T. Scanlon, "Some Mamluk Ceramic Shapes from Fustat: 'Sgraff' and 'Slip'" (hereafter cited as MCS), *Diamond Jubilee Volume of the Islamic Museum* (Cairo, 1980); five of the bowls discussed there came from the 1968 season.

4. George T. Scanlon, "Fustat Expedition: Preliminary Report 1968, Part 1" (hereafter cited as FEPR 68–1), *Journal of the American Research Center in Egypt* 11 (1974): 81–91, esp. p. 83 and n. 8. A double error has crept into its designation: (a) it is actually pit A in XI″–15/20, not XI′–15/20, a mistake in the printing of the report; and (b) before the drawing of the final plan I, it had been designated pit A in XI″–5, simply because the particular locus lay well beyond the concession area of Fustat-B. Following the permission of the Antiquities Service to proceed westward, the designation was corrected, but the photography of the contents of the pit carries the erroneous designation. As the pit is firmly in area A and related to the domicile described as centered on basin F (XI′–11), it can be none other than pit A (XI″–15/20) to be seen in plan I of the report. Its position is at center right of pl. XV-b, with basin F at the center of the photograph.

5. George T. Scanlon, "Ancillary Dating Materials from Fustat," *Ars Orientalis* 7 (1968): 9–16, and text fig. 4-b. A very fine example of the type can be seen in FEPR 68-1, fig. 15.

6. FEPR 68-1. The carved bone inlay pieces are discussed in detail by Marilyn Ereshefsky, "Bone and Ivory Carving in Early Islamic Egypt" (Master's thesis, American University in Cairo, 1980).

7. This latter evidence can be collated with that from the undisturbed pits G (XI′–12) and F (XI′–12/17), also associated with the same domicile as pit A under discussion. The absence of anything Fatimid within *any* undisturbed locus relative to this domicile forces us to see the latter as a *kharab*, that is, a ruined, abandoned residence. Cf. FEPR 68-1, p. 83 and nn. 6 and 7.

8. Cf. Pierre Olmer, *Les filtres des gargoulettes* (Cairo, 1932); George T. Scanlon, "Fatimid Filters: Archaeology and Olmer's Typology," *Annales islamologiques* 9 (1970): 37–64; and idem, "Preliminary Report: Excavations at Fustat, 1964" (hereafter cited as FEPR 64), *Journal of the American Research Center in Egypt* 4 (1965) : 7–30.

9. Other examples of the phenomenon obtained throughout Fustat-B. One of the deterrents to complete scavenging was the high water table; our fill became moist, then muddy (hence the necessity of sieving) after about 9.0 m. The same held true of pit H (VI–19) excavated in 1971, where mud appeared at 11.1 m; see W. B. Kubiak and G. T. Scanlon, "Fustat Expedition: Preliminary Report 1971, Part 1," *Journal of the American Research Center in Egypt* 16 (1979) : p. 105.

10. Bo Gyllensvard, "Recent Finds of Chinese Ceramics at Fustat. II," *Bulletin of the Museum of Far Eastern Antiquities*, no. 47 (1975) : 93–117. The fish motif can also be seen in FEPR 64, fig. 5, in my "Egypt and China: Trade and Imitation," in *Islam and the Trade of Asia*, ed. D. S. Richards (Oxford, 1971), fig. 10, and the local imitation in pls. XIII-c and XVI. The Egyptian potter sometimes reverted to colors other than the variations of celadon green: cf. plate 3, upper left, and plate 15, upper center. For an earlier demonstration of this color freedom, see "Egypt and China," pp. 81–95, esp. p. 84 and pl. X.

11. This fragment has been published in color, in "Shard Count," pl. 5. It is also discussed in "Egypt and China," p. 91 and pl. XIV-c.

12. It was a surface find in quadrant VI–22; see plan 1 in FEPR 68-1.

13. Armand Abel, *Ghaibī et les grands faïenciers égyptiens de l'époque mamlouke* (Cairo, 1930), passim; types additional to those surveyed by Abel and by Aly Bahgat and Felix Massoul, *La céramique musulmane de l'Egypt* (Cairo, 1930; hereafter cited as *CME*) and the anonymous *La céramique égyptienne de l'époque musulmane* (Cairo, 1922; hereafter cited as *CEEM*), can be assayed in Bengt Pederson, "Blue and White Imitation Pottery from the Ghaibī and Related Workshops in Medieval Cairo," *Bulletin of the Museum of Far Eastern Antiquities*, no. 52 (1980) : 65–88. For two other, albeit much smaller, imitations of Chinese models, see plates 8 and 9. Both are by al-Shāmī and neither exhibits that unfortunate pooling of the covering glaze which so often destroys the effect of Egyptian imitations of blue-and-white. The fragment in plate 8 has a phoenixlike bird at its center; comparable exemplars can be found in *CME*, pl. 112; *CEEM*, passim; and Abel, *Ghaibī*, pls. XIII–XV. Plate 9 has three fishes surrounding a motif of three dots, and other exemplars can be found in *CEM*, p. 112, upper row right, and Pedersen, "Blue and White Imitation Pottery," pl. 1 and pl. 7-XXV, where all of the fish motifs come from the Ghaibī atelier. Finally, a sense of the original as opposed to the imitation of blue-and-white can be appreciated in color: "Shard Count" (pl. 5-f shows the largest shard of the bowl in pl. 7 of this article).

14. For a comparison, see "Egypt and China," pl. XVI.

15. This subject has been most thoughtfully assayed by Amy Newhall, "Polychrome Underglaze Pottery of the Ayyubid and Bahri Periods" (Master's thesis, American University in Cairo, 1978).

16. Cf. "Shard Count," p. 230 and pl. 3; George T. Scanlon, "A Note on Fatimid–Saljuk Trade," in *Islamic History: 950–1150 A.D.*, ed. D. S. Richards (Oxford, 1973), pp. 265–74, esp. p. 271 and pl. VI.

17. Until a local waster is found, one must assume that the vessels bearing a red slip in addition to the usual black and blue ones were imports from Syria. Such must be the case for "Shard Count," pls. 3-b and 3-e.

18. "Shard Count," pp. 229, 231.

19. This bowl has been illustrated in FEPR 68-1, pl. XVI-c. Two other shards from pit A where manganese has replaced black can be seen in plate 16 herein, upper and middle rows, far right.

20. Ernst Grube, "Studies in the Survival and Continuity of Pre-Muslim Traditions in Egyptian Islamic Art," *Journal of the American Research Center in Egypt* 1 (1962): 75–97.

21. It would be more helpful to consider the shards in pl. 3 of "Shard Count" as follows:

c, i	turquoise silhouette	Syria, 13th century
h, j	turquoise silhouette	Egypt, 14th century
g	green silhouette	Egypt, 14th–15th centuries
f	cobalt silhouette	Egypt, 15th century

22. For other baraka examples, see *CME*, pls. XIII-1, XXVIII-2, and A-9; and *CEEM*, pls. 7, 20, 71, and 85.

23. MCS, type I, passim.

24. Scanlon, "Note on Fatimid–Saljuk Trade," pl. 5-c.

25. W. Y. Adams, *Nubia, Corridor to Africa* (London, 1977), pp. 495–500. A very good fragment can be seen in Wladyslaw Kubiak and George T. Scanlon, "Fustat Expedition: Preliminary Report 1966" (hereafter cited as FEPR 66), *Journal of American Research Center in Egypt* 10 (1973), fig. 7.

26. A very good example was found in 1966 (FEPR 66, fig. 8); others of the same dating were unearthed from undisturbed loci in 1978 and 1980.

27. Most particularly *CME* and *CEEM*, passim; "Shard Count," pp. 224, 225, and 228, and pls. 1, 2, and 6; MCS, where all the illustrations are of the type under discussion; and Ernst Grube, *Islamic Pottery in the Keir Collection* (London: 1976), 282–92, which contains an exhaustive bibliographic survey of these types of Mamluk pottery.

LOUISE W. MACKIE

Toward an Understanding of Mamluk Silks: National and International Considerations

Mamluk society was saturated with textiles,[1] signaling the position and wealth of the inhabitants. The significance of textiles is evident in their role as transmitters of religious, political, social, and economic messages. The annual donation of the kiswa, textile cover for the Kaaba, established the sovereignty of the Mamluk kingdom in the Islamic world.[2] Clothing styles and colors, based on court regulation, identified rank and religion.[3] Prestigious robes of honor, *khila*ʿ, were given annually by the Mamluk court, which included a bewildering variety of clothing appropriate to the recipient's rank. *Khil*ʿ*a* fabrics were distinctive for their quality and color, in silk, linen, cotton, or wool, sometimes lined with exotic fur. The actual cut of the garments, however, was the same as for daily wear.[4] Some luxurious *khil*ʿ*a* fabrics were woven in Mamluk tiraz factories, though others, such as silks from China, wool from Malatiya, and cloths from Baghdad, were imported.[5] *Khila*ʿ were shown off, and the finest textiles therefore became transmitters of artistic styles and fashions.

The conspicuous consumption and display of luxury textiles was the privilege of the wealthy elite, primarily the ruling Mamluks, while the vast majority of the population used common textiles. Average-quality textiles were woven in villages throughout the Mamluk realm, linen in Egypt, cotton in Syria. Undyed fibers were combined with blue, the most common color, to create simple patterns of stripes and bands.[6] In contrast, luxurious textiles of international acclaim were woven in only a few cities; for example, cotton was made in Aleppo and Baalbek, linen in Alexandria, and patterned silks in Damascus, Alexandria, and Cairo.[7]

The textile industry was a vital force in the prosperity and subsequent decline of the Mamluk economy. Control of this lucrative industry appears to have shifted from the pre-Mamluk practice of government ownership to partial control by privileged Mamluks[8] and weavers.[9] During the economically stable Bahri period, the Mamluk textile industry flourished and was a dominant force in the textile commerce throughout the Mediterranean and in the East-West spice trade. By the fifteenth century, however, it was corrupt; competition was strangled, quality declined, and prices rose,[10] all of which contributed to the economic depression during the Burji period. Alexandria, once acclaimed for luxurious linens and silks, suffered a devastating decline. Of the approximately twelve thousand to fourteen thousand looms active in the 1380s, only eight hundred were working in 1434.[11] In Europe, the textile industry had, by 1400, benefited from technological innovations that enabled the manufacture of finer and cheaper silks and woolens than in the Mamluk kingdom. Consequently, European textiles flooded the Mamluk market, much to the detriment of the economy. The Mamluk textile industry had become a mere shadow of its former prosperity.

Any investigation into what the once-famous Mamluk textiles looked like, a subject few have tackled,[12] involves distinguishing Mamluk silks from those woven in Italy, in China, and on the

I wish to thank the museum directors and curators who made their collections accessible for study, especially Abd al-Rauf Ali Yusuf, General Director, and Muhammad Abbas, Textile Curator, Museum of Islamic Art, Cairo; Waltraud Berner; Klaus Brisch; Volkmar Enderlein; Gisela Helmecke; Anatol Ivanov; Marilyn Jenkins; Santina Levey; Barbara Mundt; Milton Sonday; and Friedrich Spuhler. I am also grateful to Lisa Golombek, who discussed problems, and Nobuko Kajitani, who discussed technical matters concerning textiles.

Iberian peninsula during the thirteenth through fifteenth centuries. Almost nothing survives from Turkey, Iraq, and Iran in this period. In the comments that follow I will attempt to identify some distinguishing features of Mamluk silks and to consider their national and international significance.

Several hundred Mamluk silks exist today: most are fragments that have survived in the arid Egyptian ground and were purchased in the art market; few silks have been scientifically excavated (plates 2, 7).[13] Thanks to the long-term benefits of international trade, a few were also preserved in Europe, where they were held in sufficient esteem to be made into ecclesiastical vestments (plate 16).

The identification of Mamluk silks is based on establishing clusters of related fabrics in which four factors are considered: pattern, color, fiber, and structure. Some silks are in a state of limbo, awaiting the development of a cluster or evidence of Mamluk manufacture. The patterns in Mamluk silks are usually easy to perceive, both in their organization and in their design elements. The organization is typically composed of a repetition of compartments, a natural by-product of the woven structure, outlined by straight or curved contours in a variety of mathematical layouts. Vegetal, animal, and epigraphic elements form the designs. Geometric strapwork is rare, despite its overwhelming popularity in other media. Human figures and blazons are unknown in silk fabrics.[14] Surviving Mamluk silks are often limited to two or three colors, the number sometimes determined by the woven structure.[15] Blue, derived from locally available indigo plants,[16] was the most popular, an aesthetic preference also evident in illuminated pages, enameled glass, and ceramic decoration.

Identifying fibers is of significance when considering linen and cotton textiles, since Egypt and Syria each used their own indigenous fibers,[17] but that significance breaks down for silk fibers because Syrian sericulture supplied fibers for both local and Egyptian manufacture.[18] Whether a silk was woven in Egypt or Syria cannot yet be determined. Gold was used lavishly in silks, especially at the instigation of al-Nāṣir Muḥammad ibn Qalā'ūn, but few silks with gilt threads have survived (plates 1, 7, 8, 11, 12, 16).[19]

The woven structures of Mamluk silks indicate a change in loom technology in Egypt, a land already renowned for its textile production.[20] The marked change was probably introduced during the thirteenth century by experienced weavers from Iraq and Iran who fled the Mongols, were attracted to the prosperous Mamluk textile industry, or perhaps emigrated from the shrinking Islamic territory on the Iberian peninsula.

The drawlooms they introduced had mechanical patterning devices that radically altered the nature of textile patterns, in contrast to the simple looms with individual patterning devices that had dominated textile production in Egypt for well over two thousand years.[21] Mechanical patterning devices allowed an endless repetition of motifs, often in mirror image, called point repeat, when shortcuts were taken in preparing the loom (plates 3, 5, 14–17, 19; fig. 1). Repetition and mirror images affected the size of motifs and length of inscriptions: large images and long inscriptions required more time to prepare and weave, and consequently were more expensive.

The variety of structures in Mamluk silks indicates the expertise of the weavers. While the range includes some simple weaves, especially damask (plates 5, 14, 17; figs. 1–3),[22] most are compound weaves.[23] Among the most prevalent, based on chance survival, are versions of double cloth (plates 2, 3, 6, 9, 10, 12, 20).[24] Owing to the radical change in loom technology, from individual to mechanical patterning devices, there is no internal technological evidence for identifying Mamluk silks, a factor that reinforces the importance of establishing clusters of related silks.

The dating of Mamluk silks is imprecise, based primarily on stylistic comparisons with a few datable silks, all of which survive from the prosperous Bahri rather than the economically depressed Burji period. Attributions are also influenced by occasional stylistic comparisons with other media and the change of style apparent in most late Mamluk art, such as the disappearance of the figural style in metalwork after 1350.

The corpus of datable silks known to me at this time includes three Mamluk and two Chinese groups:

Twelve Mamluk silks with historical inscriptions: four with the names of sultans (plates 1, 8; figs. 2, 3); four with the titles of intended rulers (plates 9, 11; fig. 1);[25] four with titles only, which could be honorific or generic (plate 6);[26]

Three scientifically excavated Mamluk silks (plates 2, 3, 7);[27]

Two Mamluk silk patterns represented in European paintings, providing a *terminus ante quem* (plates 5,[28] 16,[29] 17);

One Chinese silk with Chinese patterns adapted for the Mamluk market with a historical inscription (plate 21);

PLATE 1. Blue and ivory silk with metallic threads, "Glory to our master the sultan al-Malik al-Manṣūr Qalā'ūn, may his victory be glorious," 1279–90; a compound weave, ground satin, pattern twill, wrapped metallic membrane; 18 × 15.5 cm. Museum of Islamic Art, Cairo, no. 15608.

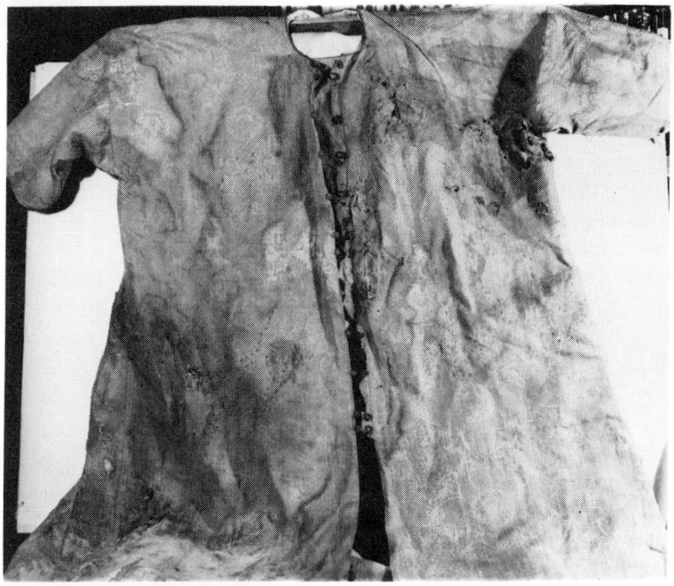

PLATE 2. Yellow and tan (formerly green) silk robe with buttons, excavated at Jabal Adda, Nubia, late 13th century; double-cloth weave; length 119 cm, width 101 cm (across hem), 122 cm (arms extended). Museum of Islamic Art, Cairo, no. 23903.

PLATE 3. Detail of plate 2, curvilinear star and cross layout.

One Chinese export silk with an Islamic layout made for the Mamluk or European market (plate 23).

ARTISTIC STYLES

The artistic vocabulary of Mamluk silks appears to shed light on the nature of the silk industry. Stylistic parallels with the other Mamluk decorative arts are fewer than might be expected. Individual design elements, such as rabbits, blossoms, and epigraphy have numerous comparisons, but combinations of elements and the overall layout often stand apart without parallel, with the exception of banded and striped layouts, which will be discussed later. This may result from the lack of a centralized court art where artists establish styles that are adopted for surface embellishment in all the decorative arts. When textile patterns are dependent on court art, they usually have parallels in the art of the book, as in Safavid silks, or in the treatment of wall decoration, as in Ottoman silks. Since the Mamluk court does not appear to have exerted strong control over the textile industry, all evidence suggests that Mamluk silks were designed in the marketplace where economic viability influenced standards of style and quality for local as well as foreign consumption.

Following well-established traditions from Iran to Spain, Arabic writing continued to be a significant feature in textile patterns. Almost half the surviving Mamluk silk fragments include Arabic words, all legible, ranging from single words, such as "the sultan" (plate 19), to historical inscriptions with the names of sultans and titles that could be honorific or generic, all attributed to the Bahri period (plates 1, 5, 6, 8, 9, 11, 16; figs. 1–3). The most frequent inscriptions invoke "glory to our master the sultan the king," a blessing that would have retained its relevance despite changes of power (plates 15 and 17). Textiles with Arabic

PLATE 5. Blue silk damask with curvilinear lattice layout, "al-Ashraf al-A," said to be from al-A'zām; pattern worn in *Enthroned Madonna with Angels and Saints*, by the Master of the Fabriano Altarpiece and Allegretto Nuzi, 1354; 12 × 14 in. Victoria and Albert Museum, London, 817-1898.

PLATE 4. Block-printed linen with silver pigments pattern same as plate 3; 12 × 24.5 cm. Museum of Islamic Art, Cairo, no. 14816.

inscriptions were prestigious and suggested that the wearer was close to the center of authority and power.[30] Such honor could even have been flaunted from head to toe; inscribed silks survive as sandals,[31] garments (plates 2, 10, 14, 19), and skull-caps (plate 13).

The comparatively short inscriptions were not strictly the result of loom technology; they continued a fashion that had evolved in the eleventh century, when short benedictory texts replaced long historical tiraz inscriptions.[32] A rare holdover from that earlier tradition of long texts woven on simple looms with individual rather than mechanical patterning devices survives in a tapestry-woven silk, inscribed with a long text and the name Ashraf Ṣalāḥ al-D[īn Khalīl], who ruled from 1290 to 1293 (plate 8).[33] Gilt thread forms the compartmentalized vegetal and interlacing patterns.

Generally speaking, inscribed silks display the same range of artistic layouts as silks without inscriptions. A tentative classification of the variety of layouts suggests four main categories.

The first group has a mathematical division of the space that is perceivable; however, the layout, design, and color interact visually so that no single element dominates (plates 1–5). All three patterns are among the earliest Mamluk silks, datable before 1300 based on a historical text (plate 1), archaeological context (plates 2, 3), and representation on metalwork (plate 5).[34] The silk inscribed "al-Malik al-Manṣūr Qalā'ūn" (1279–90, plate 1) illustrates the awkwardness of a lengthy text in an irregular, repeated area. The text layout that resembles a *y* did not persist; it was possibly displaced by more appropriate layouts in the second group.

However, a splendid example of an interactive layout survives in two different fibers and weights, one an expensive silk robe that was found folded above a corpse in a Christian burial at Jabal Adda in Upper Egypt (plates 2, 3),[35] the other a cheaper linen fabric with the pattern stamped with silver pigments (plate 4). Design elements ranging from linear motifs to animals are skillfully combined to form a dynamic pattern in which no single element dominates. Tension and balance are juxtaposed. The pattern ranks among the most sophisticated in Mamluk art.

The second and most common layout has a fluid linear organization of the space that is immediately perceivable with a clear, often dominant, foreground pattern and background space. Banded, striped, and ogival layouts are the most common (plates 6–17). The static layout of roundels that had dominated textile patterns since the seventh century appears to have gone out of fashion during the thirteenth. A rare blue damask with dodecagons is a late vestige of the earlier style (fig. 1). In mirror image, panthers are framed by a text with the name of al-Nāṣir Nāṣir al-Dunyā wa'l-D[īn], attributed to al-Nāṣir Muḥammad ibn Qalā'ūn on stylistic grounds.[36] The motif of framed birds amid lotus blossoms and vines in plate 12 suggests itself as a transition between static roundel and fluid ogival layouts. While ogival lattices usually define the layout, as in the striking blue and white silk in plate 15, occasional patterns imply it, as in the beautiful yellow silk damask robe in plate 14.

In the third layout group, dominant motifs are arranged in staggered rows on a foliate ground that sometimes includes birds or animals floating rather than framed in space (plate 19). Future research may establish this as a major group with artistic origins emanating from the naturalistic drawing in Chinese silks.

The layout of patterns in the fourth group is inconsistent with both the rigid mathematical principles that characterize the previous types of layouts and the appearance of most Mamluk art. The layout is asymmetrical, formed with free-flowing elements (plate 20; figs. 2, 3). It was introduced by the Yüan Dynasty in China (1279–1368) to the West in the medium of woven silks.[37] Two

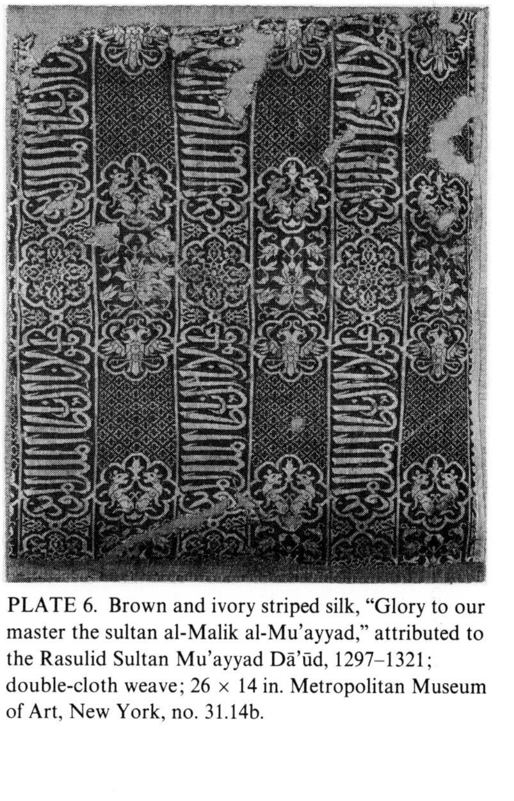

PLATE 6. Brown and ivory striped silk, "Glory to our master the sultan al-Malik al-Mu'ayyad," attributed to the Rasulid Sultan Mu'ayyad Dā'ūd, 1297–1321; double-cloth weave; 26 × 14 in. Metropolitan Museum of Art, New York, no. 31.14b.

PLATE 7. Multicolored striped silk with gilt threads, winding sheet, excavated at Jabal Adda, Nubia, "To whoever looks, I am the moon," late 13th century; complementary warp pattern weave; approx. 350 × 150 cm. Museum of Islamic Art, Cairo.

categories of Yüan silks have been found in Egypt, those with pure Chinese designs[38] and those with Chinese designs adapted for export to the Mamluk market. The latter includes a silk damask with tear-shaped blossoms growing diagonally on sinuous stems and bearing the name Muḥammad [ibn] Qalā'ūn (plate 21).[39] A gift of seven hundred Mongol textiles, according to Abu'l Fida, was brought in 1323 by Mongol ambassadors to al-Nāṣir Muḥammad, inscribed with his titles.[40] While this and other Yüan silks could have been in the recorded gift, there were probably thousands of Mongol silks in the Mamluk kingdom. Historic documents record a substantial Mongol population in Egypt and Syria, several of whom al-Nāṣir Muḥammad appointed to prestigious ranks in the Mamluk artistocracy.

The radical, free-flowing, asymmetrical layout had limited appeal to the Arabs. The drawing in a Mamluk version of the Yüan silk is more rigid and static (fig. 3). Neither the tear-shaped blossoms nor the almond-shaped leaves sway gracefully; however, the same text appears with the name Muḥammad [ibn] Qalā'ūn. The same sultan is cited in another damask whose flowing scroll layout suggests a dependence on a lost Chinese model (figure 2).[41]

Occasional evidence of asymmetrical patterns imitating Yüan silks survives elsewhere in the Islamic world: on a bedcover in a fourteenth-century Iranian miniature,[42] in a fourteenth-century Turkish carpet from Konya, and, a century later, in a Mudejar carpet from the Iberian peninsula.[43] The limited influence of these layouts in the Near East, however, contrasts with the major impact they had on Italian silk patterns, which in turn inspired the undulating vertical stem patterns in Ottoman art.[44]

When considering the artistic vocabulary in silks, it is difficult to believe that only Arabic script

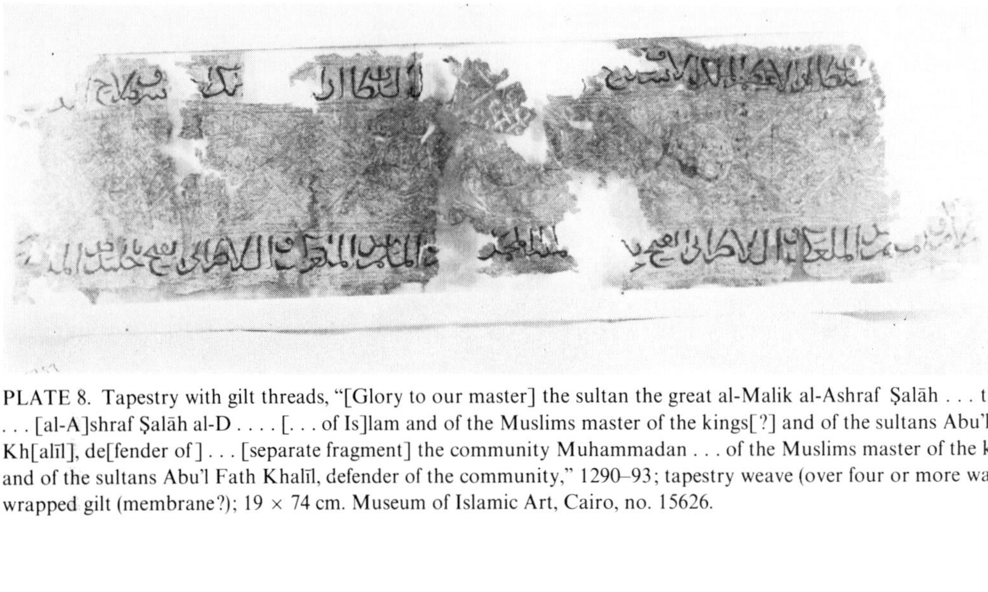

PLATE 8. Tapestry with gilt threads, "[Glory to our master] the sultan the great al-Malik al-Ashraf Ṣalāh . . . the sultan . . . [al-A]shraf Ṣalāh al-D . . . . [. . . of Is]lam and of the Muslims master of the kings[?] and of the sultans Abu'l Fath Kh[alīl], de[fender of] . . . [separate fragment] the community Muhammadan . . . of the Muslims master of the kings[?] and of the sultans Abu'l Fath Khalīl, defender of the community," 1290–93; tapestry weave (over four or more warps), wrapped gilt (membrane?); 19 × 74 cm. Museum of Islamic Art, Cairo, no. 15626.

FIGURE 1. Blue silk damask fragment, "Glory to our master the sultan al-Malik al-Nāṣir Nāṣir al-Dunya wa'l-D[īn]," attributed to al-Nāṣir Muḥammad ibn Qalā'ūn, 1293–1341 (with two interruptions); damask weave, satin and twill. Islamisches Museum, East Berlin, no. I 3211. (Drawing after Schmidt.)

was auspicious. Were other features any more meaningful than simply fashion?

Two silks have survived that are exceptional in size and condition, and in possible interpretation. Approximately 3.5 m long and 1.5 m wide, they functioned as winding sheets in two Christian graves at Jabal Adda in Upper Egypt, datable to the late thirteenth century (plate 7).[45] Well woven with many colors and gold thread in a striped layout with hares, gazelles, birds, and geometric motifs, each winding sheet bears an Arabic text for which textile parallels are lacking. Is it fortuitous that one invokes "glory and victory and long life" and that the other, perhaps folkloric in content, confesses, "to whoever looks, I am the moon"?[46] Certainly the texts are more appropriate than the omnipresent benedictions to the sultan, suggesting the possibility that textiles with specific textual, and perhaps artistic, content served specific functions.

The visual arrangement in the winding sheets of opposing orientations of one hundred and eighty degrees for the text and animals enables the pattern to be viewed from two directions and is characteristic of a group of warp-patterned silks with striped layouts.[47]

For consumers of sufficient means, specific functions and occasions required specific fabrics, such as the expensive woven silk or cheaper stamped linen (plates 3, 4). Fabrics were selected for their fiber content, weight, and woven structure, and then for their color and pattern. Within the silk industry, popular patterns were woven in different weights, structures, and colors. The length of time a single pattern was produced and remained fashionable awaits investigation.

One sophisticated ogival layout survives in two different weights and color lines with only slight differences in the proportions or details of the pattern. The expensive, heavy silks with gilt patterns exist in two color lines, blue and green, while the cheaper, light-weight silk damasks survive in three color lines, blue, rose, and pale green (plates 16, 17). Both of the expensive silks have been preserved as ecclesiastical vestments in Europe, where the pattern was recorded by an Italian painter in about 1430, thereby providing a *terminus ante quem* for the design.[48] The richness of the fabric and the sophistication of the pattern are especially evident in the silk with a gilt pattern highlighted with white on a blue ground that was made as a mantle for a

PLATE 9. Blue, ivory, and brown silk, "Glory to our master the sultan [in large script] al-Malik al-Nāṣir, may his victory be glorious [in small script]," attributed to al-Nāṣir Muḥammad ibn Qalā'ūn, 1293–1341 (with two interruptions); one warp double-cloth weave; 51 × 90.5 cm. Museum of Islamic Art, Cairo, no. 12753/1.

statue of the Virgin.[49] The complex ogival layout is composed of large lotus blossoms and small inscribed medallions on a vine framing tear-shaped blossoms, with Arabic in mirror image. The generic text bestowing benevolence on a sultan varies slightly in each silk. Only the orphrey silk suggests an intended recipient, al-Ashraf; this title, however,

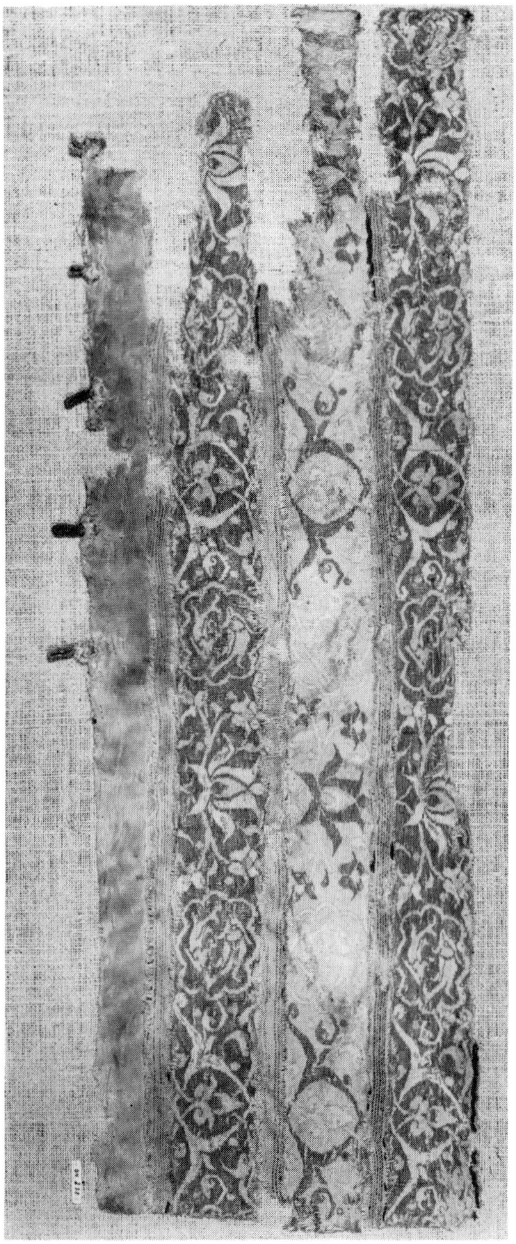

PLATE 10. Garment fragment of blue, brown, and ivory banded silk; one warp double-cloth weave; 16 × 42 cm. Kunstgewerbemuseum, West Berlin, no. 04.278a.

PLATE 11. Ivory, medium blue, and dark blue silk with metallic threads, "Glory to our master the sultan al-Malik al-Ashraf, may his supporters be glorified," possibly Ashraf Nāṣir al-Dīn Shaʿbān, 1363–76; complementary weft plain weave, wrapped metallic membrane; 36 × 22.5 cm. Museum of Islamic Art, Cairo, no. 15554.

was used by nine Mamluk sultans, four of whom ruled before the pattern was recorded in about 1430 (plate 16).

In contrast with most Mamluk silks with ogival layouts, the mathematical division of the space in this pattern is not immediately perceivable despite the clarity of the individual design elements. Two prominent motifs, the lotus and the tear-shaped blossom, compete visually in scale and orientation. Comparable representations in Mamluk art have not been found. However, a silk with a gilt parchment strip pattern woven in East Asia, probably in Yüan China, displays a remarkably similar layout and distribution of motifs (plate 18). Framing a tear-shaped blossom, the ogival layout is formed by a vine with small roundish

PLATE 12. Ivory, light blue, and medium blue silk with metallic threads; incomplete triple-cloth weave, wrapped metallic membrane; 7 × 4.5 in. Textile Museum, Washington, D.C., no. 3.238.

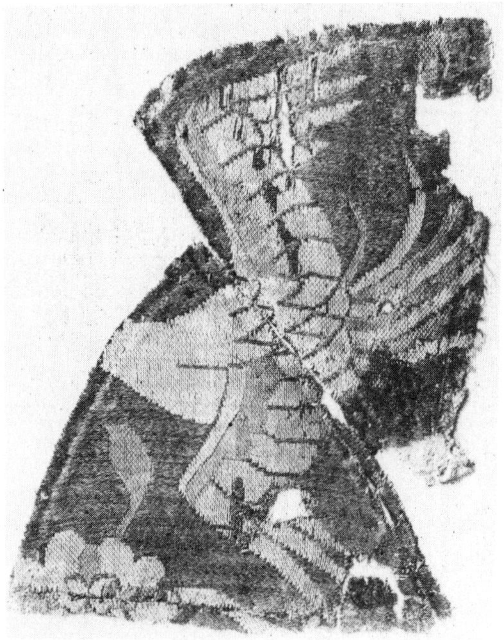

PLATE 13. Silk fragments from a cap of ivory, medium blue, and dark blue silk; a compound weave. Islamisches Museum, East Berlin, no. I 3229.

blossoms and lotus blossoms at the ends and sides of the ogee. Even the lotus and the tear-shaped blossom face in opposite directions. The delicate naturalistic drawing is consistent with Yüan art and contrasts with the more simplified, abstract, and bolder renditions in the Mamluk silks. The refined drawing of the pattern in the Yüan silk suggests that a Yüan silk was the source of inspiration for the Mamluk versions. Whether the actual layout originated in China or was woven there in imitation of Islamic layouts for export to the prosperous Mamluk market requires further investigation. The overwhelming importance of Yüan silks as transmitters of Chinese designs to the West is a topic of major significance, yet fraught with difficulties of paucity, identification, and dating.[50]

PLATE 14. Yellow silk damask robe, "the sultan" "al-Kamil"; 72 × 58 cm. Museum of Islamic Art, Cairo, no. 2740.

Stripes and Bands

One of the most fashionable layouts in Mamluk silks was the division of the space into vertical stripes or horizontal bands, sometimes of varying widths, in which a variety of elements—animal, vegetal, geometric, and epigraphic—were displayed (plates 6–11). Linear layouts reached their artistic height during the early Mamluk period not only in silks but also in inlaid metalwork and enameled glass. The concept of forming an all-over pattern by means of dividing a space into vertical or horizontal linear units in which a variety of design elements could be juxtaposed appears to have evolved slowly in a culture preoccupied with total surface embellishment. Let us consider briefly the evolution of the fashion.

Stripes and bands are inherent to textiles; they are the simplest way to introduce pattern. Stripes extend along the length of a fabric in the warp; bands occur across the width of a fabric in the weft. The combination of stripes and bands produces plaids.

In the early and medieval Islamic periods, the most common patterned textiles were probably those with stripes, which are even easier to weave than bands. The abundance is suggested by the high percentage excavated at Fustat[51] and Quseir al-Qadim.[52] Perhaps some of the striped textiles coveted by medieval authors[53] were even intended to be portrayed in Arab and Iranian miniature paintings.[54]

Despite the existence of simple striped textiles, the introduction of design elements into layouts defined by repeating lines, be they warp stripes or weft bands, did not really become fashionable until the eleventh century, when a variety of motifs appeared, foliate, figural, and linear, usually with Arabic inscriptions.[55]

Examples abound from Egypt, where bands display a variety of motifs and generic Arabic texts that are repeated at random along the length of a fabric.[56] The bands are in tapestry weave, which is the equivalent of drawing with weft yarns, on looms with manual patterning devices. In contrast, the far scarcer examples from Iran and Iraq are striped and woven on drawlooms with mechanical patterning devices that repeated the pattern in mirror image.[57] Some of the weavers who used these looms were probably responsible for transmitting the mechanical repeat technology to Egypt during the thirteenth century.

The pattern orientation in some Mamluk silks

PLATE 15. Blue and ivory silk, "the sultan, the king"; a compound weave; 14.5 × 13 in. Metropolitan Museum of Art, New York, no. 46.156.17.

PLATE 17. Pale red silk damask with European orphrey, "Glory to our master the sultan [in tear-shaped blossom] the sultan the king [in small medallion]," pattern worn in *Enthroned Madonna with Saints*, by Maestro del Bambino Vispo, c. 1430; satin damask; 16 × 15 in. Victoria and Albert Museum, London, no. 8614-1863.

continued the established tradition in Egypt of horizontal bands, despite the radical change in loom technology. The Mamluk tapestry weave in plate 8 is a rare reminder of the former weaving tradition. The artistic preference for a continuous repetition of bands along the length of a fabric is evident in the silks in plates 9 and 11, which were woven on the newly introduced drawlooms with mechanical patterning devices.

Striking rhythm and a feeling of monumentality are achieved through variations in the height, content, and drawing of the bands in the predominately blue and ivory silk in plate 9. The elegant proportions of the historic text on a foliate ground and of the eagle attacking a gazelle beside a lotus framing a deer imply a grand scale, yet the tallest band is only 8.6 cm. Integral to the success of the pattern are the narrow bands with chevrons, animals in medallions, generic texts punctuated by running animals, and the restful ivory bands. In tiny letters between the tall shafts in the large text is "al-Malik al-Nāṣir, may his victory be glorious."

PLATE 16. Green silk orphrey with gilt threads, "Glory to our master the sultan al-Malik [in tear-shaped blossom] al-Ashraf [in small medallion]," pattern worn in *Enthroned Madonna with Saints*, by the Maestro del Bambino Vispo, c. 1430; a compound weave, ground satin, pattern plain weave, wrapped gilt membrane; 114 × 19 cm. Victoria and Albert Museum, London, no. 753-1904.

PLATE 18. Chinese silk, gilt parchment strips on green ground, Yüan Dynasty (1279–1368); a compound weave; 35.2 × 60 cm. Victoria and Albert Museum, London, no. 8590-1863.

The latter words suggest that a specific sultan was intended, probably al-Nāṣir Muḥammad ibn Qalā'ūn.[58] The graceful quality of the drawing confirms the ability of the designers and weavers to adapt naturalistic features, such as the eagle, gazelle, and lotus blossom, from Yüan silks to their own repertory.[59]

The repetitive treatment of the bands in plate 11 is less refined, although wrapped metal threads enhance the pattern, along with ivory and medium and dark blue silk. Contrasting rhythm is achieved between the subdivided animated bands and the uninterrupted text bands, which extol, "Glory to our master the sultan al-Malik al-Ashraf, may his supporters be glorified." Above, the commanding knotted Kufic on a dense floral ground is reminiscent of similar drawing on mosque lamps bearing the name of Sultan Ḥasan,[60] which assists in attributing this textile to a sultan as late as Ashraf Nāṣir al-Dīn Sha'bān (1363–76).

Diverse elements are combined in mathematically organized spatial units to create a dynamic pattern in the brown and ivory striped silk in plate 6. Scale, line, pattern intensity, color, and visual orientation complement one another. The animal stripe, in mirror image, includes a transmutation

PLATE 19. Silk garment fragment, ivory simurghs amid vines and brown medallions, "the sultan"; damask weave with supplementary wefts. Hermitage Museum, Leningrad, no. Eg. 678.

PLATE 20. Ivory, medium blue, and dark blue silk; incomplete triple-cloth weave; 23 × 19 cm. Kunstgewerbemuseum, West Berlin, no. 97.224.

from an eagle's wing into a duck, while the adjacent stripe displays a prominent text at a ninety-degree angle, a feature also apparent in Iran-Iraqi silks.[61] Yet the character of the pattern is consistent with early Mamluk art, including the elegant *naskh*, "Glory to our master the sultan al-Malik

FIGURE 2. Yellow silk damask with leafy vine displaying medallions, "Glory to our master ∗ the sultan al-Malik ∗ al-Nāṣir[?] [the illustrious, al-Sharīf] ∗ the suppressor of heresy ∗ Muḥammad ibn Qalā'ūn ∗ may [Allah] perpetuate his sovereignty." Museum of Islamic Art, Cairo, no. 3899. (Drawing after Schmidt.)

al-Mu'ayyad." This stunning silk is attributed to the Rasulid Sultan Mu'ayyad Dāwūd (1297–1321), whose name also appears on Mamluk metalwork and glass with related figural decoration.[62]

The fashion for banded and striped patterns displaying a variety of design elements was not confined to the Mamluk kingdom, but spread through international commerce to Europe and Asia. In Christian Europe, Arabic script had honorific associations acquired through contact and textile trade with Muslim neighbors and the Near East during the Middle Ages. As early as the tenth century, European sources recorded the social significance of wearing garments with Arabic writing, indicating honor and a proximity to power.[63] The presence of Arabic script, rather than the content of the words, was meaningful. Testament is provided by ecclesiastical vestments made with Mamluk silks, as well as with Chinese export silks, that impart distinctly Islamic political wishes (plates 16, 22).

In Spain, striped silks with Arabic script have been found in the royal Christian tombs at Las Huelgas, Burgos, dating from the thirteenth century. They are among the earliest woven on the peninsula.[64] Following the Mamluk initiative, striped silks became increasingly popular under Nasrid rule during the fourteenth and fifteenth centuries. One silk even extols its own merits: "I am

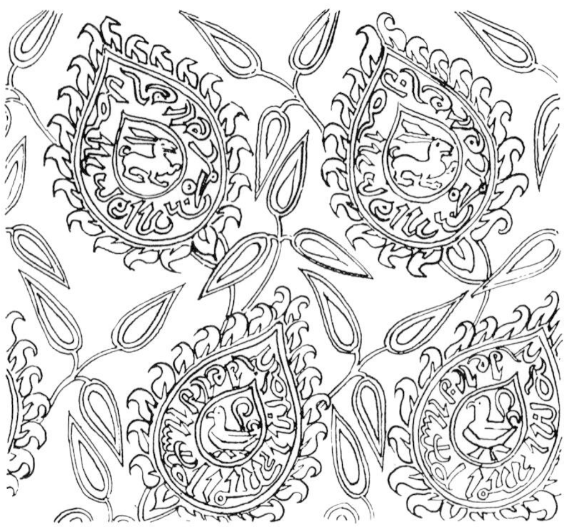

FIGURE 3. Red silk damask in two almond-shaped fragments, undulating vertical stem pattern influenced by Chinese silk patterns adapted for Mamluk market, "Glory to our master the sultan al-Malik al-Nāṣir . . . Nāṣir al-Dunya wa'l-Dīn Muḥammad Qalā'ūn," 1293–1341 (with two interruptions); satin damask. Islamisches Museum, East Berlin, no. I 3214. (Drawing after Schmidt.)

strips of gilt parchment which signal Chinese manufacture (plate 22).[68] Westerners used gilt membrane. The Chinese renditions were woven under Mongol rule (Yüan Dynasty) probably in Turkestan or farther east in Central Asia. Islamic silks with Arabic texts could have served as models for Yüan silks, since Islamic textiles and metalwork were the main imports from the Middle East in the thirteenth, fourteenth, and fifteenth centuries.[69]

Insight into Yüan striped silks may be gleaned from considering early fourteenth-century blue-and-white ceramics. Margaret Medley has shown that the methodical banded layout in early Yüan blue-and-white ceramics was based on Islamic aesthetic standards that are evident in Islamic metalwork, but were inconsistent with Chinese taste. However, the Chinese applied the banded layout to blue-and-white ceramics in order to capture the substantial Islamic market.[70]

Something comparable appears to have occurred in the silk industry. The division of the surface into methodical stripes would have been equally alien to Chinese aesthetics. Yet, as in ceramics, the Chinese appear to have copied the Islamic layout and design features, such as Arabic

for pleasure, welcome. For pleasure am I. And he who beholds me sees joy and delight."[65]

In Italy, Arabic script, usually illegible, was incorporated into numerous layouts, including striped silks, during the fourteenth century. The extensive Mamluk—and Chinese—artistic influence in this period probably occurred because the Italian industry was growing rapidly and therefore was unusually receptive to accomplished silk patterns from abroad. The auspicious associations with Arabic writing continued in many media until well into the fifteenth century, as witnessed in a Florentine painting entitled the *Death of the Virgin*, where a striped silk inscribed with pseudo-Arabic serves as the pall.[66]

Although Mamluk silks seem to have had considerable influence in Italy, little evidence exists to suggest Italian influence in the patterns of Mamluk silks, even though Italian textiles were available in Egypt and Syria, and Italian tailored garments even occasionally became fashionable. Overcoats with narrow Venetian-style sleeves were so disliked by al-Nāṣir Muḥammad that he had them banned.[67]

In the East, surviving striped silks with legible Arabic inscriptions were woven often with radiant

PLATE 21. Chinese silk damask with undulating vertical stem pattern adapted for Mamluk market, "Glory to our master the sultan al-Malik al-Nāṣir * Nāṣir al-Dunya wa'l-Dīn Muḥammad [ibn] Qalā'ūn," 1293–1341 (with two interruptions), Yüan Dynasty (1279–1368); satin damask; 10 × 10 in. Victoria and Albert Museum, London, no. 769.1898, said to be from al-A'zam.

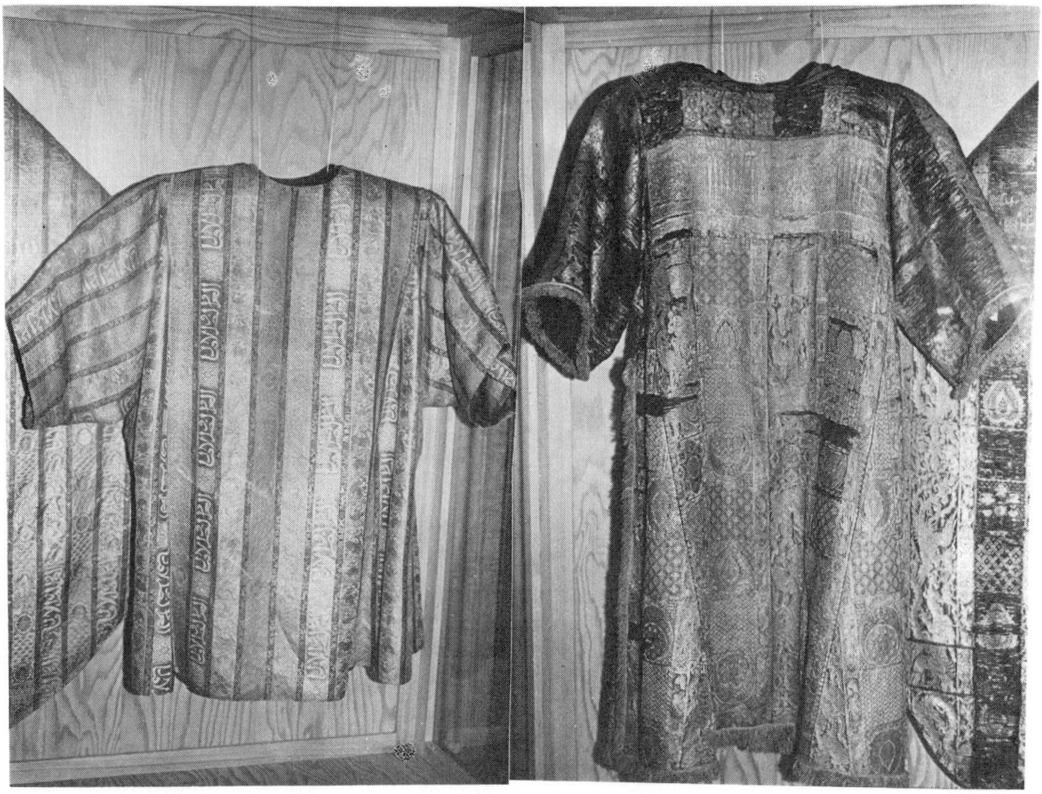

PLATE 22. Ecclesiastical vestments, Chinese export silk with gilt parchment strips, striped Islamic layout for Western market, "Glory, victory, and prosperity"; "the sultan" [backward], "work of the master ʿAbd al-ʿAziz," Yüan Dynasty (1279–1368); a compound weave. Alte Kapelle, Regensberg.

inscriptions, in order to compete successfully in the lucrative silk trade. The Chinese also added some designs from their own artistic repertory to fill the spaces. Consequently, generic Arabic texts offering "glory, victory, and prosperity" appear beside Chinese tortoises, ducks, and *feng huang* (plate 22).[71] The Chinese succeeded in weaving luxurious striped silks with radiant colors and extensive gold for export to the West, some of which have been preserved as ecclesiastical vestments.[72]

If the chance and meager survival of striped silks in Europe sheds any light on the competition between the Yüan and the Mamluk for the European market in the fourteenth century, we would have to say that the Yüan won. Perhaps the Yüan striped-silk export industry can be compared to the Japanese automobile industry today. The Japanese have combined Western preferences with their own expertise to manufacture highly successful cars for Western consumption. The Yüan export silk industry seems to have achieved comparable status and success.

Included among the striped silks woven in the East are some whose places of origin remain uncertain, owing to variations in structure, fiber content, and design elements. Whether research will clarify the problem is uncertain, but at least it will identify groups for future study.

Other Designs

Considering the economic incentives and the apparent ability of the Chinese to weave export silks for the Western market, additional silk patterns based on Islamic layouts might well be expected. One candidate with a luxurious gilt pattern on a brown ground displays features from Islamic and Chinese art (plate 23).[73] The dominant elements are Islamic: the continuous layout of dodecagons, the bold rendition of confronted parrots, and the Arabic inscription blessing, "Glory to our master the sultan, the king, the just, the wise, Nāṣir," possibly al-Nāṣir Muḥammad. The naturalistic drawing of the leaves, tendrils, and dragons are Chinese in style.

PLATE 23. Chinese export silk with gilt pattern woven with Islamic layout for Mamluk market, "Glory to our master the sultan al-Malik al-ʿĀdil al-ʿAlim Nāṣir(?), possibly Nāṣir Muḥammad ibn Qalā'ūn, 1293–1341 (with two interruptions), Yüan Dynasty (1279–1368); a compound weave (ground twill, pattern plain weave), gilt parchment strip; 70 × 21.8 cm. Kunstgewerbemuseum, West Berlin, no. 75.258.

Whether Asian weaving centers outside the vast territory Yüan had the resources to adapt patterns specifically for export during the Mongol period is doubtful. While this atypical silk has been variously attributed to Egypt, Iran, Central Asia, and China,[74] the combination of design features, the quality of the drawing, and the fiber content deny West Asian manufacture and support a Yüan attribution.

Another candidate for Yüan export is a silk with a gilt parchment pattern highlighted with medium blue on a rich blue ground (plate 24).[75] A generic Arabic text forms the ogival lattice framing staggered rows of confronted khilins and a directional composite plant. The naturalistic quality of the drawing supports Chinese rather than Islamic draftsmanship, reinforced by the Chinese character *shou* in the center of the blossom.

The significance of Yüan silks increases as research on Mamluk silks continues. At this point, Yüan silks warrant additional investigation in three main categories: Chinese silks with purely Chinese

PLATE 24. Chinese export silk, gilt parchment, ogival Islamic layout for Western market, "Glory to our master the sultan the king, the learned, the just, may his supporters be glorified," Yüan Dynasty (1279–1368); a compound weave, wrapped gilt parchment. Kunstgewerbemuseum, West Berlin, no. 68.2742.

patterns (possibly plate 18), Chinese silks with Chinese patterns adapted for the Mamluk market (plate 21), and Chinese export silks woven for the Islamic and European markets with Islamic layouts framing Islamic and Chinese design elements (plates 22–24). The extent to which the patterns in Chinese silks in any category may have transmitted designs that influenced styles in other media in the Near East deserves additional consideration in view of the many Chinese features in fourteenth- and fifteenth-century Islamic art.

Any attempt to evaluate the significance of the once thriving Mamluk silk industry clearly suffers from limited evidence and size. Hardly any silks resplendent with gold or gorgeous garments survive. Nor are they portrayed in miniature paintings, where the superficial treatment of fabric patterns in no way reflects the range and quality of existing silks. The splendid appearance of the Mamluk sultans and their courts can only be imagined through historical descriptions.

Yet the chance survival of Mamluk silks indicates high-quality production in design, dyeing, and weaving. The designers were adept at creating repeat patterns, often with only two or three colors, typically blue, ivory, and brown, that were integral to the success of a pattern rather than an additive enrichment. Whether by choice or happenstance,[76] Mamluk silks display a distinctive balance of color and design with a stylistic preference for bold and often simplified drawing. Further research will be directed toward clarifying the role of the active participants in the silk-trade triangle, headed by the Mamluk kingdom, China, and Europe.

TEXTILES AND THE DECORATIVE ARTS

One final aspect with far-reaching implications deserves to be raised concerning the significance of Mamluk textiles in a society saturated with textiles. In a pioneering study on the impact of textiles in "The Draped Universe of Islam," Lisa Golombek cites literary sources for the application of textile terminology to nontextile art and discusses several nontextile items that exhibit textile characteristics.[77] She mentions interlacing brickwork as reflecting the interlacing structure of textiles, the layout of tile revetments of buildings as reflecting the placement of wall hangings, and the location of a text on a Samarqand plate as reflecting tenth-century tiraz textiles, creating a "co-ordinated set."[78]

Turning to metalwork, we see that some early pieces, such as the roundel-patterned blanket on the Pisa griffon from the eleventh century, attempt to portray textiles.[79] Pieces from the twelfth and thirteenth centuries exhibit a fashion for total surface embellishment that suggests that some vessels were wrapped in textiles, some even having a knotted macramé fringe hanging down at the bottom.[80] Others display all-over repeat patterns, a type inherent in textiles, and even designs in mirror image, a result of loom technology. For example, an Ayyubid ewer dated A.H. 629 is enveloped in an ogival layout with adjustments for the curvature of the body.[81] A circular brass box from Mosul displays a curvilinear lattice layout (plate 5) that had to be cut severely to fit on its surface.[82]

Similarly, the organization of surface embellishment into stripes or bands suggests that textiles may have inspired the fashionable banded layout that totally envelops metalwork from the thirteenth through the fifteenth centuries. This hypothesis is supported by the appearance of a twelfth-century Khurasani bucket in the Hermitage whose surface decoration is divided into ten startling vertical stripes that even include design elements in mirror image.[83] While the vertical layout is not related to the brass material and looks incongruous on the bulbous bucket, the pattern can be readily understood as a woven silk textile.[84] Perhaps the bucket was intended to be coordinated with striped silks to form a matching set. Fortunately, however, striped metalwork did not become fashionable and banded metalwork did, bands being more complementary to an object's shape.

Design similarities between Mamluk silks and metalwork include individual details such as animal chases, calligraphy, and framing devices; however, the closest stylistic comparisons appear in the rare tapestry-woven textiles rather than the overwhelming majority of drawloom silks. There is a logical, technical reason for this (plate 8):[85] only tapestry-woven textiles have a technical freedom comparable to that of inlaid metalwork, in which fiber or metal can be inserted in a desired area to form a pattern.

In considering the hypothesis that textiles were the source of artistic influence for the banded layout of inlaid metalwork, rather than the traditional view that metalwork initiated the fashion, one final question should be raised. Was the influence direct or indirect, conscious or unconscious? Did the banded layout on metalwork, as well as on enameled glass and ceramics, reflect an existing aesthetic preference for the division of the surface into repeating bands that were so abundant in Mamluk textiles, or did prestigious, luxurious Mamluk silks directly inspire imitation? Recalling the intrinsic nature of bands in textiles, it seems highly plausible that textiles provided both unconscious and conscious influence on the banded layout of decoration applied to the surface of metalwork, glass, and ceramics.

ROYAL ONTARIO MUSEUM
TORONTO

NOTES

1. On the role of textiles, see Ira M. Lapidus, *Muslim Cities in the Later Middle Ages* (Cambridge, Mass., 1967), p. 31. On their role in Fatimid Egypt, see S. D. Goitein, *A Mediterranean Society: The Jewish Communities of the Arab World as Portrayed in the Documents of the Cairo Geniza*, vol. 3, *The Family* (Berkeley, Calif., 1978), pp. 128ff.

2. R. B. Serjeant, *Islamic Textiles: Material for a History up to the Mongol Conquest* (Beirut, 1972), p. 153 (reprint of articles in *Ars Islamica* 9–16 [1942–51]).

3. L. A. Mayer, *Mamluk Costume: A Survey* (Geneva, 1952), pp. 12, 15, 21, 49, 53, 67; Eliyahu Ashtor, "The Social Isolation of Ahl Adh-Dhimma," in *The Medieval Near East: Social and Economic History, Collected Studies* (London, 1978), pp. 76ff.

4. Mayer, *Mamluk Costume*, pp. 57ff.

5. Serjeant, *Islamic Textiles*, pp. 149, 150.

6. Jonathan Brookner, "Textiles," and Janet H. Johnson, "Appendix: Statistics," in Donald S. Whitcomb and Janet H. Johnson, *Quseir al-Qadim: Preliminary Report* (Cairo, 1979), pp. 183–95; Carl Johan Lamm, *Cotton in Medieval Textiles of the Near East* (Paris, 1937), p. 160, pl. 20, on double-cloth weave. Double cloth in Dumbarton Oaks Research Library and Collections, Washington, D.C., 33.47.

7. Serjeant, *Islamic Textiles*, pp. 150, 153.

8. Lapidus, *Muslim Cities*, p. 60.

9. Serjeant, *Islamic Textiles*, p. 8.

10. Eliyahu Ashtor, *A Social and Economic History of the Near East in the Middle Ages* (Berkeley, Calif., 1976), pp. 308–09.

11. Ibid., pp. 306ff.

12. Otto von Falke was the pioneer in 1913; see his *Decorative Silks*, 3d ed. (New York, 1936); also A. F. Kendrick, *Catalogue of Muhammadan Textiles of the Medieval Period, Victoria and Albert Museum* (London, 1924); Ernst Kühnel, *Islamische Stoffe aus ägyptischen Grabern* (Berlin, 1927); Heinrich J. Schmidt, "Damaste der Mamlukenzeit," *Ars Islamica* 1 (1934) : 99–109, and idem, *Alte Seidenstoffe* (Brunswick, Germany, 1958); Carl Johan Lamm, "Some Mamluk Embroideries," *Ars Islamica* 4 (1937) : 65–76, and idem, *Cotton*; Mohammed Taha Hussein, *Mamlukische Kunstformen in der Seidenweberei des 13. bis 15. Jahrhunderts* (Ph.D. diss., Universität zu Köln, 1963).

13. Nicholas B. Millet, "Gebel Adda Preliminary Report, 1965–66," *Journal of the American Research Center in Egypt* 4 (1967) : 53–63; Brookner, "Textiles," and Johnson, "Appendix," pp. 183–95.

14. Blazons appear in applied work, as either embroidery or fabric applique, and on printed linens; Esin Atıl, *Renaissance of Islam: Art of the Mamluks* (Washington, D.C., 1981), no. 124.

15. Two frequent examples are double-cloth weave with two colors (plates 3, 6) and incomplete triple cloth with three colors (plates 12, 20). Double-cloth weave has two coequal weave structures, usually plain weave (tabby), that are distinct from each other and are interconnected only to form a pattern. Incomplete triple cloth has a third matching warp and weft set. Each set interlaces on the face to form areas of solid color while the two warp and weft sets not in use on the face are interlaced together on the back (3/1 twill). See Irene Emery, *The Primary Structures of Fabrics: An Illustrated Classification* (Washington, D.C., 1966), pp. 155–59.

16. Serjeant, *Islamic Textiles*, pp. 119, 164; on availability of dyes, see Ashtor, *Social and Economic History*, p. 308; on the high cost of dyeing, see S. D. Goitein, *Mediterranean Society*, vol. 1, *Economic Foundations* (Berkeley, Calif., 1967), pp. 106, 107.

17. Cotton textiles were imported from India with resist-dyed and stamped patterns.

18. Sericulture prospered in Syria, and lower-grade silk was also available from Iran, but Egypt was climatically unsuitable for producing silk.

19. The type of gilt thread assists in determining provenance. Mamluk silks have gilt membrane wound around an ivory-colored silk thread, sometimes paired with a plain silk thread. Flat strips of gilt parchment were imports from East Asia, mainly China. Only ten Mamluk silks with wrapped gilt membrane have been identified: plates 1, 7, 8, 11, 12, 16; Royal Ontario Museum, Toronto, 978.76.1175; Yale University Art Gallery, New Haven, striped; Millet, "Gebel Adda," p. 60; Atıl, *Renaissance*, no. 116.

20. Comments are confined to Egyptian textiles, since Syrian textiles from preceding centuries await identification.

21. H. Ling Roth, *Ancient Egyptian and Greek Looms* (1913; reprint ed., McMinnville, Oreg., 1978), pp. 3–21. Egyptian and Syrian compound weaves in silk and wool, fifth through eighth centuries A.D., were woven on drawlooms with mechanical patterning devices. That technology appears to have been lost, based on several thousand Egyptian textiles of the ninth to twelfth centuries; Adele Coulin Weibel, *Two Thousand Years of Textiles: The Figured Textiles of Europe and the Near East* (1952; reprint ed., New York, 1972), figs. 44–54; Nancy Pence Britton, *A Study of Some Early Islamic Textiles in the Museum of Fine Arts, Boston* (Boston, 1938), pp. 30ff.

22. Damask is believed to have come from Damascus where Mamluk damasks were probably woven and exported to Europe. They are the oldest known Islamic damasks and are roughly contemporary with the Chinese; both predate European damasks. A damask is a monochrome simple weave, patterned by the contrast between the two faces of a satin or a twill weave. Simple weaves have only one set of warp and weft elements.

23. Compound weaves have more than one set of either or both warp and weft elements.

24. See n. 15. Plates 9 and 10 are one-warp double cloths.

25. The intended ruler is indicated by the blessing that follows the title. Museum of Islamic Art, Cairo, no. 8228, unpublished, *naskh*: "the sultan al-Malik al-Ṣāliḥ, the devoted [*al-'ab(d)*]," in chevron layout in brown and ivory silk double cloth, 5 by 12 cm. Two of the four Mamluk sultans with this title ruled longer than a year, Ṣāliḥ ʿImād al-Dīn Isma'īl (1342–45) and Ṣāliḥ Ṣalāḥ al-Dīn Ṣāliḥ (1351–54). The other two ruled 1381–82 and 1421–22.

26. Two banded and one striped silk attributed to al-Nāṣir Muḥammad ibn Qalā'ūn (1293–1341, with two interruptions) on stylistic grounds. Al-Nāṣir Muḥammad was the first of five Mamluk sultans with the title al-Nāṣir. The second ruled less than a year in 1342, followed by Sultan Ḥasan (1347–51, 1354–61). The Burji sultans are stylistically too late. Atıl, *Renaissance*, no. 113, "Glory to our master the sultan al-Malik al-Nāṣir"; Schmidt, "Damaste," fig. 12, "Glory to our master the sultan al-Malik al-Nāṣir"; Kühnel, *Islamische Stoffe*, 80, no. 3215, pl. 48 (cropped), "Glory to our master the sultan al-Nāṣir."

27. Millet, "Gebel Adda," p. 60, striped winding sheet with gilt threads, Jabal Adda, late thirteenth century (similar to plate 7), "Glory and victory and long life"; Ministry of Culture of the United Arab Republic, *Islamic Art in Egypt: 969–1517* (Cairo: 1969), no. 262, pl. 45; Museum of Islamic Art, Cairo, no. 23899.

28. If it is not generic, the title al-Ashraf in both examples can only refer to one of two of the nine Mamluk sultans with this title, Ashraf Ṣalāḥ al-Dīn Khalīl (1290–93), or ʿAlā' al-Dīn Kūjūk (1341–42). The layout also occurs on an inlaid brass box made sometime between 1233 and 1259; Douglas Barrett, *Islamic Metalwork in the British Museum* (London, 1949), fig. 18.

29. A mantle for a statue of the Virgin in an almost identical pattern in the same structure but with different colors is shown in Atıl, *Renaissance*, no. 116, Cleveland Museum of Art, 39.40.

30. Anthony Welch, *Calligraphy in the Arts of the Muslim World* (Austin, Tex., and New York, 1979), p. 52, Ibn Khaldūn.

31. Friedrich Spuhler, *Islamic Carpets and Textiles in the Keir Collection* (London, 1978), no. 91.

32. Lisa Golombek and Veronika Gervers, "Tiraz Fabrics in the Royal Ontario Museum," *Studies in Textile History in Memory of Harold B. Burnham*, ed. Veronika Gervers (Toronto, 1977), pp. 87–88.

33. I know of only one other Mamluk tapestry-woven textile; Maurice S. Dimand, *A Handbook of Muhammadan Art*, 3d ed. (New York, 1958), fig. 167.

34. See n. 28.

35. Millet, "Gebel Adda," p. 60.

36. Sultan Ḥasan, the only other sultan with the same title, can be rejected on stylistic grounds; his dates are too late.

37. Papal inventory listing Tartar Chinese silks in Rome before 1295; Agnes Geijer, *A History of Textile Art* (London, 1979), pp. 143, 147, 114.

38. Von Falke, *Decorative Silks*, figs. 285, 286; Schmidt, "Damaste," fig. 96; Sherman E. Lee and Wai-Kam Ho, *Chinese Art under the Mongols: The Yüan Dynasty (1279–1368)* (Cleveland, 1968), no. 300.

39. Both Yüan and Mamluk damasks have twill and satin structures.

40. Kendrick, *Catalogue of Muhammadan Textiles*, p. 40.

41. Studied only from reproductions.

42. Basil Gray, *Persian Painting* (Lausanne, 1961), p. 38.

43. Louise W. Mackie, "Rugs and Textiles," in *Turkish Art*, ed. Esin Atıl (Washington, D.C., and New York, 1980), pp. 304, 306; figs. 172, 173. Idem, "Native and Foreign Influences in Carpets Woven in Spain during the 15th Century," *Hali: The International Journal of Oriental Carpets and Textiles* 2, no. 2 (Summer 1979) : 94, 95, figs. 28–30.

44. Mackie, "Rugs and Textiles," pp. 354–55, 366, figs. 206, 218.

45. Millet, "Gebel Adda," p. 60.

46. A blue and white silk reveals "I am the moon" in angular and rounded script on the side of a fish, with a baby fish beneath; Museum of Islamic Art, Cairo, no. 7800, unpublished. Both silks read by Muhammad Abbas and Dr. David King.

47. Two rare blue and white striped cottons with similar patterns are in the Textile Museum, Washington, D.C., and the Metropolitan Museum of Art, New York, 27.169.5.

48. Enthroned Madonna and Child by the "Maestro del Bambino Vispo," in Brigitte Klesse, *Seidenstoffe in der italienischen Malerei des 14. Jahrhunderts* (Bern, 1967), pp. 72, 73, figs. 87, 88, cat. no. 226.

49. Atıl, *Renaissance*, no. 116.

50. Yüan silks survived in European treasuries and Egyptian soil; few are in China. See Hsio-Yen Shih, "Textile Finds in the People's Republic of China," *Studies in Textile History in Memory of Harold B. Burnham*, ed. Veronika Gervers (Toronto, 1977), p. 323.

51. Blue and white striped linens were the largest pattern group among about 3,000 textiles excavated in 1980 by George Scanlon and dated c. 750–1100.

52. Brookner, "Textiles," pp. 183ff.

53. Serjeant, *Islamic Textiles*, indexes: *burd*, *ḥibara*, *ḥulla*, *miḳrama*, *misḥ*, *mukhaṭṭat*, *muraiyash*.

54. *Khilʿa*, in David Talbot Rice and Basil Gray, *The Illustrations of the "World History" of Rashid al-Din* (Edinburgh, 1976), fig. 50.

55. A rare banded curtain, Egypt, 4th century, wool tapestry, in Louise W. Mackie and Anne P. Rowe, *Masterpieces in the Textile Museum* (Washington, D.C., 1976), no. 1 (10′8″ by 5′11″, no. 71.118).

56. Britton, *Some Early Islamic Textiles*, figs. 80–83, 87. Many examples in the Royal Ontario Museum, Toronto.

57. Spuhler, *Islamic Carpets and Textiles*, p. 138, no. 81 (color); Weibel, *Two Thousand Years*, fig. 111 (Cleveland).

58. Al-Nāṣir Muḥammad was the first of five

Mamluk sultans with this title. The second ruled in 1342 followed by Sultan Ḥasan (1347–61, with one interruption). The Burji sultans are too late stylistically.

59. Kendrick, *Catalogue of Muhammadan Textiles*, pl. 21, no. 995.

60. Gaston Wiet, *Lampes et bouteilles en verre émaillé, catalogue général du Musée Arabe du Caire* (Cairo, 1929), pls. 25–27.

61. See n. 57.

62. If a sultan was intended, the two fifteenth-century Mamluk sultans are too late stylistically. For comparisons, see Atıl, *Renaissance*, nos. 22, 50.

63. Irene Bierman, "Fatimid Art and Trade," paper presented at the American Research Center in Egypt Annual Meeting, Detroit, Mich., April 29–30, 1977.

64. Florence Lewis May, *Silk Textiles of Spain: Eighth to Fifteenth Century* (New York, 1957), pp. 56ff., esp. figs. 58, 64, 67, 68, also figs. 86, 101, 102. Dorothy G. Shepherd, "The Textiles from Las Huelgas de Burgos," *Needle and Bobbin Club Bulletin* (*New York*) 35, nos. 1 and 2 (1951) : 2–26.

65. Welch, *Calligraphy*, no. 18 (Textile Museum).

66. By a follower of Andrea del Castagno, Yale University Art Gallery, New Haven, no. 1871.38. For Italian silks with Mamluk influence, see von Falke, "Decorative Silks," figs 431, 426, 343, 295 (and related group 296–303), considered Spanish or possibly Italian. See also Schmidt, "Damaste," figs. 189, 193.

67. Mayer, *Mamluk Costume*, p. 22.

68. Only two non-Mamluk striped silks associated with West Asia are known, each with the name of a ruler. The Iranian Abu Sa'id (1317–35; burial garment of Duke Rudolf IV of Austria, d. 1365); Phyllis Ackerman, "The Textile Arts, Textiles of the Islamic Period, A History," in *A Survey of Persian Art*, ed. A. U. Pope (London and New York, 1939), vol. 3, p. 2056; vol. 6, pl. 1003; possibly of Iranian manufacture (silk seen only in photograph). Turkish Sultan Beyazid Han, probably Bāyazīd I (1389–1402); Mackie, "Rugs and Textiles," p. 346, fig. 199; possibly of Chinese origin (silk seen only in photograph).

69. Margaret Medley, "Chinese Ceramics and Islamic Design," in *The Westward Influence of the Chinese Arts from the 14th to the 18th Century*, ed. William Watson, Colloquies on Art and Archaeology in Asia, no. 3 (London, 1972), p. 2; based on Chinese sources.

70. Ibid., pp. 3–8; idem, *Yüan Porcelain and Stoneware* (London, 1975), pp. 33–37.

71. For details of silks in plates 23 and 24, see Ackerman, "Textile Arts," pl. 1001, and von Falke, "Decorative Silks," figs. 288, 289, 291–93.

72. None in Egypt; main collections in Gdansk and Lübeck. Walter Mannowsky, *Der Danziger Paramentenschatz*, 5 vols. (Berlin, 1931–38). A silk of comparable Mamluk luxury quality with gilt threads is shown in plate 16 in this article.

73. The gold is the flat gilt parchment strip used in East Asia, not the gilt membrane used in West Asia and Europe (misidentified as gilt membrane in Hayward Gallery, *The Arts of Islam* (London, 1976), no. 15.

74. Von Falke, "Decorative Silks," fig. 287; Ackerman, "Textile Arts," pp. 2053, 2059, no. 14, pl. 1000.

75. Gilt parchment wound around a silk core rather than typical flat gilt strips. For Chinese silks with wound gilt parchment, see Pauline Simmons, *Chinese Patterned Silks* (New York, 1958), fig. 25.

76. See n. 16.

77. Lisa Golombek, "The Draped Universe of Islam," in *Iconography: Content and Context of Visual Arts in the Islamic World*, Proceedings from the Richard Ettinghausen Memorial Colloquium, 1980 (forthcoming).

78. Ibid., MS pp. 24–30, figs. 15–23.

79. David Talbot Rice, *Islamic Art* (New York, 1965), fig. 93.

80. Inlaid brass ewer, Mosul, 1232, in *Islamic Metalwork*, fig. 12. Versions of macramé fringe pattern appear at the bottom and top of the patterned surface, or at the neck. See inlaid brass ewer, Damascus, 1258, in Ministère des Affaires Culturelles, Réunion des Musées Nationaux, *Arts de l'Islam des origines à 1700 dans les collections publiques françaises* (Paris, 1971), exhibition cat., fig. 152.

81. Freer Gallery of Art, Washington, D.C., no. 55.22, in Esin Atıl, *Art of the Arab World* (Washington, D.C., 1975), no. 26.

82. Inlaid brass box, dated c. 1233–59, in Barrett, *Islamic Metalwork*, fig. 18.

83. Ernst J. Grube, *The World of Islam* (New York, 1966), fig. 42, by Muḥammad ibn Nāṣir ibn Muḥammad al-Harawi.

84. Since twelfth-century Iranian striped silks are rare, the best comparisons can be found among slightly later silks; von Falke, "Decorative Silks," fig. 309.

85. See n. 33.

DAVID JAMES

Some Observations on the Calligrapher and Illuminators of the Koran of Rukn al-Dīn Baybars al-Jāshnagīr

The Koran of Rukn al-Dīn Baybars[1] is one of the earliest and finest examples of Mamluk book art. It has received some attention by scholars—most recently in 1976 when it was shown at the World of Islam Festival in London—but has never had a proper examination. This is unfortunate, because it contains interesting visual and documentary information linking it to other manuscripts produced in the early fourteenth century, and, while much has been written on Mamluk manuscripts over the past several decades, this writing has centered entirely on the handful of fourteenth-century picture books. It is no denigration of those scholarly efforts to say that these are isolated phenomena perpetuating an archaic (pre-1225) form of painting whose artists were uninterested in—and no doubt unaware of—the sophisticated development of that form which had occurred in the Baghdad *Maqāmāt* manuscripts between 1225 and 1258.[2] The magnificent Korans produced in the reign of Sultan Shaʿbān II, on the other hand, represent the coming together of many different strands of a vital and vigorous tradition, of which the manuscript discussed here is the earliest manifestation.

At the beginning of the fourteenth century, the Mamluk Bahri sultanate had been in existence for half a century. The defeat of the last Crusader strongholds and the stemming of the Mongol advance had secured its survival for the immediate future. Some of its ablest rulers had appeared, and some of its greatest monuments had already been erected. The surprise, then, is to learn that from this glittering half-century not a single Mamluk Koran is known. Nevertheless this hiatus is more than made up for by the appearance in 1305 of the Koran of Baybars al-Jāshnagīr.

In its size, style, quality of material, and overall appearance the manuscript seems to have all the characteristics of a deluxe Mamluk Koran. The manuscript is copied in *asbaʿ*, or "sevenths," the least popular of all the divisions used for the Koranic text.[3] As far as we know, it is the only Mamluk Koran to have been produced in this way; multipart Korans were in any case not particularly favored by the Mamluks.[4] The manuscript measures 48 by 32 cm, significantly larger than most Korans before the time of Sultan Shaʿbān and the largest of those dating from the first twenty years of the fourteenth century. The script employed is unknown elsewhere. Unlike most later Korans, this one is signed in several places by the illuminators. Finally, several of the compositions used by the artists have no precedent, so far as I am aware. Thus upon examination the manuscript turns out to be quite the opposite of typical, except in one respect: it was commissioned by a high-ranking Mamluk official with no expense spared.

The patron in question was Rukn al-Dīn Baybars, already one of the most important officers of state, and one whose importance was destined to grow even greater before his sudden demise in 1310. This *jāshnagīr*, or "taster," was appointed *ustādar*, or majordomo, of al-Nāṣir Muḥammad in 1299, during the latter's second reign. Around the time the manuscript was commissioned he is spoken of by chroniclers as *atābak al-jaysh*, "commander-in-chief." His public works are attested by the minarets of the mosque of al-Ḥākim, which he restored after the earthquake of 1302. His substantial khanqah[5] still stands nearby, though now devoid of his name in its dedicatory stone inscription: it was carefully chipped away on instructions from al-Nāṣir Muḥammad in 1310 after his return from exile, into which he had gone rather than suffer further humiliation at Baybars's hands during the shaky months of the latter's rule as sultan, under the title of al-Muẓaffar Baybars.

Although the seven-part Koran is devoid of any waqfiyya or related inscriptions, there is no doubt that it was ordered by its commissioner, Baybars, for his brand new khanqah. This we are told by Ibn Iyās in an unusually detailed account, which I will quote in full because of its interest and importance:

> In that year [705/1305–06] Atābak Baybars al-Jāshnagīr began to build his khanqah which is in the square of Bāb al-ʿĪd, opposite the Darb al-Aṣfar. It is said that when the building of the khanqah was completed, Sheikh Sharaf al-Dīn ibn al-Wāḥid wrote a copy of the Koran in seven parts for Atābak Baybars. It was written on paper of Baghdadi size, in *ashʿār* script. It is said that Baybars spent 1,700 dinars on these volumes so that they could be written in gold. It was placed in the khanqah and is one of the beauties of the age.[6]

Despite the lack of waqfiyya stating the terms under which the Koran was endowed to the khanqah, there is no doubt that this account refers to our manuscript. It was completed by Ibn al-Wāḥid in 705/1305–06. Illumination must have taken until A.H. 706 or longer. The khanqah was not completed until 709/1309. Whether the manuscript remained with Baybars in the intervening years, was kept somewhere in the khanqah while the building progressed, or remained with the craftsmen who produced it is not known.[7] In any event, the gap in time between the completion of the manuscript and the completion of the building probably explains the absence of a waqfiyya. In 1309, Baybars was also struggling to hold on to the throne he had obtained in April; within twelve months, in April 1310, he was overthrown, imprisoned, and executed. Under the circumstances it is safe to assume that the Koran was never officially endowed.

The calligraphy was executed by Ibn al-Wāḥid, and the manuscript is the only unquestionable example of his work. Born Sharaf al-Dīn Muḥammad al-Zarʿī in Damascus in 1249,[8] Ibn al-Wāḥid studied under the famous Yāqūt al-Mustaʿṣimī in Baghdad and was a master of *naskh*, *rayḥān* and *muḥaqqaq*. He soon became a teacher with pupils of his own. He was also a belle-lettrist and poet, some of whose verses have come down to us, and he composed at least one treatise in verse on calligraphy. However, his best-known writing in this field is his commentary on the poem by Ibn al-Bawwāb in praise of calligraphy.[9]

It was probably as a man of letters, rather than as a calligrapher, that biographers thought him worthy of mention. He was also a good linguist. We are told that when the Ilkhanid Sultan Ghāzān sent a letter to al-Nāṣir Muḥammad in 1301, it was Ibn al-Wāḥid who translated it. His facility in Persian, and perhaps other languages, was no doubt a result of his years in Mongol Baghdad, and it, along with his poetry and calligraphy, won him an appointment to the Mamluk chancellory sometime after 1301. Despite all these obvious recommendations, Ibn al-Wāḥid does not appear to have been much of a success as a civil servant. He was lazy, keeping work for a long time and sometimes never completing it, a laxity that can perhaps be explained by his fondness for hashish, in praise of which he wrote some verses. If negligent in his duties, he seems, however—if we are to believe a bit of malicious gossip by Ibn Ḥajar—to have been enterprising in other areas. A Koran written by him could sell for as much as a thousand dinars. According to Ibn Ḥajar, a pupil would copy his hand, and Ibn al-Wāḥid would buy the result from the pupil for four hundred dinars and then turn around and sell it for a thousand after signing the manuscript in his own hand. He was undeniably an outstanding master calligrapher, however, as the Baybars Koran shows, so perhaps we should forgive him these foibles.

The Koran was copied over a period of at least a year. The second *subʿ* (seventh) dates from Jumādā II 704/December 1304, and the final one from some time in 1305–06. Each part took about eight weeks to produce—excluding illumination—meaning that the work must have started in August or September 1304. There are six lines of text on each page, another curious feature, since Koran pages are usually copied in odd numbers of lines—seven, nine, eleven, and thirteen being the numbers most favored by Mamluk calligraphers.

The script (fig. 1)—gold outlined in black with silver diacriticals—is unique; no other known Koran employs this peculiar type.[10] Ibn Iyās refers to it as *ashʿār*. The only Mamluk writer who gives any information on *qalam al-ashʿār* is the late fifteenth-century calligrapher al-Ṭībī, according to whom it is a specific script.[11] However, *ashʿār* (*tashʿīr* in Arabic and Persian usage) normally refers to script that is outlined in hairlike strokes (Arabic *shaʿra*, a "hair"; pl., *ashʿār*), as is the script in the Baybars Koran. However, there is no mystery about the source of Ibn al-Wāḥid's choice. The script he employed was a *thuluth* type normally used in Cairo at this time for writing Koran sura headings (plate 1).

Why did he employ this unusual form?

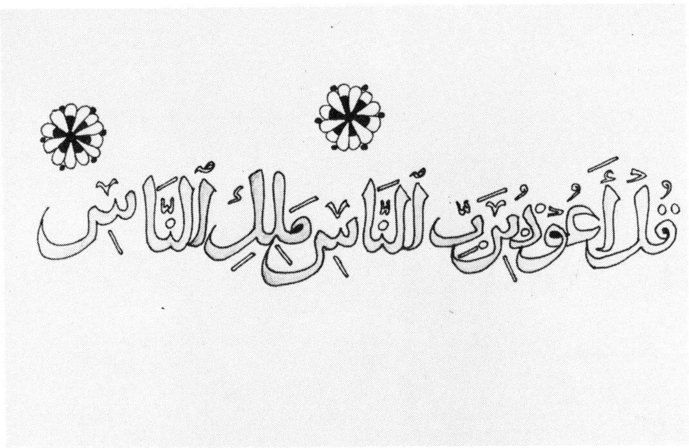

FIGURE 1. Example of the *thuluth-ash'ār* script of Ibn al-Wāḥid (Koran 113.1–2). The characters are in gold, outlined (*musha'ar*) in black; diacriticals are in silver, and other orthographic signs in red, blue, and gold. British Library MS add 22.412.

Current studies on fourteenth-century Mamluk and Ilkhanid Korans point out that the usual script for large-format manuscripts was *muḥaqqaq*, and this was certainly true for several of the manuscripts produced in Baghdad and Mosul. However, it was not the case with Mamluk Korans at this time. The earliest Mamluk Koran in *muḥaqqaq* dates from 1320, and even that is a far cry from the superb *muḥaqqaq-jalī* used in the time of Sultan Sha'bān.

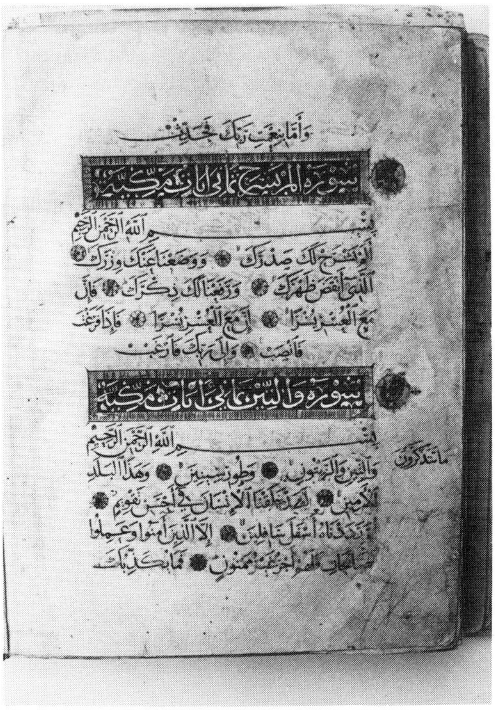

PLATE 1. Page from a Koran copied in Cairo by Muḥammad ibn 'Abdallāh al-Khazrajī, c. 1305. The script is *naskh*; sura headings are in *thuluth-ash'ār* (see also plate 3). Chester Beatty MS 1457.

Because Baybars specified that the Koran be copied in gold, presumably the calligrapher would have used the gold script with which he was most familiar, that is, the one used for sura headings. The medium may well have dictated the script used. Or did it?

There might be another explanation. Large-format, multipart Korans were certainly an Ilkhanid phenomenon, but were they ever a Mamluk one? There are several examples of enormous Ilkhanid multipart Korans in *muḥaqqaq*, in both black ink and gold paint, but no dated Mamluk Korans that can compare in any way with them until after 1350. In short, if there was no tradition of large, multipart Korans in Egypt, would there have been a traditional script? If it is argued that they could quite easily have used *muḥaqqaq* or *rayḥān*, then my answer would have to be, first, that *rayḥān* was quite apparently a script the Mamluks found unattractive. Although the famous Öljaytü Koran of 1313, written in *rayḥān*, was in Cairo from at least 1327, not a single example of a Mamluk Koran in *rayḥān* can be found.[12] As to why *muḥaqqaq* was not employed, the answer, I think, is that it was considered a "Tartar" script and was not popular as long as the Ilkhanids were in power.

We can find evidence to support this by looking at another manuscript, also from the early fourteenth century, now divided between the Chester Beatty Library[13] and the Prussian State Library (plate 2).[14] Like the British Library manuscript, it is written in a non-Koranic hand, probably *ṭūmār*, the chancellory hand. It is also multipart, uses a rare three-line division of the text, with the large gold script of the Baybars Koran for sura headings. Although the surviving illumination consists only of marginal ornaments, these are

PLATE 2. Part of a Koran copied in Cairo, probably by Ibn al-Wāḥid, and illuminated by Ṣandal or a pupil of his, c. 1306–11. The script is probably *ṭūmār*; sura headings are in *thuluth-ashʿār*. Chester Beatty MS 1437.

identical to those of the Baybars Koran. All this suggests that this is another example of the work of Ibn al-Wāḥid, produced in the period between his completion of the Baybars Koran and his death in the Manṣūrī Hospital in Cairo in 1311, and that it bears out the hypothesis that this kind of Koranic manuscript was probably a new departure for the Mamluks. Thus, it is likely that the craftsmen who illuminated the Baybars Koran were working on a relatively unfamiliar project, and perhaps had been assembled by Ibn al-Wāḥid from different places especially for the occasion. At any rate, there are wide variations in their styles.

Illumination occurs in the form of marginal ornaments to indicate each fifth and tenth verse and to mark passages where ritual prostration is required. Sura headings are not illuminated. The major areas of illumination are the opening folios, where there is a double-page composition, and the final page of each part around the colophon.

The Baybars Koran contains the signatures of three people: *subʿ* 1 bears the name Muḥammad ibn Mubādir;[15] *subʿ* 3 and *subʿ* 5 are signed by Abū Bakr, called "Ṣandal"[16] ("sandalwood"); and *subʿ* 7 bears an inscription by Aydughdī ibn ʿAbdallāh. I will consider the last inscription first, because it has led to some confusion. It is found above and below the opening pages of text and reads as follows: "This noble *subʿ* and its accompanying parts were illuminated by the poor slave desiring Allah's help—exalted be He—yearning for His pardon and mercy, Aydughdī ibn ʿAbdallāh al-Badrī, may Allah forgive him, in 705 [1305]."[17] This seems to contradict the self-evident facts that three of the parts are signed by other painters, that the style of each is very distinct, and that even this final part is obviously the work, not of Aydughdī, but of Ṣandal. The explanation, therefore, can only be that Aydughdī did not illuminate each portion of the manuscript, but performed some other task. The word used by Aydughdī to describe what he did is not the usual *dhahhaba, yudhahhib*, "to gild," but the more obscure verb *zammaka, yuzammik*, which some dictionaries translate as "to incrust" or "to illustrate." It is evident that what we have is a technical term used at the time to mean some very specific task other than illumination in the usual sense. This is not the only instance of its use by Mamluk artists in the early fourteenth century.

We are dealing, then, with a team of three craftsmen: two illuminators, Ibn Mubādir and Ṣandal, and an assistant who executed some secondary task. Four of the seven parts—1, 2, 4, and 6—appear to have been illuminated by Ibn Mubādir. The opening compositions of these parts show him to have been a rigidly precise, though in many ways quite original, painter. None of the designs he employs are otherwise known, apart from another Koran illuminated by him. Two of them—in 4 and 6 (plate 3)—are almost identical. They consist of a large central hexagon on a bed of six-pointed stars connected by white lines forming segments of a circle. The segments are bordered by plain gold alternating palmettes on a blank ground with blue and orange teardrops.

The composition in part 2 is the most unusual of all. Its main features are octagons: a large one in the center and four smaller ones surrounding it, set into an "exploded" star-tile and cross panel of the type regularly used in Iran in the twelfth and thirteenth centuries for decorating interiors with ceramic tiles. Above and below are fine white Kufic verses on gold arabesques, decorated, as is the central panel, with a tiny treble-dot motif. The

PLATE 3. Illuminated folio from the Baybars Koran, opening recto of *sub'* 6, illuminated in Cairo by Muḥammad ibn Mubādir, 1304–05. British Library MS add 22.41.

outer border is equally unusual. It consists of strapwork squares at the outer corners with intervening palmettes similar to those in parts 4 and 6.

The composition in part 1 is perhaps the least interesting, though as far as I know there is no other example of its use in a Mamluk Koran. It is based on the same star-tile and cross pattern as in part 2, with the cross shapes cut to fit into the central square panel. White Kufic inscriptions appear above and below, on a background similar to those in part 2. The outer palmette border resembles those in the other three parts, though this time the teardrops have been modeled.

Only part 1 bears Ibn Mubādir's signature, but I am quite satisfied that all four are illuminated by him. It is true that there are a number of minor differences between part 1 and the other three—the Kufic is of a slightly more squat variety, the teardrops are modeled, and so on—but even taken together they are not enough to make me believe that the unsigned parts are by another unnamed painter. Part 7, after all, is quite clearly the work of Ṣandal, though it does not bear his signature. Other illuminated pages in the four parts bear out the attribution to Ibn Mubādir. All the opening pages of text and the colophon have backgrounds composed of tight geometric patterns, reminiscent of those found on contemporary metalwork (plate 4).

That Ibn Mubādir worked on four parts, including the opening one, suggests that he was the senior painter. However, in the only two references to this Koran (in Ibn Ḥajar and al-Ṣafadī), Ṣandal's name alone is mentioned in connection with the illumination of the manuscript, indicating that he was regarded as the master painter. Nevertheless it is surprising that the influence of Ibn Mubādir on later manuscript illuminations seems to have been nonexistent. Although there are many Mamluk manuscripts dating from the next thirty years, only one has any of the features we have noted in his

PLATE 4. Detail of one of the types of composition employed by Muḥammad ibn Mubādir in the Baybars Koran. Most of these all-over geometric patterns are used in contemporary or earlier metalwork from Syria and Egypt. Chester Beatty MS 1457.

PLATE 5. Second example of the composition employed by Muḥammad ibn Mubādir in the Baybars Koran. Chester Beatty MS 1457.

work. This exception is a manuscript in the Chester Beatty Library,[18] copied by a superb master of *naskh*, Muḥammad al-Khazrajī, whose work we also know elsewhere.[19] It includes compositions identical to those in the Baybars Koran (plate 5) and is obviously by Ibn Mubādir, though his name has been obliterated. The influence of Ṣandal seems to have been stronger and much longer lasting than that of Ibn Mubādir.

Ṣandal's compositions are of a quite different type. All are based on a central star polygon with radiating arms forming a geometric trellis (plate 6) and are reminiscent of the Mamluk frontispieces of some seventy years later, though much less tightly controlled and full of highly idiosyncratic detail. Interstices in the geometric trellis are filled with curious shapes: two main types (plate 7) with a number of smaller ones. The former, which always point in toward the polygons, are based, as one would expect, on the palmette, but have a strange anatomical quality about them that makes them resemble a human pelvis. They are often covered—as are the arabesques and palmette borders—in beautifully modeled teardrops. Apart from the 'pelvic palmettes,' Ṣandal's work is distinctive in other ways. He loves to set his palmette motifs, wherever they appear, on grounds of minute parallel hatchings in black or red (plate 8). These were painstakingly drawn after the gold had been laid on. His arabesques and all vegetal material are covered in tiny lumps, bumps, and knobbles, which give the vegetation a particularly vibrant, animated quality that is entirely missing in Ibn Mubādir's polished but sterile borders. He uses them on the opening pages of text and the colophon, where Ibn Mubādir puts cold, precise geometry (plate 9). It is the work of a very different personality, and one wonders how the two got together. They must have been of equal stature as painters and quite set in their styles. Neither shows the slightest influence on the other. Another Koran in the Chester Beatty Library illuminated and signed by Ṣandal is painted in exactly the same way.[20]

Ṣandal's style was perpetuated through his pupil Aydughdī—such was the relationship between the two men. But what was the contribution of Aydughdī to the Baybars Koran? Whatever

PLATE 6. Illuminated folio from the Baybars Koran, opening recto of *sub'* 3, illuminated in Cairo by Abū Bakr, known as Ṣandal, 1304–05. British Library MS add 22408.

PLATE 7. Two motifs used as fillers by Şandal in several of his compositions, including the opening recto of *sub'* 3 of the Baybars Koran (see plate 6). Chester Beatty MS 1479.

PLATE 9. Arabesque scroll of the type frequently employed by Şandal. Chester Beatty MS 1479.

it was, it was carried out equally on every part, as his inscription tells us. The possibilities are limited. He could have outlined the gold script in black,[21] after it had been written or painted. That task would have involved tracing over what was there, so that Aydughdī's contribution would have been undetectable. He could have painted in parts of the decorated areas, such as those in gold, which had already been drawn by the illuminators. Even though the verb associated with illumination is *dhahhaba, zammaka* also had to do with illuminating rather than with writing. Al-Şafadī, for

PLATE 8. Detail of the palmette border used extensively by Şandal. Chester Beatty MS 1479.

PLATE 10. Illuminated folio from the Koran, opening recto, illuminated by Aydughdī ibn ʿAbdallāh, former pupil of Ṣandal, assisted by ʿAlī al-Rassām, dated 1313. T.I.E.M. MS 450.

example, in describing the Baybars Koran and Ibn al-Wāḥid's contribution to it, remarks, *wa zammakahā wa dhahhabahā ṣandal al-mashur*, "then the famous Sandal painted and illuminated it,"[22] indicating that the acts of *tazmīk* and *tadhhīb* were both associated with the illuminator. Thus Aydughdī, as assistant to Ṣandal, probably carried out the task of painting in areas drawn and partially painted by Ṣandal and Ibn Mubādir, and these were most likely the areas in gold.

This assumed secondary role for Aydughdī does not argue against the likelihood that he wrote the large inscription on the opening folios of *subʿ* 7, recording his contribution. He was a calligrapher as well as a painter, as we know from a copy of *al-Fawāʾid al-Jaliyya*, copied and illuminated by him in 1312, and now in the British Library.[23]

Further information on the meaning of *zammaka* and on the relationship between Ṣandal and Aydughdī can be extracted from an important Koran which I came upon recently in Istanbul.[24] It is a fine single-volume copy, characteristic of Mamluk Korans of its time (dated A.H. 713 [A.D. 1313]) and commissioned by al-Nāṣir Muḥammad, whose name appears in an elaborately worded certificate of commissioning: "For the exalted imperial library of Sultan al-Malik al-Nāṣir, may Allah prolong his days and unfurl his banners in the East and West, exalt his power and make the kings of the earth obey his limitless authority." The text is copied by one Shādhī ibn Muḥammad ibn Ayyūb[25] in a magnificent gold *naskh* favored at the time above all other scripts. The manuscript has a set of beautifully illuminated frontis- and finispieces and opening pages of text. On both the opening and the final pages of text are two minute inscriptions. The first tells us that Aydughdī ibn ʿAbdallāh illuminated the frontis- and finispieces.[26] The second tells us that another painter, ʿAlī ibn Muḥammad the draftsman (*rassām*), known as "*al-aʿsar*" ("the left-handed"), performed the action of *tazmīk*.[27] The relationship between the two painters at that time was probably that of master and pupil. In the *Fawāʾid* manuscript completed in the previous year, Aydughdī calls himself *al-mudhahhib*, "illuminator." Here ʿAlī the Left-handed refers to himself as *rassām*, "draftsman." In the Baybars Koran the main painters use the term *mudhahhib*, whereas Aydughdī does not call himself anything.

PLATE 11. Illuminated folio, opening verso, by Ṣandal. Chester Beatty MS 1479.

PLATE 12. Detail of the arabesque scrolls used by Aydughdī. T.I.E.M. MS 450.

In the eight years between completion of the Baybars Koran and the *Fawā'id* manuscript, Aydughdī had probably become a master in his own right. That his role in 1305 was that of Şandal's pupil is shown by his inscription in the Istanbul Koran where we read "trained"[28]—that is, brought up by—the *mu'allim*—that is, the master—Şandal, whom we can presume was still alive or Aydughdī would certainly have added *raḥimahu 'llāh*, "May Allah have mercy on him."

It is instructive to compare the Istanbul Koran (plate 10) with the one illuminated by Şandal in the Chester Beatty Library (plate 11). Each composition is based on a ten-pointed central polygon with the words *tanzīl min ḥakīm ḥamīd*, "It is sent down by One full of wisdom, worthy of all praise" (Koran 51.42). These are in white *thuluth* over gold arabesque scrolls with teardrop decoration. There are several differences in detail and in the realignment of the axis from vertical to diagonal. However, the palmette fillers in the interstices of the geometric trellis still resemble those of Şandal—admittedly somewhat simplified, but on the ground of hatchings favored by Şandal. In the borders both artists make use of a large trilobed motif with crossed arms. The hatched ground is still used by Aydughdī, and the palmettes in each case build up into an elaborate hasp in the center margin. Comparison with contemporary work shows that the connections between the two compositions are not simply attributable to convention. Aydughdī also continues to paint his arabesque scrolls and all vegetal decoration with the same odd protuberances we see in the work of Şandal (plate 12). We can trace many of these features in later manuscripts. Perhaps the latest we can link to the Şandal school (if we can use that term) is a Koran in the Keir Collection (plates 13, 14; dated A.H. 730 [A.D. 1329–30]),[29] which, although much inferior, is clearly the work of someone trained in the style of Aydughdī and Şandal.

What can we conclude from these observations? First, that we have a substantial body of manuscripts, the work of several scribes and illuminators working in clearly identifiable styles over a period of two or three decades. This, I believe, is an

PLATE 13. Illuminated folio, opening verso, dated 1330. Although technically inferior to the work of Şandal and Aydughdī, this illumination follows directly in their tradition. Keir Collection MS VII.9.

PLATE 14. An opening verso folio from the same manuscript shown in plate 14. Keir Collection MS VII.9.

important corpus for the study of Mamluk manuscript illumination. It gives us the earliest detailed framework from which to begin a fuller investigation of Koran production in Mamluk Egypt and perhaps Syria as well. Second, the information contained in the various manuscripts enables us to work out the relationships existing among the various scribes and craftsmen involved. This information can help in the investigation of later related groups of Mamluk Korans that do not possess the same documentary evidence.

Finally, it should be remembered that there are still many unanswered questions relating to manuscripts produced in these early years of the fourteenth century. The most obvious one is why a manuscript commissioned by Baybars should be so completely unlike any other Mamluk Koran in its seven-part presentation, script, and illumination. Related questions pertain to the origins of the styles evidenced by the work of Ṣandal and Ibn Mubādir, practitioners of mature, fully developed, yet very different, styles of illumination. Were they established Cairo artists whose earlier work has simply disappeared? Did either, or both, come from elsewhere, perhaps specifically for the purpose of participating in the grand project being organized by Baybars and Ibn al-Waḥid? The answers to these questions will have to await another study.[30]

CHESTER BEATTY LIBRARY
DUBLIN

NOTES

1. British Library, MS Add 22406-13. See *Catalogus codicum manuscriptorum orientalium*, pt. 2, *Codices arabici*, 3 vols. (1846–71); Stanley Lane-Poole, *Art of the Saracens of Egypt* (London, 1886), pp. 255–56; Martin Lings and Y. S. Safadi, *The Qur'an*, British Library Exhibition, 1976, nos. 66–69; Martin Lings, *The Qur'anic Art of Calligraphy and Illumination* (London, 1976), no. 62; Hayward Gallery, *The Arts of Islam* (London, 1976), no. 527.

2. For a full discussion of this, see David James, "Spaceforms in the Work of the Baghdād *Maqāmāt* Illustrators," *Bulletin of the School of Oriental and African Studies* (University of London) 28, pt. 2 (1974) : 305–20; idem, "Arab Painting," *Marg* 29, no. 3 (June 1976) : 11–50. See also Oleg Grabar, "Pictures or Commentaries: The Illustrations of the *Maqāmāt* of al-Hariri," in *Studies in the Art and Literature of the Near East*, ed. P. Chelkowski (Provo, Utah, 1974).

3. Korans in two, four, seven, thirty, and even sixty parts are known, and of these those in thirty parts appear to have been the most popular and those in seven parts the rarest.

4. Many enormous multipart Korans were produced in Iran during the first half of the fourteenth century. Mamluk ones from the same period are far fewer. Apart from the Baybars manuscript only two thirty-part copies are dated during the reign of al-Nāṣir Muḥammad, though three extant metal cases (Ar. sing. *rab'a*) dating from his reign were made to hold such copies. Numerous manuscripts of this type, in addition to the famour Öljaytü Koran of 1313, can be shown to be Ilkhanid, though they are commonly regarded as Mamluk.

5. See K. A. C. Creswell, *The Early Muslim Architecture of Egypt* (Oxford, 1959), 2:249–54.

6. Ibn Iyās, *Badā'i' al-Zuhur fī Waḳā'i' al-Duhūr*, ed. Muhammad Mostafa (Weisbaden, 1975), pp. 418–19.

7. The explanation is probably to be found in the accounts of Ibn Ḥajar and al-Ṣafadī. Al-Ṣafadī, *Wāfī bi'l-Wafayāt*, ed. S. Dedering (Damascus, 1953), 3:151: "I saw [the Koran] in the Mosque of al-Ḥākim and in the *diwān al-inshā'* at the Citadel more than once. It was made a waqf of the Ḥākim mosque. I do not believe that anyone could now write and illuminate a manuscript like this. In script and illumination it was unique in its time." Ibn Ḥajar, *al-Durar al-Kāmina*, ed. Muhammad Sayid Jad al-Haqq (Cairo, 1965–66), 4:73: "[al-Jāshnagīr] endowed [the Koran] to the library of the mosque of

al-Ḥākim and it is unrivaled in excellence." The explanation would seem to be that Baybars commissioned it for the khanqah, but as the manuscript was completed well before the building was, he may have decided to endow it (or simply deposit it temporarily, as there is no waqf inscription) in the mosque of al-Ḥākim, which he had restored after a great earthquake a few years earlier.

8. The fullest accounts of the life of Ibn al-Wāḥid are found in Ṣafadī, *Wāfī bi'l Wafayāt*, no. 1104, and Ibn Ḥajar, *al-Durar al-Kāmina*, no. 3704.

9. *Sharḥ Ibn al-Wāḥid 'alā ra'iyyat Ibn al-Bawwāb*, ed. Hilal Naji (Tunis, 1967).

10. There is one thirty-part Koran with similar, though much smaller, script, a few parts of which are dispersed among various collections: Archaeological Museum, Bursa, Koran 19; Bibliothèque Nationale, Paris, MS 5949; Chester Beatty Library, Dublin, MS 1481. See also A. J. Arberry, *The Koran Illuminated* (Dublin, 1961), pl. 34; David James, *Qur'ans and Bindings from the Chester Beatty Library* (London, 1980), no. 22; Sotheby Catalogue 29.4.81, lot 271 (illustrated). Although these sections are regularly described as Mamluk, the illumination is quite unlike illumination in other Mamluk Korans.

11. Al-Ṭībī, *Jamī' Mahāsin Kitābat al-Kuttāb*, ed. Salahuddin al-Munajjed (Beirut, 1962). For his example of *ash'ar*, see pp. 90–93, and for his description, p. 18: "You can use either the pen suitable for *muḥaqqaq* or *naskh* because *ash'ar* (or *mu'anniq*) is formed [*murakkab*] in the same way."

12. The Mamluk Koran in the Oriental Institute, Chicago, A.12068, is in a script described as *thuluth khafīf* (see Nabia Abbott, *The North Arabian Script and Its Kur'anic Development* [Chicago, 1933]), though it closely resembles, on a larger scale, the classic *rayḥān* hand of the Yāqūt Korans. This is the only Bahri Mamluk example of which I am aware.

13. MS 1437; see Arberry, *Koran Illuminated*, pl. 33; James, *Qur'ans and Bindings*, no. 24.

14. MS KB 31.559; see Annemarie Schimmel, *Islamic Calligraphy* (Leiden, 1970), pl. 23.

15. In the medallions on the final folio: *dhahhabahu Muḥammad ibn Mubādir 'afā 'llāh 'anhu.*

16. *Sub'* 3, in the medallions on the final folio, *bi-tadhhīb Ṣandal*; *sub'* 5, in the large palmettes on the opening pages of illumination, *tadhhīb abū bakr* [sic] *'urifa bi-Ṣandal.*

17. *Zammaka hadhā 'l-sub' al-sharīf wa akhawātihi al-'abd al-faqīr ilā 'llāh ta'ālā al-rājī 'afw allāh wa raḥmatahu aydughdī ibn 'abdillāh al-badrī 'afā 'llāh 'anhu fī sanat 705.*

18. MS 1457; see James, *Qur'ans and Bindings*, nos. 26–27.

19. Sotheby Catalogue 9.10.78, lot 122.

20. MS 1479; see Arberry, *Koran Illuminated*, pl. 2; James, *Qur'ans and Bindings*, no. 25.

21. Lane-Poole, *Art of the Saracens*, p. 256.

22. Al-Ṣafadī, *Wāfī bi'l-Wafayāt*, 10:350.

23. MS Or 3025.

24. Türk ve Islam Eserleri Müzesi, MS 450. Some pages from this manuscript are in the Freer Gallery, Washington, D.C., and the Boston Museum of Fine Arts.

25. The calligrapher of this manuscript, whose full genealogy is given in the colophon, was a grandson of al-Malik al-Ẓāhir Shādhī (d. 681/1281) of the house of al-'Ādil. The probable royal Ayyubid origins of Shādhī ibn Muḥammad, the calligrapher, were suggested to me by Dr. Steven Humphreys at the Mamluk conference in Washington, D.C., May 1981. Ibn Ḥajar, who records the only other information we have on Shādhī, tells us that he was born in 681/1282 and died suddenly in 742/1341–42; *Durar*, no. 1921. Quatremère, *Histoire des sultans mamloukes* (Paris, 1837), 2:58, n. 456, informs us that Shādhī's grandfather al-Malik al-Ẓāhir was buried in Jerusalem.

26. *Hadhihi 'l-fawātiḥ wa'l-ghawāliq min idmān al-'abd al-faqīr ilā 'llāh ta'ālā al-rājī 'afw rabbihi aydughdī bn 'abdillāh al-badri nashu'a al-mu'allim ṣandal 'afā 'llāh 'anhum.*

27. *Zammaka hādhihi 'l-khatma al-sharīfa aqall 'abīd illāh ta'ālā 'alī bn muḥammad al-rassām 'urifa bi'l-a'sar 'afā 'llāh 'anhum.*

28. Although the reading of the latter part of the inscription in n. 26 is open to several variations (*nashu'a, nushū'*, "emerge," "derive from"; *nashsha'a*, "bring up," "raise"), the interpretation can only be that Aydughdī, who wrote it, was taught by the master (*mu'allim*) Ṣandal.

29. See B. W. Robinson, Ernst J. Grube, G. M. Meredith-Owens, and R. W. Skelton, *Islamic Painting and the Arts of the Book* (London, 1976), MS VII.9.

30. These and related questions are examined in my forthcoming book on Koranic illumination and calligraphy in the fourteenth century.

ESIN ATIL

Mamluk Painting in the Late Fifteenth Century

The Mamluk period has long been recognized as the second classical age of illustrated Arabic manuscripts. The majority of the paintings in works dating from the Bahri period (1250–1390) were based on pictorial cycles established in the first classical age. The painters copied such already popular texts as the *Automata*, *Kalīla wa Dimna*, and *Maqāmāt* and relied on the compositions, figure types, and settings created in the first half of the thirteenth century. Although in the midfourteenth century a number of texts on animals (including the fables of Ibn Ẓafar and treatises on zoology written by al-Jāḥiẓ and Ibn al-Durayhim) were illustrated for the first and often the only time, even the paintings in those volumes were inspired by contemporary manuscripts devoted to similar topics and do not reveal iconographical or stylistic innovations. The illustrations in some of these works (particularly the 1315 *Automata*, 1334 *Maqāmāt*, and several midfourteenth-century works on animals) display a refined technique of execution at the hands of highly competent painters, but they were conceived solely as decorative paintings to enhance the manuscripts and are devoid of originality.

Mamluk painting flourished in the first half of the fourteenth century and then showed a noticeable decline in the following years. Paintings from the Burji period (1382–1517) reveal a limited repertory and are generally poor copies of the *Automata*, *Kalīla wa Dimna*, or al-Āqsara'i's manual on horsemanship and warfare entitled *Nihayat al-Su'l wa'l-Umniyya: Ta'allum 'Amal al-Furūsiyya*, which was illustrated sometime after the 1360s and became a very popular work. By the midfifteenth century the tradition of Mamluk painting would no doubt have exhausted itself, had it not been for a remarkable group of manuscripts originating in Cairo but written in Turkish and illustrated by artists trained in the Turkoman courts. Two of these manuscripts were commissioned by Sultan Qānṣūh al-Ghawrī in the 1510s, indicating the existence of an active court studio in the capital.

Although close to sixty illustrated Arabic texts are known to have been produced in the Mamluk period, the provenance of very few of them can be determined. For the most part, attributing a manuscript to Egypt or to Syria is a purely arbitrary procedure, and even for the handful of manuscripts that do indicate place of origin, the information provided is not sufficient to establish painting ateliers or to assign manuscripts to specific centers. Obviously, painters traveled all over the empire, setting up their workshops wherever and for as long as there was a demand for their work.

Only a few illustrated manuscripts have dedications, but those few indicate that they were made for second-generation mamluks, that is, for the sons of former mamluks who were born Muslim and raised within an Islamic society. These patrons and their fathers are generally otherwise unknown: their names appear only in single manuscripts and are not mentioned in the sources.[1]

Since none of the manuscripts with dedications can be grouped according to period or location, a typology of their patronage cannot be established. Nevertheless, they tell us that interest in illustrated manuscripts among the upper classes was sufficient to enable painters to find commissions and to keep the tradition alive. But they also tell us that that activity was very different from the remarkable reflorescence of painting at the very end of the Mamluk empire, which was based on imperial patronage, an active court studio housed in the capital, and the emergence of a new literary genre written in a new language and illustrated in a

PLATE 1. Rider exercising with a lance, from a manual on horsemanship, c. 1465. Keir Collection, London, II.8.

new style. It is perhaps not surprising that that new style made its first appearance in a *furūsiyya* manuscript, since the *furūsiyya* genre was unique to the Mamluks and enjoyed great popularity among them in the fourteenth and fifteenth centuries, appealing as it did to their preoccupation with horsemanship and warfare.

The undated and fragmentary *furūsiyya* work divided between the Keir Collection in London (thirty-one paintings, nos. II 7–37) and the Museum of Islamic Art in Cairo (three paintings, nos. 18019 and 18235–36) which introduces the new style consists mainly of paintings showing figures practicing combat techniques with various weapons.[2] Delicately drawn, slender, and agile figures are placed against a blank ground to demonstrate the use of different pieces of military equipment (plate 1). They were executed by an artist who excelled in painting single figures but appears to have lacked expertise in developing compositions. His well-proportioned figures are dressed in tunics, boots, and furry caps; their faces are remarkably well rendered with softly tinted pink cheeks, arched eyebrows, almond-shaped eyes, small red lips, and finely drawn mustaches and beards. He was particularly adept at portraying faces in three-quarter view, but had difficulty with profiles and tended to exaggerate noses. He was also somewhat inexperienced in depicting movement, volume, and drapery.

Identical subjects are illustrated in a *furūsiyya* manuscript transcribed in Muḥarram 871/August 1466, owned by the Topkapi Palace Museum (R 1933).[3] This work, originally composed by ʿAbd al-Raḥman ibn Aḥmad al-Ṭabarī (died 1295), contains sixty-two paintings, all of them crude copies of the ones in the Keir manuscript, and many schematic drawings of military maneuvers. There is no doubt that the artist who painted the scenes in the Topkapi Palace Museum work had access to the Keir Collection manuscript, and that therefore the latter must have been produced before 1466.

The same stylistic features found in the Keir Collection *furūsiyya* reappear in a significant work, the *Iskandarnāma* of Aḥmadī, written in Turkish.[4] The manuscript, now in the Istanbul University Library (T 6044), was dedicated to the Mamluk official Khushqadam ibn ʿAbdallāh, the treasurer (*khaznadār*) of Sayfīʿ Alī Bay, who was the secretary (*dawādār*) of Sultan Timurbughā. Although the work is not dated, it must have been completed during the two-month reign of Timurbughā (December 1467–January 1468).

Aḥmadī, the author of the *Iskandarnāma*, was a native of Amasya. After two years of study in Cairo (1334–35) he returned to Anatolia and in time entered the service, first of the Germiyan amir Süleyman Shah (r. 1367–86) and then, after the amir's death in 1390, of Süleyman Chelebi (later

Süleyman I, r. 1403–10 in Rumelia), the son of the Ottoman sultan Bāyazīd I. Aḥmadī probably dedicated the *Iskandarnāma*, which, after recounting the life of Alexander the Great, provides a world history up to the Islamic era, to either the Germiyan amir or the Ottoman prince.

The work remained quite popular in the Ottoman and Mamluk courts during the fifteenth and sixteenth centuries. Its earliest illustrated version was made in the author's native Amasya three years after his death in 1413.[5] This work reused paintings from fourteenth-century Ilkhanid and Inju manuscripts and added only a few original scenes. Its second illustrated copy was produced in the Ottoman court at the end of the fifteenth century.[6] The third was the one made for Khushqadam ibn ʿAbdallāh. Aḥmadī's *Iskandarnāma* was also illustrated in the Aqqoyunlu and Safavid courts of Shiraz: three copies were produced for the Aqqoyunlus and four for the Safavids.[7]

The Mamluk *Iskandarnāma* contains twelve paintings and a diagram of the zodiac. Its frontispiece represents the entertainment of a prince who is seated in a domed iwan attached to a two-story structure with a marble terrace in front; the iwan has a central window opening onto a garden in the background (plate 2). This architectural setting with its tiled walls, pseudo-Kufic carpet, window grilles, balustrades, and stone pavement is typical of the enthronement scenes found in Timurid and Turkoman manuscripts. The figure types—

PLATE 2. Frontispiece, *Iskandarnāma* of Aḥmadī, 1467–68. Istanbul University Library, T 6044, fol. 1b.

PLATE 3. Illuminated heading, *Iskandarnāma* of Aḥmadī, 1467–68. Istanbul University Library, T 6044, fol. 2a.

musicians, wine stewards, servants, courtiers, and attendants—are also found in fifteenth-century manuscripts produced in Herat, Baghdad, and Shiraz. In contrast, the illuminated folio with the dedication that faces the illustration of the enthroned prince is executed in a typical Mamluk style (plate 3).

All the paintings in the *Iskandarnāma* represent the life of Alexander, including his acts of justice, love affairs, battles, and other heroic achievements (plates 4 and 5). Although carefully rendered, the figures are haphazardly placed within the scenes. Like the painter of the Keir Collection *furūsiyya*, this artist was not very proficient in composition. In the entertainment of Iskandar and Gulshah (plate 4), the faces are finely drawn with large almond-shaped eyes, arched eyebrows, straight noses, and small lips, but the figures are not fully integrated into the composition, and spatial development and clearly defined planes are notably lacking. Some of the ladies have tattoos between their eyebrows, and all the courtly females wear a high, cylindrical hat that is tied at the back with a ribbon. This headdress is not found in Timurid and Turkoman paintings; it is possible that the painter was attempting to represent a local headgear used by Mamluk ladies. It is also conceivable that he had access to fourteenth-century Ilkhanid or Mongol paintings in which courtly women also wear tall, cylindrical hats.[8] The composition of some scenes, such as that depicting Iskandar hunting, however, is typical of Turkoman painting; the artist appears to have used as his model a formulaic hunt frequently encountered in fifteenth-century Turkoman manuscripts (plate 5). Relying on his expertise as a figure painter, he attempted to create original compositions when the proper models were not available, but used existing prototypes for his generalized, formulaic scenes.

If we are correct in assuming that the painters of the *furūsiyya* and of the *Iskandarnāma* arrived in Cairo around 1466, their appearance at the Mamluk court coincided with the political upheaval in the Qaraqoyunlu state that had led to the collapse of Pīr Būdāq's principality. Pīr Būdāq, the son of the Qaraqoyunlu sultan Jahān Shāh, had been an enthusiastic patron of the arts.[9] Given the rule of Fars by his father, he established a prolific court atelier in Shiraz that was enriched by artists from Herat after its conquest and brief occupation by the Qaraqoyunlus in 1458. Pīr Būdāq's independent attitudes compelled his father to march against him in 1462, and the success of that attack forced the prince to move his court to Baghdad. The enmity between father and son continued until 1466, when the prince was killed and his painting studio dispersed.

Only two of the illustrated manuscripts dating from Pīr Būdāq's last court indicate in their colophons that they were produced in Baghdad: the *Khamsa* of Amīr Khusraw Dihlavī, dating from 1463,[10] and the *Khamsa* of Jamālī, dating from 1465.[11] The paintings in those manuscripts combine Qaraqoyunlu and Timurid traditions in the full blossoming of Pīr Būdāq's atelier.

Pīr Būdāq's death and the dispersal of his court studio in Baghdad coincide with the appearance of the Turkoman style in Cairo, and that suggests that some of his painters sought employment in the Mamluk capital. In the Turkoman court these painters were accustomed to working in an atelier with master designers and relying on a wealth of models. When assigned to work on the *furūsiyya* and *Iskandarnāma* illustrations, they reused a number of themes (such as landscapes sprinkled with clusters of vegetation and schematic enthronement, hunting, and battle scenes) and attempted to make the most of their training as figure painters.

The Mamluk *Iskandarnāma* is important on several counts. It proves that Turkoman artists came to Cairo after the fall of Pīr Būdāq's court and were immediately put to work. It introduces Turkish epic historiography as a subject for illustration, a genre that was to reach its full development under the Ottomans several generations later. It provides us with one of the earliest illustrated copies of Aḥmadī's work and with paintings specifically created for his text. Finally, it points to the development in the Mamluk court of an interest in illustrating Turkish texts.

Turkoman artists, and perhaps their local apprentices, were employed in the creation of another unusual manuscript, the first Turkish translation of the *Shāhnāma* of Firdawsī.[12] This two-volume work, now in the Topkapi Palace Museum (H 1519), was transcribed by Ḥusayn ibn Ḥasan ibn Muḥammad al-Ḥusaynī al-Ḥanafī and contains sixty-two paintings. The work was translated into Turkish verse by Sharīf, who states in his introduction that he was asked to undertake the task by Sultan Qānṣūh al-Ghawrī.

The author writes in his own introduction that the sultan was devoted to books, particularly to those on history and science, and had many copies of the *Shāhnāma* in his library. He himself read Persian, but since he wanted others to appreciate this renowned epic he insisted that a Turkish translation be made so that it could be read with ease by everyone. Sharīf began the translation in the first year of Qānṣūh al-Ghawrī's reign (1501) and presented the complete work to the sultan ten years later.

At the end of the first volume the calligrapher states that he finished it on 1 Shaʿbān 913 (6 December 1507) in the Qubbat al-Ḥusayniyya; at the end of the second, that he completed it on 2 Dhūl'l-Ḥijja 916 (2 March 1511) at the al-Mu'ayyad Mosque. From this it appears that the

PLATE 4. Iskandar and Gulshāh, *Iskandarnāma* of Aḥmadī, 1467–68. Istanbul University Library, T 6044, fol. 66b.

PLATE 5. Iskandar hunting, *Iskandarnāma* of Aḥmadī, 1467–68. Istanbul University Library, T 6044, fol. 99b.

PLATE 6. Enthronement of Gayūmarth, *Shāhnāma* of Firdawsī, 1511. Topkapi Palace Museum, Istanbul, H 1519, fol. 13b.

PLATE 7. Enthronement of Gayūmarth, *Shāhnāma* of Firdawsī, 1486. Topkapi Palace Museum, Istanbul, H 1506, fol. 15a.

PLATE 8. Enthronement of Jamshīd, *Shāhnāma* of Firdawsī, 1511. Topkapi Palace Museum, Istanbul, H 1519, fol. 22b.

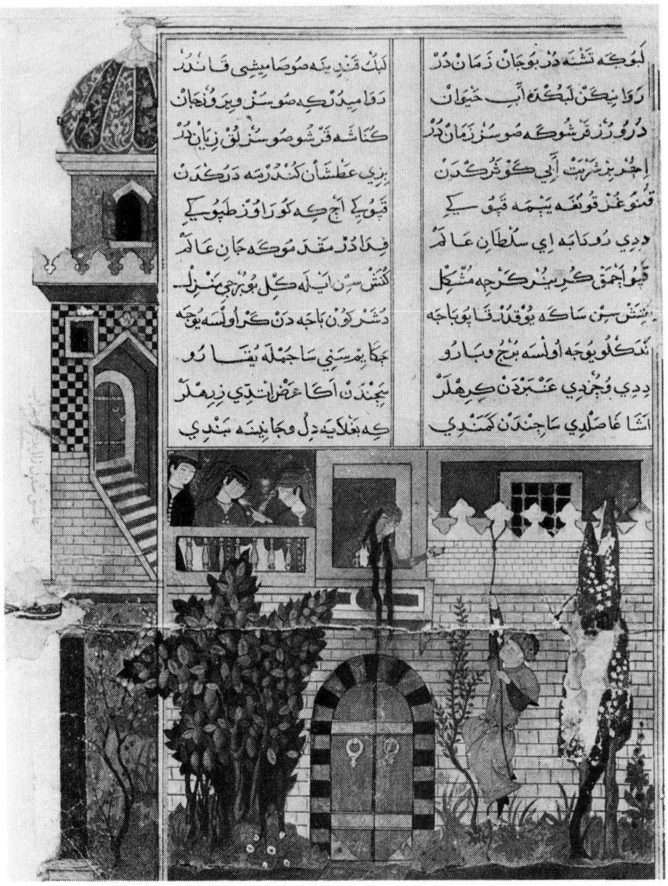

PLATE 9. Zāl climbing the wall to reach Rūdāba, *Shāhnāma* of Firdawsī, 1511. Topkapi Palace Museum, Istanbul, H 1519, fol. 115a.

calligrapher was transcribing the text as fast as Sharīf could translate it and handing it over to the painters to add the illustrations.

It is possible that some of the illustrations were executed by Aqqoyunlu Turkoman artists who joined the Mamluk court at the beginning of the sixteenth century when the Aqqoyunlu empire collapsed with the rise of the Safavids. After Tabriz, the capital, was captured by Shah Ismāʿil in 1501, other major Aqqoyunlu centers, including Shiraz, accepted the Safavid rule. Some of the painters in these cities might have sought the protection of the Mamluk sultan. If they did, their timing would have been most opportune for the *Shāhnāma* project.

The artists of the *Shāhnāma* were more fortunate than their predecessors in that they had an Aqqoyunlu manuscript to use as a model. A copy of the *Shāhnāma* with fifty-three paintings, also in the Topkapi Palace Museum and dating from 1486, must have been one of the Persian manuscripts in Qānṣūh al-Ghawrī's library mentioned by Sharīf in his introduction.[13] About a quarter of the illustrations in the Mamluk *Shāhnāma* are copies of the Aqqoyunlu work (plates 6–7), though a number of them are more elaborate than their models and show richer landscapes, more intense colors, and more dramatic movement. A second group constitutes scenes not found in the 1486 Aqqoyunlu work; these, however, depict such stock compositions as hunts, combats, and enthronements commonly seen in other late fourteenth-century Aqqoyunlu manuscripts. The third and most remarkable group displays an extraordinarily acute observation of the court and represents the ceremonies and settings with a realism not hitherto achieved in Mamluk painting. These scenes are by far the most interesting and show a divergence from stereotypical *Shāhnāma* illustrations.

Among the most outstanding of this last group is the enthronement of Jamshīd. It takes place on a terrace in front of a garden (plate 8); a gold throne is pushed to the right, exposing a high wall decorated with gazelles running in a landscape. On the wall, placed in a prominent position and emphasized by a lush and colorful fruit tree, is an oblong blue cartouche with gold inscriptions bestowing traditional Mamluk benedictions; below is a circular epigraphic shield divided into three fields. The *sāqī* (cupbearer) in the foreground leans over a low table and pours wine from a gold bottle into a small gold cup. On the table is a large blue-and-white footed bowl (identical in shape to the cup used in the blazon of the *sāqī*), a blue-and-white bottle, and a gold rosewater sprinkler. The *ṣilāḥdār* (swordbearer) holding the imperial sword stands next to the king, while a lute player and two attendants appear on the far left. The blue-and-white ceramics and the inscriptions on the wall are characteristic of the period, although the figure types are taken from the Aqqoyunlu repertory. The placement of the imperial blazon and the inscribed cartouche in such a significant position, almost overshadowing the enthroned figure, suggests that Qānṣūh al-Ghawrī is being likened to Jamshīd, because he, like the legendary ruler, is a great patron of the arts.

The lush tree in the background is of a type alien to Turkoman art, but it reappears in the scene depicting Zāl climbing the wall to reach his beloved Rūdāba (plate 9). There its fruit resembles the mangos native to Egypt. The architecture was also inspired by local structures and is decorated with trefoil crenellations, mashrabiyya balustrades, inlaid marble panels, and ablaq arches. The pavilion in the left margin has a ribbed dome with a golden bird perched on top.

The ribbed dome with a bird is also seen on the balcony jutting into the left margin of the painting representing Rustam slaying the wild elephant with a single blow (plate 10). This scene takes place in a Mamluk interior: a heavy metal door with a blue-and-white tile panel at the top leads into a narrow vaulted corridor lit by a cylindrical glass lamp; beyond the corridor is a fully furnished bedroom. The bed, a platform with a headboard resting on four high feet, is decorated with turned wooden grilles and has two pillows with a brocaded quilt encased in a sheet. A bulky knotted curtain hangs above the bed. The group of figures observing Rustam's remarkable feat from the pavilion on the left represent diverse types and includes two women, each wearing an unusual headdress: a small cap tied with a band and embellished with a central ornament. The same cap appears on the heads of the ladies watching Siyawush's ordeal by fire from the roof of a cut-stone building with trefoil crenellations (plate 11).

Several enthronement scenes reflect an interest in representing local ceremonial settings. The enthronement of Kay-Khusraw takes place in front of a wall adorned with colorful marble panels and columns (plate 12). Although it is difficult to conceive the structural components of this backdrop (there seems to be a window in the center overlooking a garden), the interior decoration with rectangular and circular marble inlays is characteristic of Mamluk architecture.

PLATE 10. Rustam killing the elephant, *Shāhnāma* of Firdawsī, 1511. Topkapi Palace Museum, Istanbul, H 1519, fol. 146a.

PLATE 11. The ordeal of Siyāwush, *Shāhnāma* of Firdawsī, 1511. Topkapi Palace Museum, Istanbul, H 1519, fol. 326a.

PLATE 12. Enthronement of Kay-Khusraw, *Shāhnāma* of Firdawsī, 1511. Topkapi Palace Museum, Istanbul, H 1519, fol. 425b.

PLATE 13. Enthronement of Kay-Qubād, *Shāhnāma* of Firdawsī, 1511. Topkapi Palace Museum, Istanbul, H 1519, fol. 188a.

The enthronement of Kay-Qubād shows an elaborate throne resting on two gold sphinxes (plate 13). The throne is placed on a marble platform raised by three steps and is covered by a ribbed dome carried by four marble columns. This structure is so unusual that it must have been inspired by an actual Mamluk throne.

The painters of Qānṣūh al-Ghawrī's *Shāhnāma*, trained in the Qaraqoyunlu school of Baghdad and the Aqqoyunlu school of Shiraz, must have been enchanted with the court of their new patron. Exceptional artists all, they set out to represent their new environment, adjusting the settings and ceremonies of the Mamluk capital to the established iconography of the *Shāhnāma* and depicting the architecture and furnishings of Cairo with the fascination of newcomers.

One of them was also employed to paint the frontispiece of an undated anthology of Turkish poetry commissioned by Sultan Qānṣūh al-Ghawrī. The work, now in the Staatsbibliothek in Berlin (MS or. oct. 2744), is a compilation of *ghazal*s and *qaṣīda*s written by such renowned Turkish poets as Aḥmad Pasha, Shaykhī, and Aḥmadī. It also includes the *ghazal*s composed by Sultan Qānṣūh al-Ghawrī himself.[14]

Its frontispiece represents an enthroned ruler accompanied by two attendants, who hold a bottle and a cylindrical box (plate 14). The crowned figure sits in an elaborate square pavilion with a ribbed dome surmounted by a bird, a feature observed in several *Shāhnāma* illustrations. The dome rests on four marble columns, and the spandrels on the façade are decorated with inlaid marble panels. A window opening onto a garden appears behind the king, and a fountain and a round table with a bottle, a cup, and what appears to be a box are placed in the foreground.

Combining traditional Turkoman features with local elements, the artist is obviously attempting to recreate the court of his patron. Unfortunately, the faces of the figures have been rubbed out, and we cannot determine whether the ruler represented here is the elderly Qānṣūh al-Ghawrī, who was sixty years old when he ascended the throne, or merely a stereotypical ruler.

Qānṣūh al-Ghawrī was not the only Mamluk sultan to show an interest in Turkish literature. His predecessor Barqūq commissioned Darir of Erzurum to write a voluminous biography of the Prophet Muḥammad in 1388. This work, entitled the *Siyar-i Nabī*, was illustrated with over 750 paintings in the Ottoman court at the end of the sixteenth century.[15]

Sultan Qānṣūh al-Ghawrī was an innovative patron. He was the only Mamluk sultan to reveal a strong interest in illustrated manuscripts; he encouraged development of a new genre in literature; and he supported the first imperial Mamluk painting atelier. His patronage came to an end, however, when the Ottomans conquered Cairo, and Sultan Selim I must have shipped Qānṣūh al-Ghawrī's painters along with his library to Istanbul.[16] There they would have joined the other Turkoman painters who had fled from the fallen Aqqoyunlu state or were taken when Tabriz was

PLATE 14. Frontispiece, from an anthology of Turkish poetry, c. 1510. Staatsbibliothek, Berlin, MS or. oct. 3744, fol. 2a.

captured. Together with artists from all corners of the Ottoman Empire, from Hungary to Iran, they helped to create the classical style of Ottoman painting that was established in the midsixteenth century and survived until the end of the nineteenth.

FREER GALLERY OF ART
SMITHSONIAN INSTITUTION
WASHINGTON, D.C.

NOTES

1. For a discussion of these patrons and a survey of Mamluk painting with relevant publications, see Esin Atıl, *Renaissance of Islam: Art of the Mamluks* (Washington, D.C., 1981), pp. 250–65, 279.

2. These paintings have been published in Mohamed Mostafa, "Miniature Paintings in Some Mamluk Manuscripts," *Bulletin de l'Institut Égyptien* 52 (1970–71) : 5–15, pls. 23, 25, 27, 29, 31, 33, 35, and 37; idem, *Unity in Islamic Art: Guide to the Second Temporary Exhibition* (Cairo, 1958), p. 39; Ernst J. Grube, "Pre-Mongol and Mamluk Painting," in *Islamic Painting and the Arts of the Book*, by B. W. Robinson, Ernst J. Grube, G. M. Meredith-Owens, and R. W. Skelton (London, 1976), pp. 72–81, pl. 12 and color pl. 4; Duncan Haldane, *Mamluk Painting* (Warminster, England, 1978), pp. 72–73.

3. Fehmi Edhem Karatay, *Topkapı Sarayı Müzesi Kütüphanesi Arapça Yazmalar Kataloğu* (Istanbul, 1962–69), vol. 3, no. 7416; Mostafa, "Miniature Paintings," pls. 24, 26, 28, 30, 32, 34, 36, and 38.

4. Fehmi Edhem and Ivan Stchoukine, *Les manuscrits orientaux illustrés de la Bibliothèque de l'Université de Stamboul* (Paris, 1933), no. 44; Güner İnal, "Kahirede Yapılmış bir Hümâyünnâmenin Minyatürleri," *Belleten* 40, no. 159 (July 1976) : 439–65, figs. 21–22, idem, "Ahmedînin İskendernâmesinin Minyatürlü Nüshaları," paper presented at II. Uluslar Arası Türkoloji Kongresi, Istanbul, 1976 (proceedings forthcoming).

5. The manuscript, which is in Paris, Bibliothèque Nationale, is described in Esin Atıl, "Ottoman Miniature Painting under Sultan Mehmed II," *Ars Orientalis* 9 (1973) : 103–20.

6. The work, now in Venice, was discussed by Ernst J. Grube during the Second International Congress of Turkology, II (Uluslar Arası Türkoloji Kongresi, Istanbul, 1976), proceedings forthcoming.

7. It is surprising that this Turkish work was more popular among the Aqqoyunlus and Safavids than it was at the Ottoman court. For a discussion of these manuscripts, see İnal, "Ahmedînin İskendernâmesinin Minyatürlü Nüshaları."

8. These high hats are seen in some *Jami al-Tawarikh* illustrations incorporated into albums. M. Ş. İpşiroğlu, *Saray-Alben* (Wiesbaden, 1964), pls. 7–8; Filiz Çağman and Zeren Tanındı, *Topkapı Saray Museum: Islamic Miniature Painting* (Istanbul, 1979), fig. 3.

9. Qaraqoyunlu and Aqqoyunlu paintings are discussed in Basil W. Robinson, "The Turkman School to 1503," in *The Arts of the Book in Central Asia*, ed. Basil Gray (London, 1979), pp. 215–47.

10. Topkapi Palace Museum, Istanbul, H 1021; Çağman and Tanındı, *Topkapı Saray Museum*, no. 38, fig. 17, with bibliography.

11. India Office Library, London, MS 138; Basil W. Robinson, *Persian Paintings in the India Office Library* (London, 1976), nos. 74–79.

12. Nurhan Atasoy, "1510 Tarihli Memluk Şehnamesinin Minyatürleri," *Sanat Tarihi Yıllığı*, 1966–68, 49–69; idem, "Un manuscrit mamluk illustré de Šahnama," *Revue des études islamiques* 37 (1969) : 151–58; Mostafa, "Miniature Paintings," pls. 20–22; Atıl, *Renaissance*, no. 5.

13. Fehmi Edhem Karatay, *Topkapı Sarayı Müzesi Kütüphanesi Farsca Yazmalar Kataloğu* (Istanbul, 1961), no. 338.

14. Ivan Stchoukine, Barbara Fleming, Paul Luft, and Hanna Sohrweide, *Illuminierte islamische Handschriften* (Wiesbaden, 1971), no. 111; *Islamische Buchkunst aus 1000 Jahren* (Berlin, 1980), no. 017.

15. This manuscript, completed in 1594–95, was conceived as a six-volume set. Barqūq's patronage was commemorated in the frontispiece depicting Darir kissing the hand of his Mamluk patron (Topkapi Palace Museum, Istanbul, H 1221, fol. 12a). Esin Atıl, "The Art of the Book," in *Turkish Art*, ed. Esin Atıl (Washington, D.C., and New York, 1980), pp. 198, 206–07, figs. 100–01.

16. The seal of Sultan Selim I appears on both volumes of the Mamluk *Shāhnāma*, which was the first Turkish translation of the work in the Istanbul court until the 1560s; Atıl, "The Art of the Book," pp. 168–69.

IRA M. LAPIDUS

Mamluk Patronage and the Arts in Egypt: Concluding Remarks

The symposium that produced the essays published here was an important occasion in Islamic art history, for it was, as far as I know, the first devoted entirely to the Mamluk period. The work of so many specialized scholars assembled in one place now makes it possible to survey the "state of the art." The research presented ranges from preliminary reconnaissances to monographic additions to the literature. Certain areas, such as the study of the Mamluk military and political system, Mamluk monuments—mosques, colleges, Sufi convents, shrines, and other structures—are already relatively well known. Mamluk-period heraldry, glass, and metalwork have received a fair amount of attention, but ceramics, textiles, and illuminated manuscripts still lack basic research. Some of these studies therefore contribute to the identification and dating of ceramics, textiles, and other works of art that have hitherto been studied hardly at all. Other contributions deal with historical problems concerning internal and international influences upon the development of Egyptian arts.

Almost all the work presented in this volume raises important methodological questions about the relationship between basic research into specific topics and generalization about broader aesthetic and historical issues. Many of the contributors hew to the straight and narrow path, and rightly so. It is apparent that in some areas too little is known to venture any important generalizations about the quality or provenance of, or the influences on, a particular set of objects. Too little is known to speculate about their artistic or social meaning. Nonetheless, it is important to raise the kinds of general questions that do not depend upon the state of our knowledge but are guides to the development of further research. It is crucial to ask how a particular contribution fits into the whole. What do objects or groups of objects tell us about the larger class of works of art to which they belong? What does a particular contribution tell us about Mamluk-era society, its functions, its values, and the kind of people and human experiences it embodies? The issue is not whether we are ready to generalize our knowledge, but whether we locate our research in its artistic, cultural, or historical context so that we may pose significant rather than trivial questions for investigation. No research is meaningful without an implicit or explicit sense of the whole from which it is abstracted. All research, regardless of the state of knowledge, requires artistic and historical imagination to guide us toward the type of data that must be gathered and the questions that need to be addressed.

Though the articles in this volume do not always address the social and cultural context, to a social historian they suggest a number of considerations. One is the responsiveness of Mamluk-period art to international influences. Egyptian arts evolved along with the transformation of Egypt's position in the Middle Eastern and Mediterranean world from the thirteenth through the sixteenth centuries. The history of Mamluk arts reveals how much Mamluk Egypt was part of an international religious community, related to Muslim regimes in Iran and Anatolia, and tied to an international trading economy.

Egypt's position in the Muslim, Middle Eastern, and Mediterranean worlds falls into three major phases. The first lasted from about 1250 to 1350, when Egypt became heir to the scholarly and artistic legacy of the Muslim Middle East. In an age when the Mongol invasions left Iran, Iraq, and Anatolia in political turmoil and economic collapse, when the Byzantine empire was crumbling before Turkish and Latin onslaughts and Europe had yet to emerge from the fragmentation of its feudal era, the Mamluk regime emerged as one of the strongest and most stable of Muslim Middle Eastern and Mediterranean states. The Mamluks expelled the remaining Crusader principalities from Palestine and Syria, defended Syria and Egypt against Mongol invasions, and extended their power to the Cilician Gates and to the upper Euphrates valley in order to defend them against renewed invasions. By 1323 the Mamluks, by a treaty with Abū Saʿīd, ended hostilities with the Ilkhanid state of Anatolia and Iran on terms favorable to the security of Syria and Egypt.

The war against the Crusaders, the struggle against the Mongols, the suppression of Shiism, and anti-Christian and anti-Jewish riots generated intense religious fervor. As a leading Muslim power, the Egyptian regime became the protector of the caliphate and the suzerain of the holy places; Egypt organized the pilgrimage and provided the cover of the Kaaba. Egypt and Syria became refuges for scholars, artisans, and merchants from the embattled parts of the Muslim world. Muslim peoples, uprooted by non-Muslim conquests in Central Asia, Iran, and Spain and unsettled by the political turmoil in Anatolia, Mesopotamia, and North Africa, brought their scholarly abilities and artistic skills to Syria and Cairo. Egypt became a leading center of Muslim religious scholarship, especially in the study of hadith and law. Migrant workers in metal, textiles, ceramics, glass, and the building crafts revived Mamluk industry. Metalworkers from Mosul, for example, created a flourishing industry of inlaid brass, and architects from Tabriz worked in Damascus in the 1330s. Patterns for ceramics came from Sultanabad; silk designs from Iran; geometric motifs from Iran and Anatolia. The Baghdadi and Mesopotamian tradition of illuminated manuscripts was continued in early Mamluk copies of *Automata*, *Kalīla wa Dimna*, and *Maqāmāt*. The Mamluks also inherited the astronomical traditions of Rakka and Damascus as well as of Fatimid Cairo.

The second phase of Egypt's sensitive relation to world conditions came as a response to the Black Death of 1348 and succeeding epidemics that destroyed a substantial portion of the Egyptian population. The Mamluk elite, deprived of resources, turned to factional warfare and exploitation of the subject population. Regimes turned over rapidly, and Mamluk patronage for the arts and quality crafts declined. The history of metalworking, as reviewed by James W. Allan, gives a good illustration of this era: between 1360 and 1382 quantity but not quality suffered. The decline of patronage, however, showed itself in quality between 1382 and 1450, when very few distinguished pieces were produced. In the early fifteenth century the production of gold belts for Mamluks, horse trappings, spurs, and ornate inlaid saddles also declined. A similar decline took place in architecture, glassware, illuminated manuscripts, and other fine crafts and arts.

The third phase of Egyptian arts was a glorious outburst during the reigns of Qāytbāy (1468–96) and Qānṣūh al-Ghawrī (1501–16). European fashion became an important influence on Egyptian glass, metalwork, pottery, and textiles in the late fifteenth century, when Italian and Spanish goods were both imported and imitated in the Mamluk empire. The predominant international influences, however, were Anatolian and Iranian. Ottoman expansion in eastern Anatolia opened the way for trade, overseas and overland through Aleppo, and provided the Mamluk empire with new sources of luxury goods and new markets for Mamluk products. The collapse of the Timurid regimes, and the rise and rapid demise of Turkoman states, such as the Aqqoyunlu, once again sent Iranian artists westward. Marilyn Jenkins, analyzing Mamluk underglaze-painted pottery, points out that artisans from Tabriz in the second quarter of the fifteenth century were manufacturing tiles in Damascus and Fustat. An Egyptian rug industry began in the late fifteenth century as a result of the migration of craftsmen from northwestern Iran. Esin Atıl discusses the development of a new Mamluk style of illuminated manuscript under the influence of the Turko-Persian courts of northwestern Iran and the Ottoman empire. With the breakup of the Aqqoyunlu court in the midfifteenth century, an influx of Iranian artists led to the production of Turkish versions of the conquests of Alexander and of the *Shāhnāma*, as court painters seeking new patronage began to compose epic histories for Mamluk sultans. Other Iranian painters came from Shiraz after the Safavid conquest. Baghdadi influences were also felt in Mamluk Egypt.

Late Mamluk artistic activity was generated by some of the same forces that inspired the late thirteenth- and early fourteenth-century period of greatness in Egyptian art—the migration of craftsmen from disturbed regions of Iran to the stable court of the Mamluks and the international fashions and patterns of trade. The late fifteenth century, however, introduced new motives for the production of Mamluk masterpieces. For over a century and a half the Mamluk empire had been the leading Middle Eastern Muslim regime. By the fifteenth century, however, new large-scale empires were being formed by the Ottomans in Anatolia and the Balkans and by Tamerlane and his successors in Iran. These new empires introduced a period of intensified Middle Eastern rivalry for political power and prestige. The Mamluks in this case benefited not only from the migration of artisans and from enhanced trade but from being forced by political competition to reassert their own imperial claims and to rededicate themselves to the creation of Islamic architectural monuments and the cultivation of imperial arts such as illuminated histories of ancient kings. Mamluk patrons and artists thus responded to the cultural achievements of their Iranian and Ottoman rivals.

The artistic and cultural style of Egypt was also influenced by international trade. Despite the establishment of the Mongol empire in Central Asia and the opening of new routes to China, the Mamluks managed to keep open the Red Sea–Alexandria route to Europe. By the middle of the fourteenth century, the closure of Central Asian routes again favored Egyptian ports. By 1375 a regular trade with Venice was reestablished in Alexandria, and the international spice and luxury trade flourished in Syria. Throughout most of the fifteenth century, Syria and Egypt traded regularly with Italian, French, Spanish, and Balkan ports.

International trade led to an internationalization of fashion in textiles and ceramics. Mamluk striped silks with bands of Arabic text became fashionable in Spain and Italy and were commonly reproduced in excellent quality and resold in Egypt. Islamic metalworks and textiles sold in China inspired Chinese weavers to copy Arabic striped silks for sale in both Egyptian and European markets. Chinese blue-and-white ceramics were also greatly admired and widely reproduced in Egypt. By the fifteenth century, Egyptian domestic production was virtually overwhelmed by Chinese, European, and Anatolian products.

From the viewpoint of social history, another important theme in this volume is the profound commitment of the Mamluk regime to two kinds of art, one cosmopolitan and imperial, the other religious. These two major dimensions of Mamluk art have their origin not only in the international situation, but also in the peculiarities of the Mamluk political and social system. This system is well enough known. Egyptian society in the Mamluk period was ruled by a regime of slave soldiers. In 1250, these slaves had revolted against their masters, replaced the previous ruling family with a slave general, and established a government run by slaves and former slaves. In principle no one could be a member of the military or political elite unless he was of foreign (usually Turkish or Circassian) origin, purchased and raised as a slave, and trained to be a soldier and administrator in a slave army barracks. No native of Egypt or Syria could ever belong to this elite, nor in principle could the son of the slave inherit the position of his father. The slave system assured the ruler complete control over the army and the administration, since the slaves had no ties and no loyalties to the subject society, but were isolated from the people they ruled. These slaves were able to dominate their subjects because they ruled a society that could not itself organize for political purposes.

The subject society was peculiarly fragmented. Though united by Islam, Egyptians and Syrians were divided by family, tribe, quarters, youth gangs, and other parochial associations and could not generate a regional political leadership. The ulema, who had the widest range of influence, were themselves divided into several schools of law and were attached to numerous local communities. The combination of alien rule and a fragmented society created intense problems of coordination, communication, and legitimation, as well as peculiar problems of expressing identity and world view. In the Mamluk period these problems were handled on a political and social level by an informal collaboration between the Mamluk state elites and the ulema religious elites. The state elites patronized Islamic causes and took the ulema into the service of the government; the ulema in turn legitimated and supported the political regime. Mamluk patronage of popular quarters and youth gangs also helped achieve a political equilibrium between the regime and its subjects.

On a symbolic level the problem of integration was handled through public ceremonies and the creation of a religious and a royal art. The Mamluk regime had to balance competing considerations. To generate political cohesion within the military elite and to express the supremacy of the regime over its subjects, the Mamluks had to glorify their nobility and win recognition of their sovereignty and their right to rule. However, because the political and military elites were foreigners, the Mamluks also had to articulate their dedication to Islam and their concern for the whole society. Mamluk art, therefore, was channeled into both royal and religious forms.

The royal forms of Mamluk art express class identity and imperial claims. The Mamluk court was organized to dramatize and celebrate the glory of royalty. Karl Stowasser points to regal Mamluk pageantry, such as the ceremonies for the accession of a new sultan, at which the caliph would invest the sultan with his office. There were special protocols for the reception and greeting of the caliph, the treatment of visiting ambassadors, the review and payment of troops, including the distribution of honorary garments, the review of military exercises, public audiences in the House of Justice, celebrations of the birthday of the Prophet, and banquets for the military elite, at which gifts were distributed to soldiers and officials. Royal processions reached out from the court to the general public. The annual *mahmal*, the weekly procession to Friday prayers, the processions to mark the passing of the agricultural year, the measuring of the high tide of the Nile, and the breaking of the dam to mark the summer cultivating season were all occasions for the public to witness the glory of the regime. Sultans also attended hunting excursions and polo games. On these occasions sultans and amirs were accompanied by *ṭablkhāna*, or bands of drummers and cymbalists, whose presence signified the high rank of officials.

The glorification of the ruler and the elite was also expressed through the production and ownership of splendid apparel, weapons, furnishings, and utensils. The Mamluks wore different costumes for royal receptions, parades, hunting, polo, and tournaments. Their banners, cloaks, blankets, and saddlecloths were all woven with blazons—lions, swords, rosettes, epigraphy, and geometric designs—which signified the rank and court function of the amirs and their place in the Mamluk hierarchy. Early Mamluk ceramics and metalwork were also decorated to signify the glory of the regime. In the late thirteenth century, there were figural representations of court life, as well as animal, bird, and floral arabesque decoration. Blazons were incorporated into Mamluk metalwork in the early fourteenth century. Inscriptions dedicate the objects to Mamluk amirs. Much metalwork art was also devoted to arms and armor, helmets, coats of mail, shields, swords, and drums.

Mamluk painting was the royal art, par excellence. The illuminated manuscripts of the late thirteenth and early fourteenth centuries reflect the classical style of Baghdad and Mosul. Early Mamluk manuscripts are copies of *Automata* and of the tales of the *Kalīla wa Dimna* and the *Maqāmāt*. These works were probably composed by artisans who fled from Iraq and Mesopotamia to Mamluk domains. From the late fourteenth century, however, new forms of art more characteristic of Mamluk interests became popular. *Furūsiyya*, literary works devoted to military concerns, were illustrated in the late fourteenth and early fifteenth centuries. After the middle of the fifteenth century, epic histories, including the history of Alexander the Great and the *Shāhnāma*, were produced in Turkish translation. These works assert royal prerogative, the grandeur of monarchy, and the identification of Mamluk rulers with Turkish princes throughout the Middle East. By choosing themes such as the histories of Alexander and ancient Persian kings, told in Turkish, the Mamluks asserted their claim to Turko-Persian and Middle Eastern traditions of royalty. Like other Turkish and Iranian rulers, they became the patrons of works that celebrated imperial conquests and court life. In the last decade of Mamluk rule, Qānṣūh al-Ghawrī established the first Mamluk court studio to produce manuscripts for the royal library. The royal artists were supplemented by Mamluk youngsters, who produced copies of manuscripts as part of their education.

Mamluk cultural consciousness had an ethnic and personal as well as a regal aspect. The Mamluk court listened to Sufi orations in Turkish. Circassian poetry was recited; Persian and Arabic manuscripts were translated into the language of the Mamluk elite. Even an element of personal vanity shows through. Laila ʿAli Ibrahim points to the decoration of Mamluk halls with pictures of conquered citadels and portraits of important amirs. Heraldry and armaments, with their distinctive and original blazons, were a way to assert the personal vanity, pride, and power of the Mamluk warrior.

Alongside royal art, the Mamluks cultivated a commitment to religion. The sultan, as Karl Stowasser points out, had important religious functions. He upheld the suzerainty of the Abbasid caliphate. He maintained the four major schools of law. He was the guardian of the departure of the *mahmal* (pilgrimage caravan) and the protector of the holy places; he sat in the Hall of Justice supported by his *qadis* in order to hear the grievances of his subjects. He celebrated the Id feasts and other religious occasions, such as the birthday of the Prophet.

The most striking expression of the Mamluk commitment to Islam was the construction of great numbers of mosques, colleges, Sufi khanqahs, and other religious buildings. Mamluk sultans and amirs prepared monumental tombs for themselves, surmounted by large domes, each one the centerpiece of a complex of mosques, schools, and convents endowed with agricultural incomes and urban rents. These were designed to win popular favor, to assure the memory of the good name of the benefactor, and perhaps to please God in the world to come. All the major cities of the Mamluk empire were provided with dozens and even hundreds of buildings dedicated to religious purposes. Vast sums were appropriated to provide permanent endowments for worship and teaching.

John Alden Williams and André Raymond illustrate how the growth of Cairo as a metropolis centered around religious constructions. Both study the way in which the building of new suburbs was determined by Mamluk investment in economic and religious facilities. Wherever a religious center—consisting of a tomb, a mosque, a college, or a khanqah, and often including soup kitchens and residences—supported by permanent endowments was created, a neighborhood could grow up. Whenever Mamluk amirs invested in canals, gardens, markets, caravanserais, and baths, a new center of urban life came into being. Religious and economic facilities were closely related. Markets, caravanserais, and baths were often built to provide an income for the support of mosques, colleges, and khanqahs, and reciprocally the construction of religious facilities stimulated settlement and the development of a neighborhood economy.

Jerusalem was a particularly favored place because it was a holy city to Muslims. Endowments for hadith schools, colleges, khanqahs, mausolea, orphanages, hospices for travelers, baths, and other public facilities were supported by commercial constructions, such as markets and hotels. The Ḥaram was an important center of Ayyubid and Mamluk period buildings. Donald P. Little calls our attention to a hitherto unknown and precious collection of 875 documents, dating from the period 1393–97, which comes from the records of a Jerusalem judge and administrator of endowments and includes royal decrees, deeds of sale, endowment records, and inventories of waqf properties and private estates.

The patronage of religious institutions also inspired auxiliary arts. Building parts, including mihrabs, portals, windows, screens, shutters, and cupboards, display splendid achievements in metal, wood, and stonework. Religious furniture, including minbars and *kursīs* (Koran stands), inspired fine metal- and woodwork. Marble paneling was an important decorative feature for the mihrab and qibla walls of mosques, and was also used for pavements and fountains. Other furnishings included candlesticks, Koran boxes, doors, windows, and glass lamps.

Illuminated Korans were another Mamluk contribution to religious art. In the early fourteenth century, Korans were prepared in large-format, thirty-volume editions dedicated to mosques and khanqahs, to be read and recited by Sufi Koran readers. David James analyzes the first major Mamluk work of this type, possibly inspired by Ilkhanid conceptions. Similar works called forth the cooperation of calligraphers, illuminators, bookbinders, and auxiliary craftsmen who made lecterns, Koran boxes, and candlesticks. Mamluk patronage of illuminated Korans continued throughout the fifteenth century, though in the later period it shifted to smaller, multivolume sets and large, one-volume manuscripts.

Mamluk astronomy was also inspired by religious interests. While Fatimid and Timurid astronomy was carried out in special observatories under royal patronage, Mamluk astronomy, as David A. King shows, was concentrated in mosques. The major astronomical interest was the calculation of the times of daily prayer, and the major astronomical achievement was the construction of *zījs*, or tables, defining the positions of the planets. Sundials helped keep the time of prayer.

In this volume, the studies of Mamluk arts are organized by object, building, or city. There are, however, other ways to proceed that would focus our attention on important questions about the relations of Mamluk art and architecture to Mamluk religious culture. First, we may note different types of religious motivation and symbolism. Mosques and colleges and other facilities served the intellectual and legal forms of Islamic study and worship. Sufi khanqahs, mausolea, and the participation of the ruler and his amirs in such festivals as the birthday of the Prophet or the pilgrimage appealed to the popular veneration of saints and to faith in the magical presence of God's power in the world. Ceremonies such as the measuring of the waters of the Nile and the breaking of the dam at the beginning of the agricultural season symbolized the importance of the ruler as a channel for the powers of nature. Alongside the Muslim Sunni and Sufi types of veneration were a pagan glorification of kingship and a belief in the ruler who controlled the powers of the universe; whose goodness could bring rain, abundant harvest, and prosperity; whose evil deeds could bring ruin.

Moreover, the tremendous proliferation of mosques, colleges, khanqahs, hospitals, and mausolea suggests social and religious concerns of a personal nature. As Oleg Grabar points out, whole streets in the centers of old Cairo and Damascus were occupied by religious buildings. How can we explain the extraordinary proliferation of buildings, out of proportion to apparent social need? Why does the impulse to religious expression outdo even the desire for courtly embellishment and luxury?

The need for political legitimation and for the political and religious support of the ulema explains some of the construction, but there were also personal reasons for Mamluk patronage. Mamluks after all were people torn away from their homes at an early age, raised in a masculine, violent, militaristic society, exposed in a foreign land to death in battle or to death by plague. They did not easily establish families and reproduce themselves; the children of those who did were relegated to a second-class career of religious teaching or service in an auxiliary military corps. The religious endowments were about the only useful thing the Mamluks could do with their accumulated wealth, apart from forfeiting it to the state upon death. Endowments enabled them to develop local ties as property owners and donors, to transfer wealth and give employment to their children, and to win the favor of scholars, holy men, and the common people. One feels that Mamluk patronage was aimed at overcoming the isolation and despair inherent in a glorious but brutalizing life; it was a way of entering the fellowship of ordinary human beings.

Thus to understand Mamluk religious art we must not only review the history of objects, buildings, and cities but also consider these arts as expressions of Muslim belief and social relations, and in relation to the routines of Muslim worship, ritual, and religious mentality. Full understanding of religious art in the Mamluk period will require a combination of art-historical, textual, and religious studies, going far beyond the study of inscriptions found on buildings and objects, in order to bring alive our insight into the meaning and uses of any particular object or building.

Mamluk arts reveal a complex identity. They mix religious commitments with cosmopolitan imperial themes, ethnic identity with personal vanity. The creation of this varied art raises important questions. What kind of religious and monarchical vision does this production represent? What is the place of the Mamluks in the history of elite Muslim cultures? How does Mamluk elite culture compare with that of other Muslim regimes?

The juxtaposition of religious and royal iconography in Mamluk art is not, of course, unique. Almost every Muslim regime beginning with the early caliphate cultivated the arts in order to articulate religious commitments, imperial authority, and the superiority of the governing classes. A comparison of Mamluk with Fatimid and Ottoman arts—both of them being, at least in part, Egyptian arts—may bring out the distinctive qualities of Mamluk culture.

One of the striking features of both Fatimid and Ottoman cosmopolitan culture is the universality of religious and imperial claims. The Fatimid caliphs claimed to be successors to the Prophet Muḥammad and the true caliphs of all Muslims, and they rivaled the Byzantine and Abbasid empires for world imperium. The Fatimids advanced their claims in the several vocabularies of Mediterranean civilization. They used Abbasid, Byzantine, and Isma'ili symbols of political authority.

Emulating the great rival empires, the palace of the ruler was decorated with extraordinary splendor. Gold rafters supported the ceiling; rare birds and animals decorated the walls and furniture; fountains of cascading water cooled the air. The ruler himself sat on a gold throne protected by a screen in a fashion inspired by the Abbasids and resembling Byzantine enthronement. He was entitled to special clothing—a crown, a sword, a scepter, a parasol, weapons, and other implements—which were signs of his sovereignty. Court decorations, many of which were the gifts of foreign ambassadors, some of Byzantine manufacture and some Abbasid relics, depicted the glory of the ruler. A huge hanging silk map of all the lands and their rulers expressed the Fatimid claim to belong to the family of kings which governed the world. Fatimid paintings in both palace decoration and illuminated manuscripts show the influence of Samarra and, through Samarra, of Central Asia.

Equally important in the palace symbolism was Islam. The palace contained halls for the preaching and instruction of Isma'ili Islamic beliefs. Religious functionaries, such as judges, missionaries, reciters of the Koran, and prayer leaders, were regularly present for court ceremonies. Formal religious processions symbolized in both religious and cosmopolitan terms the sublime importance of the monarchy. Palace receptions, such as audiences with the caliph, the review of soldiers, or the reception of ambassadors, and public processions, such as the Ramaḍān and New Year processions and formal openings of the Nile canal, brought the caliph and his entourage to the major mosques of the city, where he delivered the sermon, celebrated the festivals, and displayed the magnificent and sacred objects of the Fatimid treasury. Thus the caliph brought home to the populace the importance of the ruler in both the secular universe of war and politics and the magical universe of religion and nature. In these processions were strong survivals of Byzantine, Iranian, and other Eastern influences.

The public architecture of the Fatimids was also an extension of the ceremonial aspect of the royal court. The new city, al-Qāhira, constructed by the Fatimids with magnificent palaces, colossal halls, and grand mosques, was itself an architectural model of the universe of Fatimid rule. It was an imperial city designed for imperial pageants. The principal mosques, al-Azhar and al-Ḥākim, were constructed with minarets and cupolas that symbolized the preeminence of the imam and recalled the construction of the holy places of Mecca and Medina as a way of glorifying the ruler in the service of God and Islam.

The Fatimids further cultivated an aura of religious glory by sponsoring the cult of the family of ʿAlī and by trying to inculcate a mass enthusiasm for shrines and relics. The caliphs constructed numerous mausolea in order to encourage pilgrimage. Koranic inscriptions encouraged obedience to the imam and called upon people to accept his authority as an expression of God's will.

Ottoman culture had a somewhat different vision of the relationship between religious and monarchical claims. The Ottomans did not claim to be imams, but rather portrayed themselves as the defenders and enforcers of Muslim law. Thus they organized Muslim judicial administration and education and provided for the endowment of Sufi shrines and religious facilities, much in the fashion of the earlier Mamluk regime. Ottoman monarchical claims, however, matched and exceeded Fatimid ambitions. The Ottomans were the self-conscious heirs to the Turkish empires of Central Asia, to the Seljuq and Middle Eastern Islamic empires, and to the Byzantine empire. They engaged in wars of conquest reaching into Eastern and Central Europe, across the Mediterranean to North Africa, and into the Indian Ocean, defending and enlarging Muslim positions on a world scale. The vast imperial ambitions of the Ottomans led them to absorb Arabic and Persian religious, literary, and scientific culture and to accept elements of Byzantine and European styles in architecture and painting. They patronized historical scholarship concerning the origins of the dynasty and universal histories beginning with the creation of Adam. The Ottomans chronicled court life and were the first great Muslim rulers to appoint official historians. Their geographies reflected the expansion of Ottoman naval power throughout the Mediterranean and the Indian Ocean.

Furthermore, the Ottomans imitated Ilkhanid and Timurid precedents by creating court studios to employ calligraphers, painters, illuminators, and bookbinders to produce illuminated manuscripts and designs for Ottoman ceramics, tiles, wood- and metalwork, textiles, and carpets. Both Persian and Turkish literary classics were illuminated, but a new emphasis upon history and illustrations of court life defined a self-conscious Ottoman style. Histories of kings, books of victories, genealogies, biographies of sultans, and descriptions of festivals, accessions of sultans, receptions of ambassadors, royal processions, battles, sieges, banquets, and celebrations were all the subjects of manuscript illumination. Viziers, janissaries, cavalrymen, scholars, guildsmen, merchants, and sultans appear in profusion. Ottoman manuscript art reflects and celebrates the self-consciousness of the Ottoman elite as a world-historical force.

The universalist and imperial emphases in Fatimid and Ottoman art and the balances between religion and imperium seem very different from those of Mamluk art. Mamluk art retreats from the Fatimid pretensions to be a Muslim world caliphate, heir to the Abbasid and rival of the Byzantine empire. The more restricted Mamluk claims had a restraining effect on courtly and royal arts. In the Mamluk period, cosmopolitan culture was severely constrained in favor of Islamic symbolism. There are important continuities with the Fatimid period in the Mamluk emphasis upon court ceremonies and public processions, the state sponsorship of religious education and scholarship, the endowment of mosques, the preservation of funerary monuments and tombs—all of which become a permanent part of Egyptian-Islamic royal culture. No longer, however, do geographic symbols, as in Fatimid and Ottoman maps, express worldwide ambitions; no longer does interest in philosophy and astronomy symbolize universal rationality. Rather, in Mamluk art there is a frank acceptance of a local political destiny.

The Mamluk attitude toward Islam is also different. The Fatimids claimed to be imams—not only guardians, but objects of faith. The Mamluks were more humble servants of religion. Thus Fatimid patronage concentrated upon the religious glory of the dynasty and focused on the patronage of four great mosques, processions, tombs for the family of ʿAlī, and the construction of a monumental capital. In contrast, the Mamluks devoted their energies to innumerable small buildings and endowments, which focus attention not so much on royal or official patrons as on the religious activity itself. They expressed care for social purposes rather than world glory. The intent of the monuments was more social and ideological than aesthetic and regal.

The restricted style in both cosmopolitan and religious arts is also related to limitations of resources. In the Mamluk era Egypt held a position of importance in the Muslim world on a very fragile economic base. It sustained its cultural and Middle Eastern–wide political responsibilities on the basis of a small territory and a relatively small capital city population. André Raymond has demonstrated that the population of greater Cairo before the Black Death of 1348 was on the order of from 200,000 to 250,000, and that in 1420 it was probably between 150,000 and 200,000. This compares with a population in Istanbul at the beginning of the sixteenth century of over 700,000. Moreover, the shallow demographic and economic base of Egyptian prosperity was shattered in the middle of the fourteenth century by repeated plagues and the progressive loss of economic opportunities to bigger trading and political competitors. By the end of the fifteenth century, Egypt would have to give up an excessive historic burden to the Ottoman empire. In the meantime the limitations of demography and economy restricted the capacity of Egypt to generate glorious architectural and artistic treasures.

This volume opens yet another important issue for social history—art and popular culture. These papers provide abundant information about the material culture of Egyptian society—clothing and textiles, ceramics, utensils, and decorations. Esin Atıl has illustrated how real life can be viewed in manuscript illuminations. Laila ʿAli Ibrahim describes domestic architecture, showing how public halls and private rooms were designed. Such important features as screens, vestibules, outlook to the street, and the disposition of walls and courtyards not only made up a housing form but expressed a concept of the relation of the family to the outside world. David A. King discusses aspects of domestic architectural planning, including ventilation and the calculation of the orientation of streets, public buildings, and private residences. André Raymond and John Alden Williams have analyzed the distribution of baths, markets, and religious facilities. A study of the Ḥaram documents, presented by Donald P. Little, contains inventories of the property of deceased people, a rare glimpse into private fortunes and individual tastes.

Even a few examples make clear that the art historian holds a key to understanding the culture of all classes that may surpass the sources available to historians who deal only with texts. This volume is replete with tantalizing suggestions about the taste, style, and sensibility of Mamluk Egyptian society. Egyptian metal- and glasswares, decorated in the late thirteenth century with figural motifs, came to be dominated in the fourteenth century by epigraphy and the blazons of amirs. Before 1300 Mamluk glassware was decorated with animal forms, pictures of musicians, and heraldic symbols such as lions and eagles. After 1300 epigraphy and the blazons of sultans and amirs decorate bottles, goblets, bowls, basins, and beakers. Mamluk textiles, which at first favored vegetal, animal, and epigraphic designs, were restyled with emphasis upon mathematically precise bands of decoration based on repetition of motifs and short inscriptions. Much of this change of style may be due to the introduction of new looms with mechanical patterning devices.

Ceramics give us important information about Mamluk taste. Bahri Mamluk ceramics, like Bahri glass- and metalware, stress animal and bird decorations and figural and narrative representations of court life. Some fourteenth-century potteries follow metalwork designs and are decorated with inscriptions and blazons. However, as George T. Scanlon points out, by the fifteenth century Mamluk taste had changed considerably, and Chinese influences had become extremely important. Mamluk pottery imitates Chinese blue-and-white wares and celadon, and underglaze pottery duplicates Ming porcelains. In the middle to late fifteenth century, with the decline of patronage for quality wares, cheaper forms of unglazed pottery abounded. Popular or mass tastes seem to have favored green, red, and brown clays, sometimes covered with brown or green color. Although the subject has hardly been explored, perhaps the most striking change in taste is the shift from decoration with animal and figural motifs to epigraphic, arabesque, and geometric decoration.

Before the Mamluk period, Egyptian art showed little interest in geometric designs; most Islamic geometric design was Iranian. However, the first hundred years of Mamluk rule brought a vast explosion of geometric decoration in Egypt. This decoration was at first based on patterns coming from Iran and Anatolia, but after 1350 Egypt became the pioneer Muslim region in the development of new patterns and in the use of geometrical decoration for architectural surfaces, Koran manuscripts, and mosque furniture. Geometric decoration seems to be a prime Egyptian contribution to Islamic art.

The stylistic qualities of Egyptian art and the changes they underwent in the Mamluk period raise a number of important and still unanswered questions. Is there an Egyptian art distinct from that of other Muslim provinces? Are there stylistic distinctions between public and official forms of art and private and intimate modes of art? Is there a distinction between the Mamluk style of art pertaining to the political elite and the art favored by the mass of the native population? Does this art unfold as the autonomous expression of the specialized tradition of craftsmanship, or does it reflect the cast of mind of the populace as a whole? What does this art tell us about values, and to what does it correspond in other levels of Egyptian religious and popular culture?

These questions about the sociology of Egyptian art remain at the frontier of art-historical investigation, not only in Egyptian but in Islamic art history generally. Michael Baxandall's *Painting and Experience in 15th-Century Italy* illustrates the fruitful potentialities of an approach to art history that seeks out the mentality and the culture of peoples from the study of their art. He shows, for example, how the gestures, postures, and positions of figures in Italian Renaissance painting are a revelation of Renaissance ideas about social relationships and the emotions that should be conveyed among people. He shows also how the fascination with perspective and proportions and the portrayal of complex geometric forms mirrored the involvement of the mercantile elites of Florence in gauging the sizes of irregular bales, boxes, sacks, and barrels. Renaissance art also reflects the calculating world of partnerships, profits, dowries, and inheritances. Renaissance art, then, can be understood in relation to other forms of culture, including other forms of art and literature, and the experiences of everyday life. In Mamluk art history the materials for similar investigations are abundant, but the questions have yet to be asked.

What kind of people and what kind of society have given us this treasure of artistic and documentary remains? In the artistic legacy of Mamluk Egypt we have clues to the political culture, the religious goals, and even the very mentality or sensibility of the civilization. If we are to understand this, our researches must be pursued on two levels. There must be an exhaustive examination of specific bodies of data, including texts and artifacts; but these investigations must be carried out with a sense of the relation of the arts to other forms of culture and to the historical context in which they were produced. To be meaningful, facts must be accumulated as contributions to illuminating the broader cultural themes and the total history of a particular civilization. The study of facts is not preliminary to, but integral with, questions of meaning.

University of California
Berkeley, California